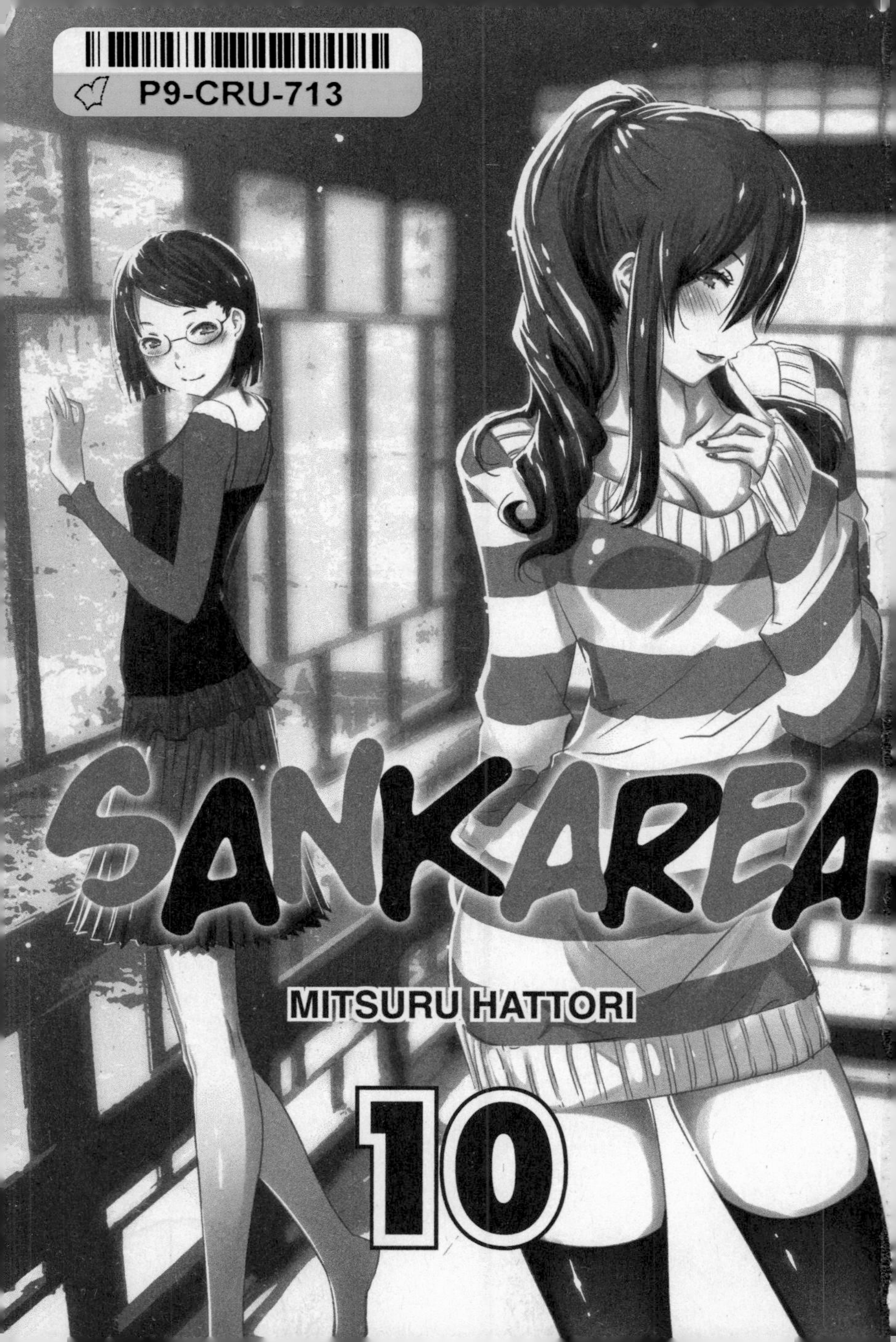
SANKAREA
MITSURU HATTORI
10

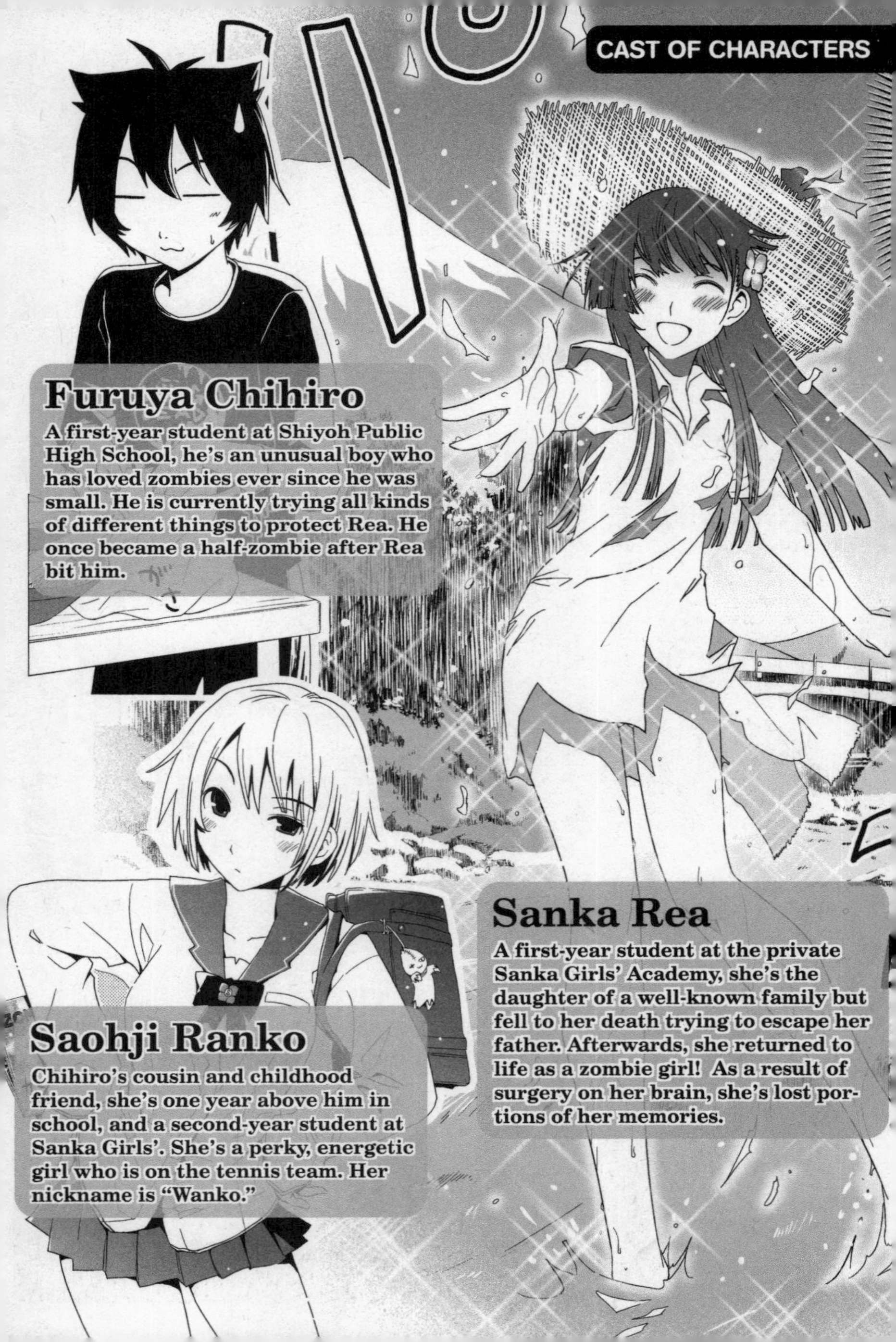

Furuya Chihiro

A first-year student at Shiyoh Public High School, he's an unusual boy who has loved zombies ever since he was small. He is currently trying all kinds of different things to protect Rea. He once became a half-zombie after Rea bit him.

Sanka Rea

A first-year student at the private Sanka Girls' Academy, she's the daughter of a well-known family but fell to her death trying to escape her father. Afterwards, she returned to life as a zombie girl! As a result of surgery on her brain, she's lost portions of her memories.

Saohji Ranko

Chihiro's cousin and childhood friend, she's one year above him in school, and a second-year student at Sanka Girls'. She's a perky, energetic girl who is on the tennis team. Her nickname is "Wanko."

THE FURUYA FAMILY

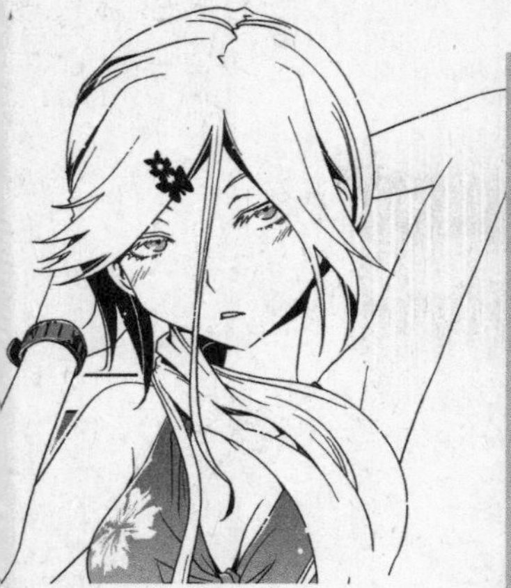

Kurumiya Darin Arciento

An expert in zombie research who came to Japan from the southern islands to visit Professor Boyle (Grandpa). She has a strange passion for her research. Despite her looks, she's younger than Rea.

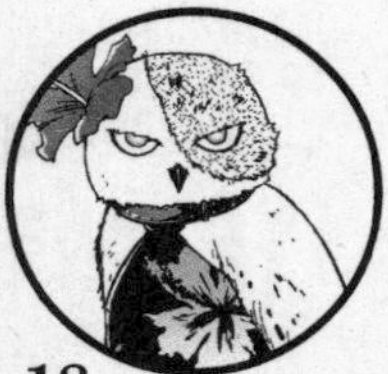

18

Darin's faithful pet. It's been zombified and half-mechanized.

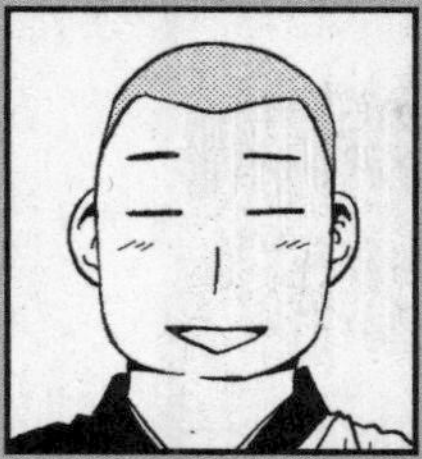

Dad

His real name is Furuya Dohn. He's the head priest at Shiryohji Temple. He agreed to Rea and Darin living in their home, saying only, "Should be fine, right?"

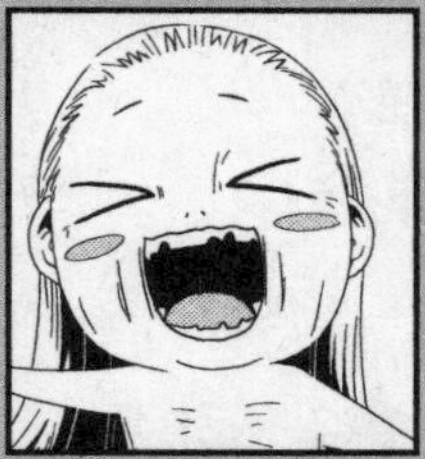

Grandpa

The very person who first created the reanimation elixir. His name is Jogoroh, but at ZoMA he was called Professor Boyle.

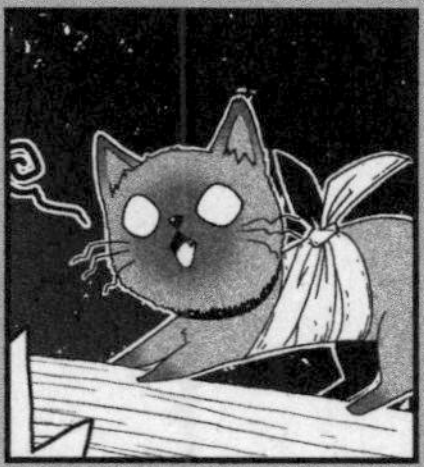

Bub

He was hit by a car and died, but came back to life thanks to the elixir Chihiro and Rea made.

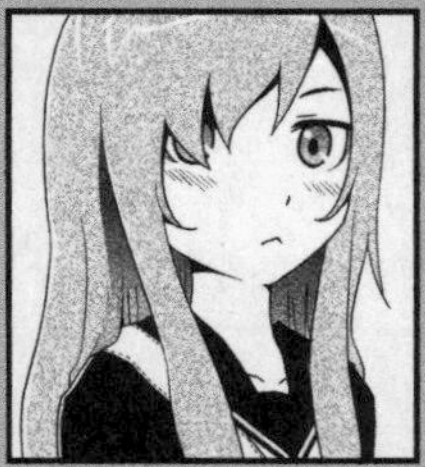

Furuya Mero

A reliable first-year middle school student, she manages all the housework for the Furuya family. She loves to read the Heart Sutra.

STORY

With Rea's "potential" clearly identified at ZoMA, Chihiro is eager to confirm the hope brought on by this discovery, but due to Rea's memory loss, Chihiro is instead treated by Rea as someone suspicious. After learning about what happened, Ranko attempts to use shock therapy on Rea by setting her up as an idol and reenacting a scene from the past at "the ruins" where it all began. Ultimately, this ends in failure, but Rea becomes aware of the "hunger" and "memories" hiding deep within her. As this occurs, Chihiro, following instructions found in a letter from Jogoroh, makes his way to an ice cavern and discovers a frozen zombie. He then revives Otoki, who has named herself as Jogoroh's wife!

MITSURU HATTORI presents

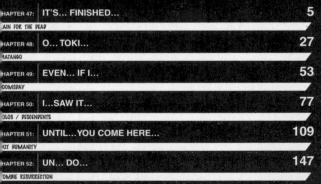

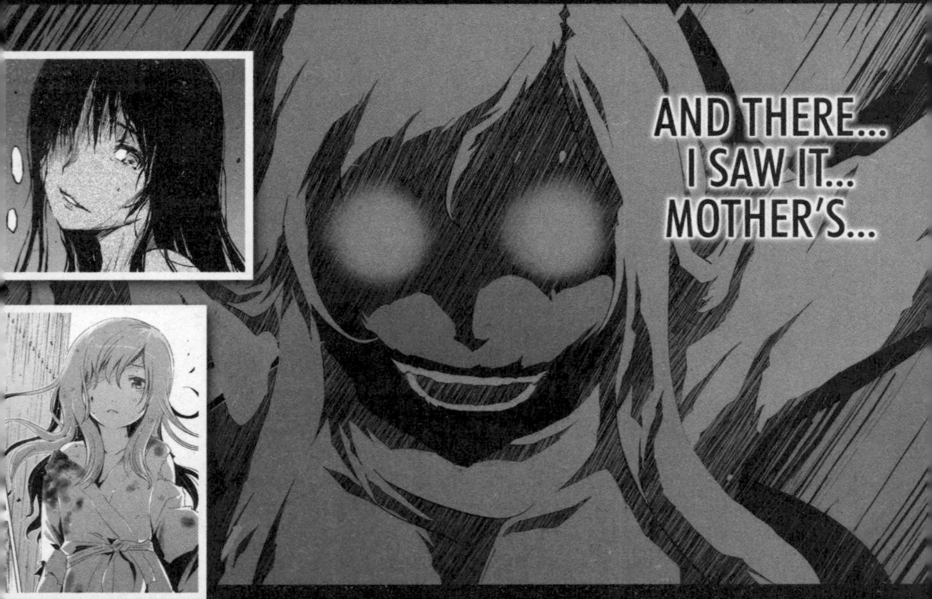

AND THERE...
I SAW IT...
MOTHER'S...

CONTENTS

SERIALIZED IN BESSATSU
SHONEN MAGAZINE,
JANUARY 2014 - JUNE 2014.

SANKAREA **10**

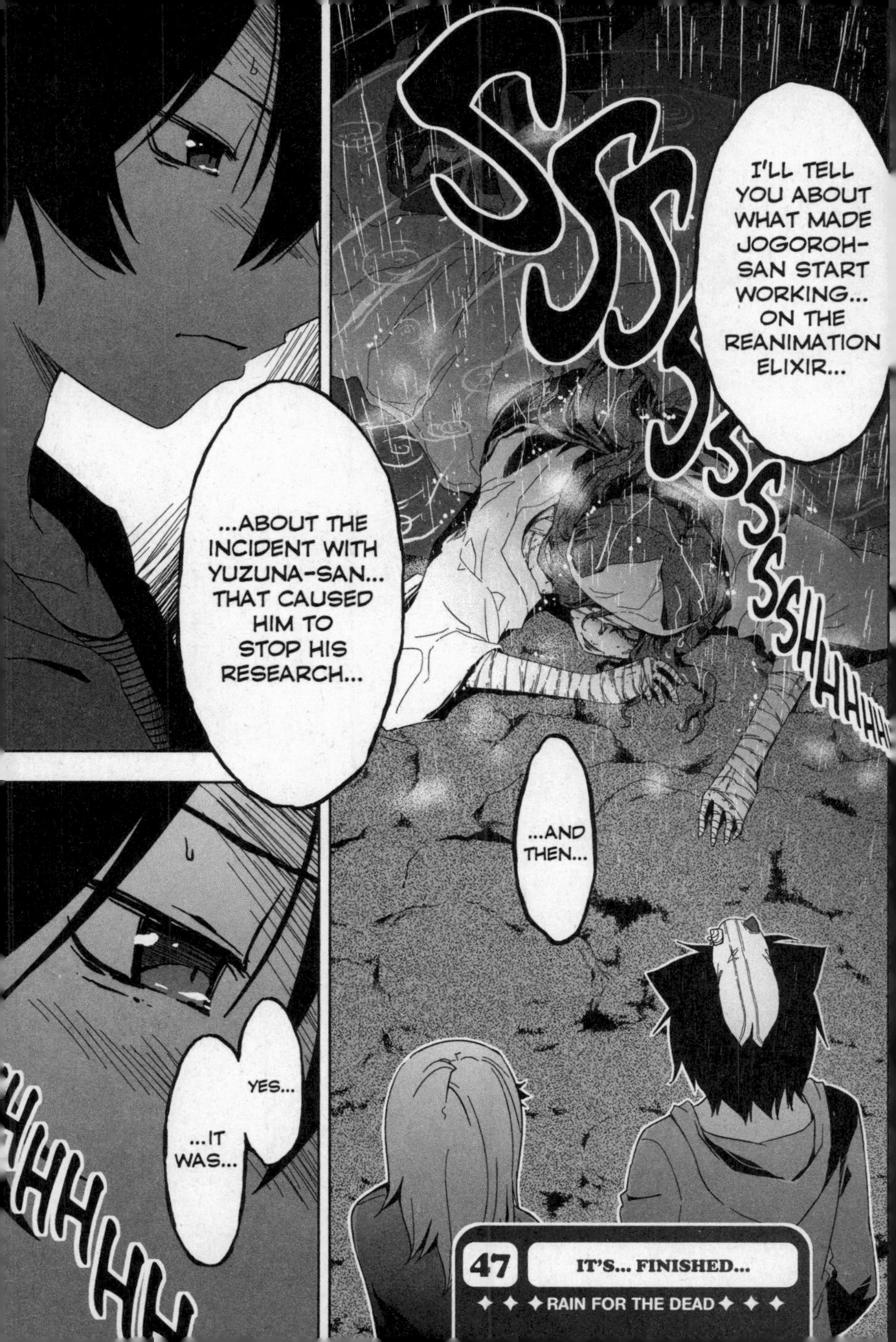
SSSSSSSSHHHHH
I'LL TELL YOU ABOUT WHAT MADE JOGOROH-SAN START WORKING... ON THE REANIMATION ELIXIR...
...ABOUT THE INCIDENT WITH YUZUNA-SAN... THAT CAUSED HIM TO STOP HIS RESEARCH...
...AND THEN...
YES...
...IT WAS...
HHHHHHH
47
IT'S... FINISHED...
RAIN FOR THE DEAD

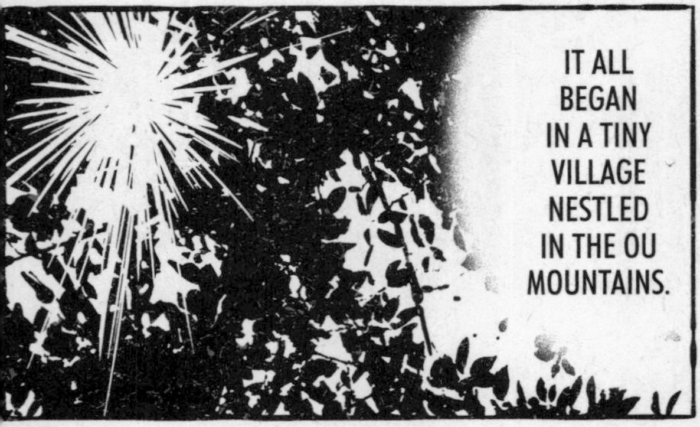
IT ALL BEGAN IN A TINY VILLAGE NESTLED IN THE OU MOUNTAINS.

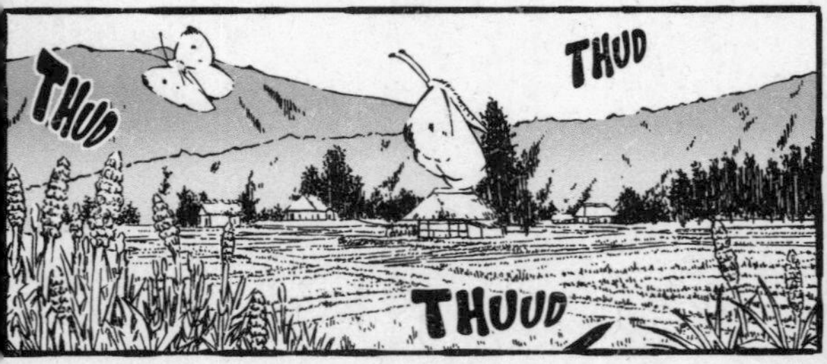
THUD
THUD
THUUD

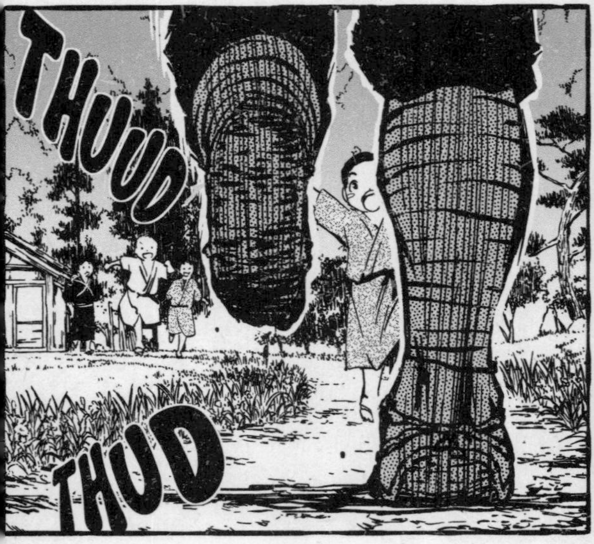
THUUUD
THUD

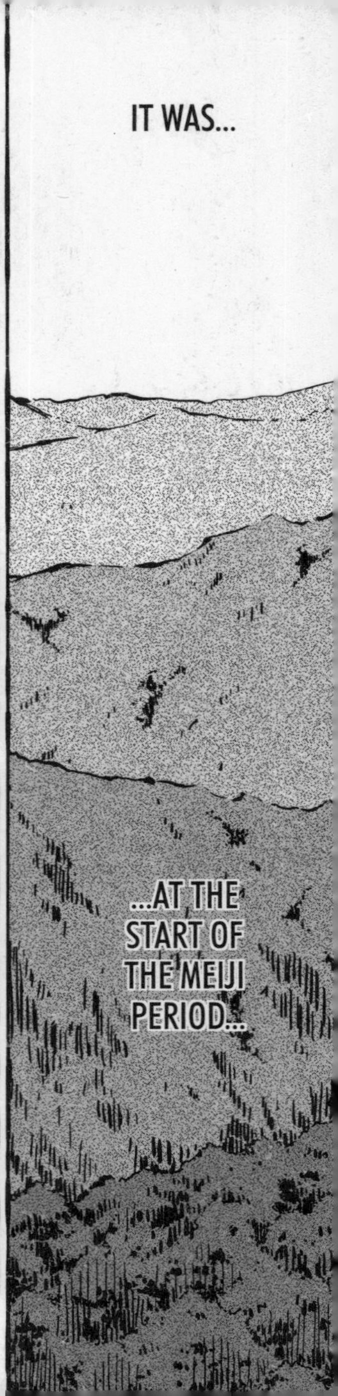
IT WAS...
...AT THE START OF THE MEIJI PERIOD...

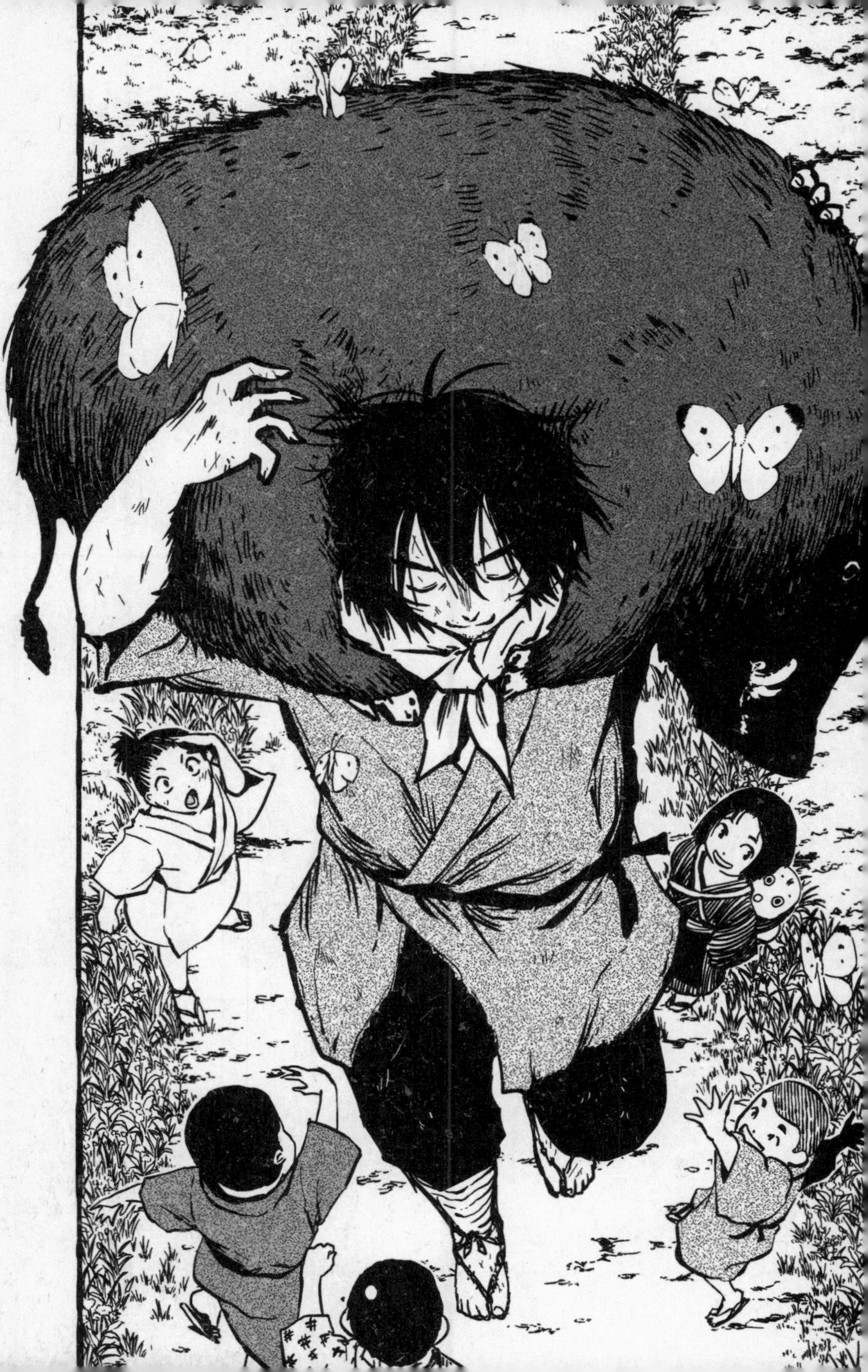

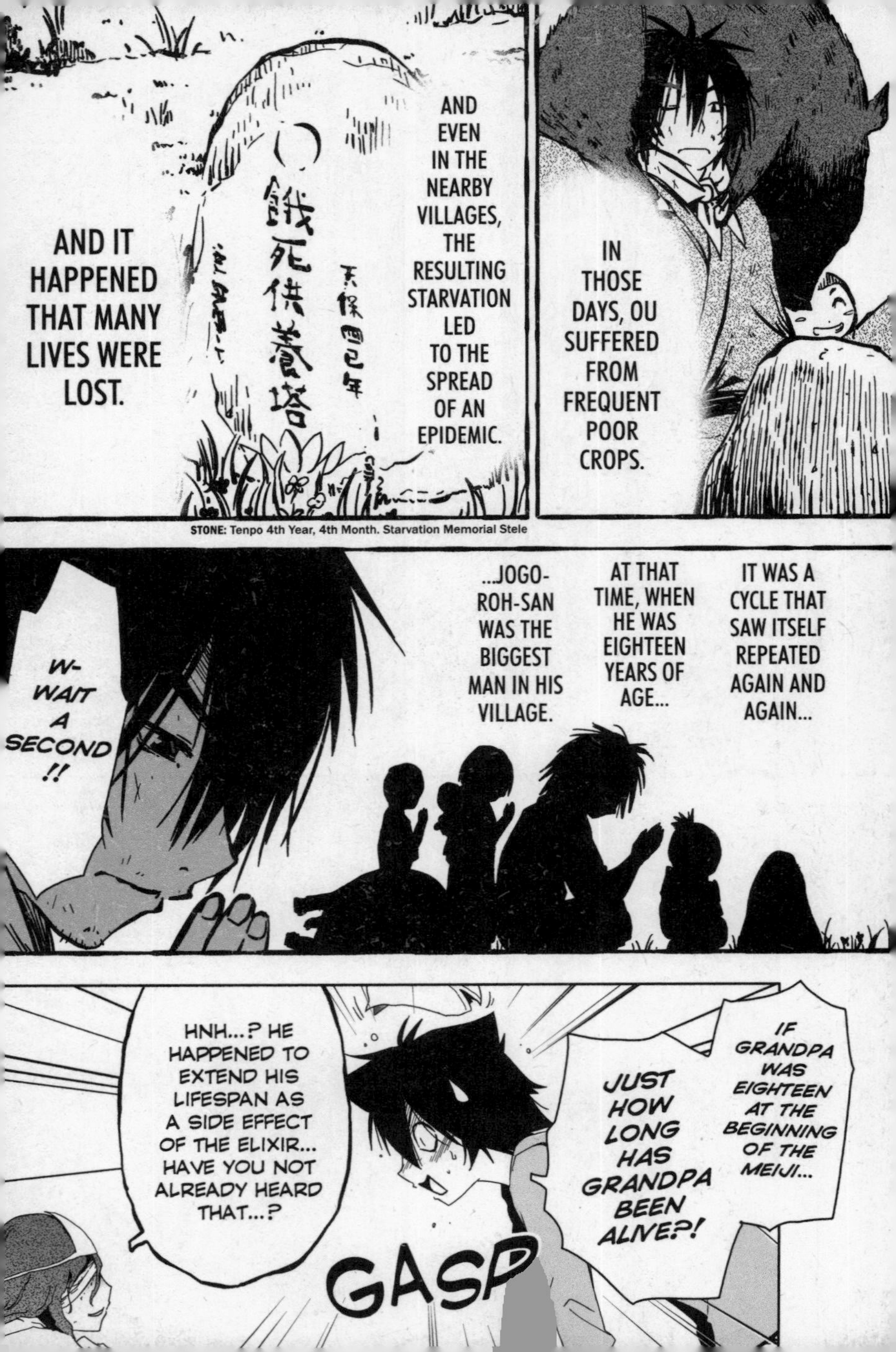
IN THOSE DAYS, OU SUFFERED FROM FREQUENT POOR CROPS.
AND EVEN IN THE NEARBY VILLAGES, THE RESULTING STARVATION LED TO THE SPREAD OF AN EPIDEMIC.
天保四巳年
餓死供養塔
AND IT HAPPENED THAT MANY LIVES WERE LOST.
STONE: Tenpo 4th Year, 4th Month. Starvation Memorial Stele
IT WAS A CYCLE THAT SAW ITSELF REPEATED AGAIN AND AGAIN...
AT THAT TIME, WHEN HE WAS EIGHTEEN YEARS OF AGE...
...JOGO-ROH-SAN WAS THE BIGGEST MAN IN HIS VILLAGE.
W-WAIT A SECOND!!
IF GRANDPA WAS EIGHTEEN AT THE BEGINNING OF THE MEIJI...
JUST HOW LONG HAS GRANDPA BEEN ALIVE?!
HNH...? HE HAPPENED TO EXTEND HIS LIFESPAN AS A SIDE EFFECT OF THE ELIXIR... HAVE YOU NOT ALREADY HEARD THAT...?
GASP

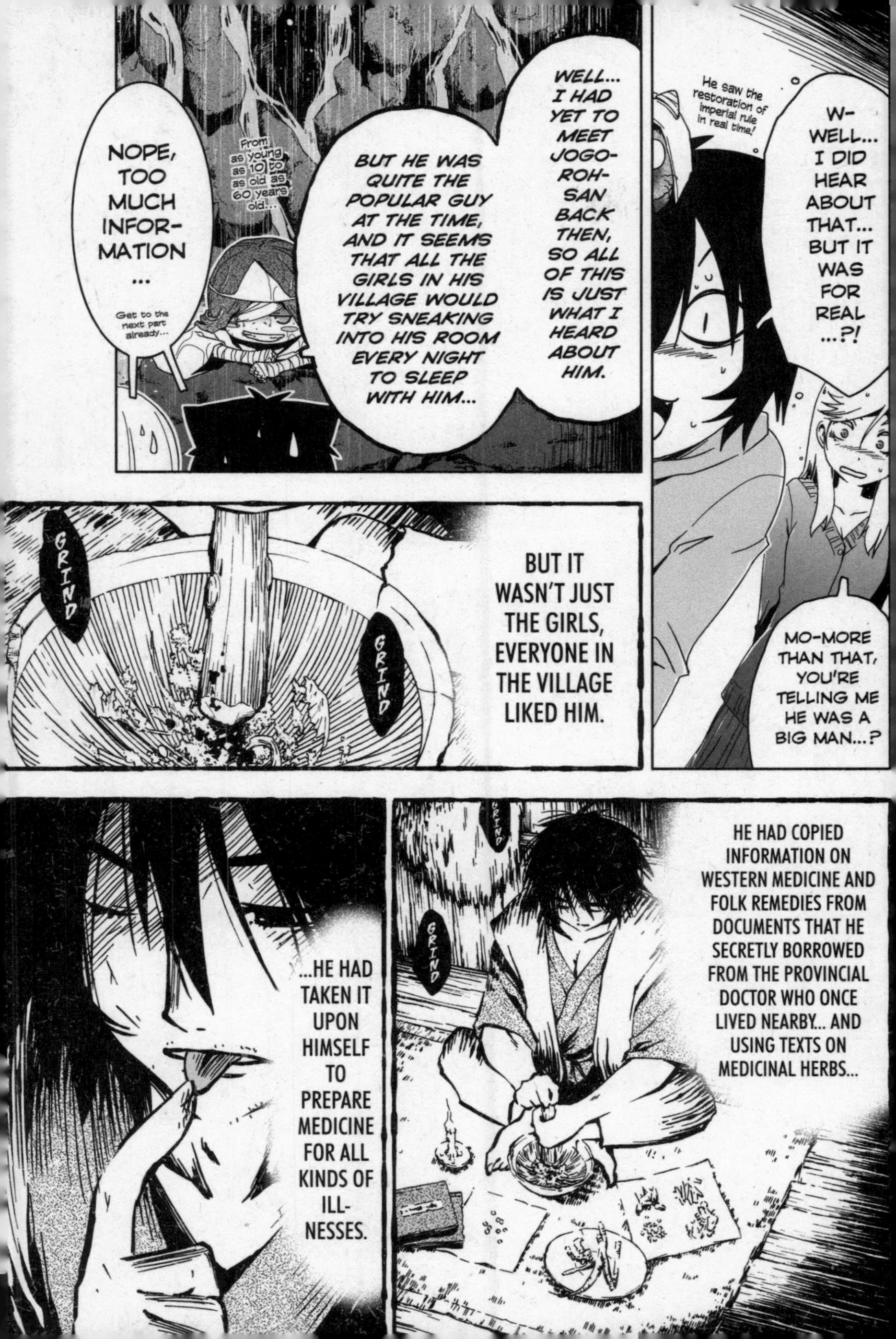
He saw the restoration of imperial rule in real time!
W-WELL... I DID HEAR ABOUT THAT... BUT IT WAS FOR REAL...?!
MO-MORE THAN THAT, YOU'RE TELLING ME HE WAS A BIG MAN...?
WELL... I HAD YET TO MEET JOGOROH-SAN BACK THEN, SO ALL OF THIS IS JUST WHAT I HEARD ABOUT HIM.
BUT HE WAS QUITE THE POPULAR GUY AT THE TIME, AND IT SEEMS THAT ALL THE GIRLS IN HIS VILLAGE WOULD TRY SNEAKING INTO HIS ROOM EVERY NIGHT TO SLEEP WITH HIM...
From as young as 10 to as old as 60 years old...
NOPE, TOO MUCH INFORMATION...
Get to the next part already...
GRIND
GRIND
BUT IT WASN'T JUST THE GIRLS, EVERYONE IN THE VILLAGE LIKED HIM.
GRIND
HE HAD COPIED INFORMATION ON WESTERN MEDICINE AND FOLK REMEDIES FROM DOCUMENTS THAT HE SECRETLY BORROWED FROM THE PROVINCIAL DOCTOR WHO ONCE LIVED NEARBY... AND USING TEXTS ON MEDICINAL HERBS...
GRIND
...HE HAD TAKEN IT UPON HIMSELF TO PREPARE MEDICINE FOR ALL KINDS OF ILLNESSES.

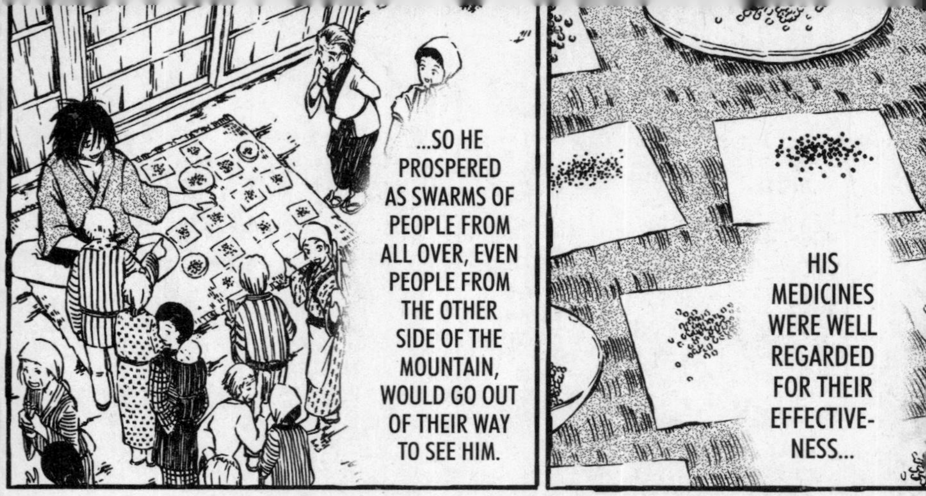
HIS MEDICINES WERE WELL REGARDED FOR THEIR EFFECTIVE-NESS...
...SO HE PROSPERED AS SWARMS OF PEOPLE FROM ALL OVER, EVEN PEOPLE FROM THE OTHER SIDE OF THE MOUNTAIN, WOULD GO OUT OF THEIR WAY TO SEE HIM.

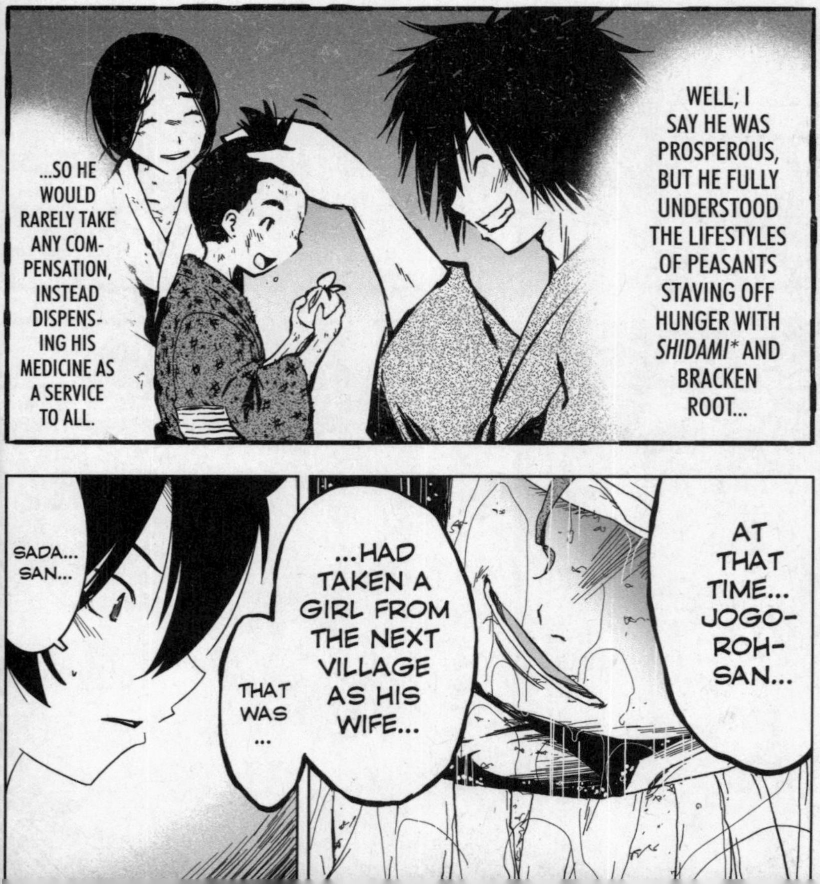
WELL, I SAY HE WAS PROSPEROUS, BUT HE FULLY UNDERSTOOD THE LIFESTYLES OF PEASANTS STAVING OFF HUNGER WITH *SHIDAMI** AND BRACKEN ROOT...
...SO HE WOULD RARELY TAKE ANY COM-PENSATION, INSTEAD DISPENS-ING HIS MEDICINE AS A SERVICE TO ALL.
AT THAT TIME... JOGO-ROH-SAN...
...HAD TAKEN A GIRL FROM THE NEXT VILLAGE AS HIS WIFE...
THAT WAS ...
SADA... SAN...

Shidami is the seed of the Japanese oak. During this time period, it was eaten as a substitute in situations where even common millet and Japanese millet couldn't be harvested.

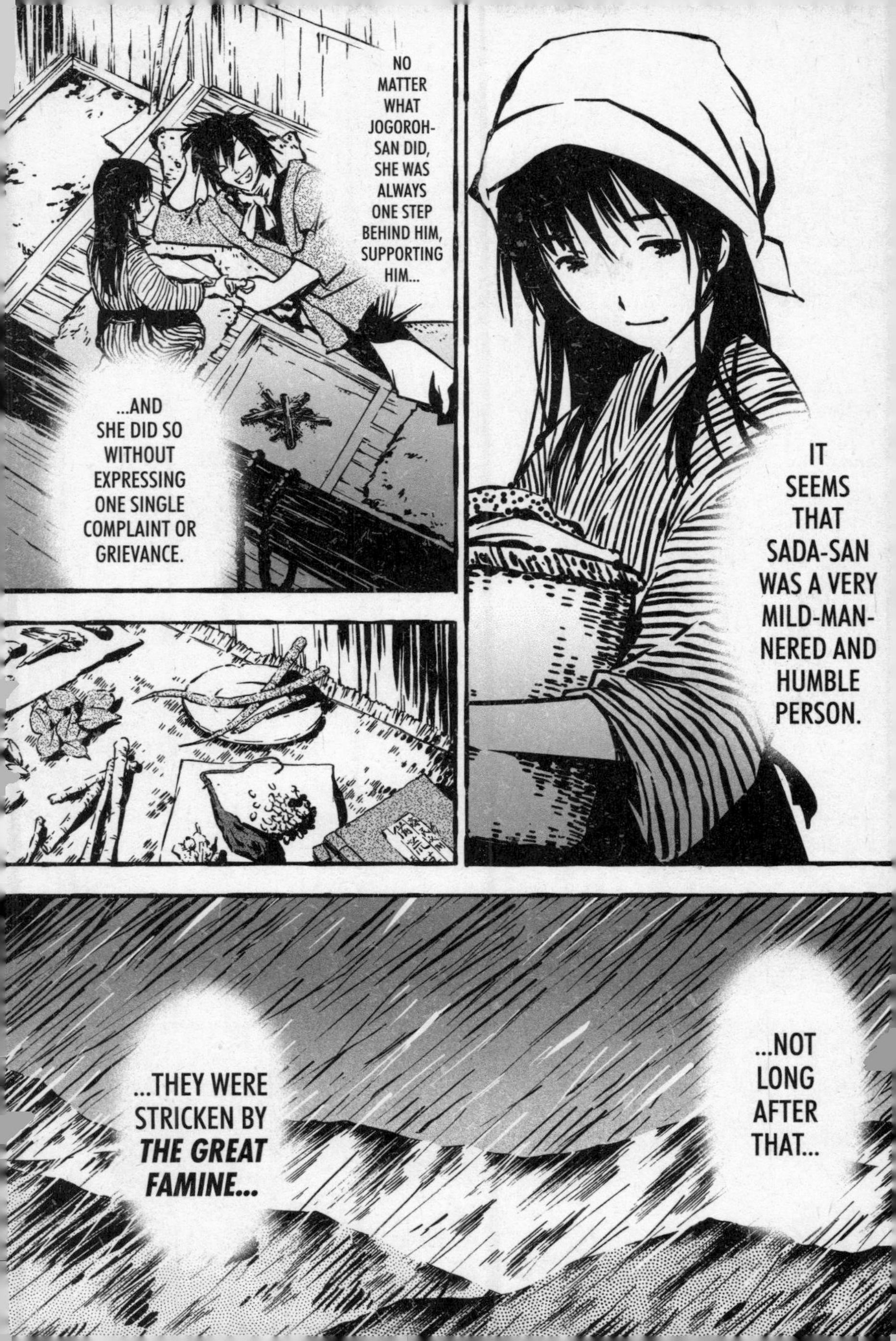
IT SEEMS THAT SADA-SAN WAS A VERY MILD-MAN-NERED AND HUMBLE PERSON.
NO MATTER WHAT JOGOROH-SAN DID, SHE WAS ALWAYS ONE STEP BEHIND HIM, SUPPORTING HIM...
...AND SHE DID SO WITHOUT EXPRESSING ONE SINGLE COMPLAINT OR GRIEVANCE.
...NOT LONG AFTER THAT...
...THEY WERE STRICKEN BY ***THE GREAT FAMINE...***

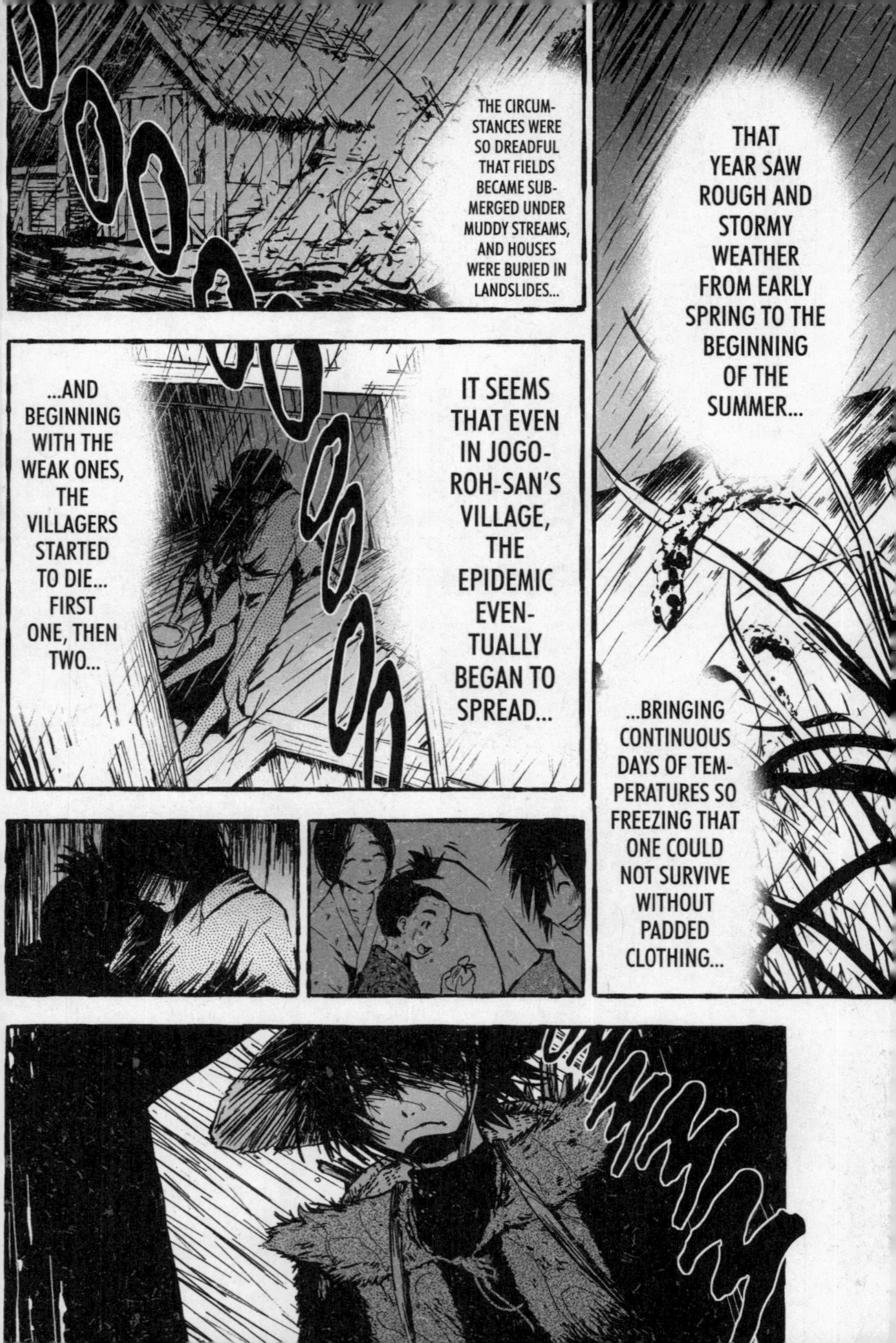
THAT YEAR SAW ROUGH AND STORMY WEATHER FROM EARLY SPRING TO THE BEGINNING OF THE SUMMER...
...BRINGING CONTINUOUS DAYS OF TEMPERATURES SO FREEZING THAT ONE COULD NOT SURVIVE WITHOUT PADDED CLOTHING...
THE CIRCUMSTANCES WERE SO DREADFUL THAT FIELDS BECAME SUBMERGED UNDER MUDDY STREAMS, AND HOUSES WERE BURIED IN LANDSLIDES...
IT SEEMS THAT EVEN IN JOGOROH-SAN'S VILLAGE, THE EPIDEMIC EVENTUALLY BEGAN TO SPREAD...
...AND BEGINNING WITH THE WEAK ONES, THE VILLAGERS STARTED TO DIE... FIRST ONE, THEN TWO...

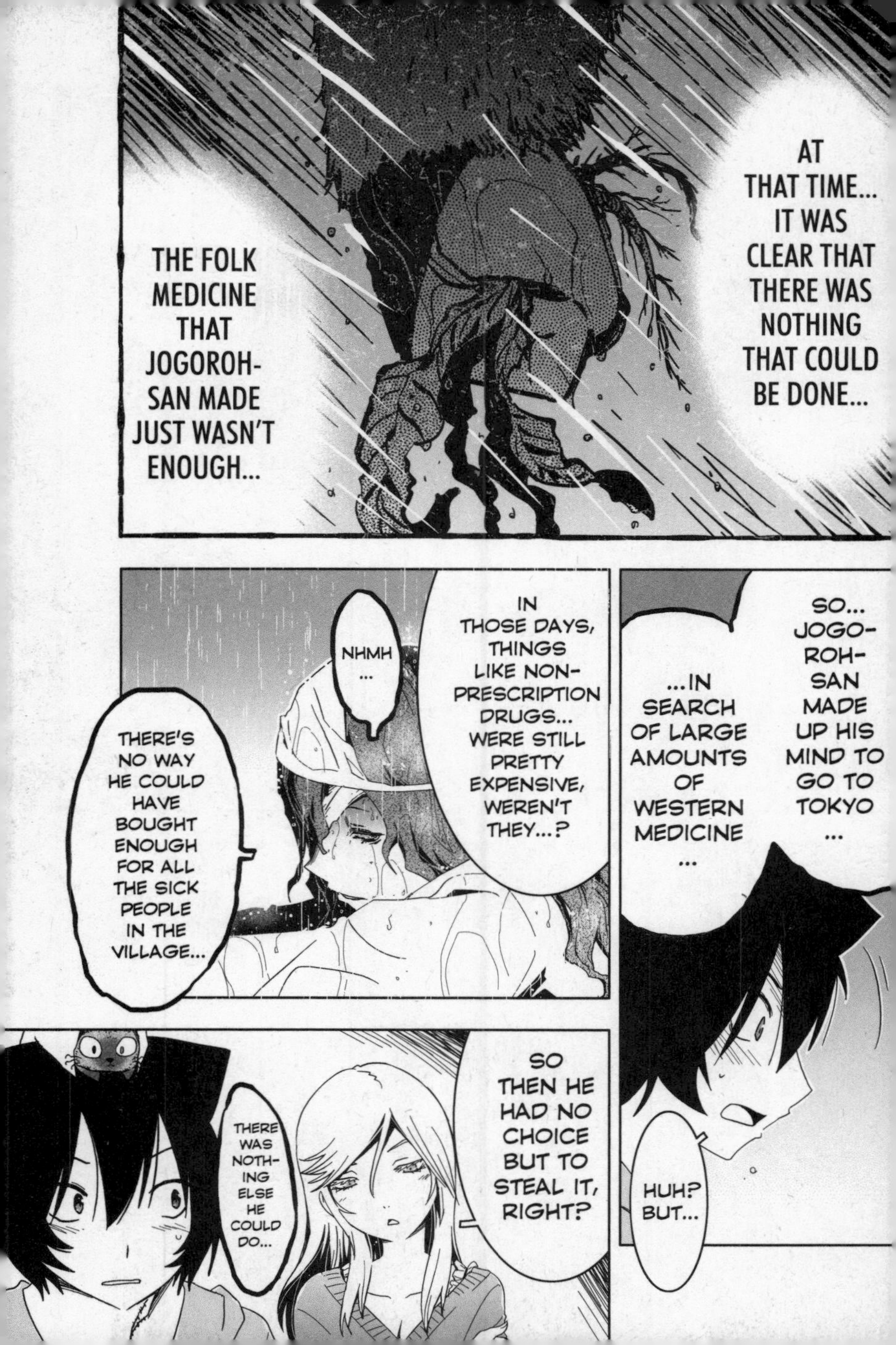
AT THAT TIME... IT WAS CLEAR THAT THERE WAS NOTHING THAT COULD BE DONE...
THE FOLK MEDICINE THAT JOGOROH-SAN MADE JUST WASN'T ENOUGH...
SO... JOGOROH-SAN MADE UP HIS MIND TO GO TO TOKYO...
...IN SEARCH OF LARGE AMOUNTS OF WESTERN MEDICINE...
IN THOSE DAYS, THINGS LIKE NON-PRESCRIPTION DRUGS... WERE STILL PRETTY EXPENSIVE, WEREN'T THEY...?
NHMH...
THERE'S NO WAY HE COULD HAVE BOUGHT ENOUGH FOR ALL THE SICK PEOPLE IN THE VILLAGE...
HUH? BUT...
SO THEN HE HAD NO CHOICE BUT TO STEAL IT, RIGHT?
THERE WAS NOTHING ELSE HE COULD DO...

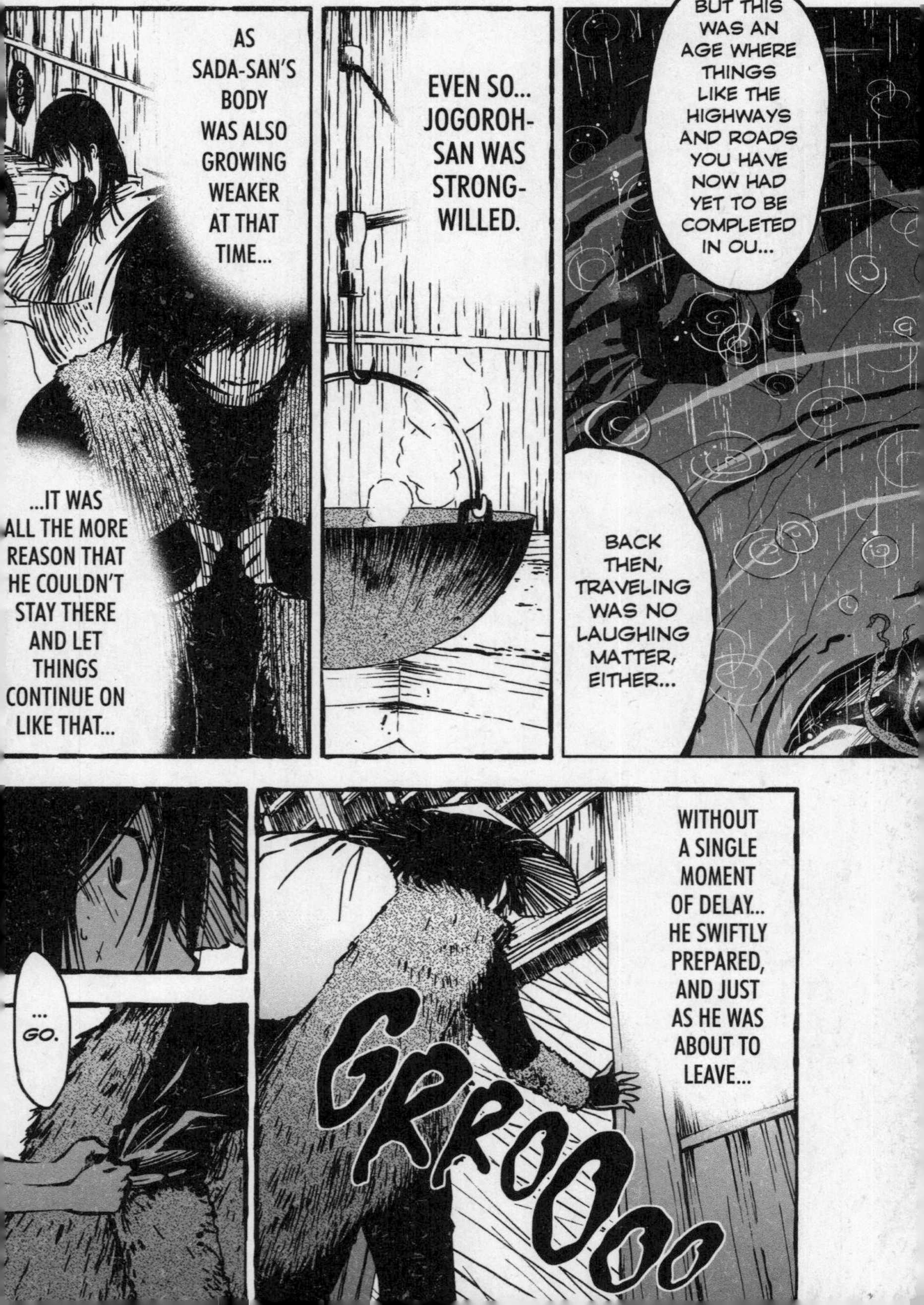
BUT THIS WAS AN AGE WHERE THINGS LIKE THE HIGHWAYS AND ROADS YOU HAVE NOW HAD YET TO BE COMPLETED IN OU...
BACK THEN, TRAVELING WAS NO LAUGHING MATTER, EITHER...
EVEN SO... JOGOROH-SAN WAS STRONG-WILLED.
COUGH
AS SADA-SAN'S BODY WAS ALSO GROWING WEAKER AT THAT TIME...
...IT WAS ALL THE MORE REASON THAT HE COULDN'T STAY THERE AND LET THINGS CONTINUE ON LIKE THAT...
WITHOUT A SINGLE MOMENT OF DELAY... HE SWIFTLY PREPARED, AND JUST AS HE WAS ABOUT TO LEAVE...
GROOOOOO
... GO.

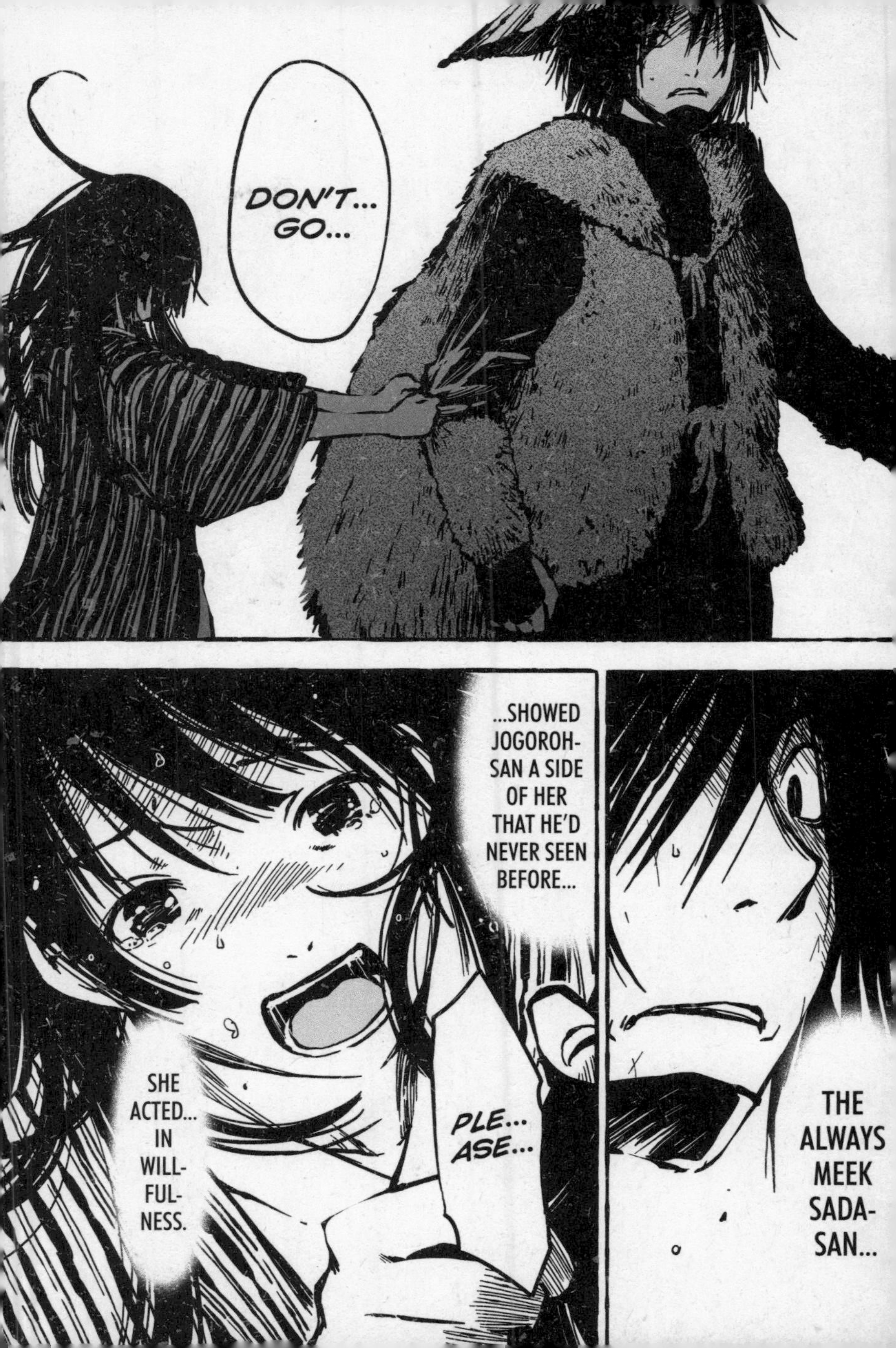
DON'T... GO...
THE ALWAYS MEEK SADA-SAN...
...SHOWED JOGOROH-SAN A SIDE OF HER THAT HE'D NEVER SEEN BEFORE...
PLE... ASE...
SHE ACTED... IN WILL-FUL-NESS.

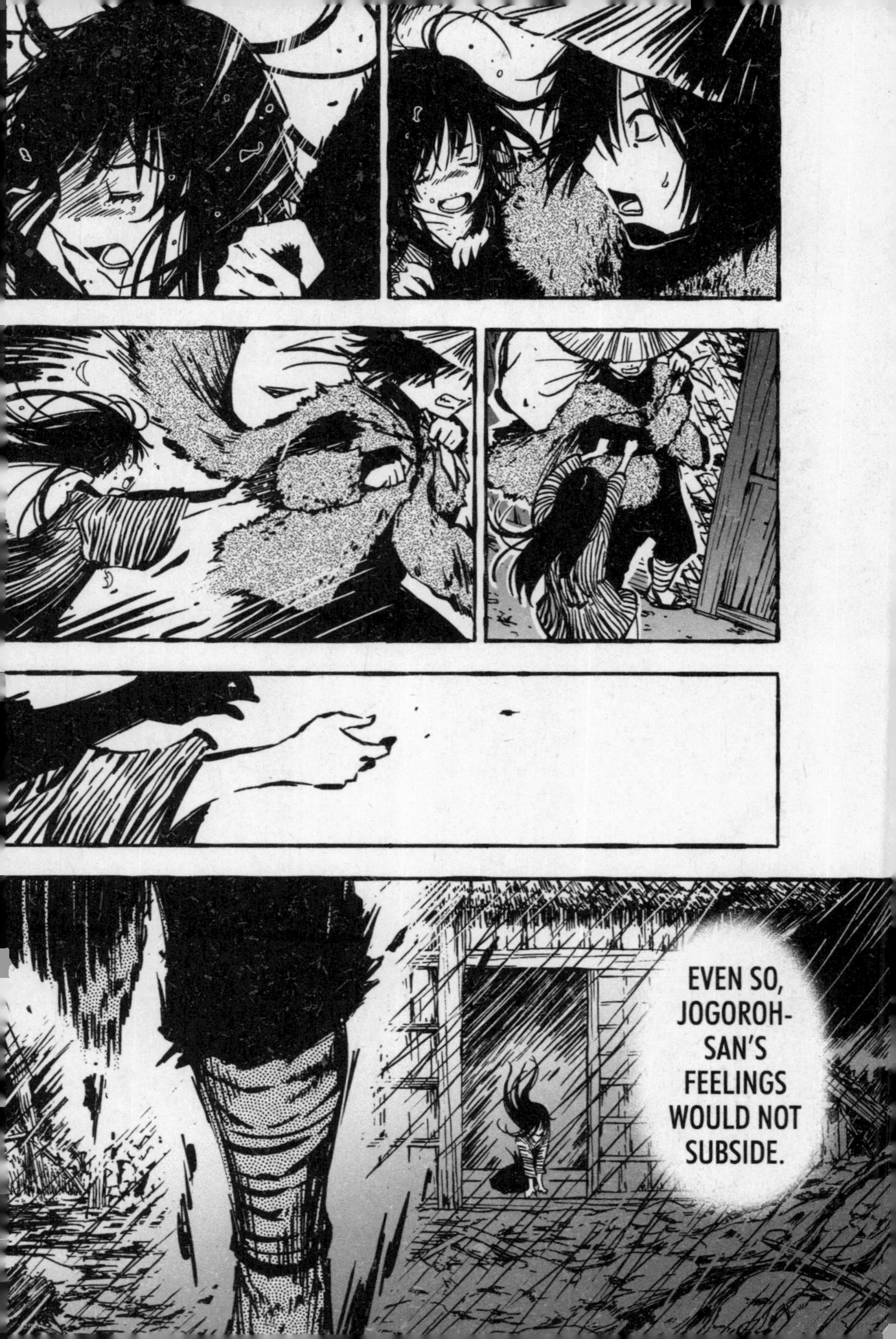
EVEN SO, JOGOROH-SAN'S FEELINGS WOULD NOT SUBSIDE.

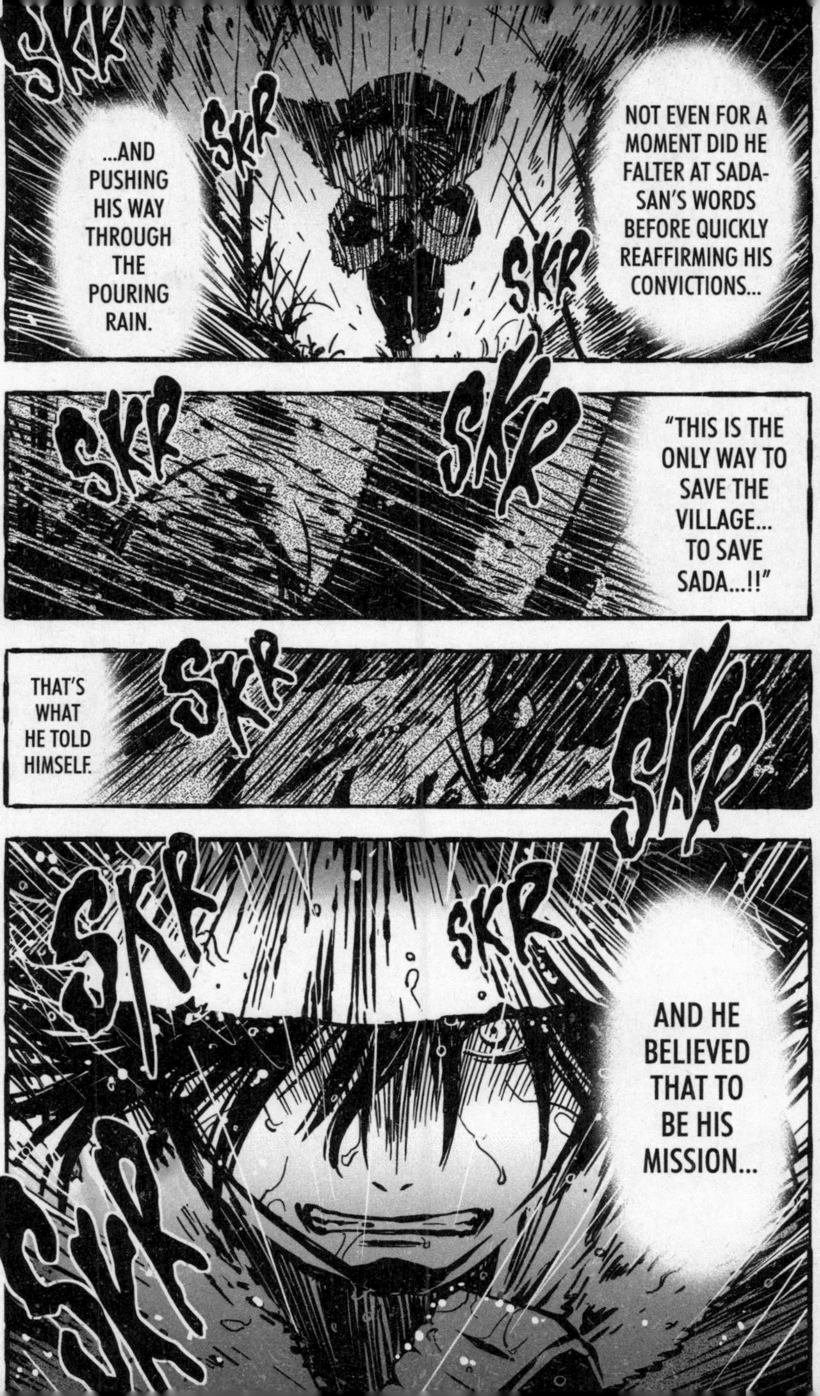
SKR
SKR
NOT EVEN FOR A MOMENT DID HE FALTER AT SADA-SAN'S WORDS BEFORE QUICKLY REAFFIRMING HIS CONVICTIONS...
SKR
...AND PUSHING HIS WAY THROUGH THE POURING RAIN.
SKR
"THIS IS THE ONLY WAY TO SAVE THE VILLAGE... TO SAVE SADA...!!"
SKR
SKR
SKR
SKR
THAT'S WHAT HE TOLD HIMSELF.
AND HE BELIEVED THAT TO BE HIS MISSION...
SKR
SKR
SKR

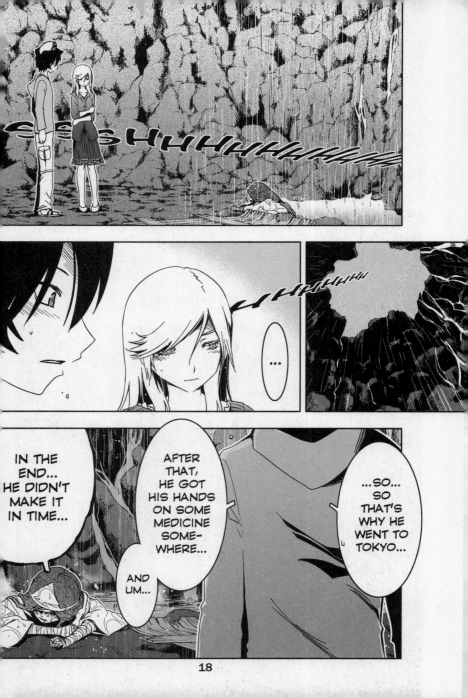

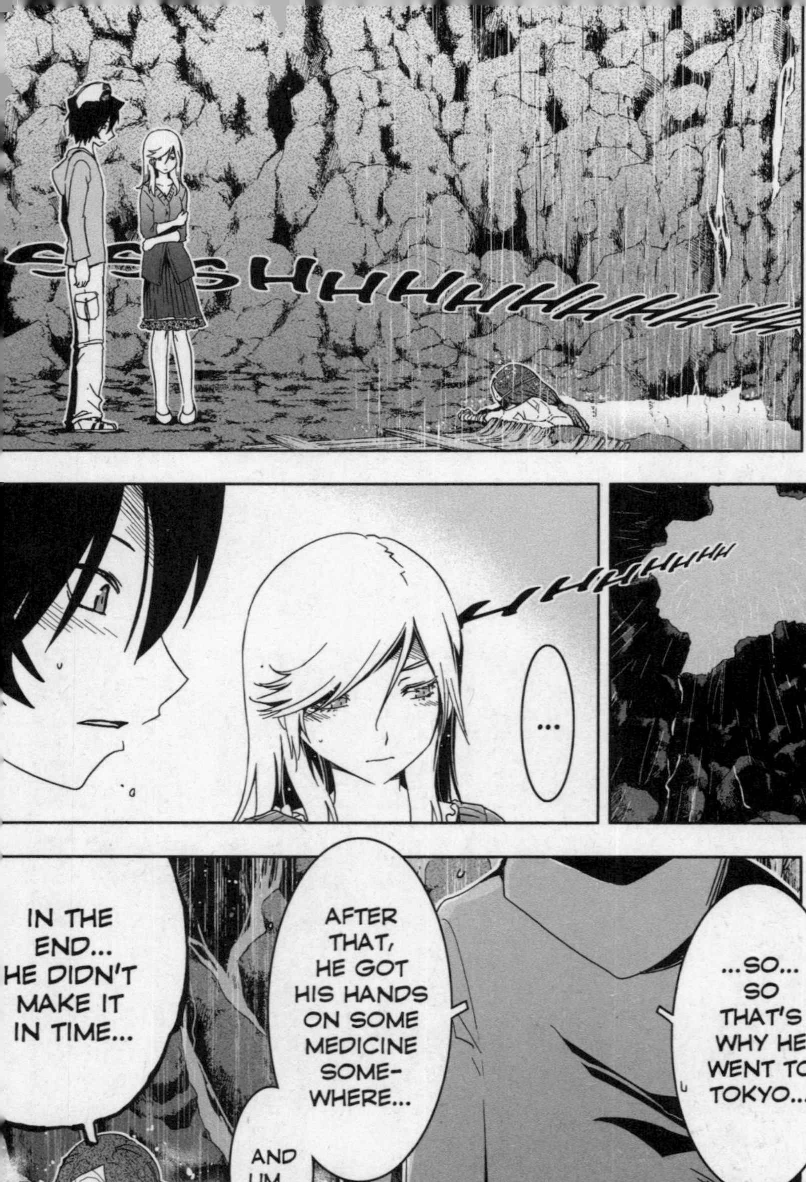
SHHHHHHHHHHHHHH
HHHHHHHHH
...
...SO... SO THAT'S WHY HE WENT TO TOKYO...
AFTER THAT, HE GOT HIS HANDS ON SOME MEDICINE SOME-WHERE...
AND UM...
IN THE END... HE DIDN'T MAKE IT IN TIME...

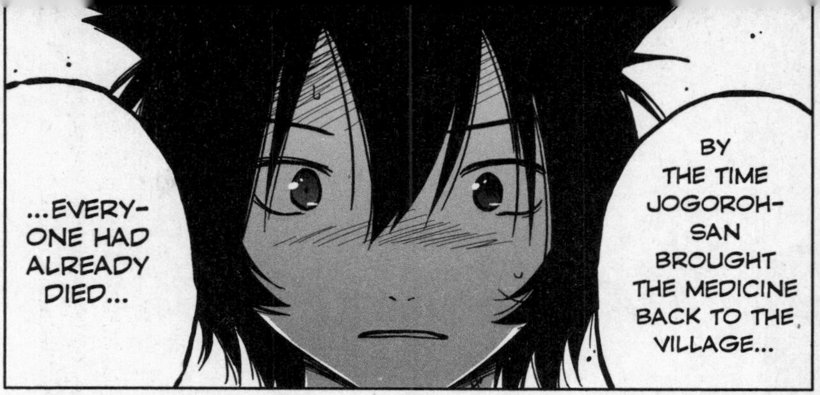
BY THE TIME JOGOROH-SAN BROUGHT THE MEDICINE BACK TO THE VILLAGE...
...EVERYONE HAD ALREADY DIED...
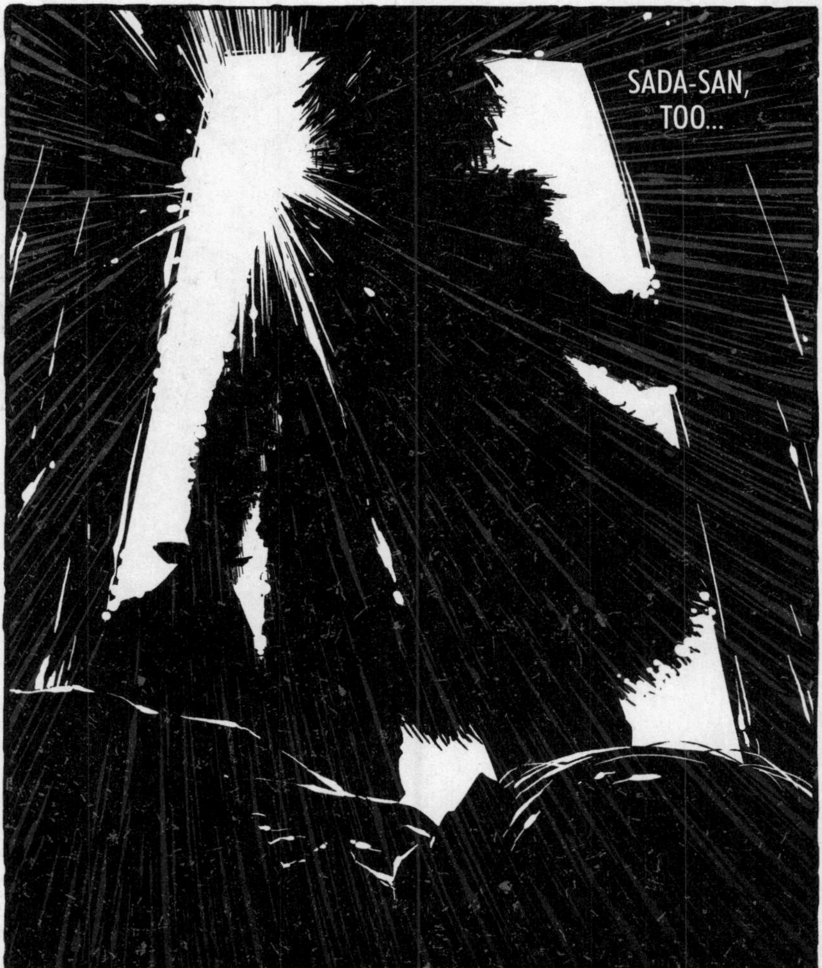
SADA-SAN, TOO...

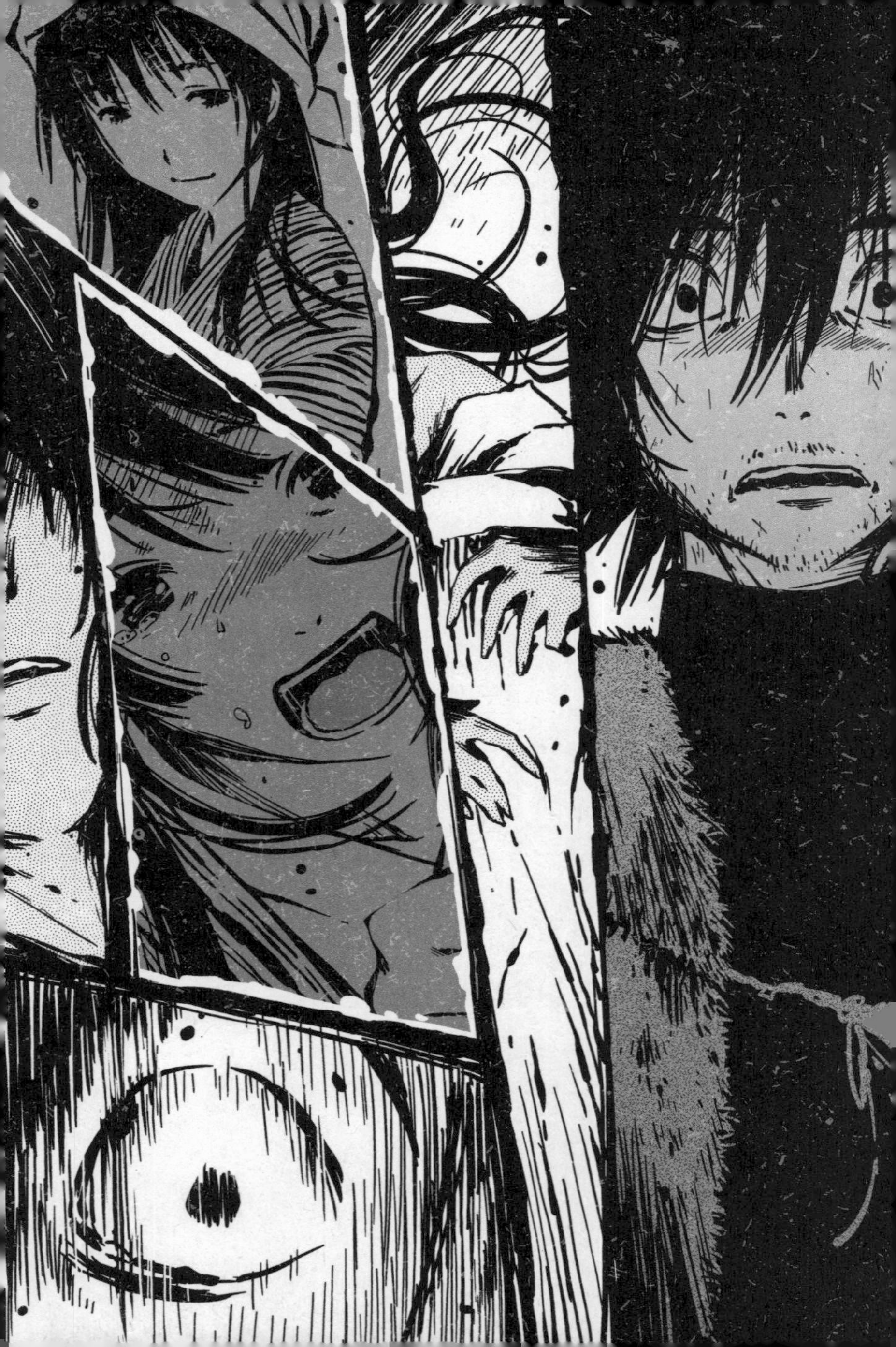

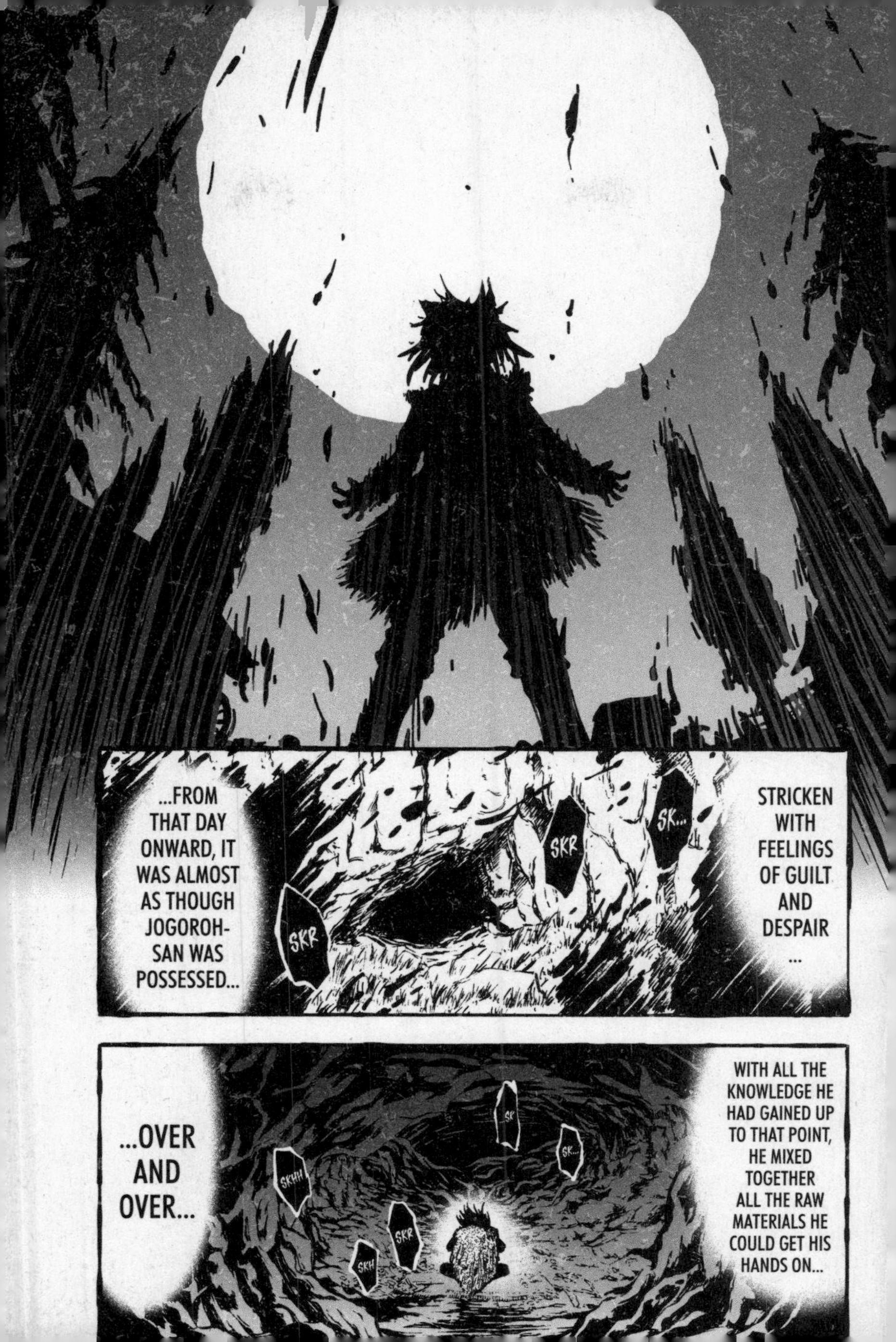
STRICKEN WITH FEELINGS OF GUILT AND DESPAIR ...
SK...
SKR
SKR
...FROM THAT DAY ONWARD, IT WAS ALMOST AS THOUGH JOGOROH-SAN WAS POSSESSED...
WITH ALL THE KNOWLEDGE HE HAD GAINED UP TO THAT POINT, HE MIXED TOGETHER ALL THE RAW MATERIALS HE COULD GET HIS HANDS ON...
SK...
SK
SKR
SKH
SKHH
...OVER AND OVER...

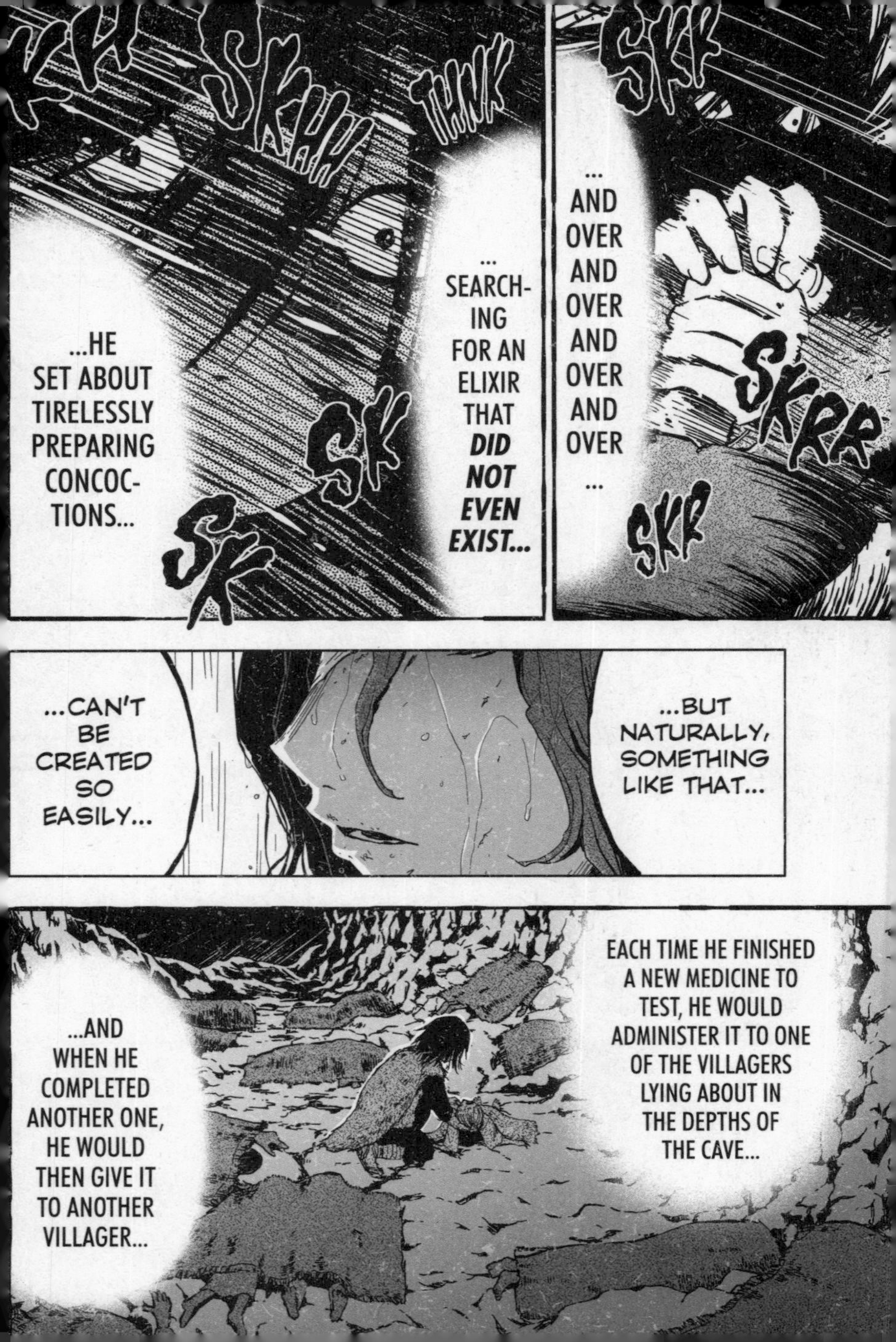
SKF
...AND OVER AND OVER AND OVER AND OVER AND OVER...
SKRR
SKR
THUNK
SKHH
SKH
...SEARCHING FOR AN ELIXIR THAT ***DID NOT EVEN EXIST...***
SK
SK
...HE SET ABOUT TIRELESSLY PREPARING CONCOCTIONS...
...BUT NATURALLY, SOMETHING LIKE THAT...
...CAN'T BE CREATED SO EASILY...
EACH TIME HE FINISHED A NEW MEDICINE TO TEST, HE WOULD ADMINISTER IT TO ONE OF THE VILLAGERS LYING ABOUT IN THE DEPTHS OF THE CAVE...
...AND WHEN HE COMPLETED ANOTHER ONE, HE WOULD THEN GIVE IT TO ANOTHER VILLAGER...

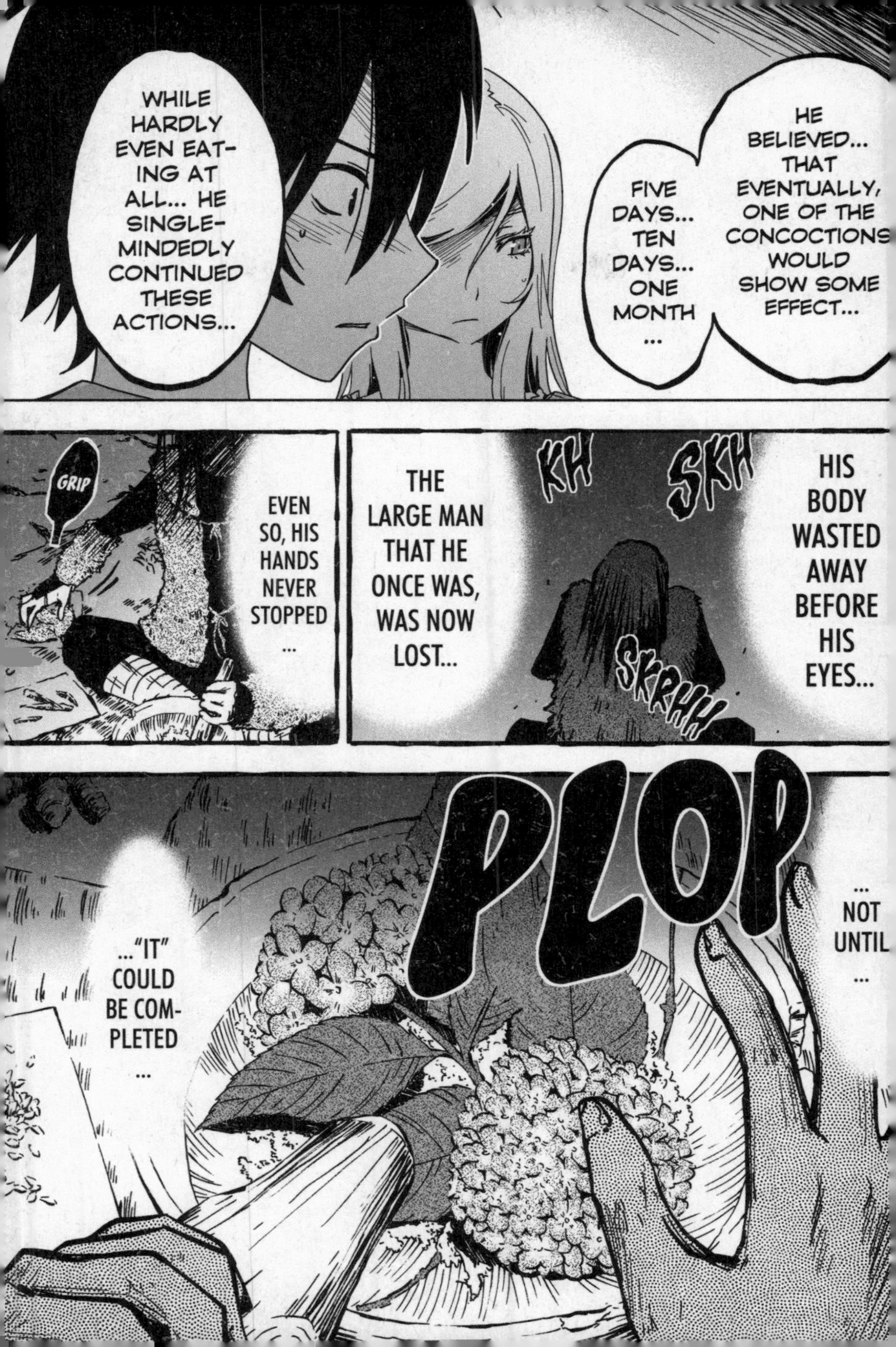
HE BELIEVED... THAT EVENTUALLY, ONE OF THE CONCOCTIONS WOULD SHOW SOME EFFECT...
FIVE DAYS... TEN DAYS... ONE MONTH ...
WHILE HARDLY EVEN EATING AT ALL... HE SINGLE-MINDEDLY CONTINUED THESE ACTIONS...
HIS BODY WASTED AWAY BEFORE HIS EYES...
SKH
KH
SKRHH
THE LARGE MAN THAT HE ONCE WAS, WAS NOW LOST...
EVEN SO, HIS HANDS NEVER STOPPED ...
GRIP
... NOT UNTIL ...
PLOP
..."IT" COULD BE COMPLETED ...

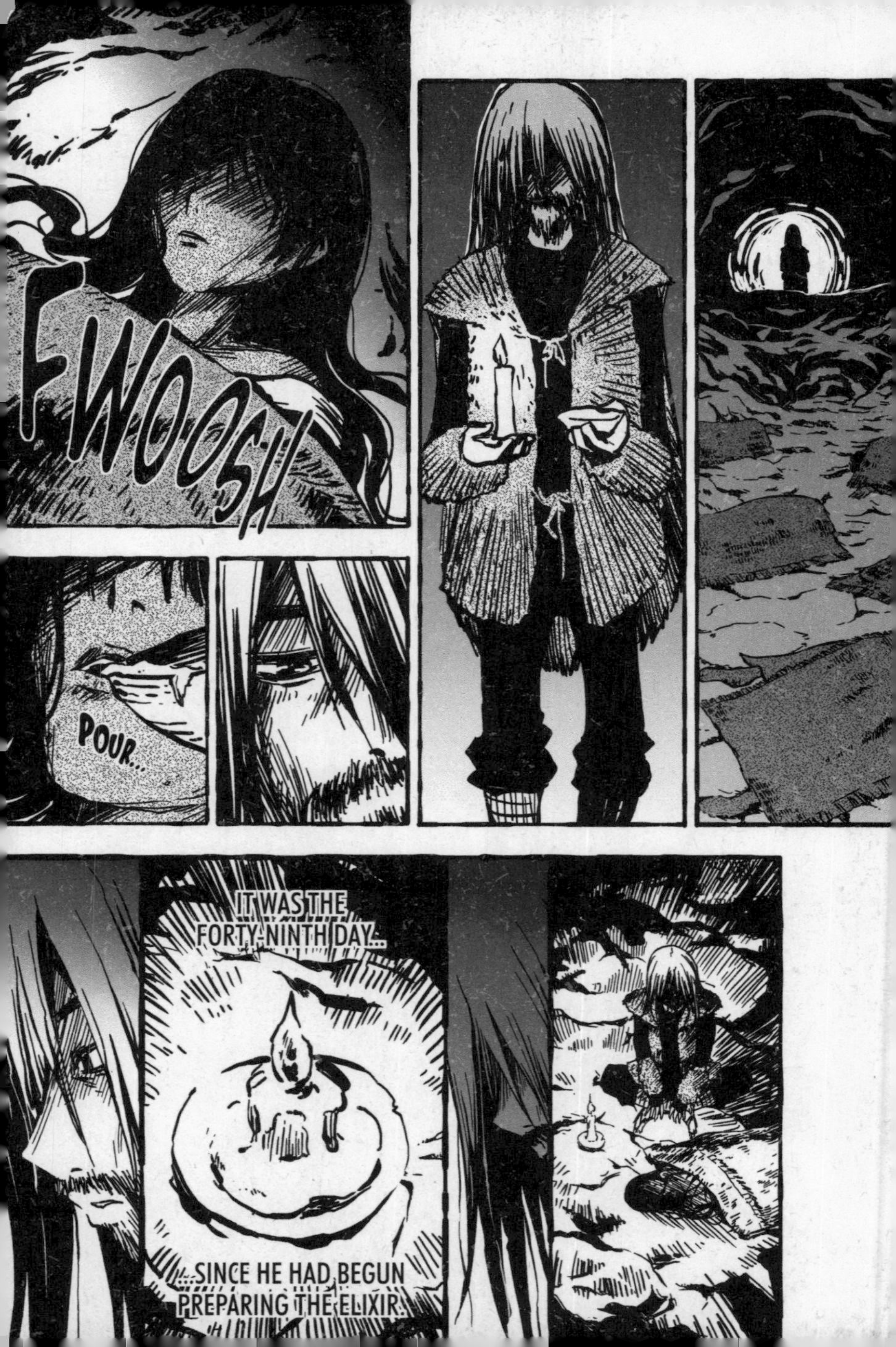
FWOOSH
POUR...
IT WAS THE FORTY-NINTH DAY...
...SINCE HE HAD BEGUN PREPARING THE ELIXIR.

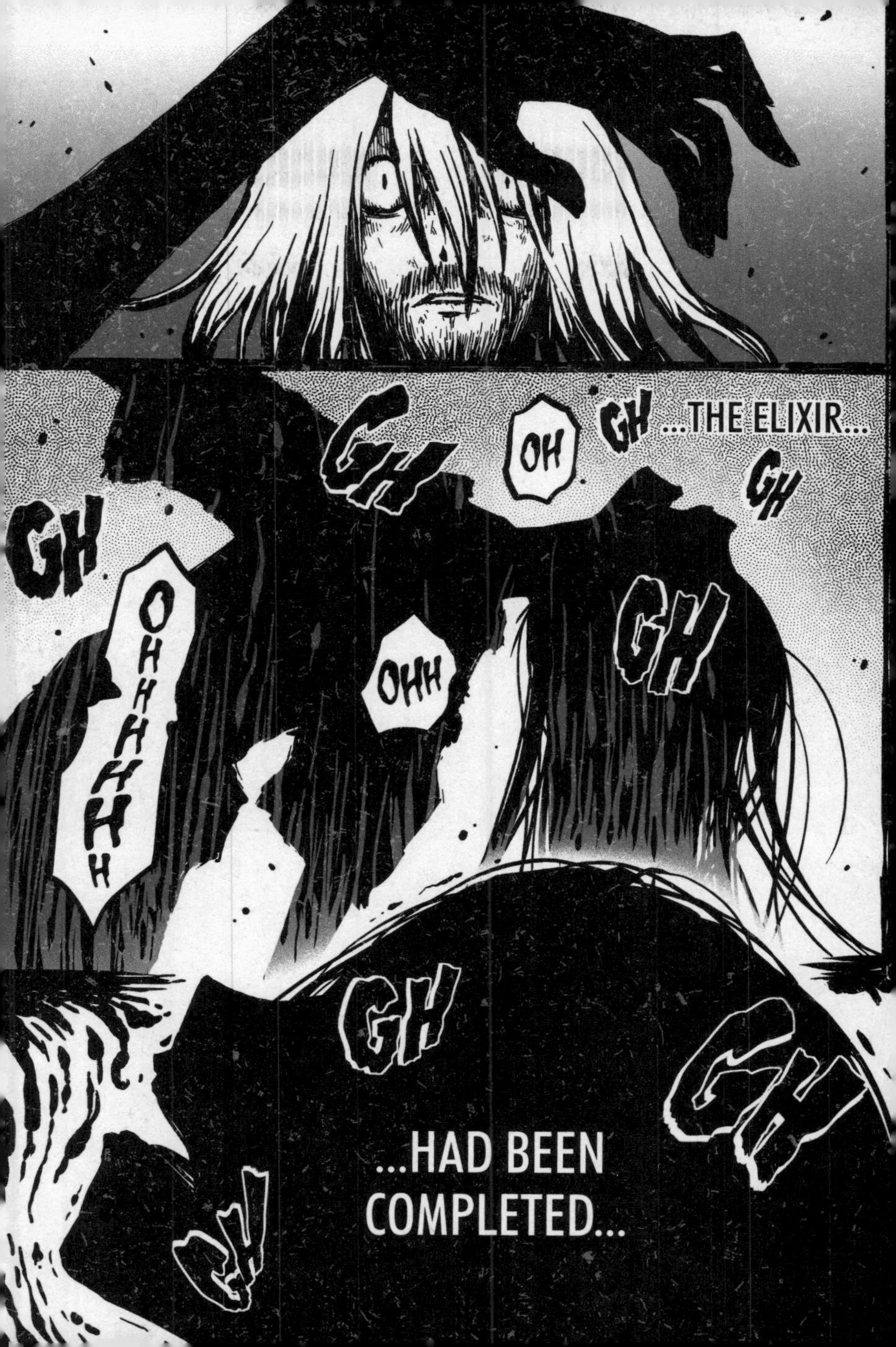
GH
...THE ELIXIR...
GH
OH
GH
GH
GH
OHH
OHHHHHHH
GH
GH
...HAD BEEN COMPLETED...

SANKAREA

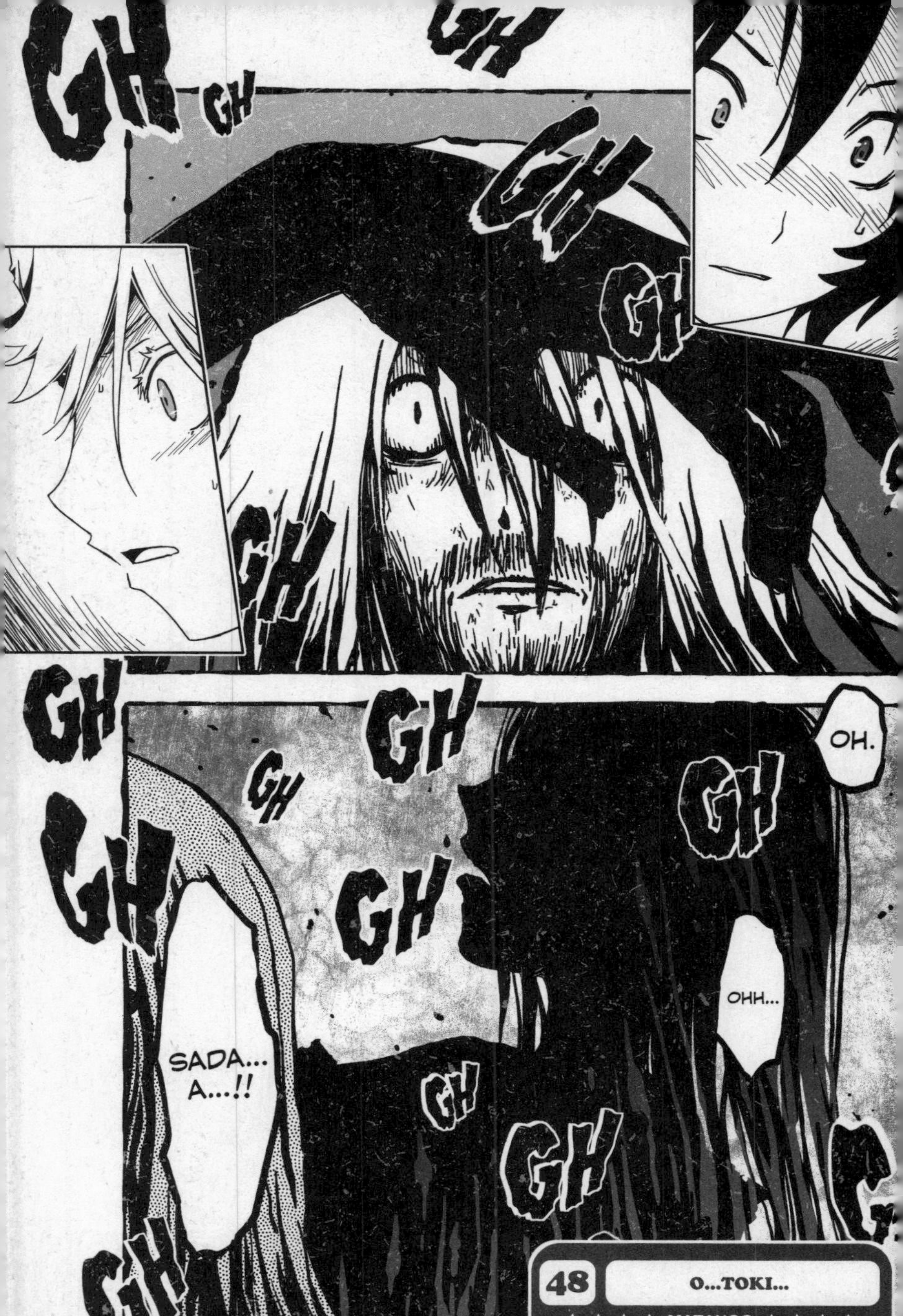
GH
GH
GH
GH
GH
GH
GH
GH
OH.
GH
GH
GH
GH
OHH...
GH
GH
GH
SADA... A...!!
GH

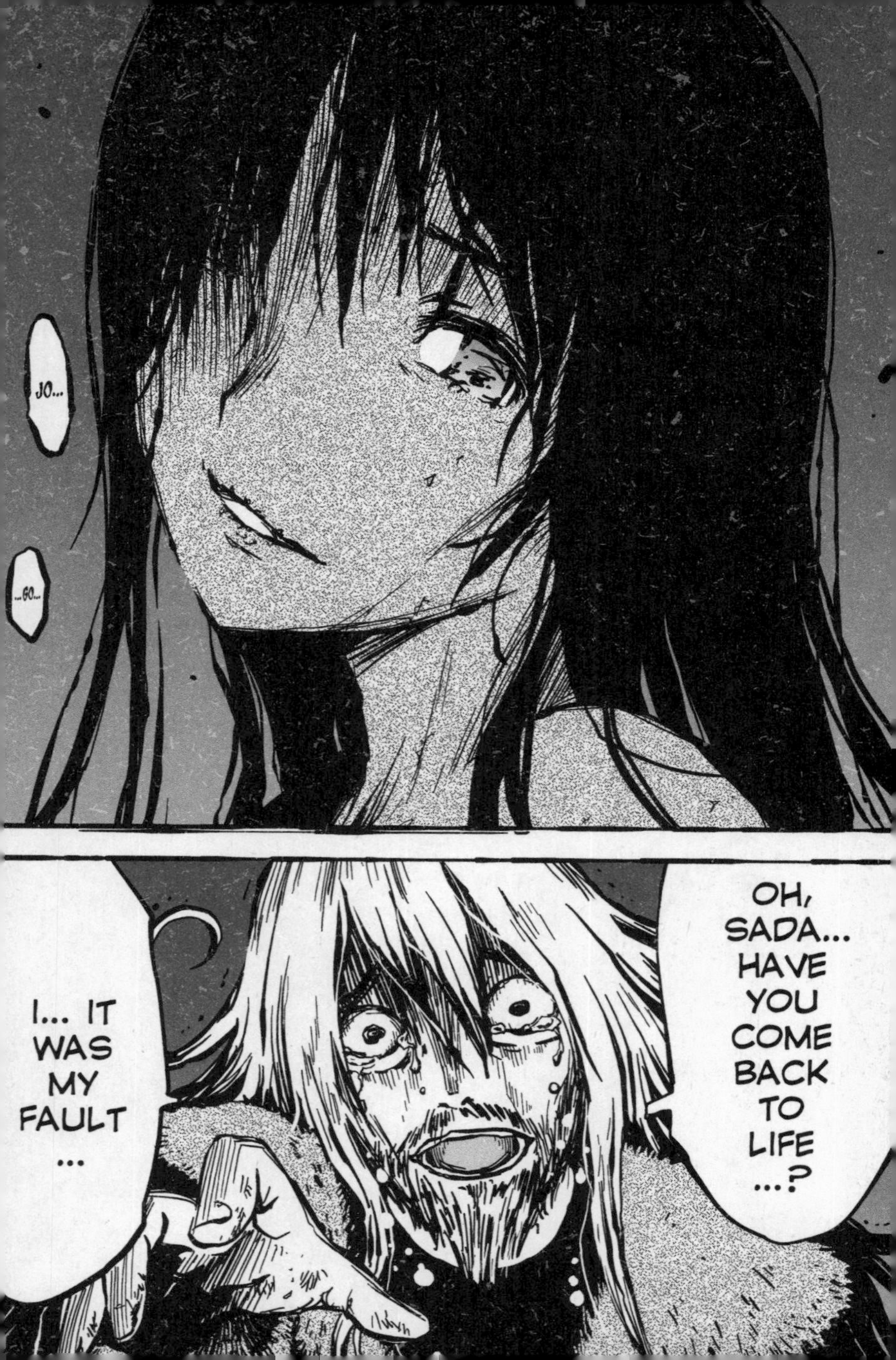
JO...
...GO...
OH, SADA... HAVE YOU COME BACK TO LIFE ...?
I... IT WAS MY FAULT ...

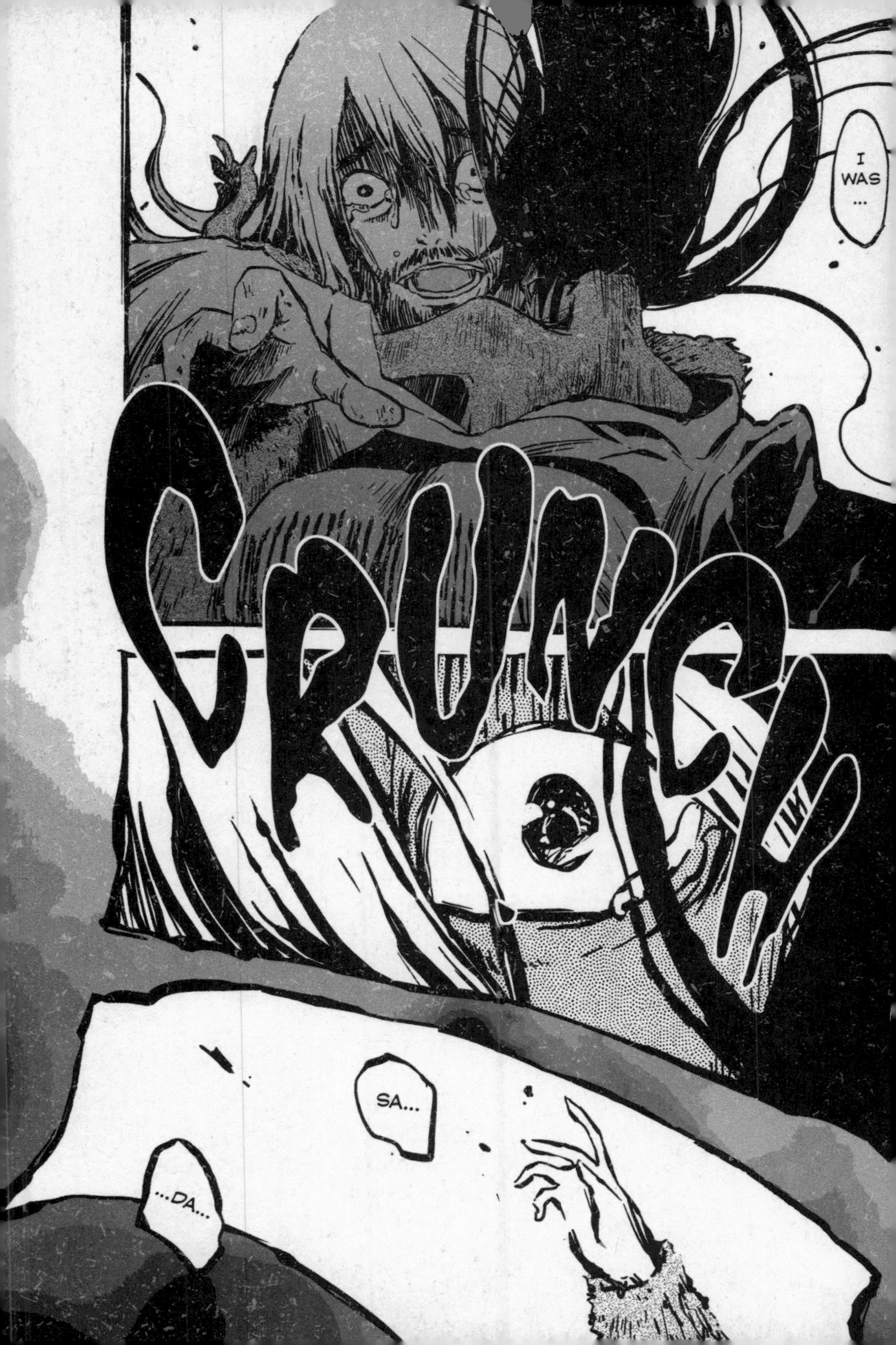
I WAS ...
CRUNCH
SA...
...DA...

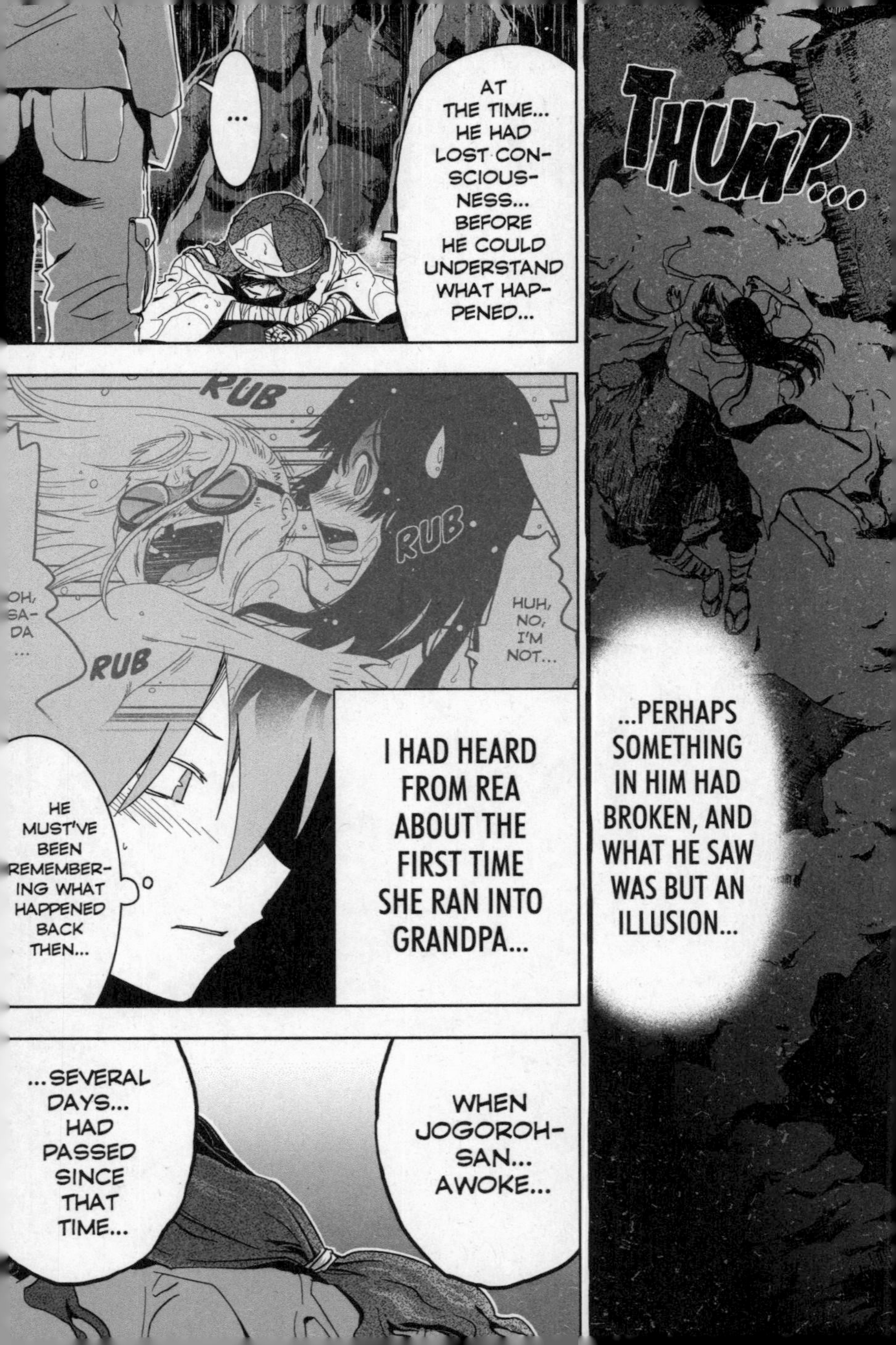
THUMP...
...PERHAPS SOMETHING IN HIM HAD BROKEN, AND WHAT HE SAW WAS BUT AN ILLUSION...
AT THE TIME... HE HAD LOST CONSCIOUSNESS... BEFORE HE COULD UNDERSTAND WHAT HAPPENED...
...
RUB
RUB
HUH, NO, I'M NOT...
OH, SADA...
RUB
I HAD HEARD FROM REA ABOUT THE FIRST TIME SHE RAN INTO GRANDPA...
HE MUST'VE BEEN REMEMBERING WHAT HAPPENED BACK THEN...
WHEN JOGOROH-SAN... AWOKE...
...SEVERAL DAYS... HAD PASSED SINCE THAT TIME...

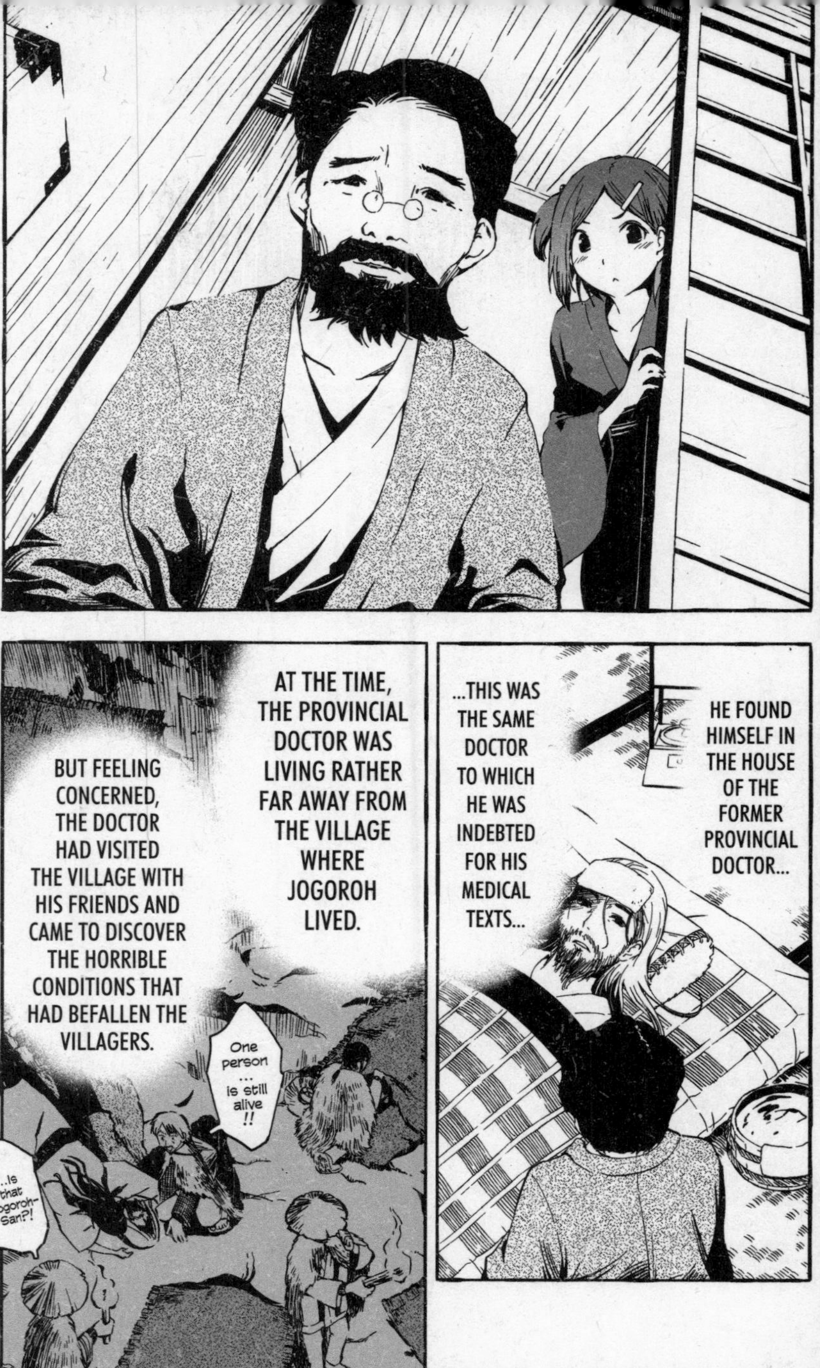
HE FOUND HIMSELF IN THE HOUSE OF THE FORMER PROVINCIAL DOCTOR...
...THIS WAS THE SAME DOCTOR TO WHICH HE WAS INDEBTED FOR HIS MEDICAL TEXTS...
AT THE TIME, THE PROVINCIAL DOCTOR WAS LIVING RATHER FAR AWAY FROM THE VILLAGE WHERE JOGOROH LIVED.
BUT FEELING CONCERNED, THE DOCTOR HAD VISITED THE VILLAGE WITH HIS FRIENDS AND CAME TO DISCOVER THE HORRIBLE CONDITIONS THAT HAD BEFALLEN THE VILLAGERS.
One person ... is still alive!!
...Is that Jogoroh-San?!

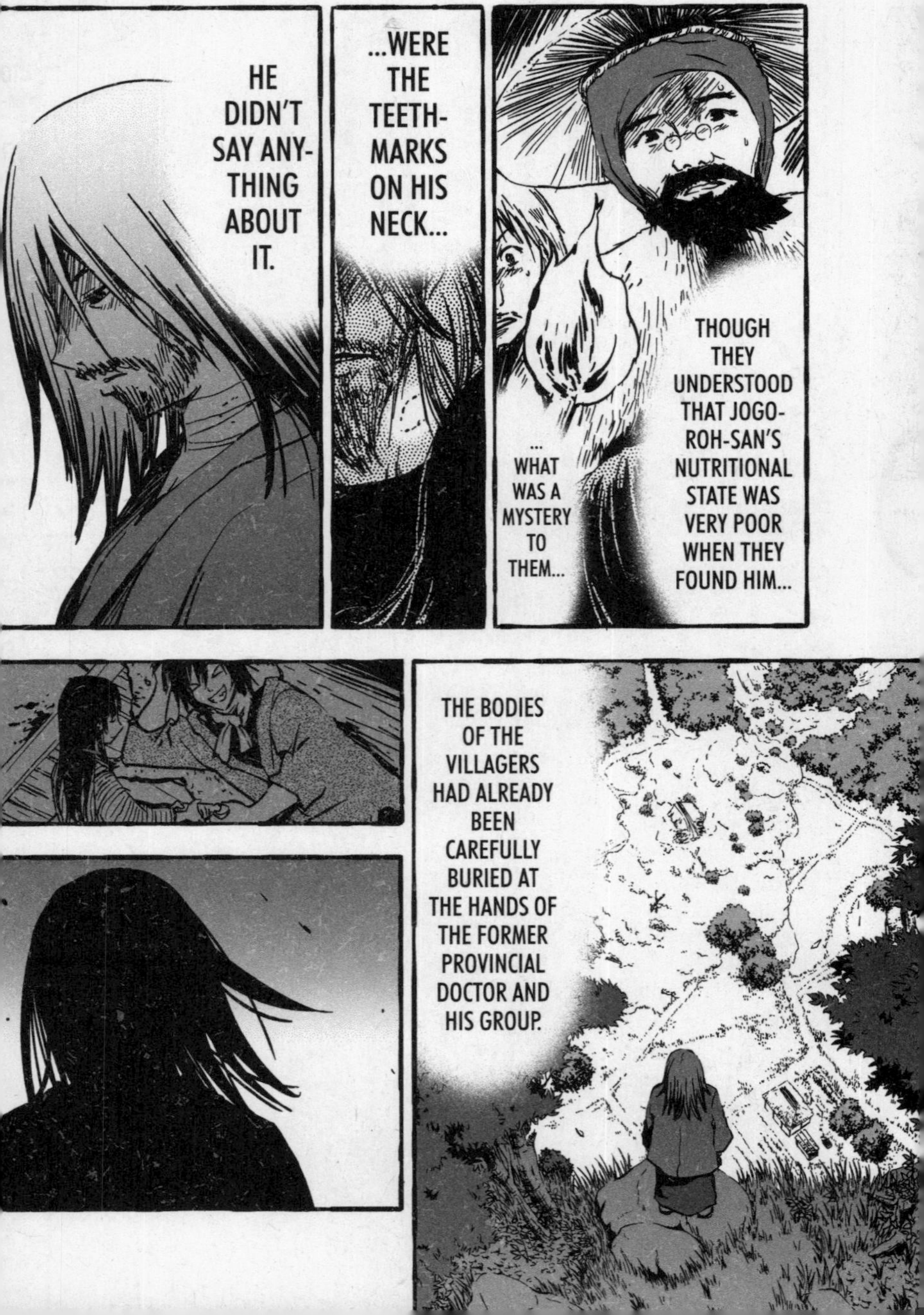
THOUGH THEY UNDERSTOOD THAT JOGO-ROH-SAN'S NUTRITIONAL STATE WAS VERY POOR WHEN THEY FOUND HIM...
... WHAT WAS A MYSTERY TO THEM...
...WERE THE TEETH-MARKS ON HIS NECK...
HE DIDN'T SAY ANY-THING ABOUT IT.
THE BODIES OF THE VILLAGERS HAD ALREADY BEEN CAREFULLY BURIED AT THE HANDS OF THE FORMER PROVINCIAL DOCTOR AND HIS GROUP.

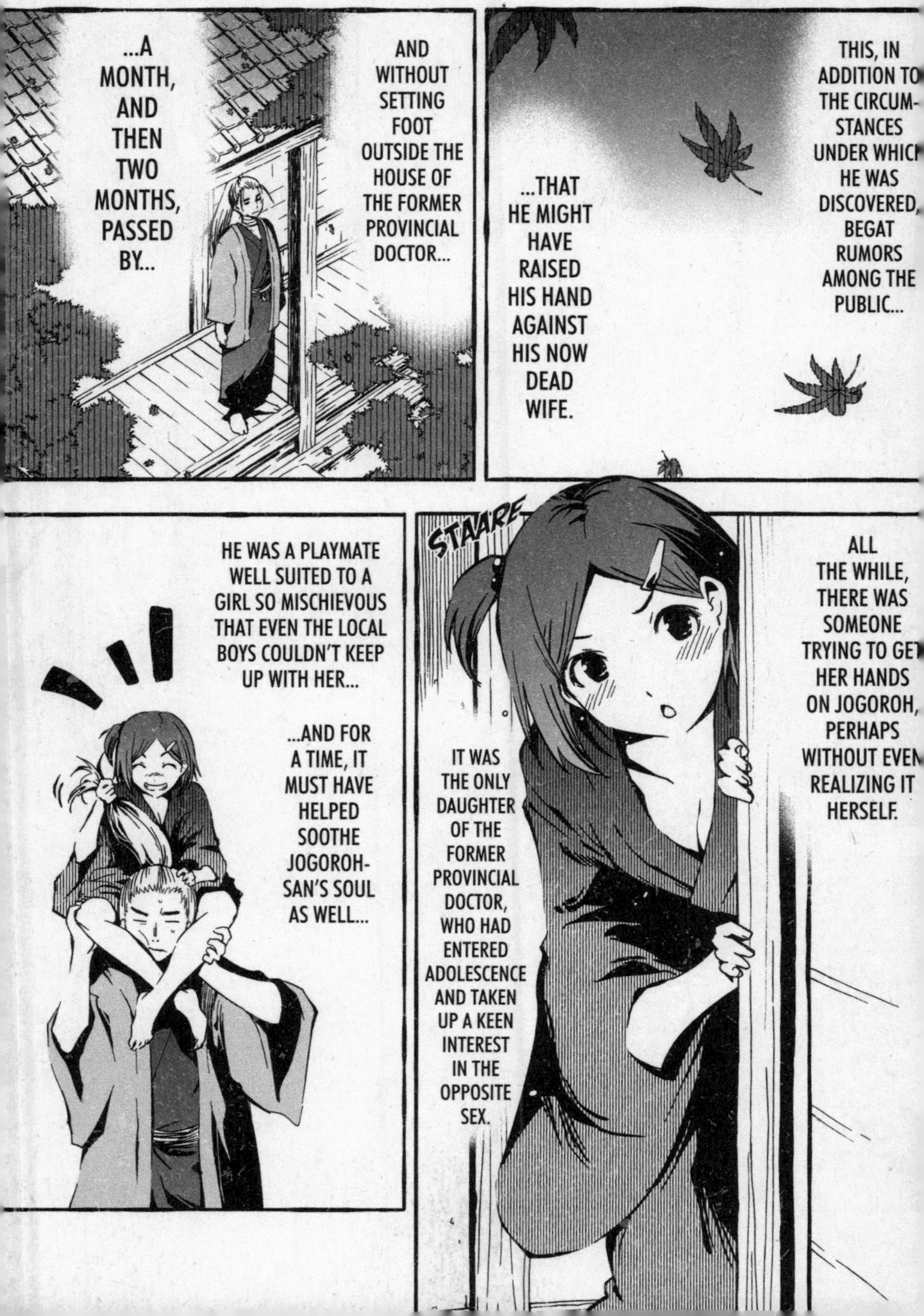
THIS, IN ADDITION TO THE CIRCUM-STANCES UNDER WHICH HE WAS DISCOVERED, BEGAT RUMORS AMONG THE PUBLIC...
...THAT HE MIGHT HAVE RAISED HIS HAND AGAINST HIS NOW DEAD WIFE.
AND WITHOUT SETTING FOOT OUTSIDE THE HOUSE OF THE FORMER PROVINCIAL DOCTOR...
...A MONTH, AND THEN TWO MONTHS, PASSED BY...
STAARE
ALL THE WHILE, THERE WAS SOMEONE TRYING TO GET HER HANDS ON JOGOROH, PERHAPS WITHOUT EVEN REALIZING IT HERSELF.
IT WAS THE ONLY DAUGHTER OF THE FORMER PROVINCIAL DOCTOR, WHO HAD ENTERED ADOLESCENCE AND TAKEN UP A KEEN INTEREST IN THE OPPOSITE SEX.
HE WAS A PLAYMATE WELL SUITED TO A GIRL SO MISCHIEVOUS THAT EVEN THE LOCAL BOYS COULDN'T KEEP UP WITH HER...
...AND FOR A TIME, IT MUST HAVE HELPED SOOTHE JOGOROH-SAN'S SOUL AS WELL...

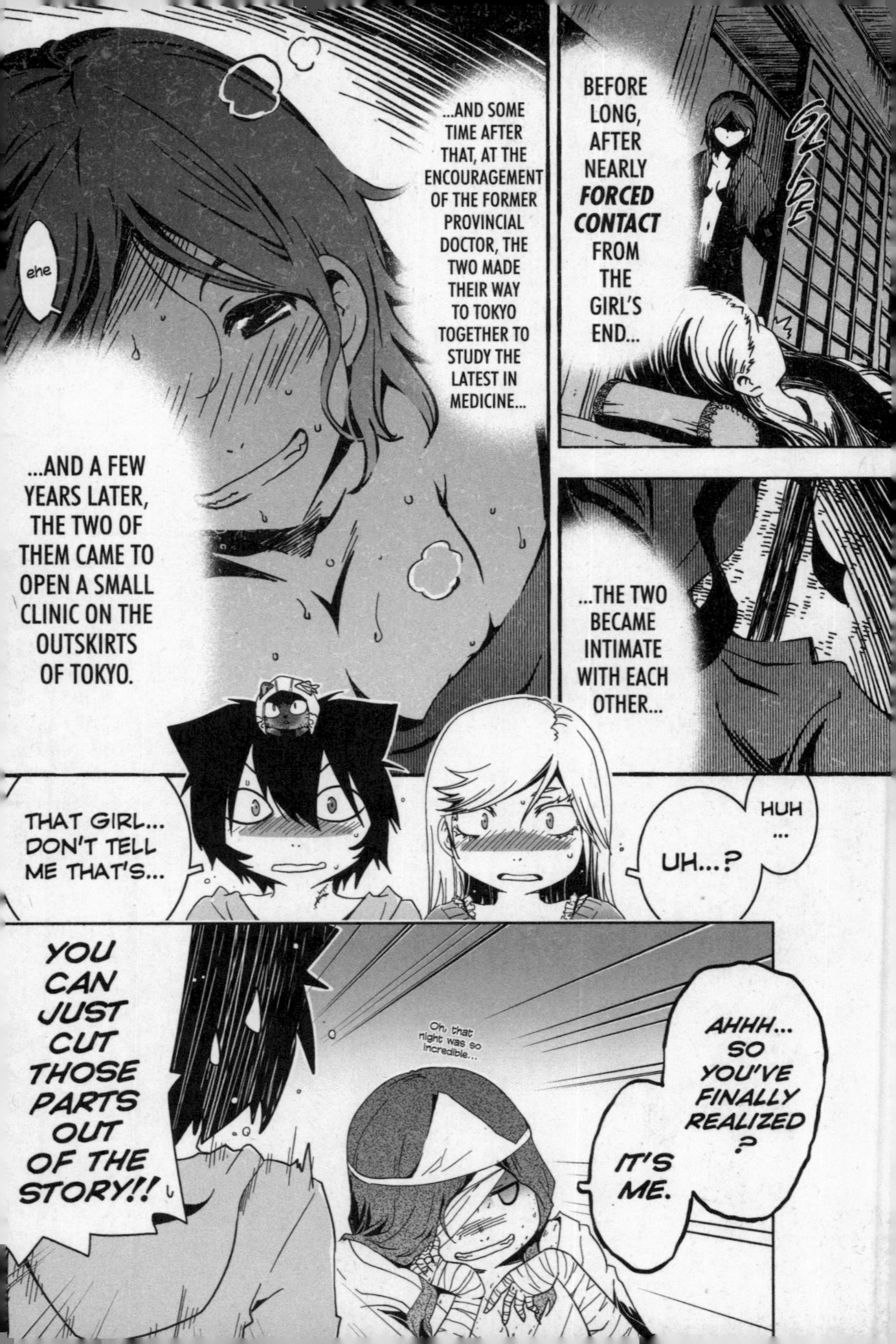
BEFORE LONG, AFTER NEARLY ***FORCED CONTACT*** FROM THE GIRL'S END...
GLIDE
...THE TWO BECAME INTIMATE WITH EACH OTHER...
ehe
...AND SOME TIME AFTER THAT, AT THE ENCOURAGEMENT OF THE FORMER PROVINCIAL DOCTOR, THE TWO MADE THEIR WAY TO TOKYO TOGETHER TO STUDY THE LATEST IN MEDICINE...
...AND A FEW YEARS LATER, THE TWO OF THEM CAME TO OPEN A SMALL CLINIC ON THE OUTSKIRTS OF TOKYO.
HUH... UH...?
THAT GIRL... DON'T TELL ME THAT'S...
AHHH... SO YOU'VE FINALLY REALIZED? IT'S ME.
Oh, that night was so incredible...
YOU CAN JUST CUT THOSE PARTS OUT OF THE STORY!!

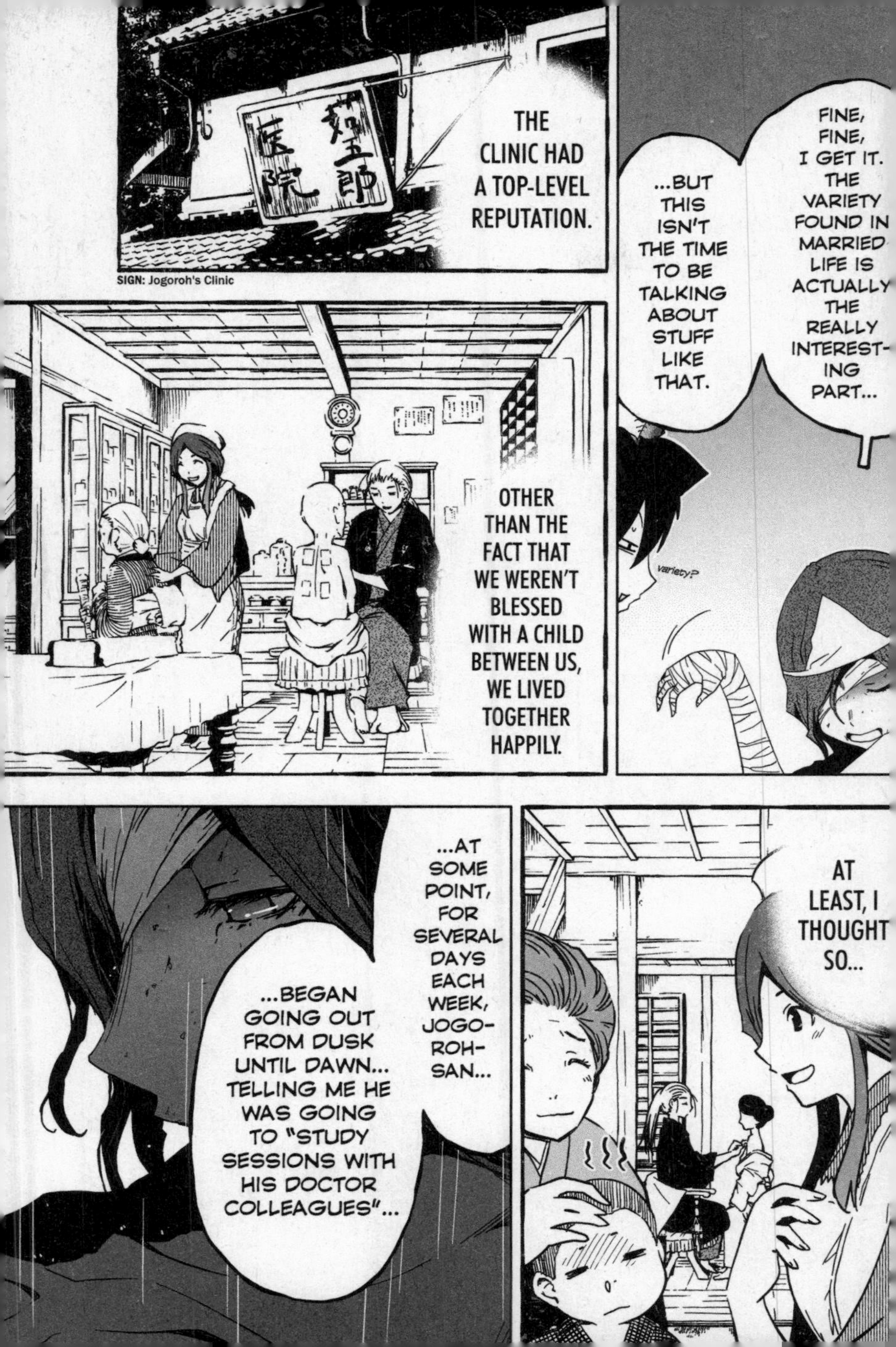
FINE, FINE, I GET IT. THE VARIETY FOUND IN MARRIED LIFE IS ACTUALLY THE REALLY INTEREST-ING PART...
...BUT THIS ISN'T THE TIME TO BE TALKING ABOUT STUFF LIKE THAT.
variety?
THE CLINIC HAD A TOP-LEVEL REPUTATION.
SIGN: Jogoroh's Clinic
OTHER THAN THE FACT THAT WE WEREN'T BLESSED WITH A CHILD BETWEEN US, WE LIVED TOGETHER HAPPILY.
AT LEAST, I THOUGHT SO...
...AT SOME POINT, FOR SEVERAL DAYS EACH WEEK, JOGO-ROH-SAN...
...BEGAN GOING OUT FROM DUSK UNTIL DAWN... TELLING ME HE WAS GOING TO "STUDY SESSIONS WITH HIS DOCTOR COLLEAGUES"...

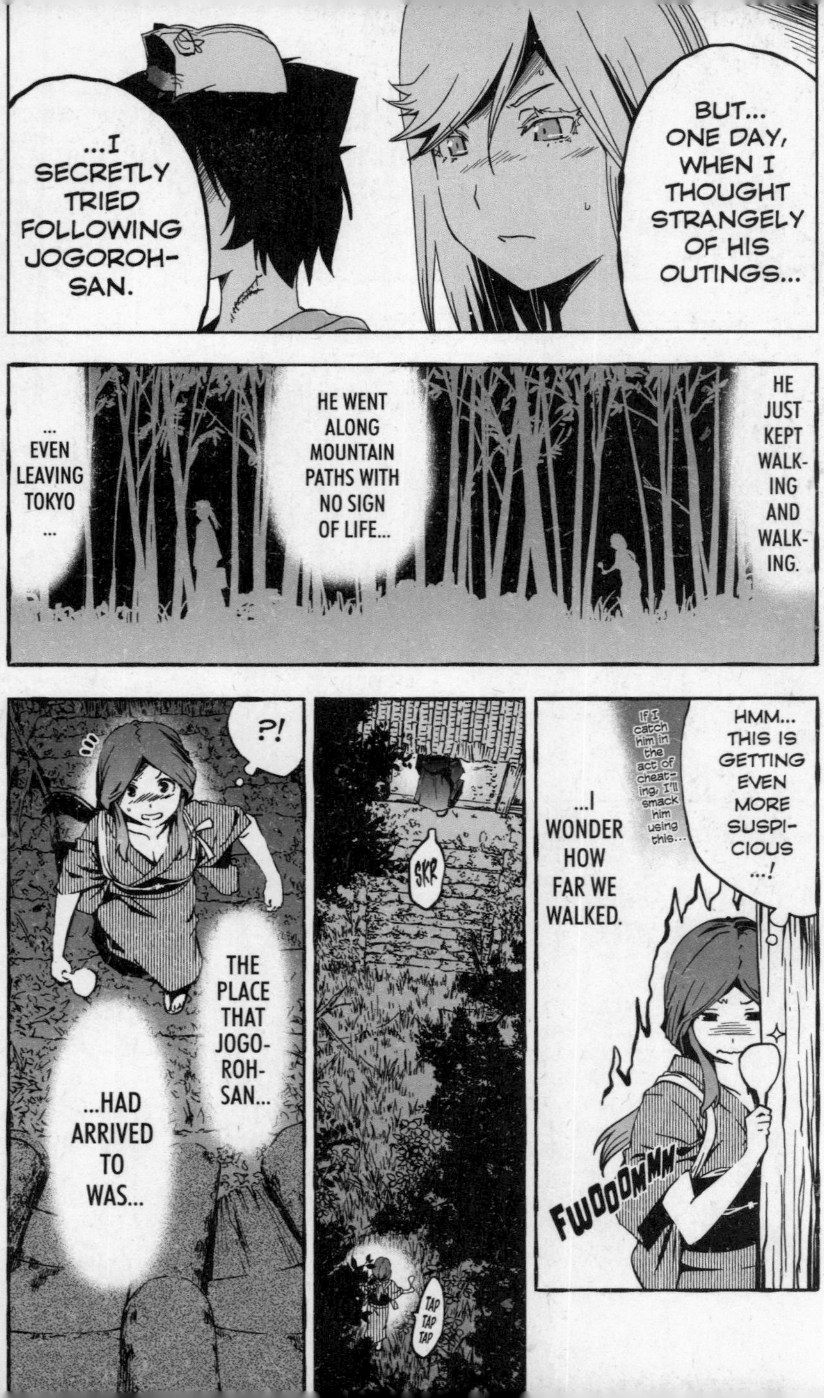
BUT... ONE DAY, WHEN I THOUGHT STRANGELY OF HIS OUTINGS...
...I SECRETLY TRIED FOLLOWING JOGOROH-SAN.
HE JUST KEPT WALKING AND WALKING.
HE WENT ALONG MOUNTAIN PATHS WITH NO SIGN OF LIFE...
...EVEN LEAVING TOKYO...
HMM... THIS IS GETTING EVEN MORE SUSPICIOUS...!
If I catch him in the act of cheating, I'll smack him using this...
...I WONDER HOW FAR WE WALKED.
FWOOOMMN
SKR
TAP TAP TAP
?!
THE PLACE THAT JOGOROH-SAN...
...HAD ARRIVED TO WAS...

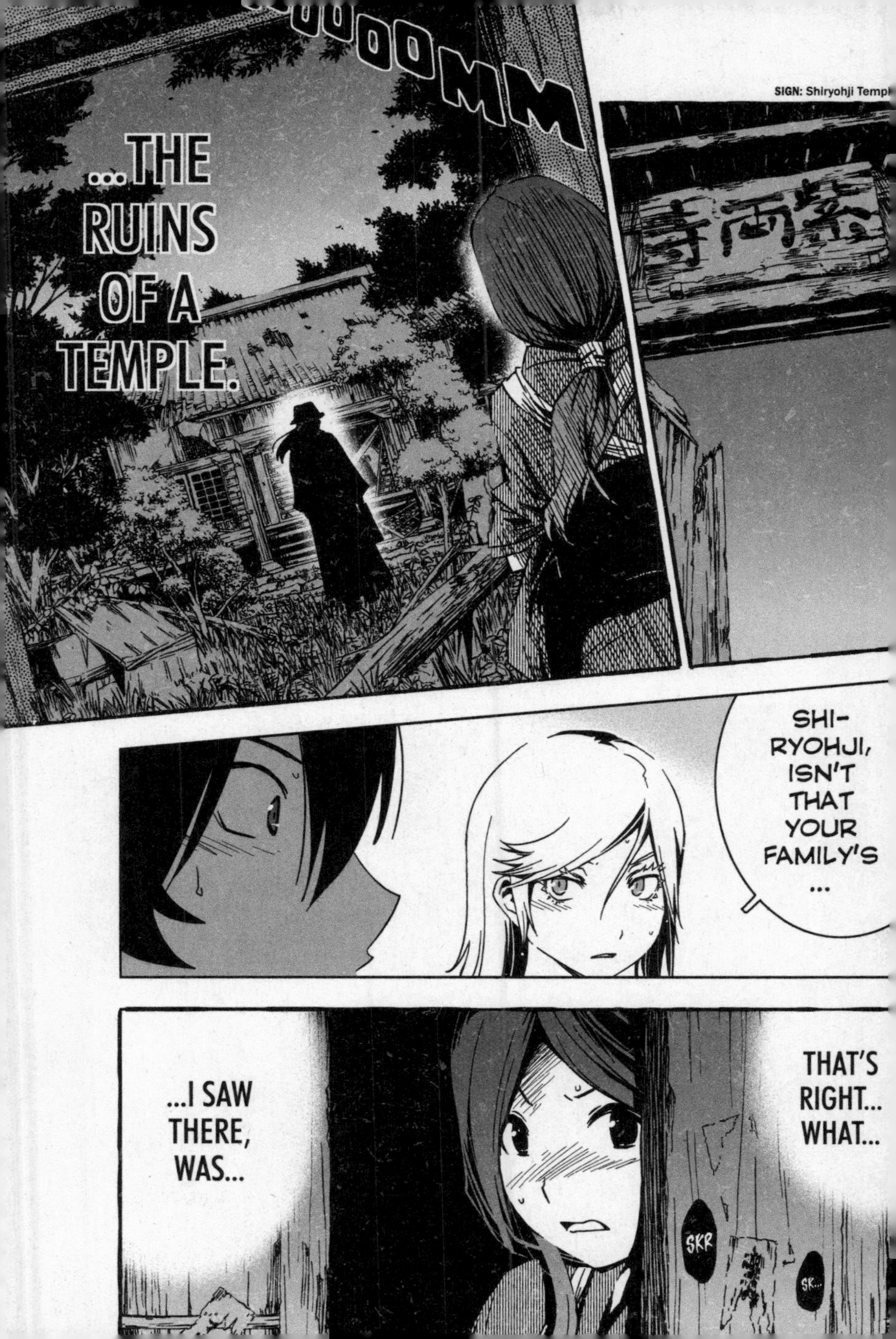
SIGN: Shiryohji Templ
...OOOOMM
...THE RUINS OF A TEMPLE.
SHI-RYOHJI, ISN'T THAT YOUR FAMILY'S ...
THAT'S RIGHT... WHAT...
SKR
SK...
...I SAW THERE, WAS...

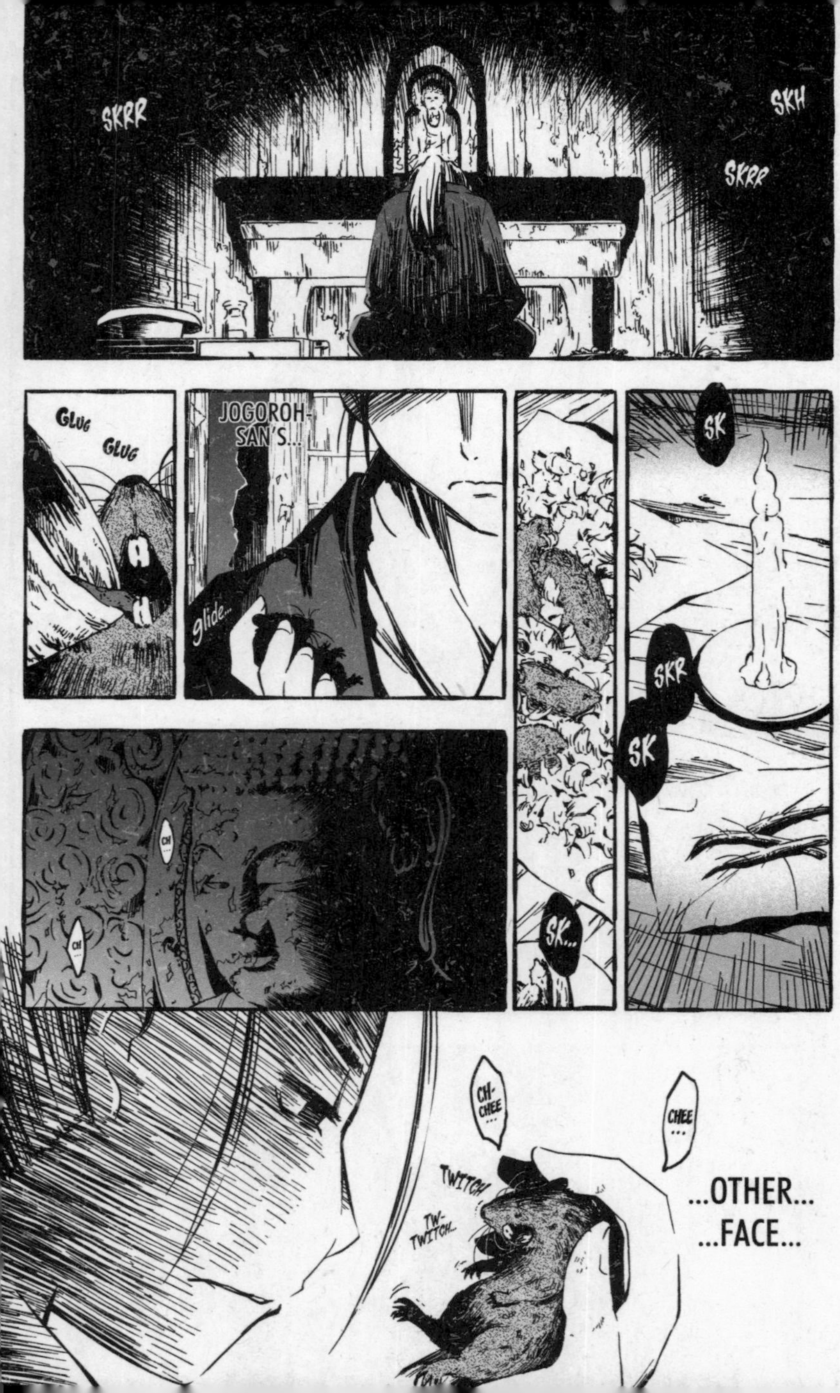
SKH
SKRR
SKRR
SK
SKR
SK
SK...
JOGOROH-SAN'S...
glide...
GLUG GLUG
CH...
CH...
CHEE...
CH-CHEE...
TWITCH
TW-TWITCH...
...OTHER...
...FACE...

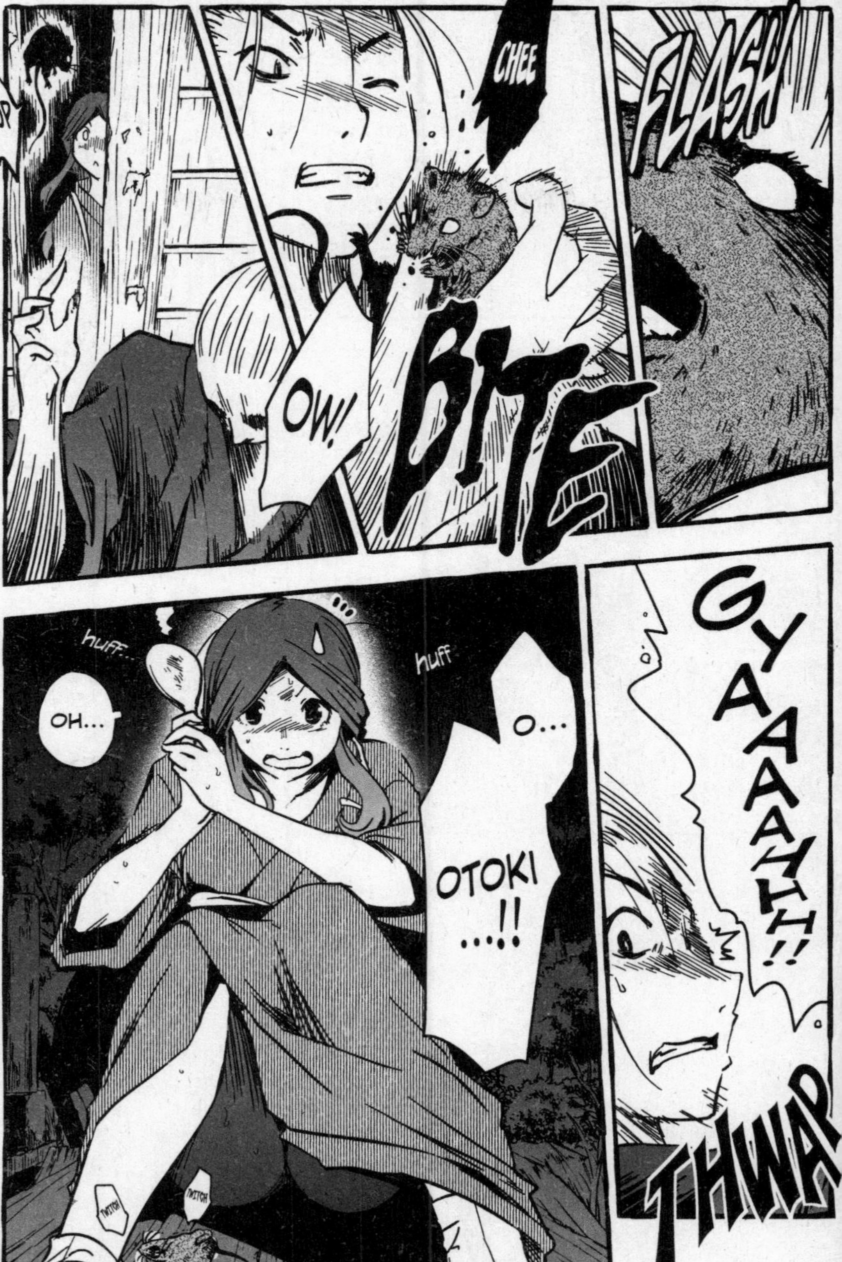
FLASH
CHEE
BITE
OW!
HOP
GYAAAAHH!!
THWAP
huff
O... OTOKI ...!!
huff...
OH...
TWITCH
TWITCH

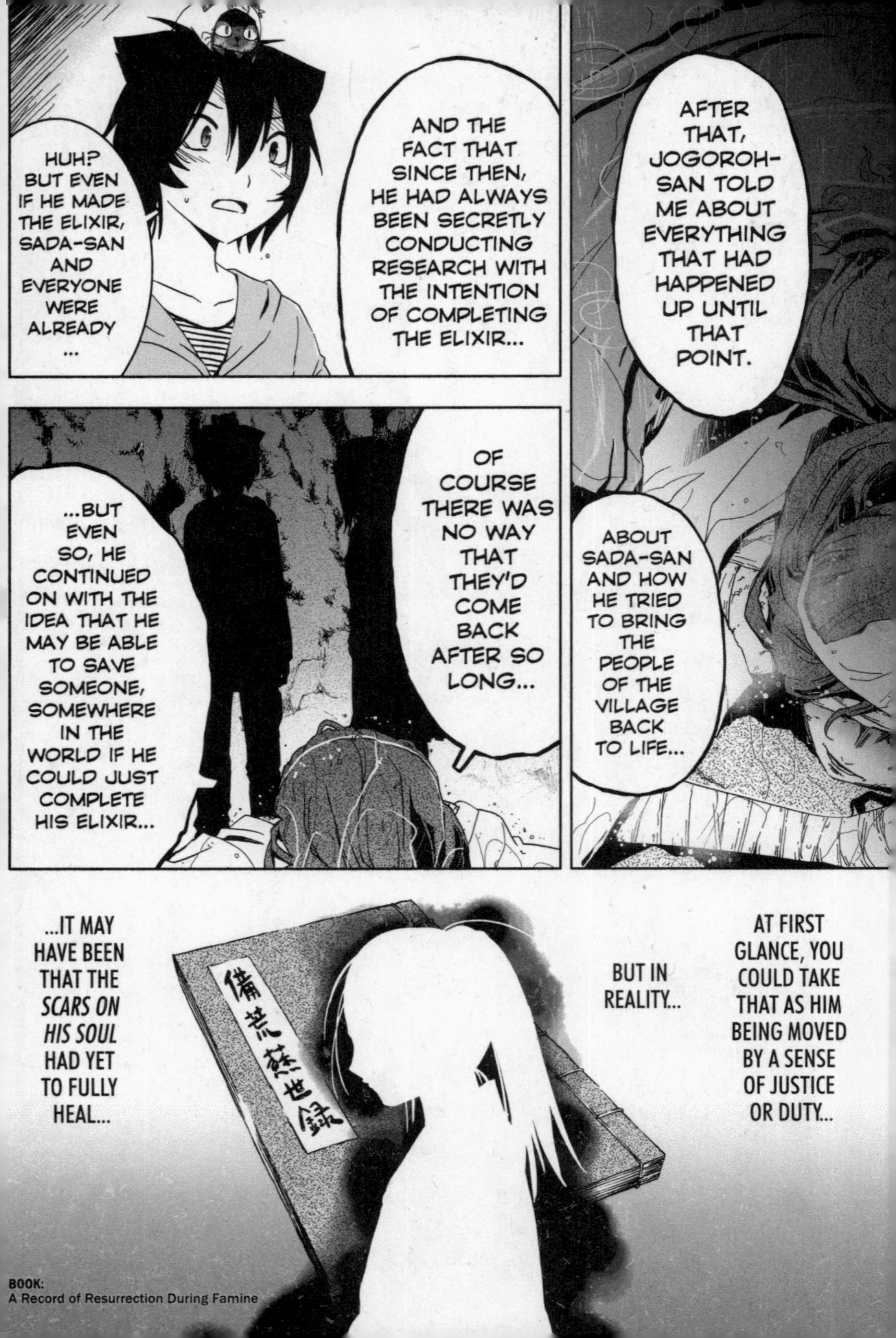
AFTER THAT, JOGOROH-SAN TOLD ME ABOUT EVERYTHING THAT HAD HAPPENED UP UNTIL THAT POINT.
ABOUT SADA-SAN AND HOW HE TRIED TO BRING THE PEOPLE OF THE VILLAGE BACK TO LIFE...
AND THE FACT THAT SINCE THEN, HE HAD ALWAYS BEEN SECRETLY CONDUCTING RESEARCH WITH THE INTENTION OF COMPLETING THE ELIXIR...
HUH? BUT EVEN IF HE MADE THE ELIXIR, SADA-SAN AND EVERYONE WERE ALREADY ...
OF COURSE THERE WAS NO WAY THAT THEY'D COME BACK AFTER SO LONG...
...BUT EVEN SO, HE CONTINUED ON WITH THE IDEA THAT HE MAY BE ABLE TO SAVE SOMEONE, SOMEWHERE IN THE WORLD IF HE COULD JUST COMPLETE HIS ELIXIR...
AT FIRST GLANCE, YOU COULD TAKE THAT AS HIM BEING MOVED BY A SENSE OF JUSTICE OR DUTY...
BUT IN REALITY...
...IT MAY HAVE BEEN THAT THE *SCARS ON HIS SOUL* HAD YET TO FULLY HEAL...
備荒蘇世録
BOOK:
A Record of Resurrection During Famine

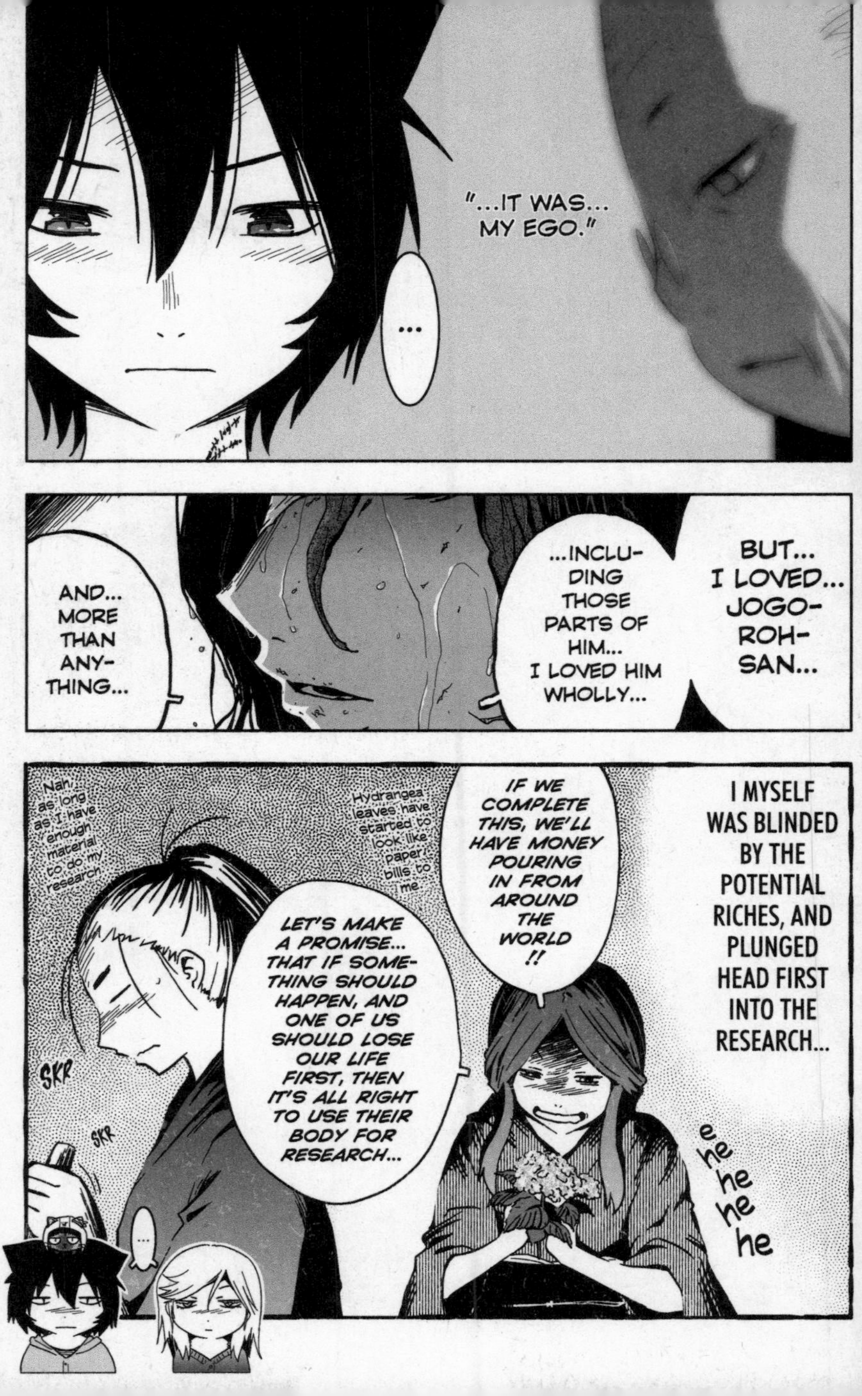
"...IT WAS... MY EGO."
...
BUT... I LOVED... JOGO-ROH-SAN...
...INCLU-DING THOSE PARTS OF HIM... I LOVED HIM WHOLLY...
AND... MORE THAN ANY-THING...
I MYSELF WAS BLINDED BY THE POTENTIAL RICHES, AND PLUNGED HEAD FIRST INTO THE RESEARCH...
IF WE COMPLETE THIS, WE'LL HAVE MONEY POURING IN FROM AROUND THE WORLD !!
Hydrangea leaves have started to look like paper bills to me
LET'S MAKE A PROMISE... THAT IF SOME-THING SHOULD HAPPEN, AND ONE OF US SHOULD LOSE OUR LIFE FIRST, THEN IT'S ALL RIGHT TO USE THEIR BODY FOR RESEARCH...
Nah, as long as I have enough material to do my research
SKR
SKR
ehe he he he
...

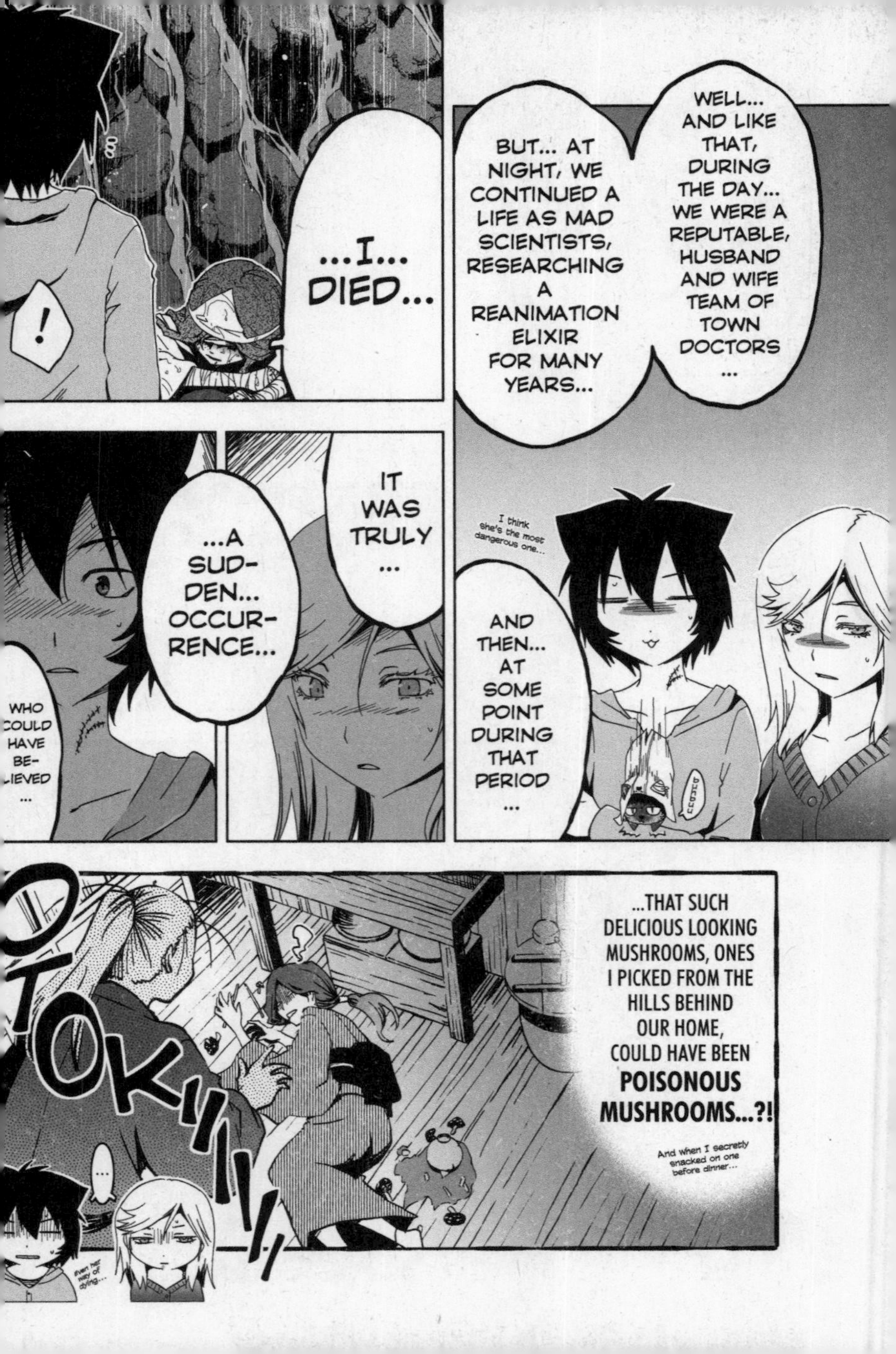
WELL... AND LIKE THAT, DURING THE DAY... WE WERE A REPUTABLE, HUSBAND AND WIFE TEAM OF TOWN DOCTORS ...
BUT... AT NIGHT, WE CONTINUED A LIFE AS MAD SCIENTISTS, RESEARCHING A REANIMATION ELIXIR FOR MANY YEARS...
I think she's the most dangerous one...
AND THEN... AT SOME POINT DURING THAT PERIOD ...
...I... DIED...
IT WAS TRULY ...
...A SUDDEN... OCCURRENCE...
WHO COULD HAVE BELIEVED ...
...THAT SUCH DELICIOUS LOOKING MUSHROOMS, ONES I PICKED FROM THE HILLS BEHIND OUR HOME, COULD HAVE BEEN **POISONOUS MUSHROOMS...?!**
TOKI!!
And when I secretly snacked on one before dinner...
...
Even her way of dying...

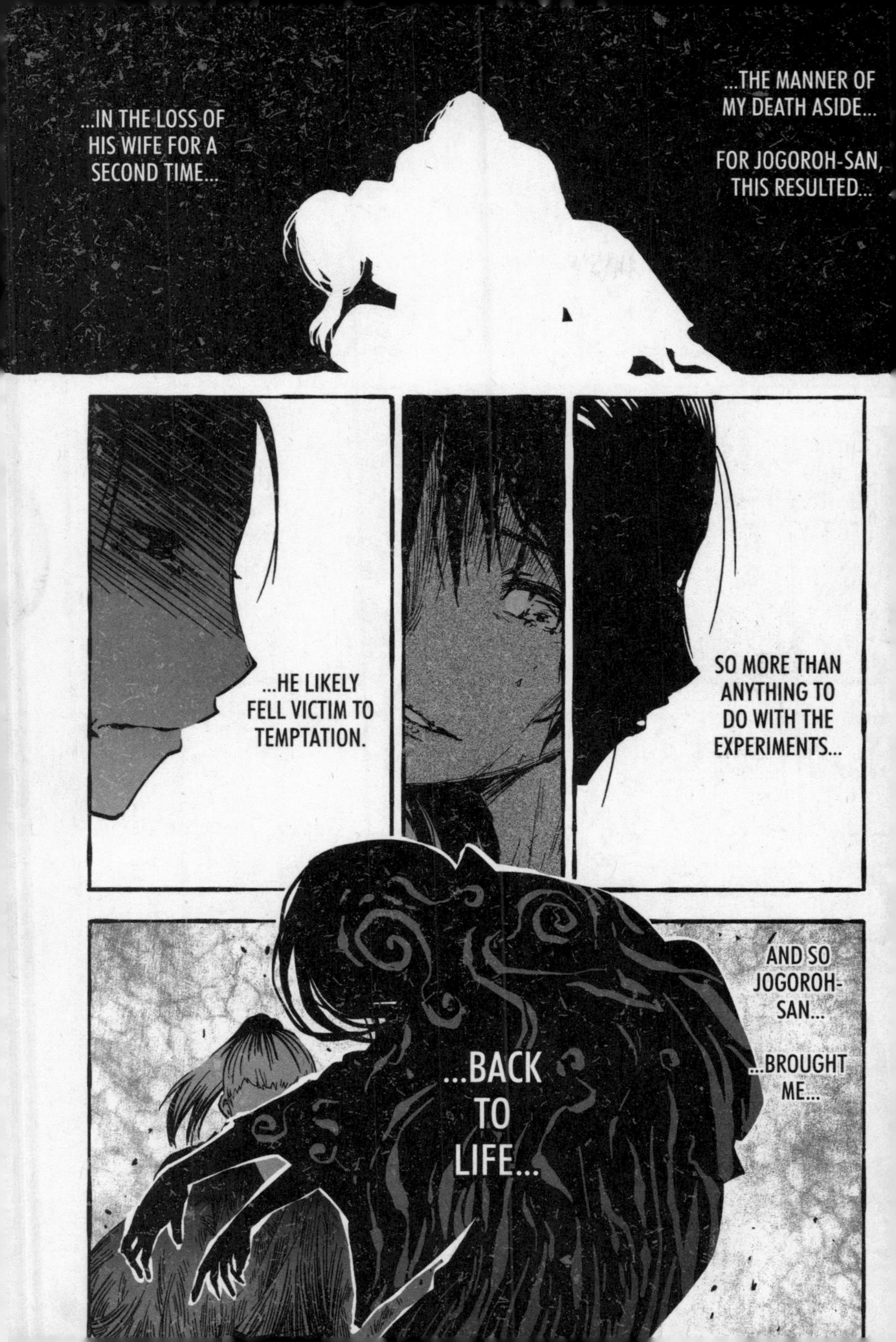
...THE MANNER OF MY DEATH ASIDE...
FOR JOGOROH-SAN, THIS RESULTED...
...IN THE LOSS OF HIS WIFE FOR A SECOND TIME...
SO MORE THAN ANYTHING TO DO WITH THE EXPERIMENTS...
...HE LIKELY FELL VICTIM TO TEMPTATION.
AND SO JOGOROH-SAN...
...BROUGHT ME...
...BACK TO LIFE...

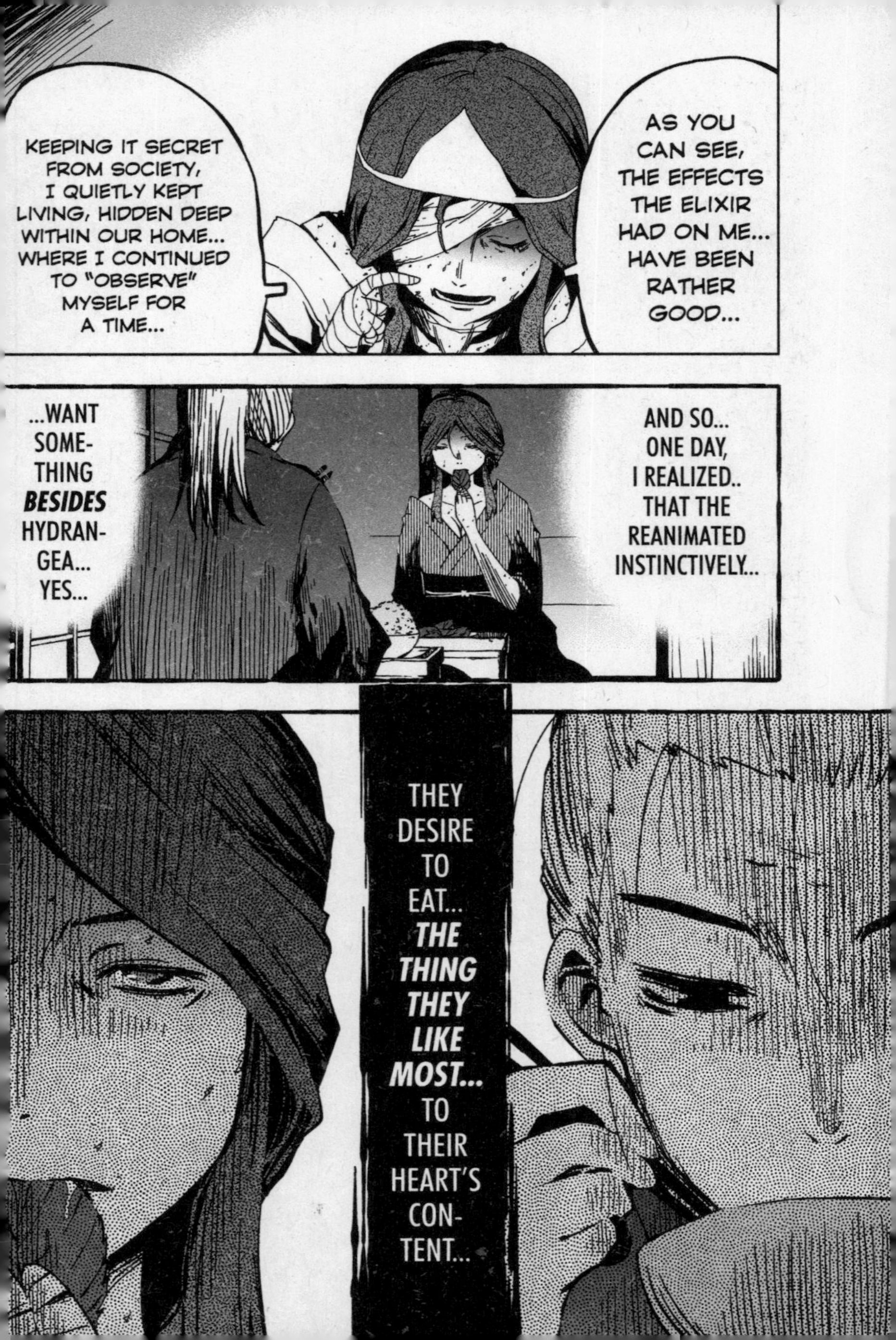
AS YOU CAN SEE, THE EFFECTS THE ELIXIR HAD ON ME... HAVE BEEN RATHER GOOD...
KEEPING IT SECRET FROM SOCIETY, I QUIETLY KEPT LIVING, HIDDEN DEEP WITHIN OUR HOME... WHERE I CONTINUED TO "OBSERVE" MYSELF FOR A TIME...
AND SO... ONE DAY, I REALIZED.. THAT THE REANIMATED INSTINCTIVELY...
...WANT SOME-THING ***BESIDES*** HYDRAN-GEA... YES...
THEY DESIRE TO EAT... ***THE THING THEY LIKE MOST...*** TO THEIR HEART'S CON-TENT...

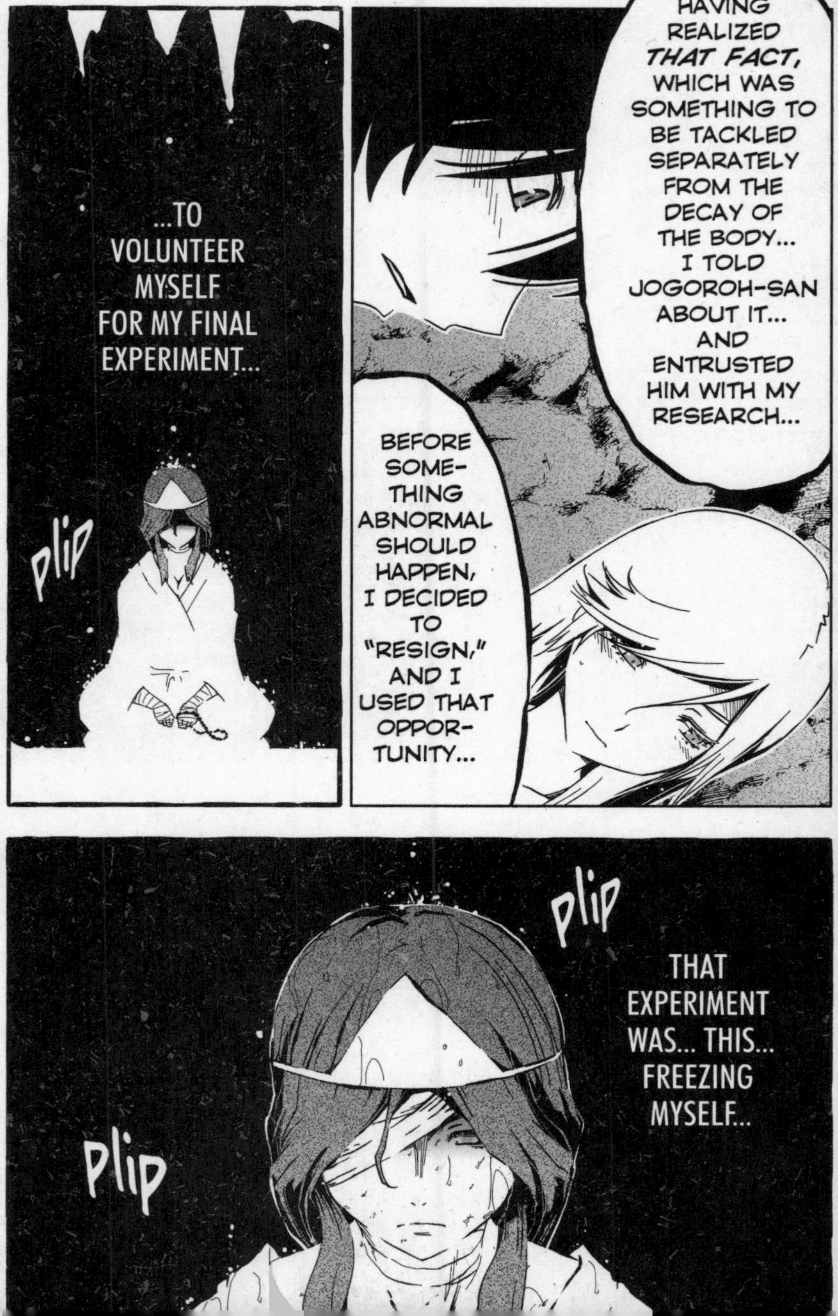
HAVING REALIZED *THAT FACT,* WHICH WAS SOMETHING TO BE TACKLED SEPARATELY FROM THE DECAY OF THE BODY... I TOLD JOGOROH-SAN ABOUT IT... AND ENTRUSTED HIM WITH MY RESEARCH...
BEFORE SOME-THING ABNORMAL SHOULD HAPPEN, I DECIDED TO "RESIGN," AND I USED THAT OPPOR-TUNITY...
...TO VOLUNTEER MYSELF FOR MY FINAL EXPERIMENT...
plip
plip
THAT EXPERIMENT WAS... THIS... FREEZING MYSELF...
plip

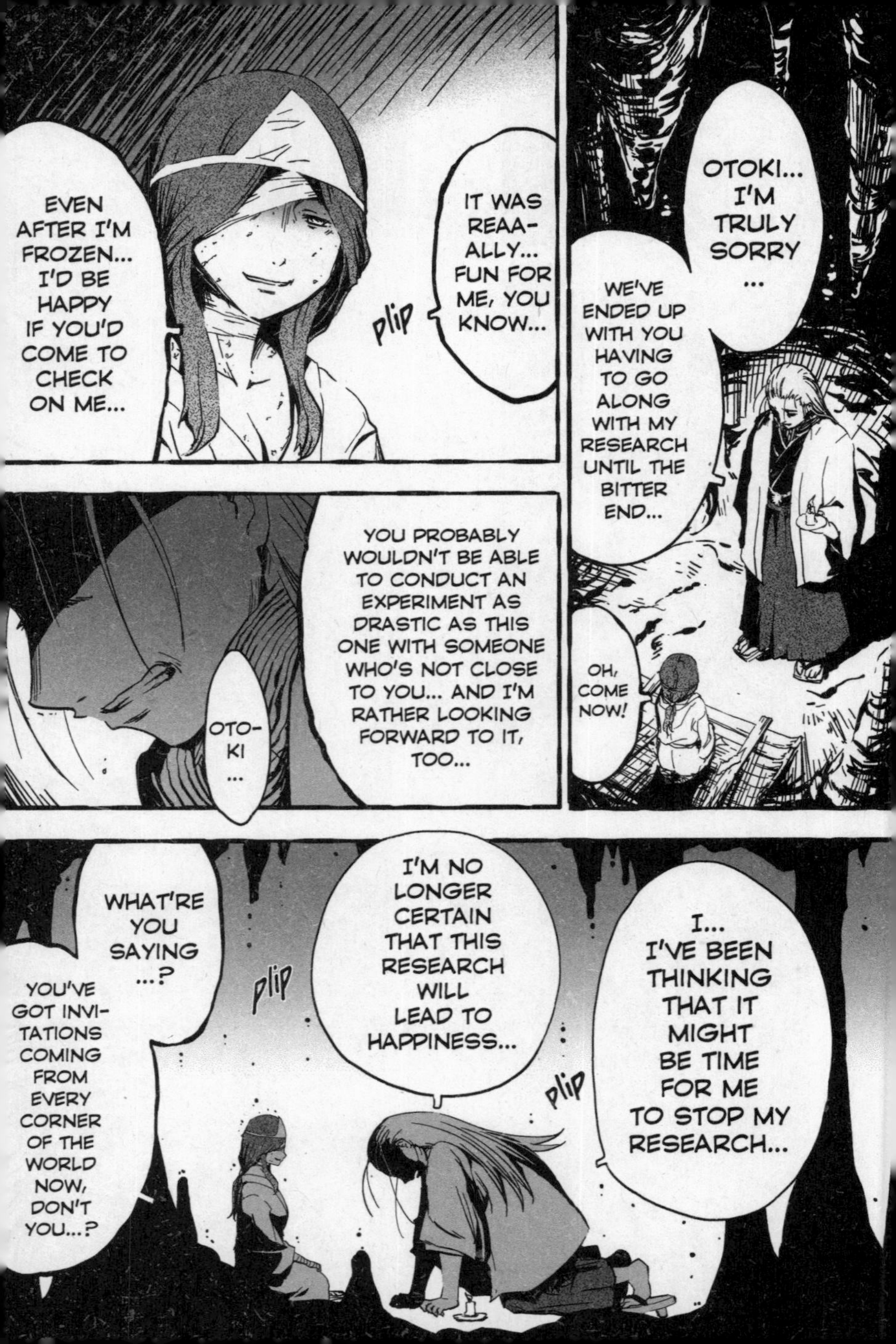
OTOKI... I'M TRULY SORRY ...
WE'VE ENDED UP WITH YOU HAVING TO GO ALONG WITH MY RESEARCH UNTIL THE BITTER END...
OH, COME NOW!
IT WAS REAA-ALLY... FUN FOR ME, YOU KNOW...
plip
EVEN AFTER I'M FROZEN... I'D BE HAPPY IF YOU'D COME TO CHECK ON ME...
YOU PROBABLY WOULDN'T BE ABLE TO CONDUCT AN EXPERIMENT AS DRASTIC AS THIS ONE WITH SOMEONE WHO'S NOT CLOSE TO YOU... AND I'M RATHER LOOKING FORWARD TO IT, TOO...
OTO-KI ...
I... I'VE BEEN THINKING THAT IT MIGHT BE TIME FOR ME TO STOP MY RESEARCH...
plip
I'M NO LONGER CERTAIN THAT THIS RESEARCH WILL LEAD TO HAPPINESS...
plip
WHAT'RE YOU SAYING ...?
YOU'VE GOT INVI-TATIONS COMING FROM EVERY CORNER OF THE WORLD NOW, DON'T YOU...?

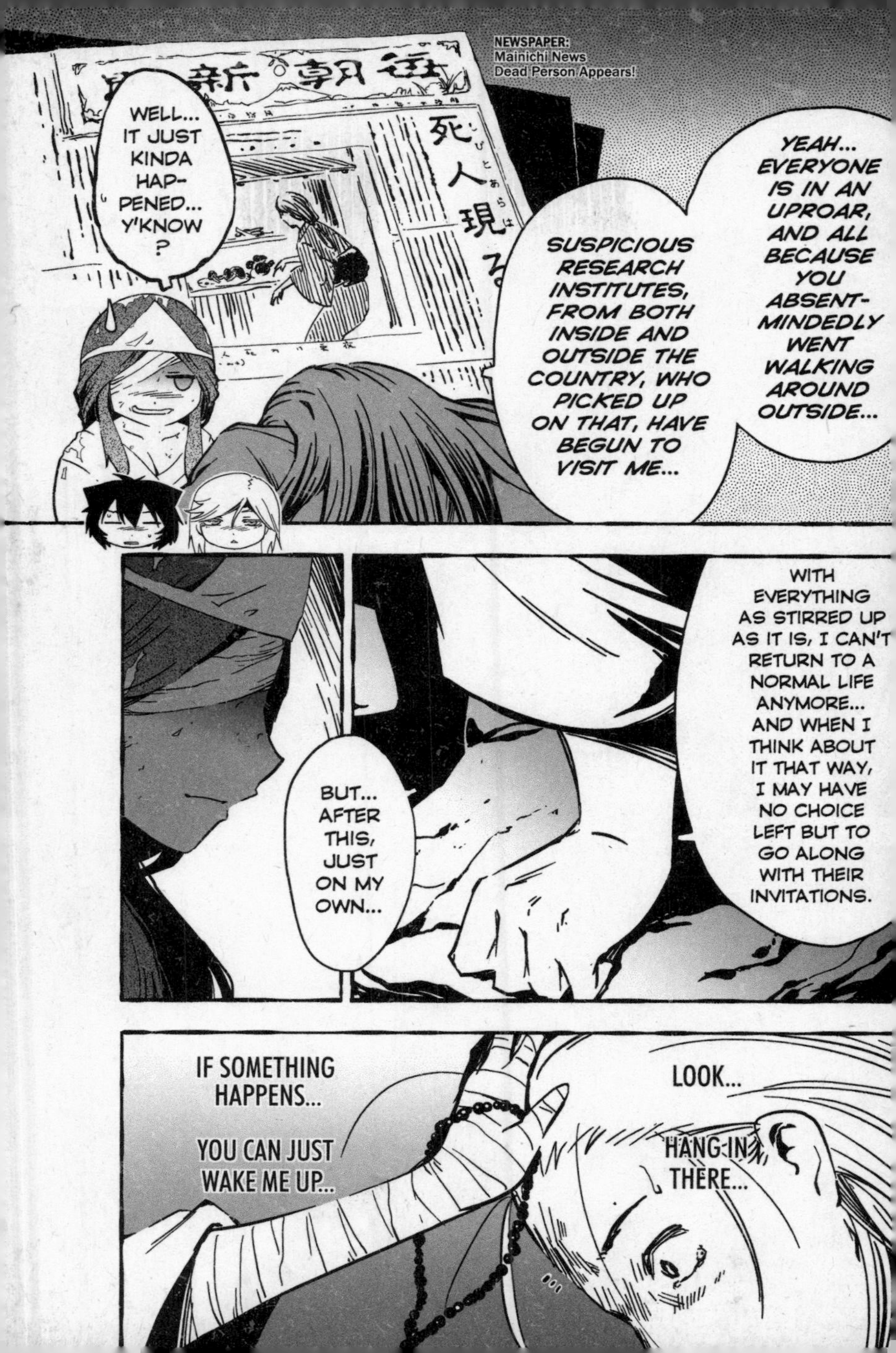
NEWSPAPER: Mainichi News Dead Person Appears!
YEAH... EVERYONE IS IN AN UPROAR, AND ALL BECAUSE YOU ABSENT-MINDEDLY WENT WALKING AROUND OUTSIDE...
SUSPICIOUS RESEARCH INSTITUTES, FROM BOTH INSIDE AND OUTSIDE THE COUNTRY, WHO PICKED UP ON THAT, HAVE BEGUN TO VISIT ME...
WELL... IT JUST KINDA HAP-PENED... Y'KNOW?
WITH EVERYTHING AS STIRRED UP AS IT IS, I CAN'T RETURN TO A NORMAL LIFE ANYMORE... AND WHEN I THINK ABOUT IT THAT WAY, I MAY HAVE NO CHOICE LEFT BUT TO GO ALONG WITH THEIR INVITATIONS.
BUT... AFTER THIS, JUST ON MY OWN...
LOOK...
HANG IN THERE...
IF SOMETHING HAPPENS...
YOU CAN JUST WAKE ME UP...
...

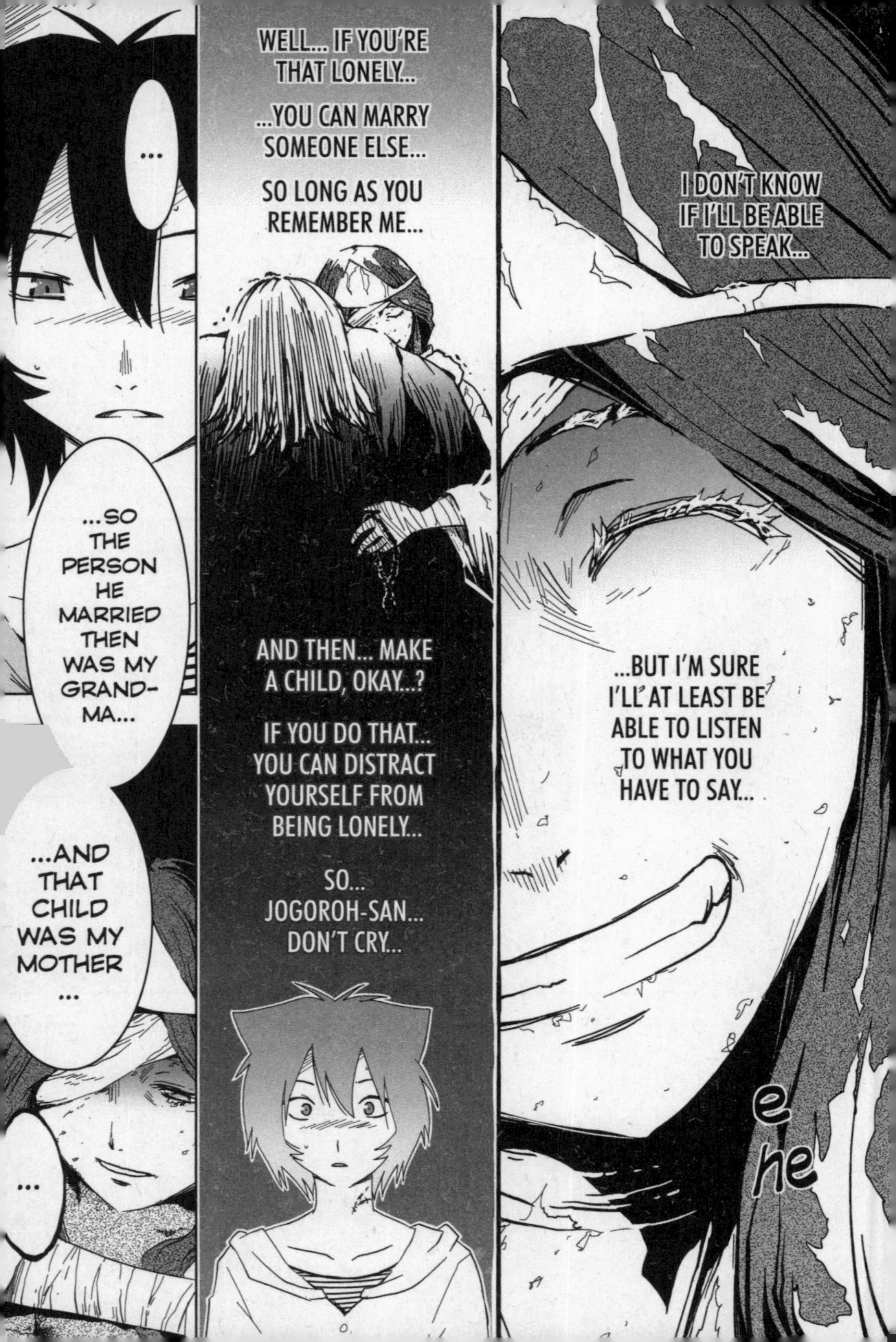
I DON'T KNOW IF I'LL BE ABLE TO SPEAK...
...BUT I'M SURE I'LL AT LEAST BE ABLE TO LISTEN TO WHAT YOU HAVE TO SAY...
e he
WELL... IF YOU'RE THAT LONELY...
...YOU CAN MARRY SOMEONE ELSE...
SO LONG AS YOU REMEMBER ME...
AND THEN... MAKE A CHILD, OKAY...?
IF YOU DO THAT... YOU CAN DISTRACT YOURSELF FROM BEING LONELY...
SO... JOGOROH-SAN... DON'T CRY...
...
...SO THE PERSON HE MARRIED THEN WAS MY GRAND-MA...
...AND THAT CHILD WAS MY MOTHER...
...

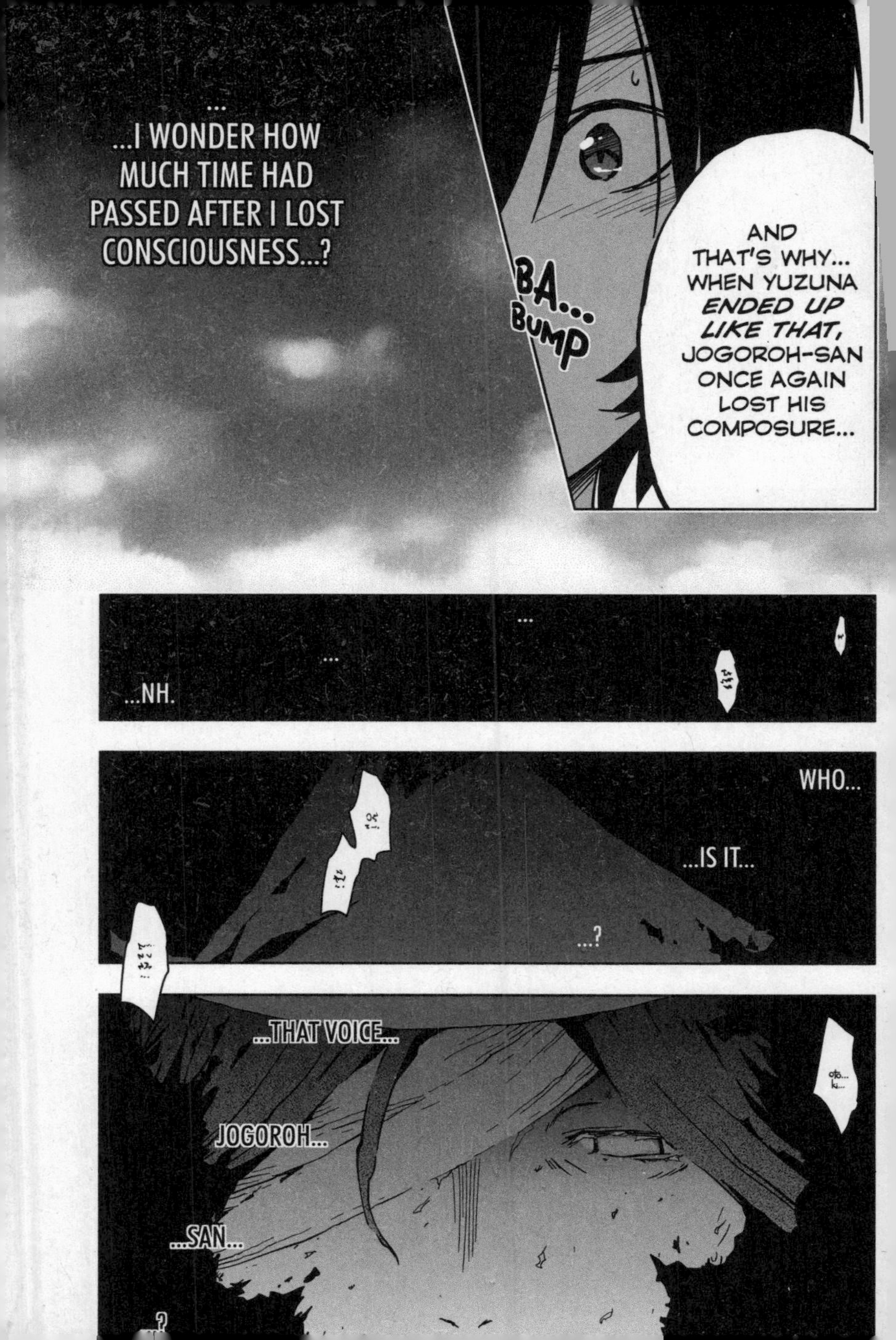
AND THAT'S WHY... WHEN YUZUNA ENDED UP LIKE THAT, JOGOROH-SAN ONCE AGAIN LOST HIS COMPOSURE...
BA... BUMP
...
...I WONDER HOW MUCH TIME HAD PASSED AFTER I LOST CONSCIOUSNESS...?
...
...
...NH.
WHO...
...IS IT...
...?
oto... ki...
...THAT VOICE...
JOGOROH...
...SAN...
...?

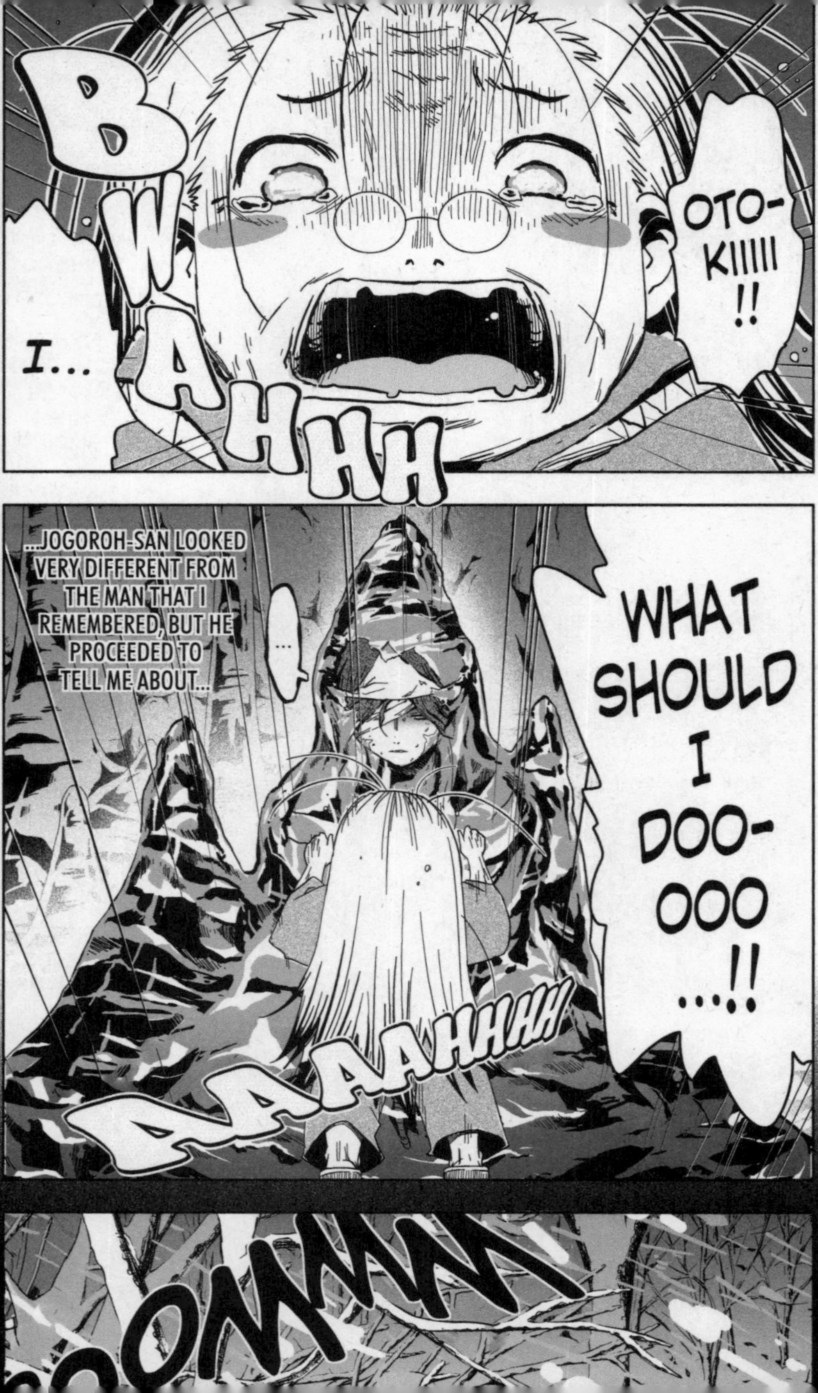
OTO-KIIIII!!
BWAHHH
I...
WHAT SHOULD I DOO-OOO!! ...!!
...
...JOGOROH-SAN LOOKED VERY DIFFERENT FROM THE MAN THAT I REMEMBERED, BUT HE PROCEEDED TO TELL ME ABOUT...
AAAAHHHH

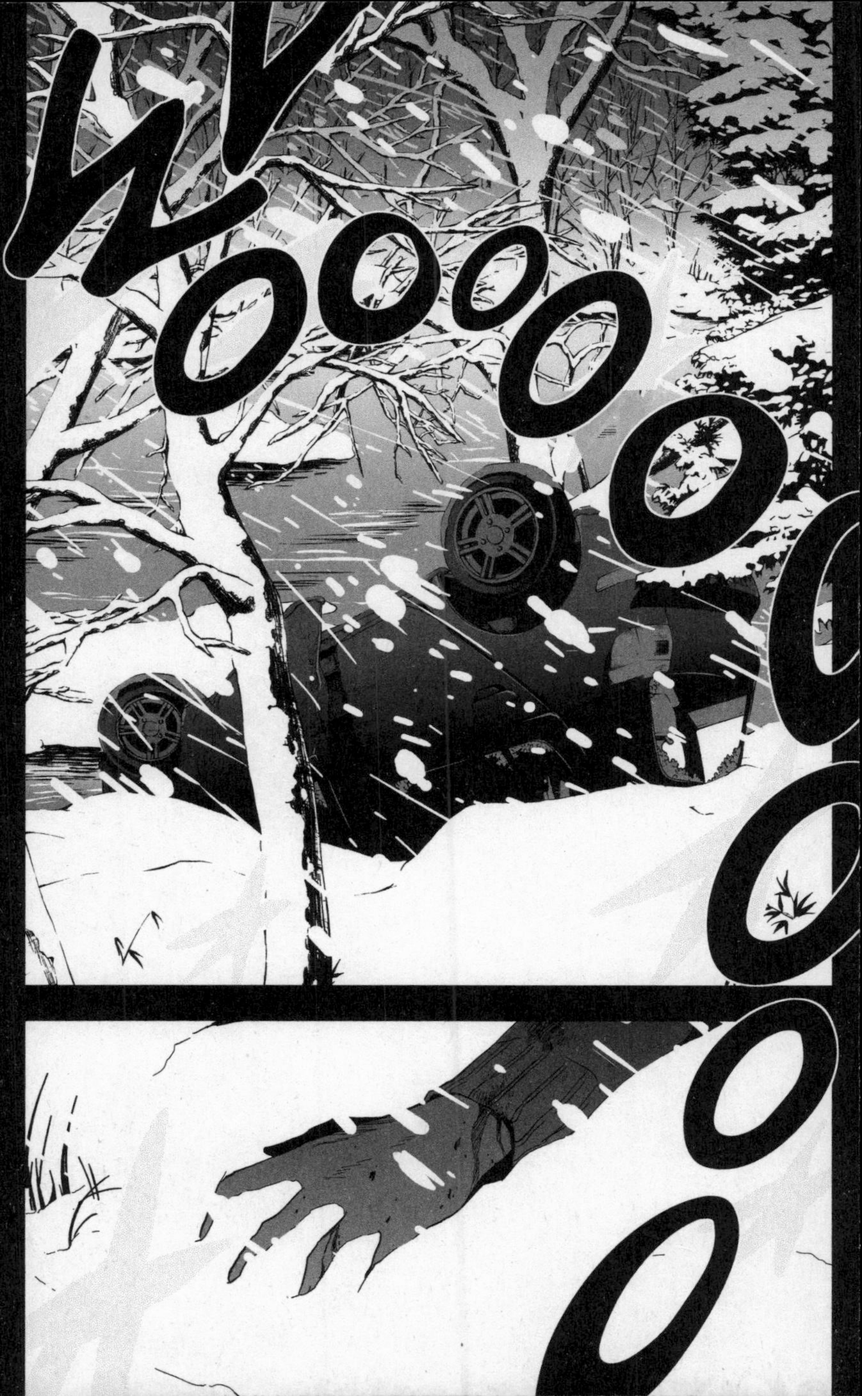
WOOOOOOOOOO

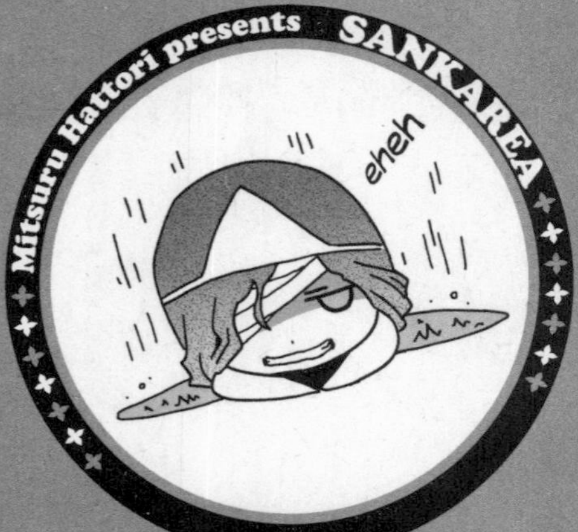
Mitsuru Hattori presents SANKAREA
eheh

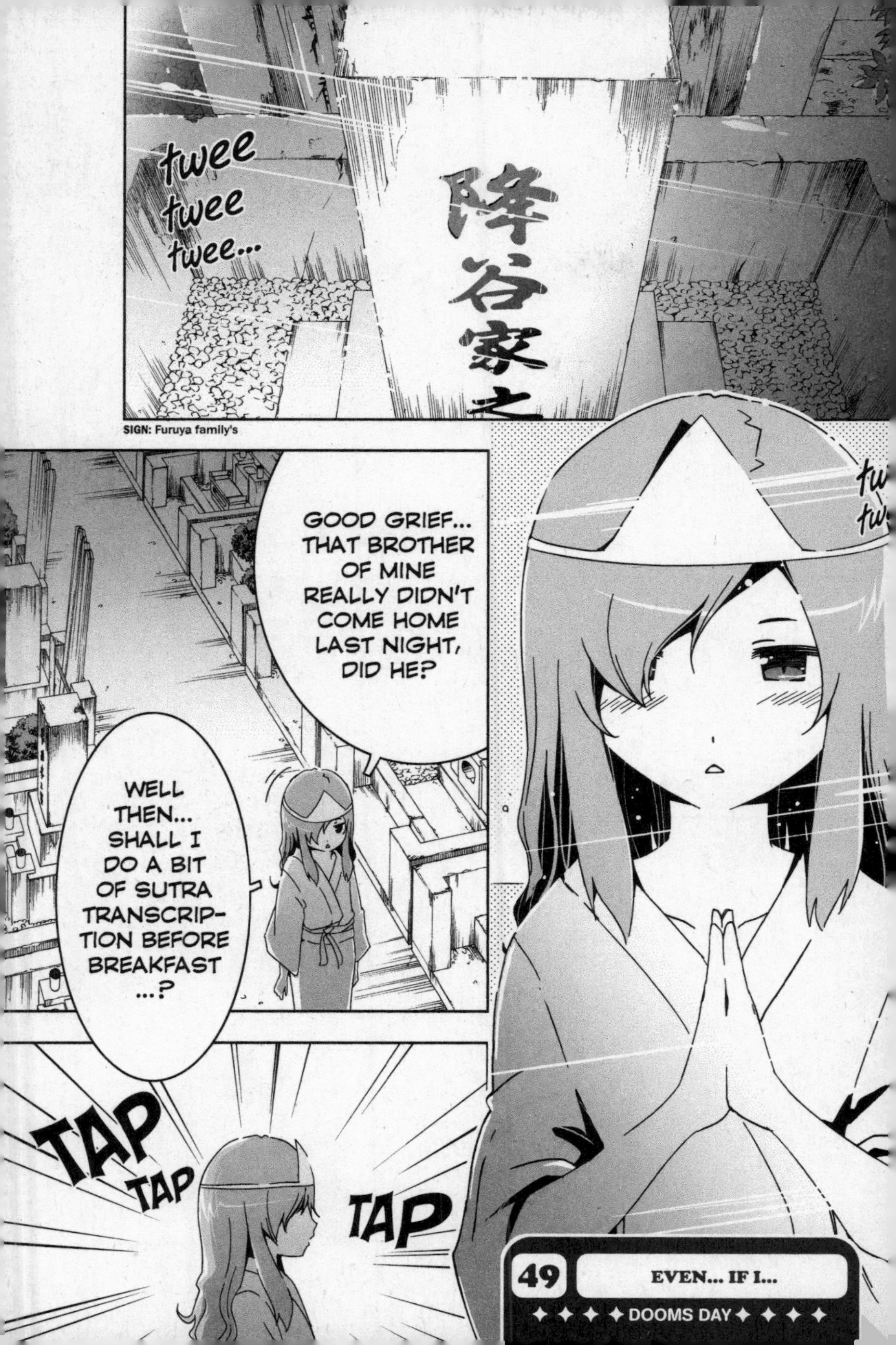
twee twee twee...
降谷家之
49
EVEN... IF I...
✦ ✦ ✦ ✦ DOOMS DAY ✦ ✦ ✦ ✦
GOOD GRIEF... THAT BROTHER OF MINE REALLY DIDN'T COME HOME LAST NIGHT, DID HE?
WELL THEN... SHALL I DO A BIT OF SUTRA TRANSCRIP-TION BEFORE BREAKFAST ...?
TAP TAP
TAP

SIGN: Furuya family's

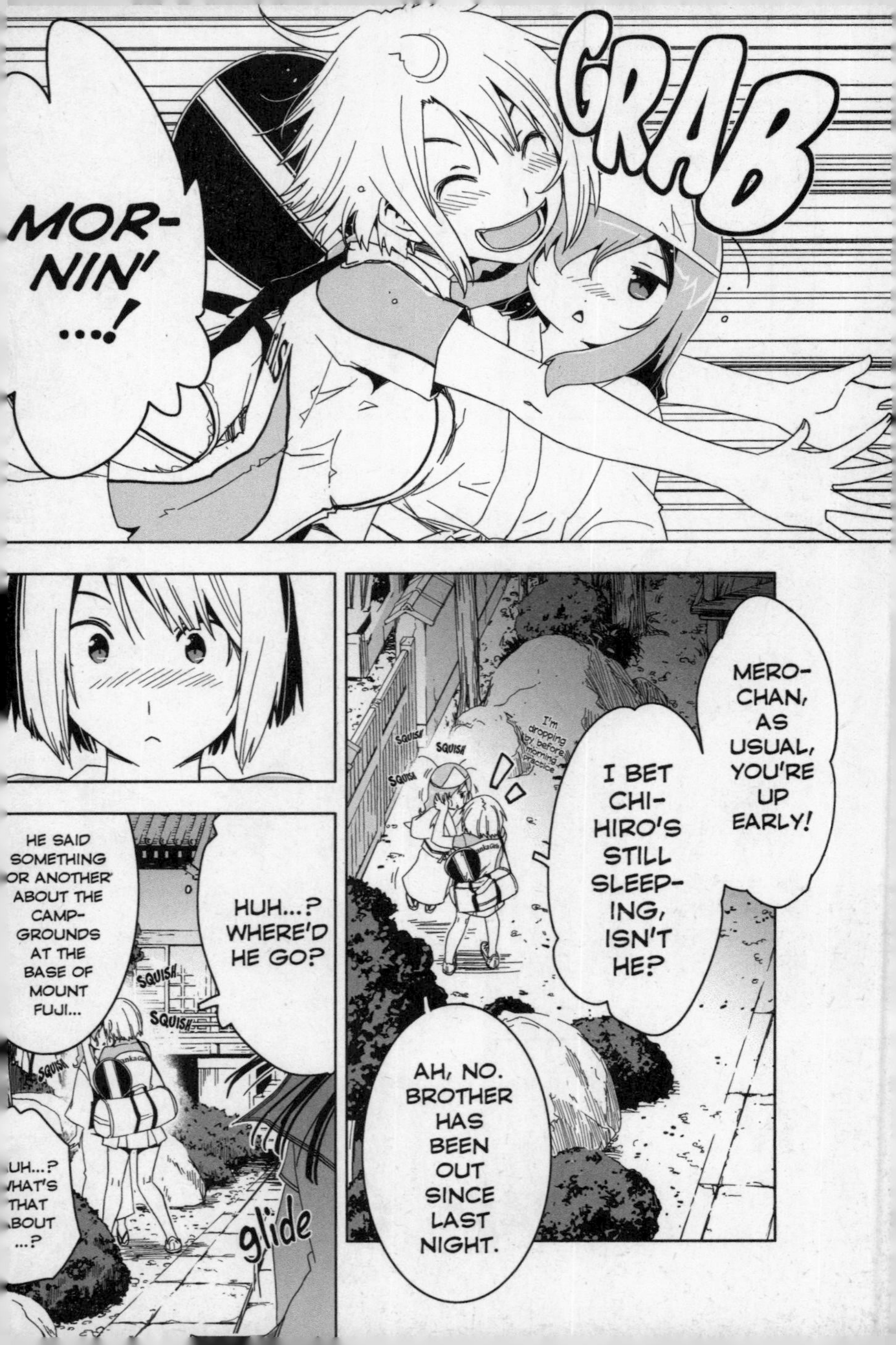
GRAB
MOR-NIN'...!
MERO-CHAN, AS USUAL, YOU'RE UP EARLY!
I BET CHI-HIRO'S STILL SLEEP-ING, ISN'T HE?
I'm dropping by before morning practice
SQUISH
SQUISH
SQUISH
!
AH, NO. BROTHER HAS BEEN OUT SINCE LAST NIGHT.
HUH...? WHERE'D HE GO?
HE SAID SOMETHING OR ANOTHER ABOUT THE CAMP-GROUNDS AT THE BASE OF MOUNT FUJI...
SQUISH
SQUISH
SQUISH
glide
UH...? WHAT'S THAT ABOUT ...?

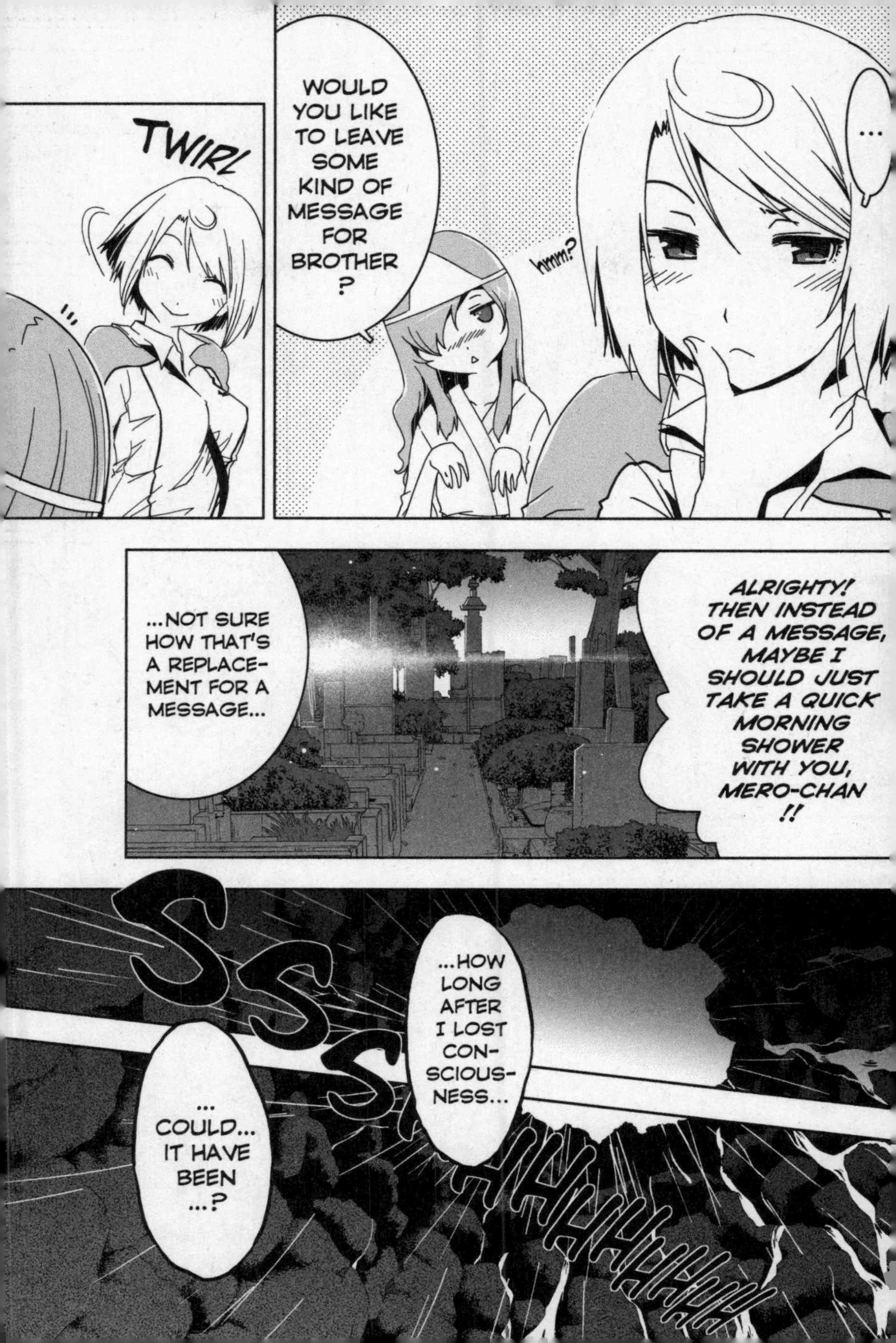
...
WOULD YOU LIKE TO LEAVE SOME KIND OF MESSAGE FOR BROTHER ?
hmm?
TWIRL
!!
ALRIGHTY! THEN INSTEAD OF A MESSAGE, MAYBE I SHOULD JUST TAKE A QUICK MORNING SHOWER WITH YOU, MERO-CHAN !!
...NOT SURE HOW THAT'S A REPLACE-MENT FOR A MESSAGE...
SSSHHHHHHHHHHHH
...HOW LONG AFTER I LOST CON-SCIOUS-NESS...
... COULD... IT HAVE BEEN ...?

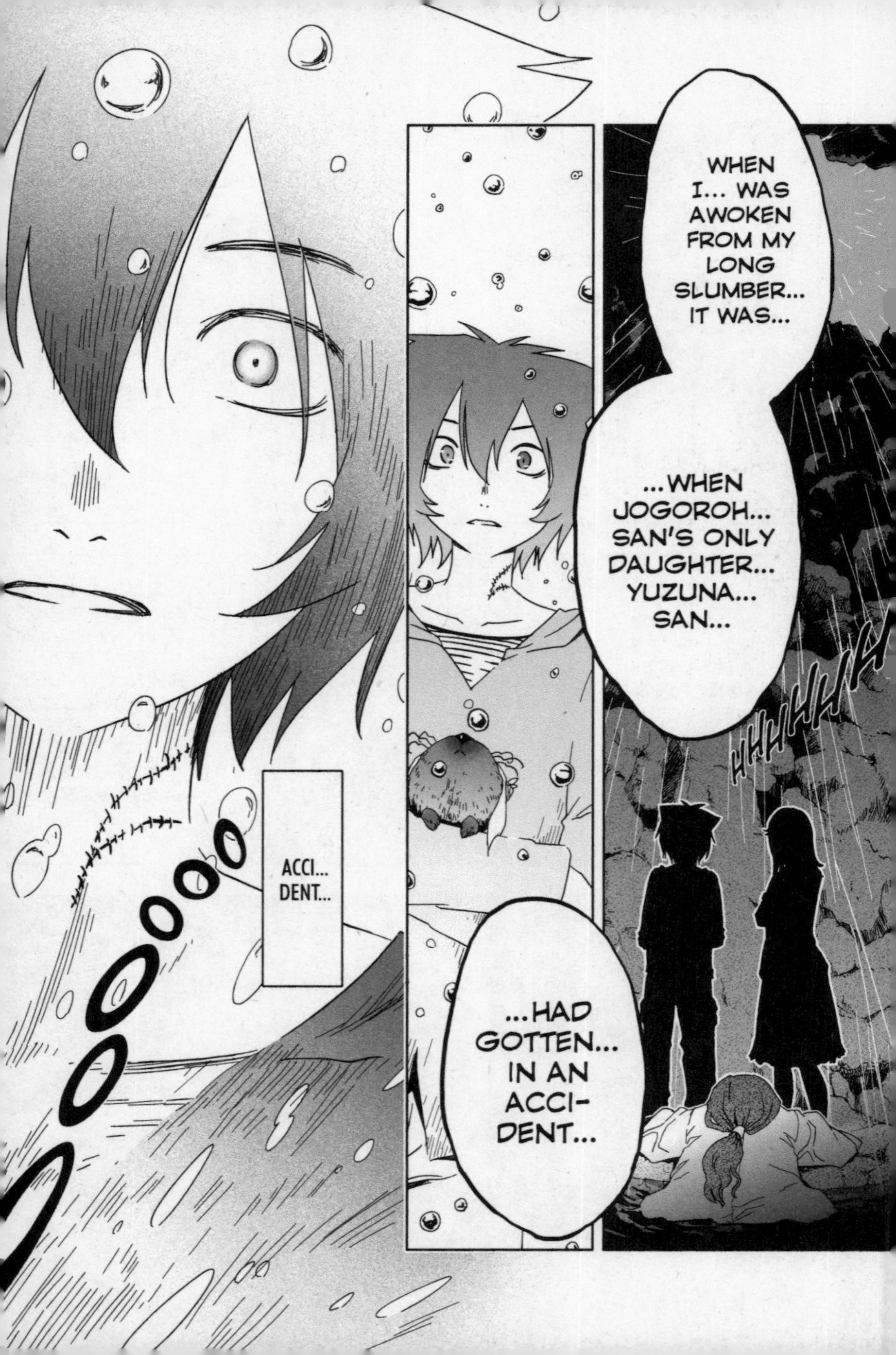
WHEN I... WAS AWOKEN FROM MY LONG SLUMBER... IT WAS...
...WHEN JOGOROH... SAN'S ONLY DAUGHTER... YUZUNA... SAN...
HHHHHHA
...HAD GOTTEN... IN AN ACCI-DENT...
ACCI... DENT...

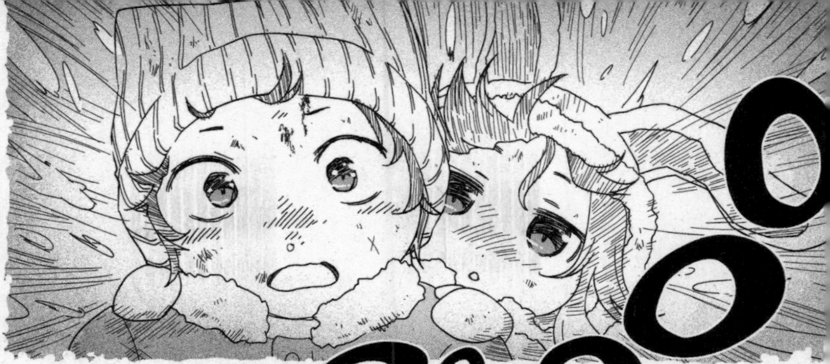

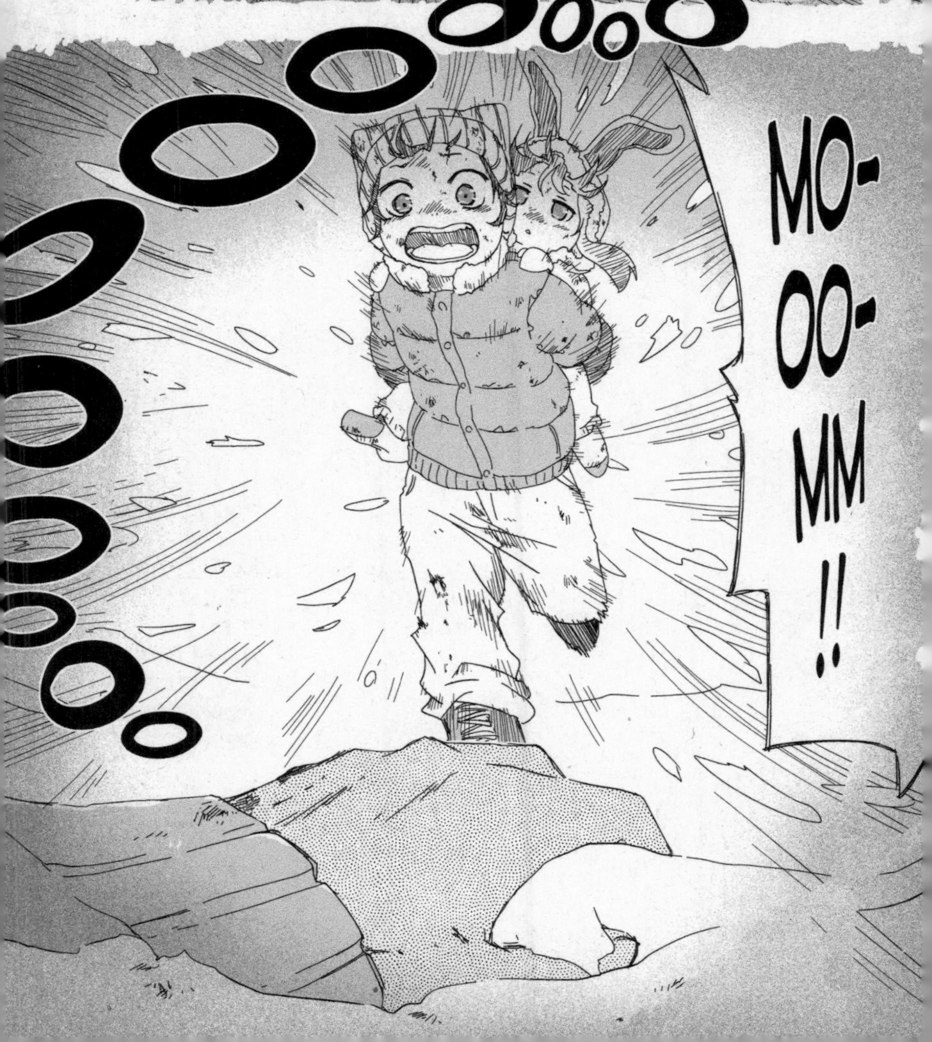
MO-OO-MM!!

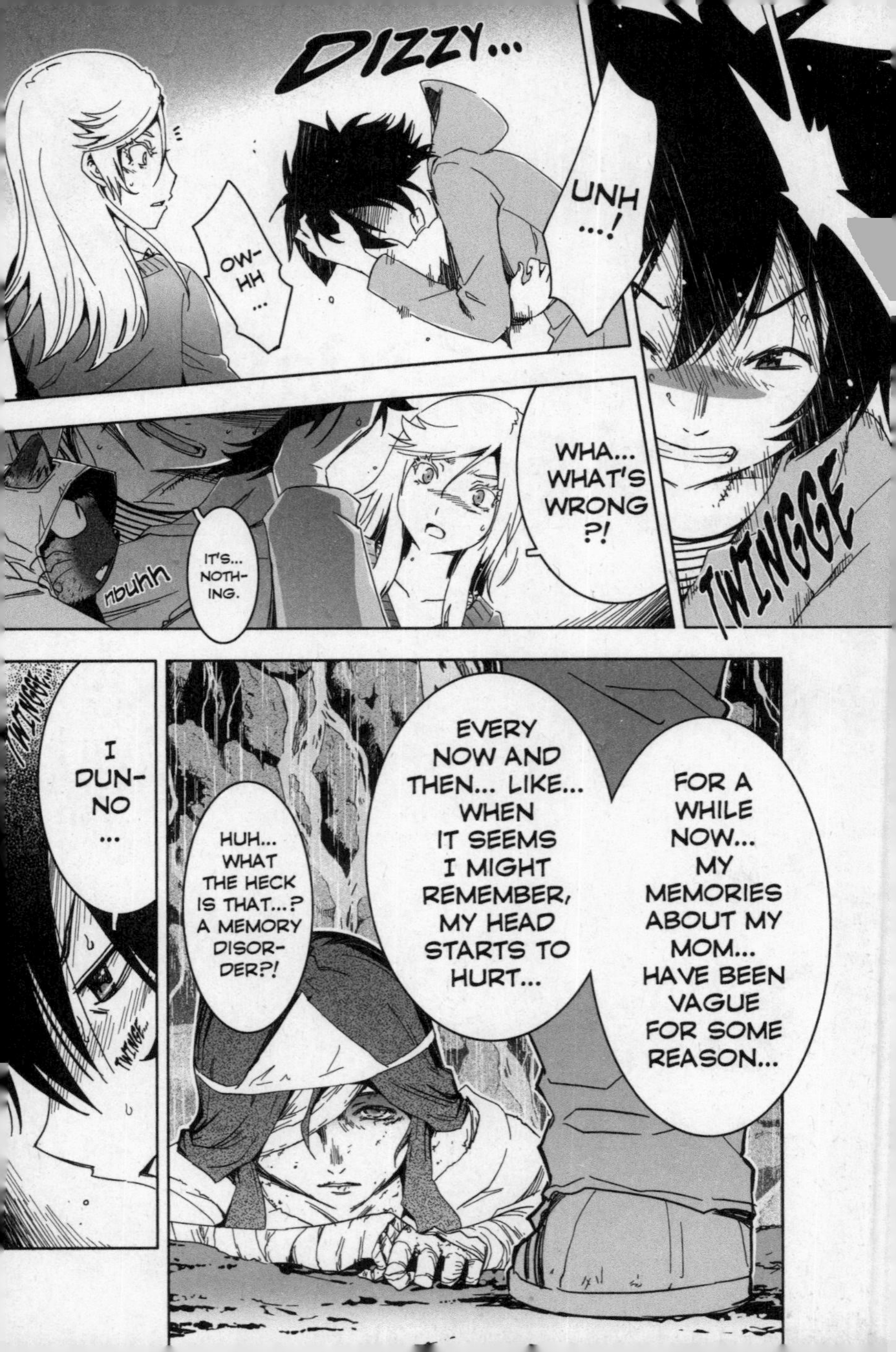
UNH ...!
TWINGGE
DIZZY...
OW-HH ...
WHA... WHAT'S WRONG ?!
IT'S... NOTH-ING.
nbuhh
FOR A WHILE NOW... MY MEMORIES ABOUT MY MOM... HAVE BEEN VAGUE FOR SOME REASON...
EVERY NOW AND THEN... LIKE... WHEN IT SEEMS I MIGHT REMEMBER, MY HEAD STARTS TO HURT...
HUH... WHAT THE HECK IS THAT...? A MEMORY DISOR-DER?!
I DUN-NO ...
TWINGE...
TWINGE...

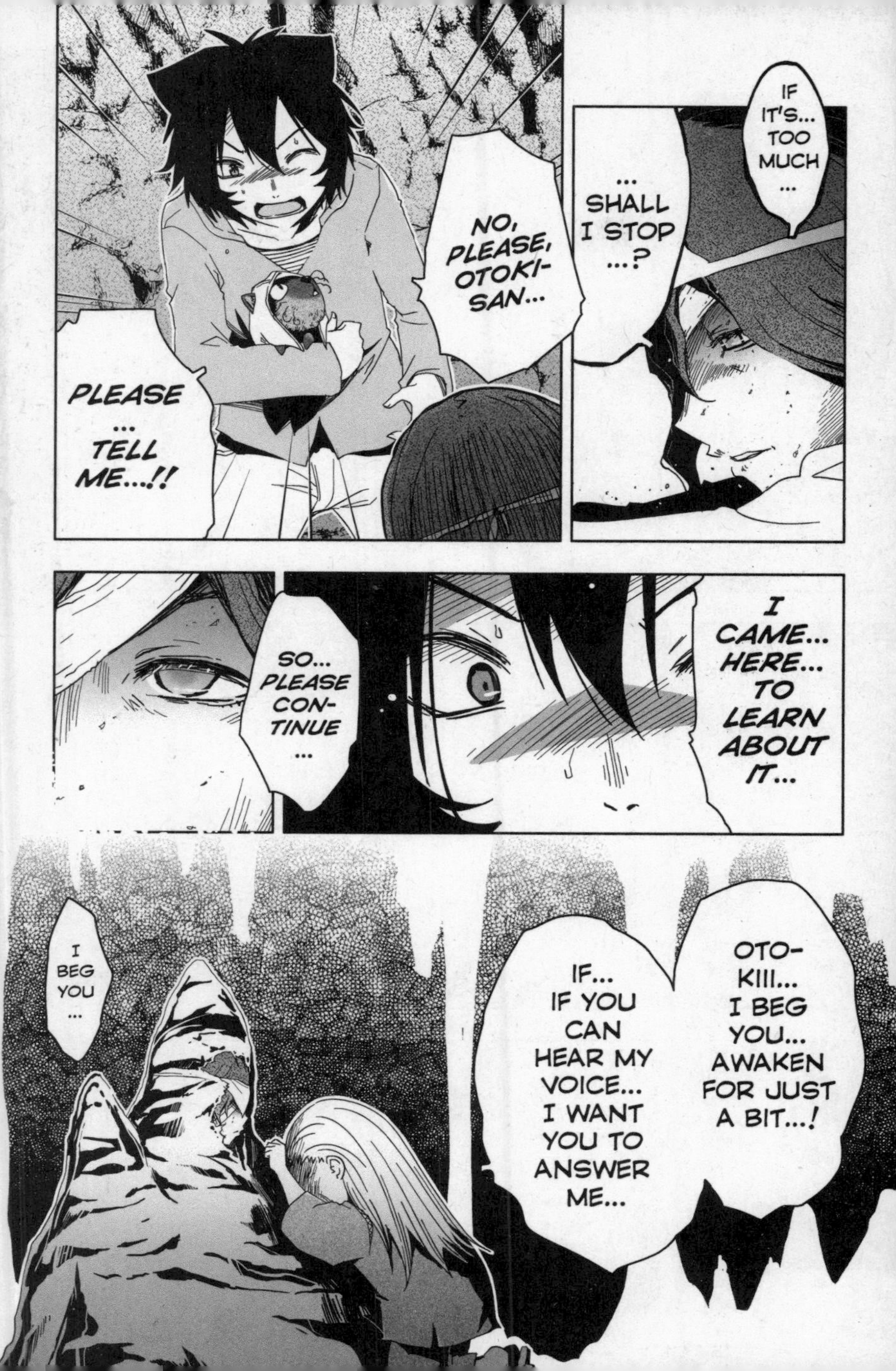
IF IT'S... TOO MUCH...
...SHALL I STOP...?
NO, PLEASE, OTOKI-SAN...
PLEASE ... TELL ME...!!
I CAME... HERE... TO LEARN ABOUT IT...
SO... PLEASE CON-TINUE...
OTO-KIII... I BEG YOU... AWAKEN FOR JUST A BIT...!
IF... IF YOU CAN HEAR MY VOICE... I WANT YOU TO ANSWER ME...
I BEG YOU...

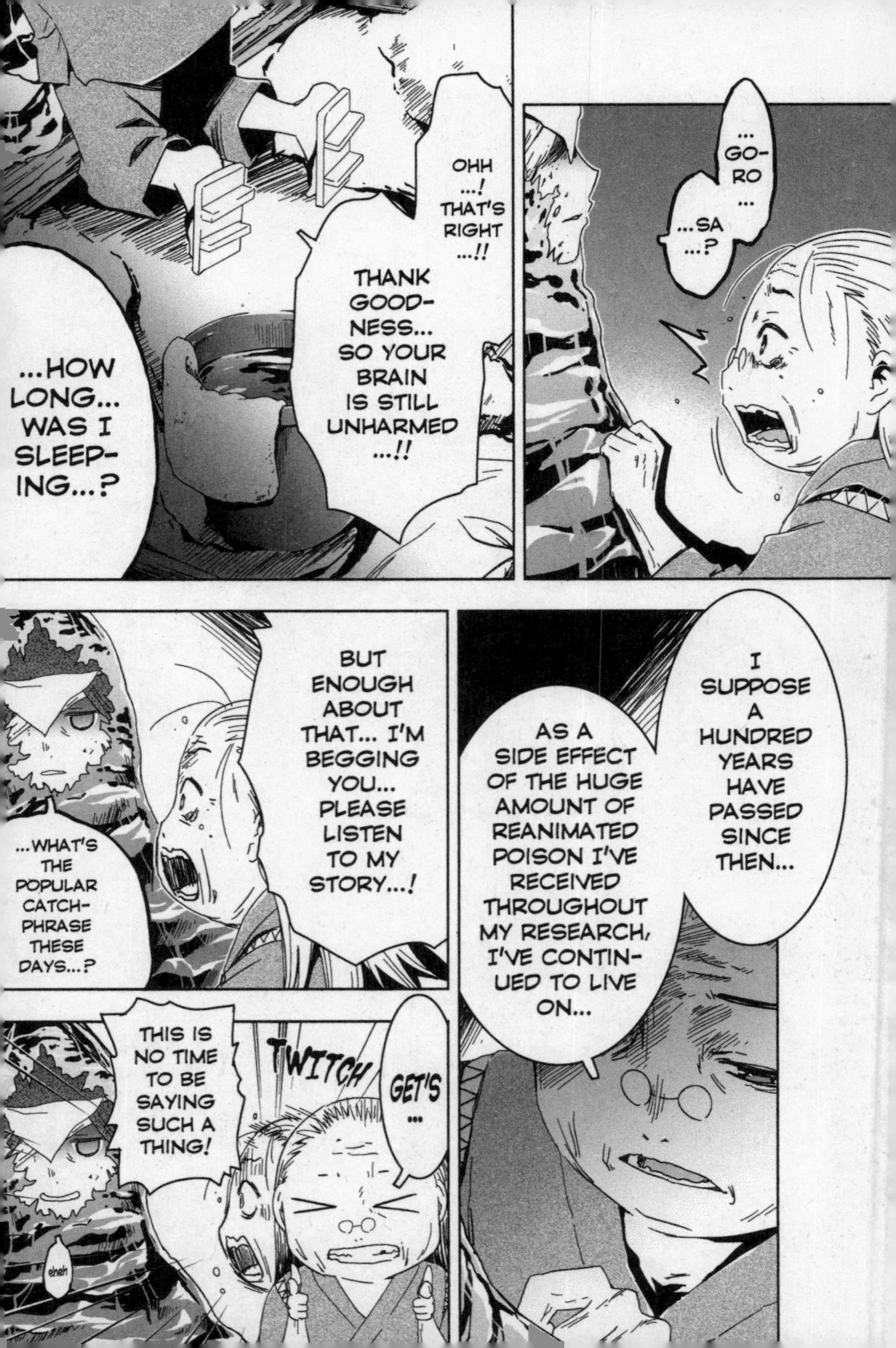
...GO-RO...
...SA...?
OHH...! THAT'S RIGHT...!!
THANK GOODNESS... SO YOUR BRAIN IS STILL UNHARMED...!!
...HOW LONG... WAS I SLEEPING...?
I SUPPOSE A HUNDRED YEARS HAVE PASSED SINCE THEN...
AS A SIDE EFFECT OF THE HUGE AMOUNT OF REANIMATED POISON I'VE RECEIVED THROUGHOUT MY RESEARCH, I'VE CONTINUED TO LIVE ON...
BUT ENOUGH ABOUT THAT... I'M BEGGING YOU... PLEASE LISTEN TO MY STORY...!
...WHAT'S THE POPULAR CATCHPHRASE THESE DAYS...?
GET'S...
TWITCH
THIS IS NO TIME TO BE SAYING SUCH A THING!
eheh

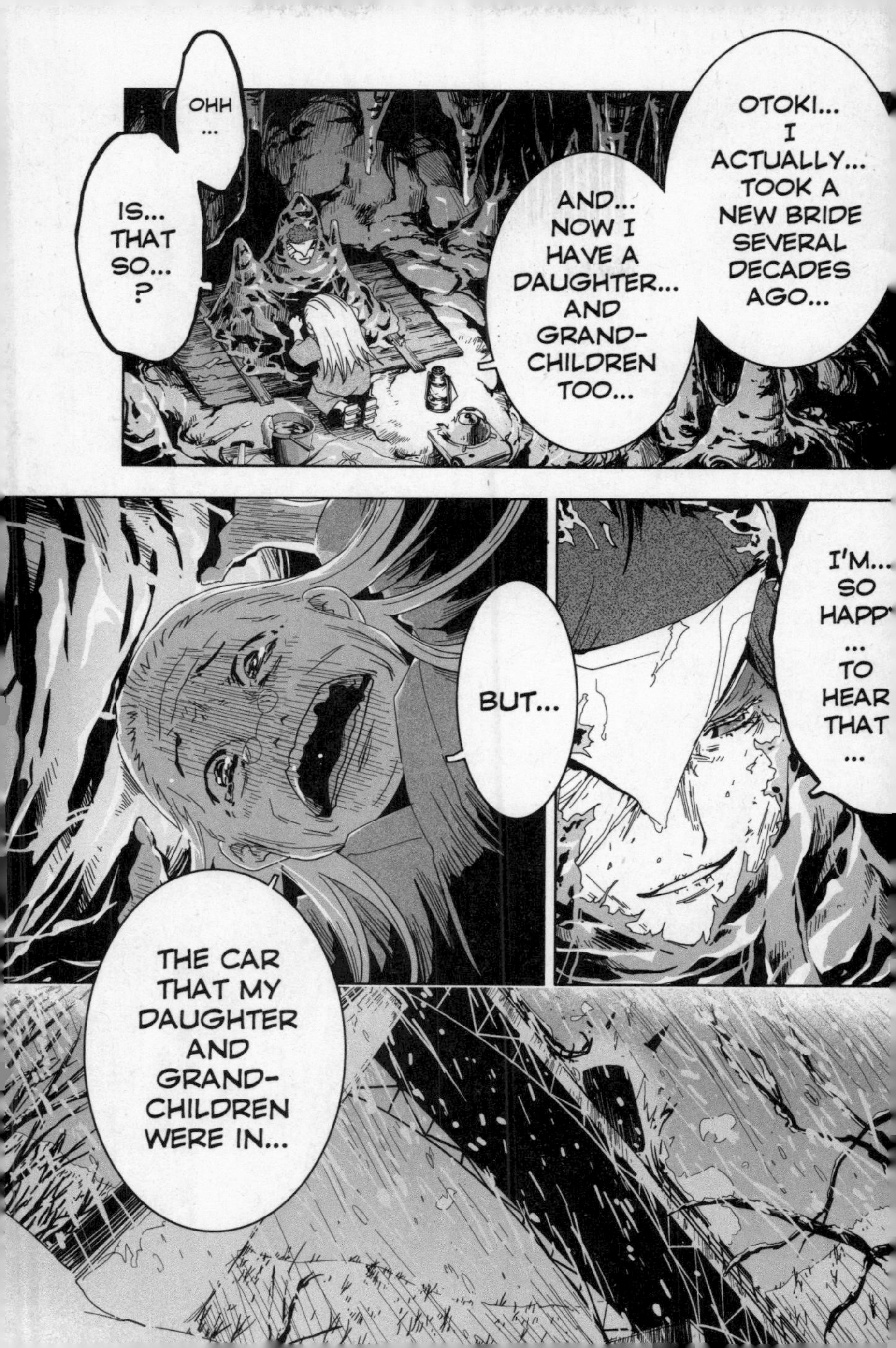
OTOKI... I ACTUALLY... TOOK A NEW BRIDE SEVERAL DECADES AGO...
AND... NOW I HAVE A DAUGHTER... AND GRAND-CHILDREN TOO...
OHH ...
IS... THAT SO... ?
I'M... SO HAPP' ... TO HEAR THAT ...
BUT...
THE CAR THAT MY DAUGHTER AND GRAND-CHILDREN WERE IN...

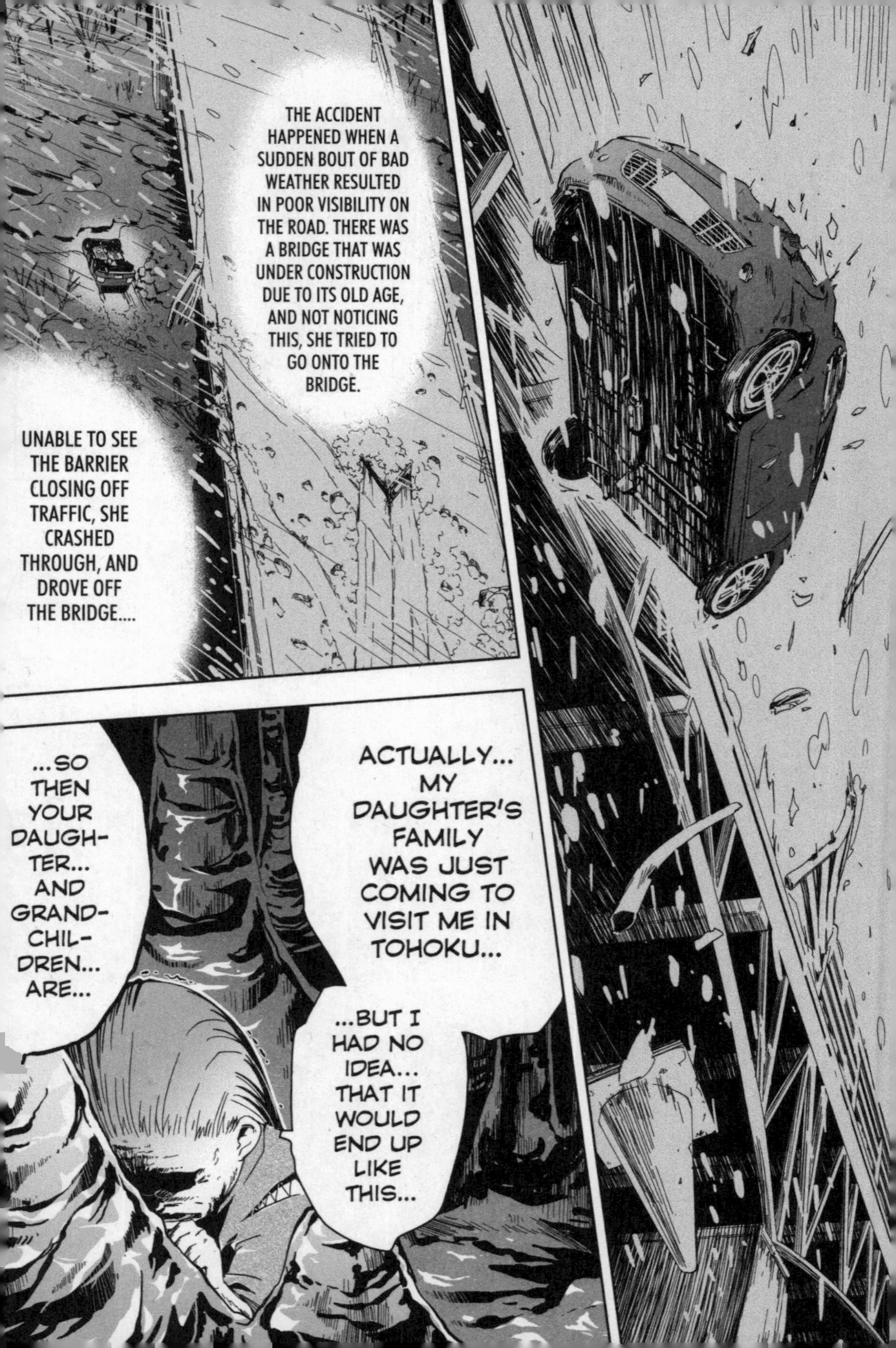
THE ACCIDENT HAPPENED WHEN A SUDDEN BOUT OF BAD WEATHER RESULTED IN POOR VISIBILITY ON THE ROAD. THERE WAS A BRIDGE THAT WAS UNDER CONSTRUCTION DUE TO ITS OLD AGE, AND NOT NOTICING THIS, SHE TRIED TO GO ONTO THE BRIDGE.
UNABLE TO SEE THE BARRIER CLOSING OFF TRAFFIC, SHE CRASHED THROUGH, AND DROVE OFF THE BRIDGE....
ACTUALLY... MY DAUGHTER'S FAMILY WAS JUST COMING TO VISIT ME IN TOHOKU...
...SO THEN YOUR DAUGHTER... AND GRANDCHILDREN... ARE...
...BUT I HAD NO IDEA... THAT IT WOULD END UP LIKE THIS...

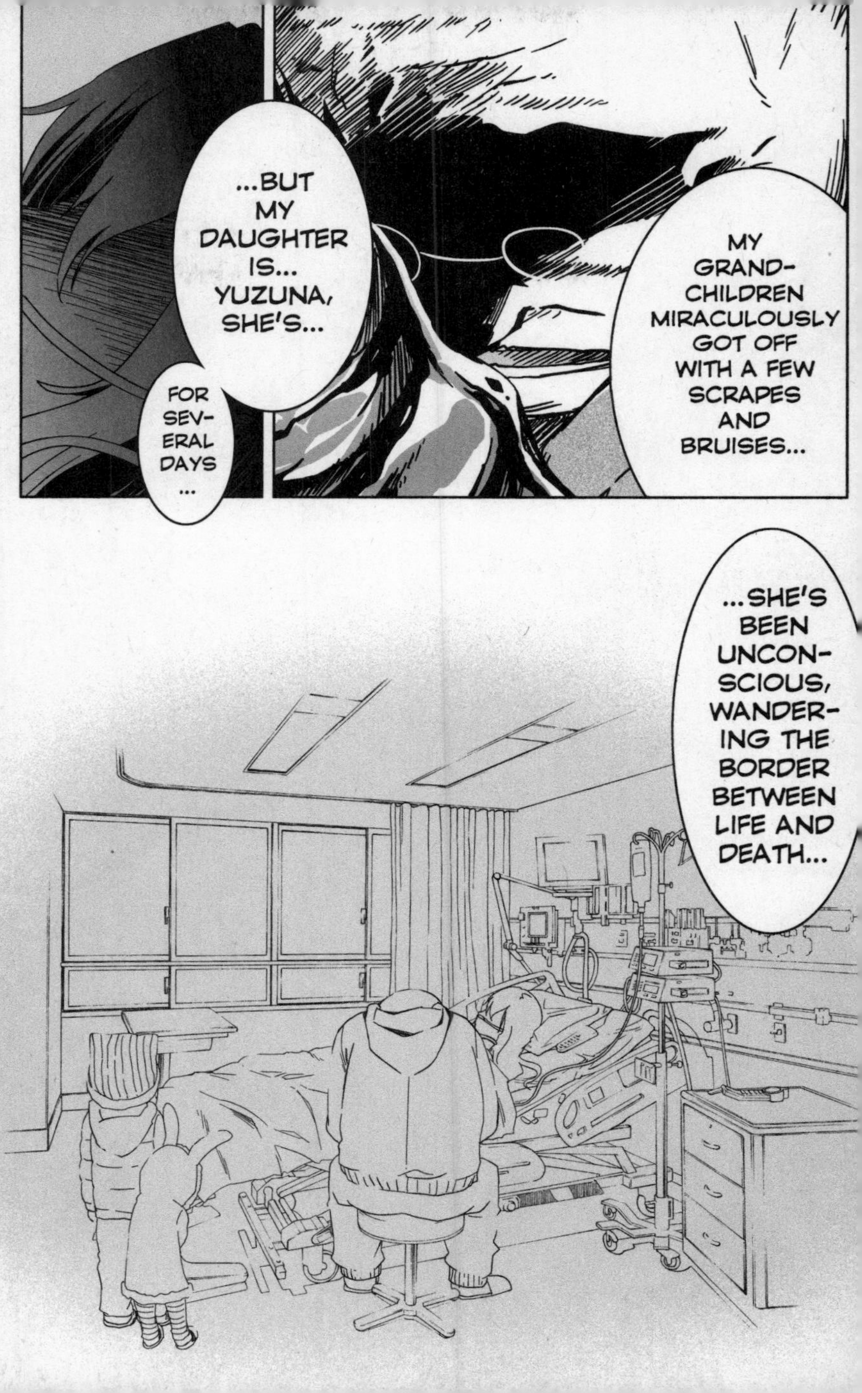
MY GRANDCHILDREN MIRACULOUSLY GOT OFF WITH A FEW SCRAPES AND BRUISES...
...BUT MY DAUGHTER IS... YUZUNA, SHE'S...
FOR SEVERAL DAYS...
...SHE'S BEEN UNCONSCIOUS, WANDERING THE BORDER BETWEEN LIFE AND DEATH...

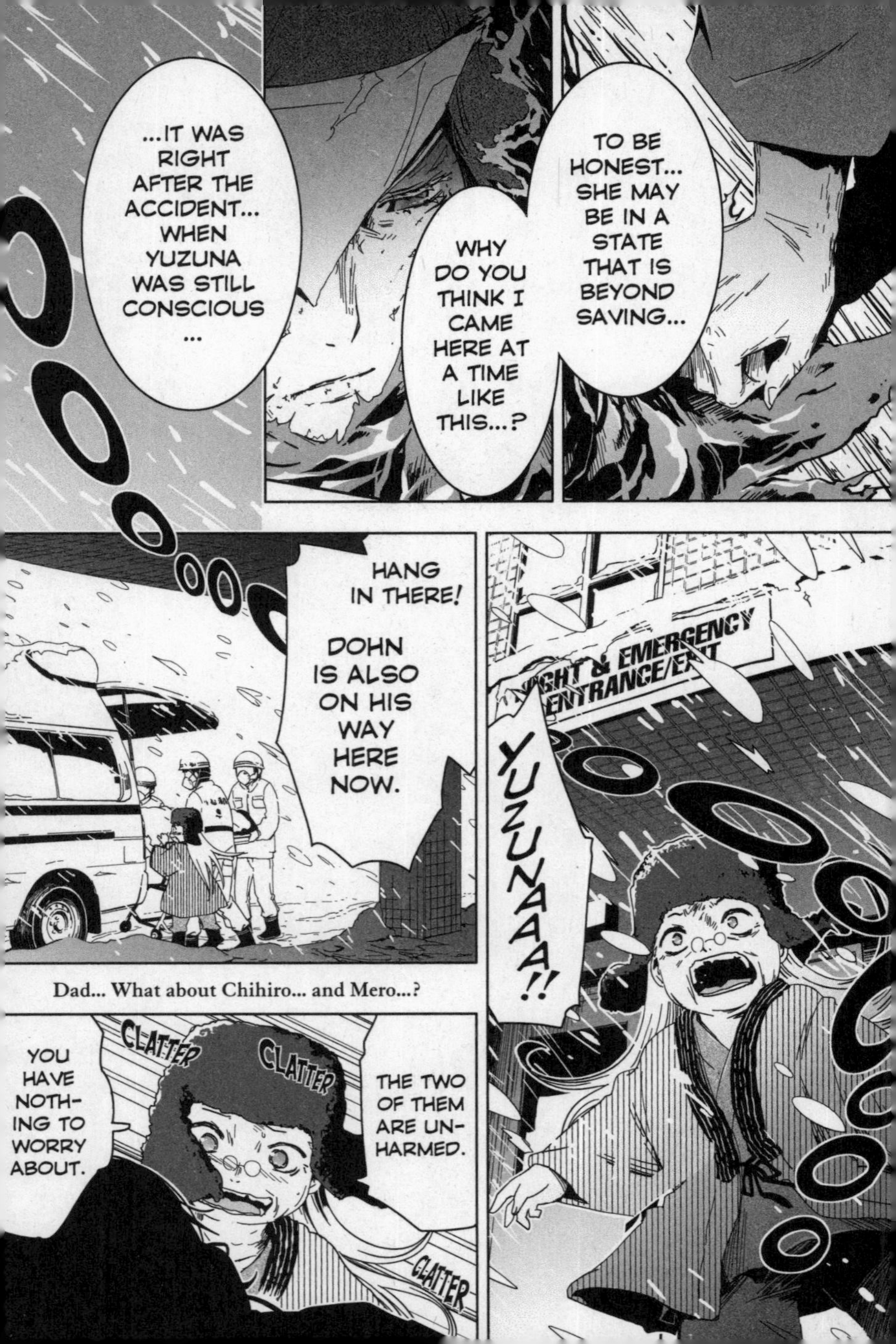
TO BE HONEST... SHE MAY BE IN A STATE THAT IS BEYOND SAVING...
WHY DO YOU THINK I CAME HERE AT A TIME LIKE THIS...?
...IT WAS RIGHT AFTER THE ACCIDENT... WHEN YUZUNA WAS STILL CONSCIOUS...
& EMERGENCY
ENTRANCE/
YUZUNAAA!!
HANG IN THERE!
DOHN IS ALSO ON HIS WAY HERE NOW.
Dad... What about Chihiro... and Mero...?
CLATTER
CLATTER
THE TWO OF THEM ARE UN-HARMED.
YOU HAVE NOTH-ING TO WORRY ABOUT.
CLATTER

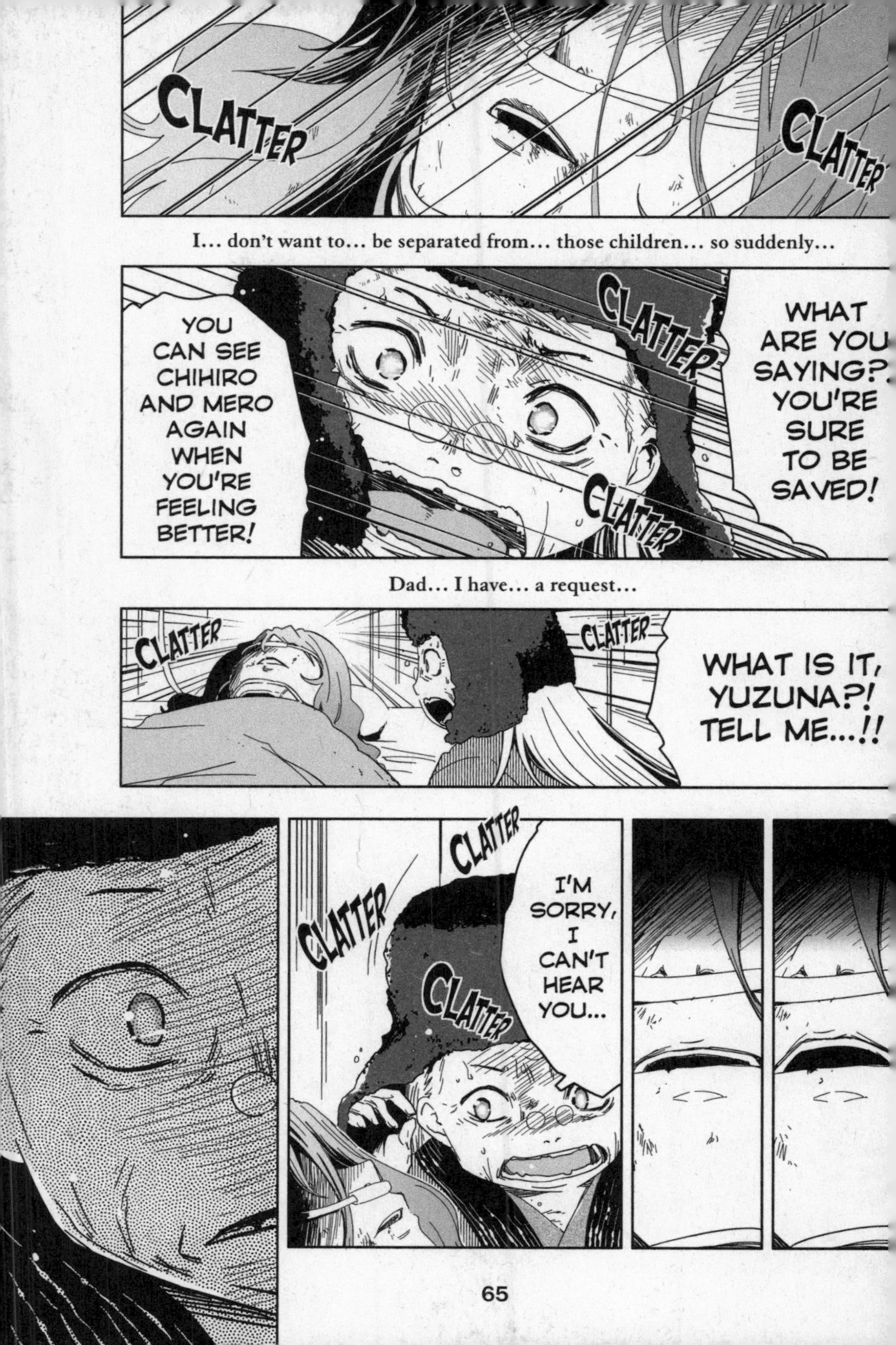
CLATTER
CLATTER
I… don't want to… be separated from… those children… so suddenly…
WHAT ARE YOU SAYING?! YOU'RE SURE TO BE SAVED!
CLATTER
CLATTER
YOU CAN SEE CHIHIRO AND MERO AGAIN WHEN YOU'RE FEELING BETTER!
Dad… I have… a request…
WHAT IS IT, YUZUNA?! TELL ME...!!
CLATTER
CLATTER
CLATTER
CLATTER
CLATTER
I'M SORRY, I CAN'T HEAR YOU...

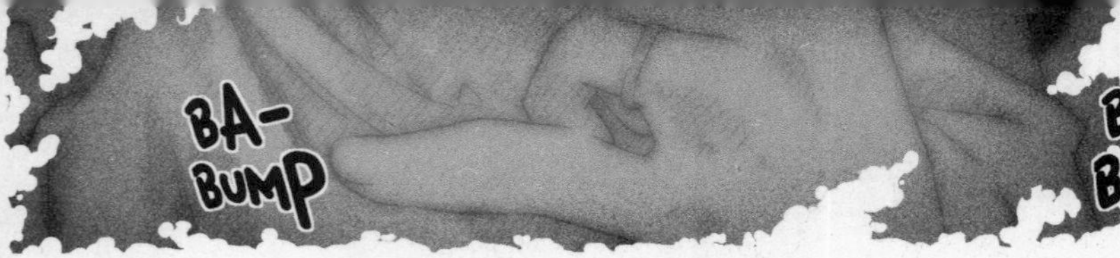
BA-
BUMP
BA-
BUMP

I… made a promise… with the children…

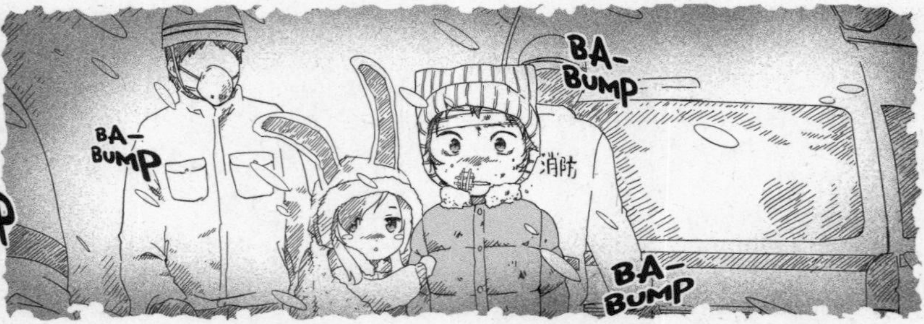
BA-
BUMP
BA-
BUMP
消防
BA-
BUMP

Next week… We'd go to the amusement park… They've been looking forward to it for a long time…

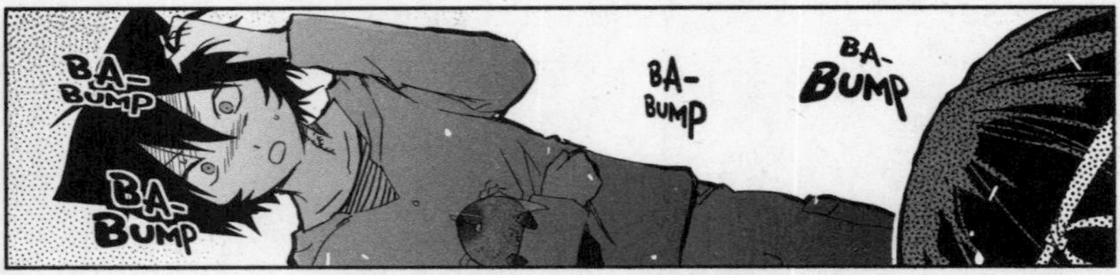
BA-
BUMP
BA-
BUMP
BA-
BUMP
BA-
BUMP
BA-
BUMP

So… I want to be… here… just a little longer…

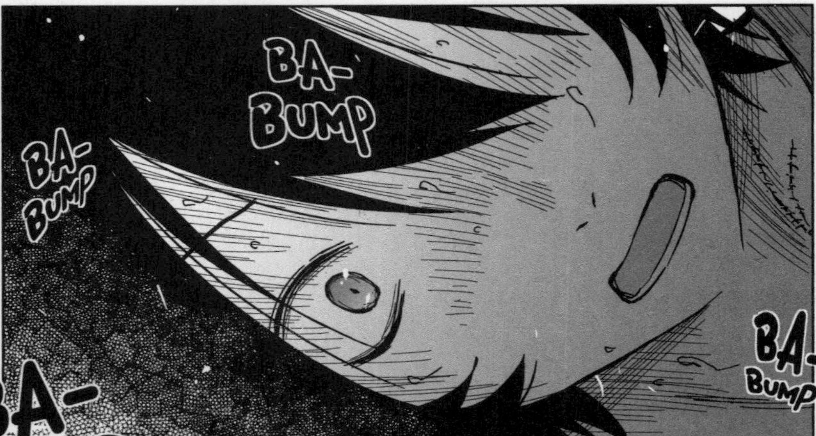
BA-
BUMP
BA-
BUMP
BA-
BUMP
BA-
BUMP

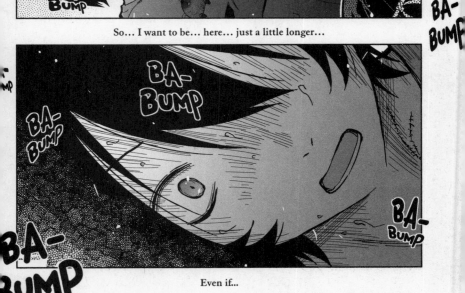

Even if...

I... become...

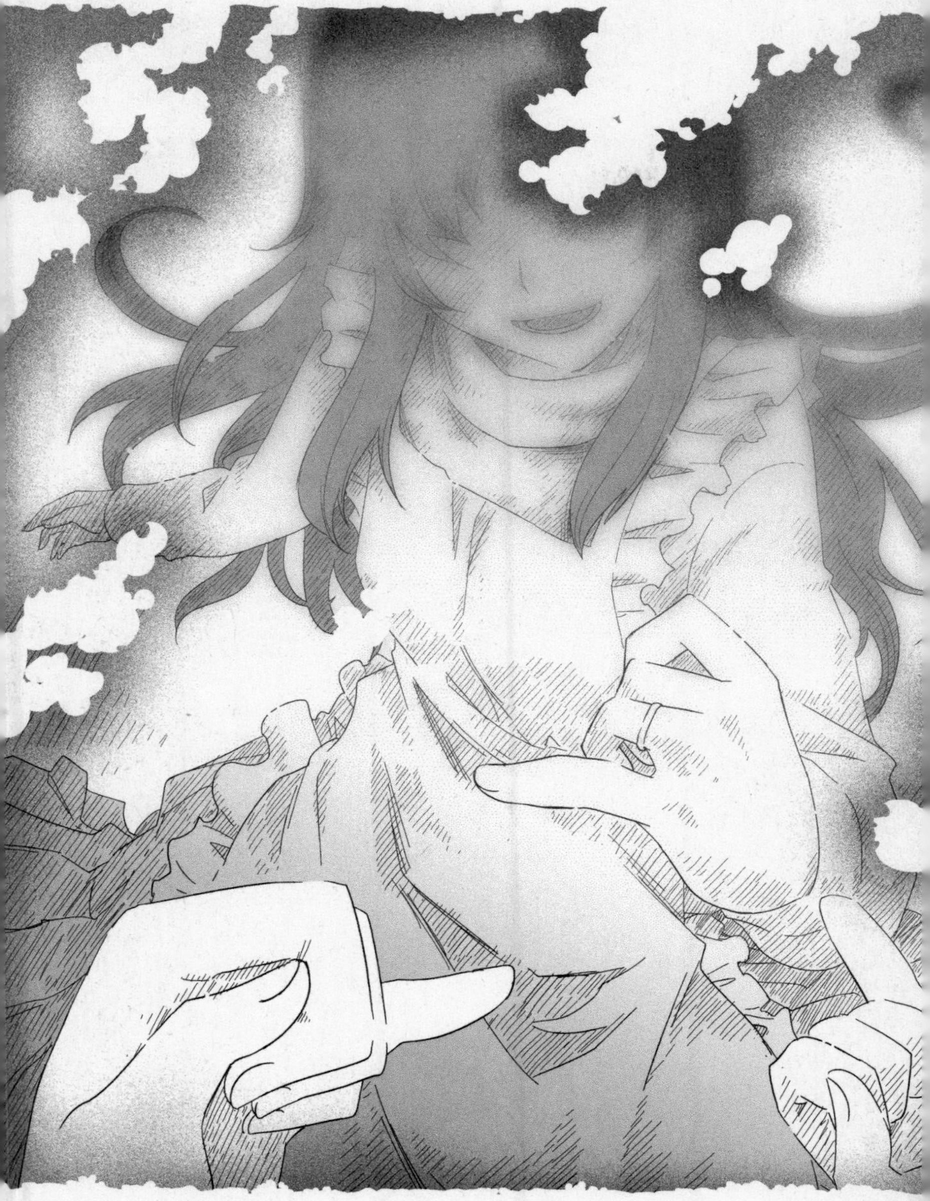

...a... zombie...

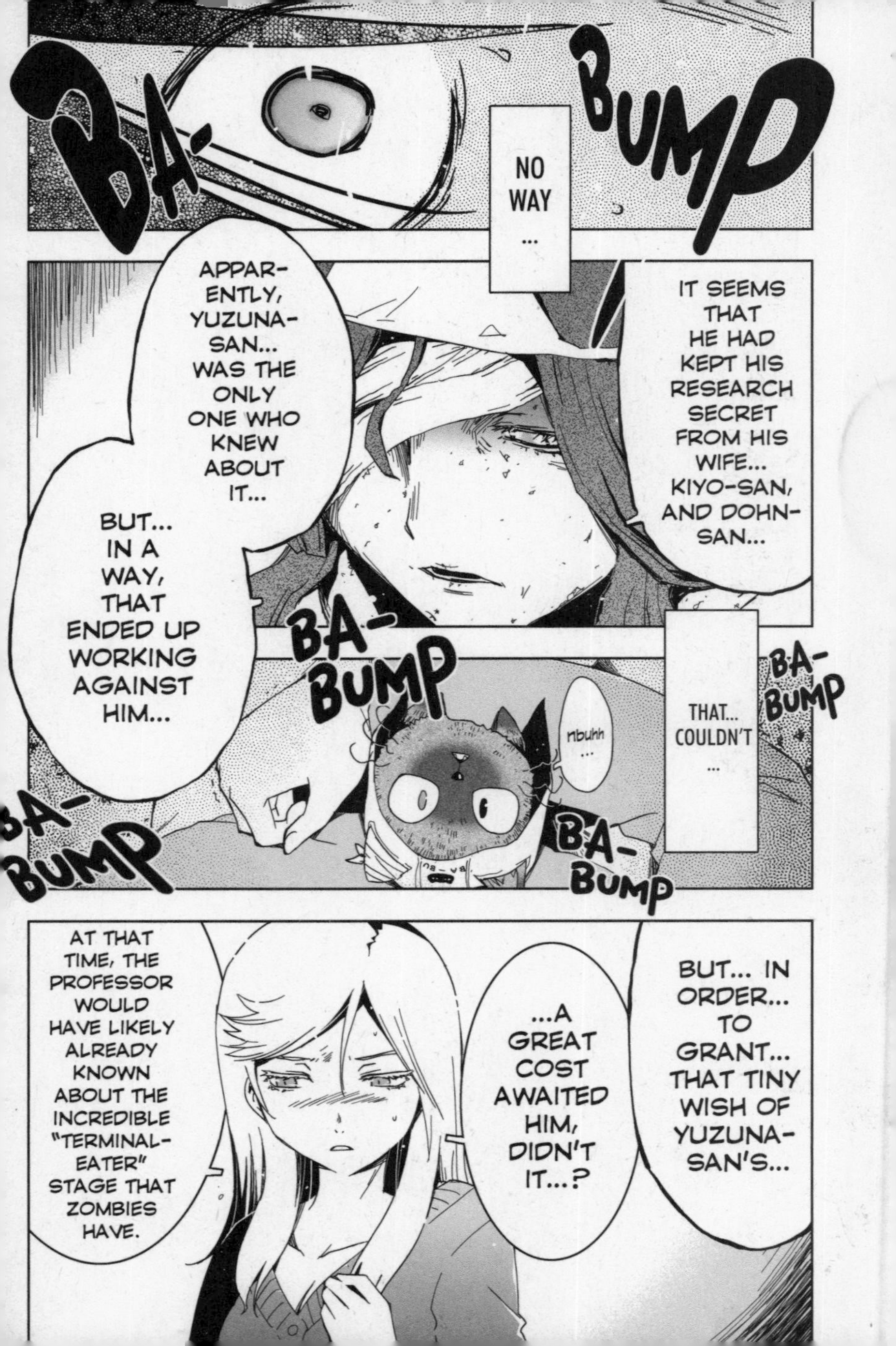
BA-BUMP
NO WAY ...
IT SEEMS THAT HE HAD KEPT HIS RESEARCH SECRET FROM HIS WIFE... KIYO-SAN, AND DOHN-SAN...
APPARENTLY, YUZUNA-SAN... WAS THE ONLY ONE WHO KNEW ABOUT IT...
BUT... IN A WAY, THAT ENDED UP WORKING AGAINST HIM...
THAT... COULDN'T ...
BA-BUMP
nbuhh ...
BA-BUMP
BA-BUMP
BA-BUMP
BUT... IN ORDER... TO GRANT... THAT TINY WISH OF YUZUNA-SAN'S...
...A GREAT COST AWAITED HIM, DIDN'T IT...?
AT THAT TIME, THE PROFESSOR WOULD HAVE LIKELY ALREADY KNOWN ABOUT THE INCREDIBLE "TERMINAL-EATER" STAGE THAT ZOMBIES HAVE.

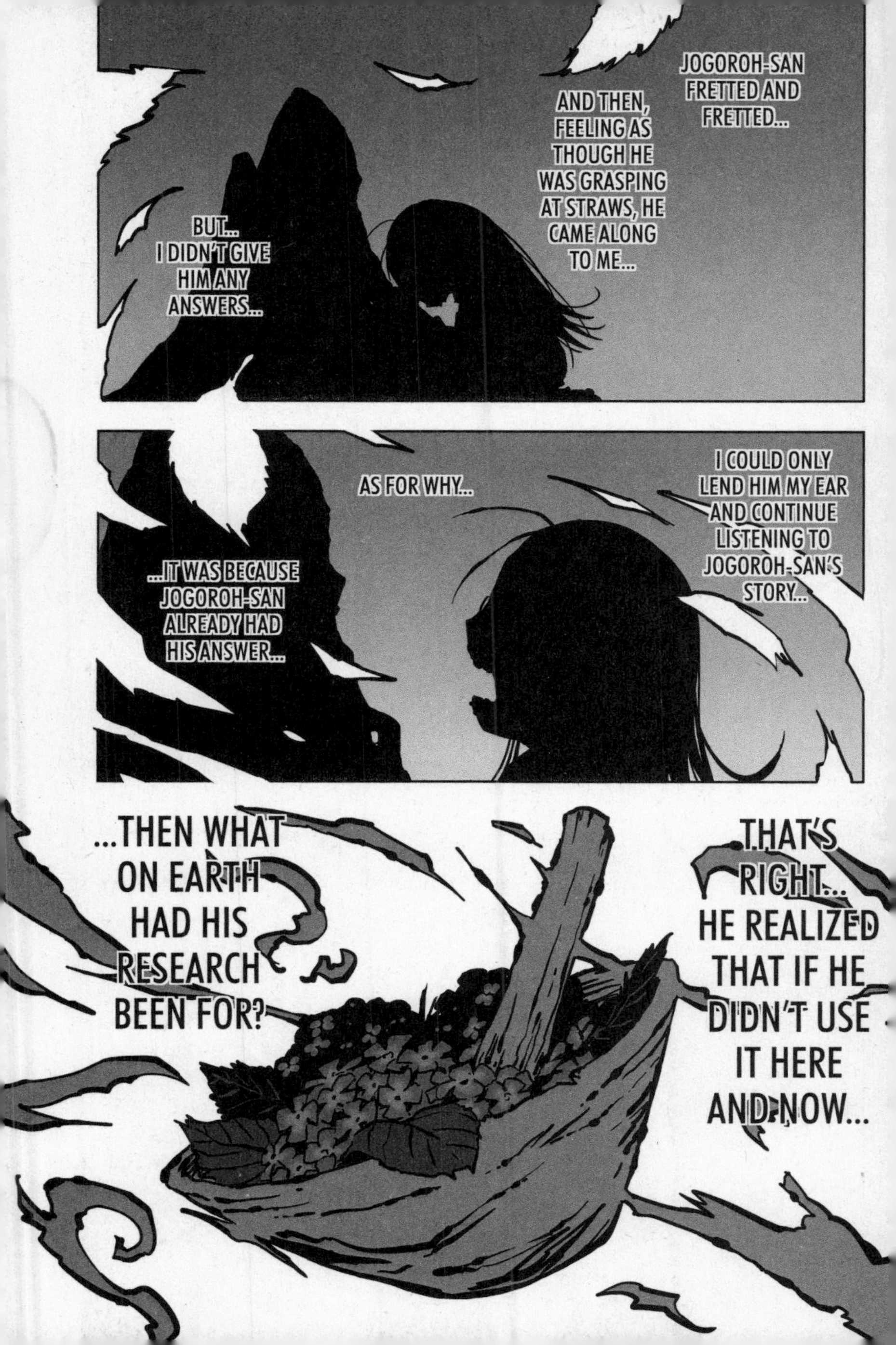
JOGOROH-SAN FRETTED AND FRETTED...
AND THEN, FEELING AS THOUGH HE WAS GRASPING AT STRAWS, HE CAME ALONG TO ME...
BUT... I DIDN'T GIVE HIM ANY ANSWERS...
I COULD ONLY LEND HIM MY EAR AND CONTINUE LISTENING TO JOGOROH-SAN'S STORY...
AS FOR WHY...
...IT WAS BECAUSE JOGOROH-SAN ALREADY HAD HIS ANSWER...
THAT'S RIGHT... HE REALIZED THAT IF HE DIDN'T USE IT HERE AND NOW...
...THEN WHAT ON EARTH HAD HIS RESEARCH BEEN FOR?

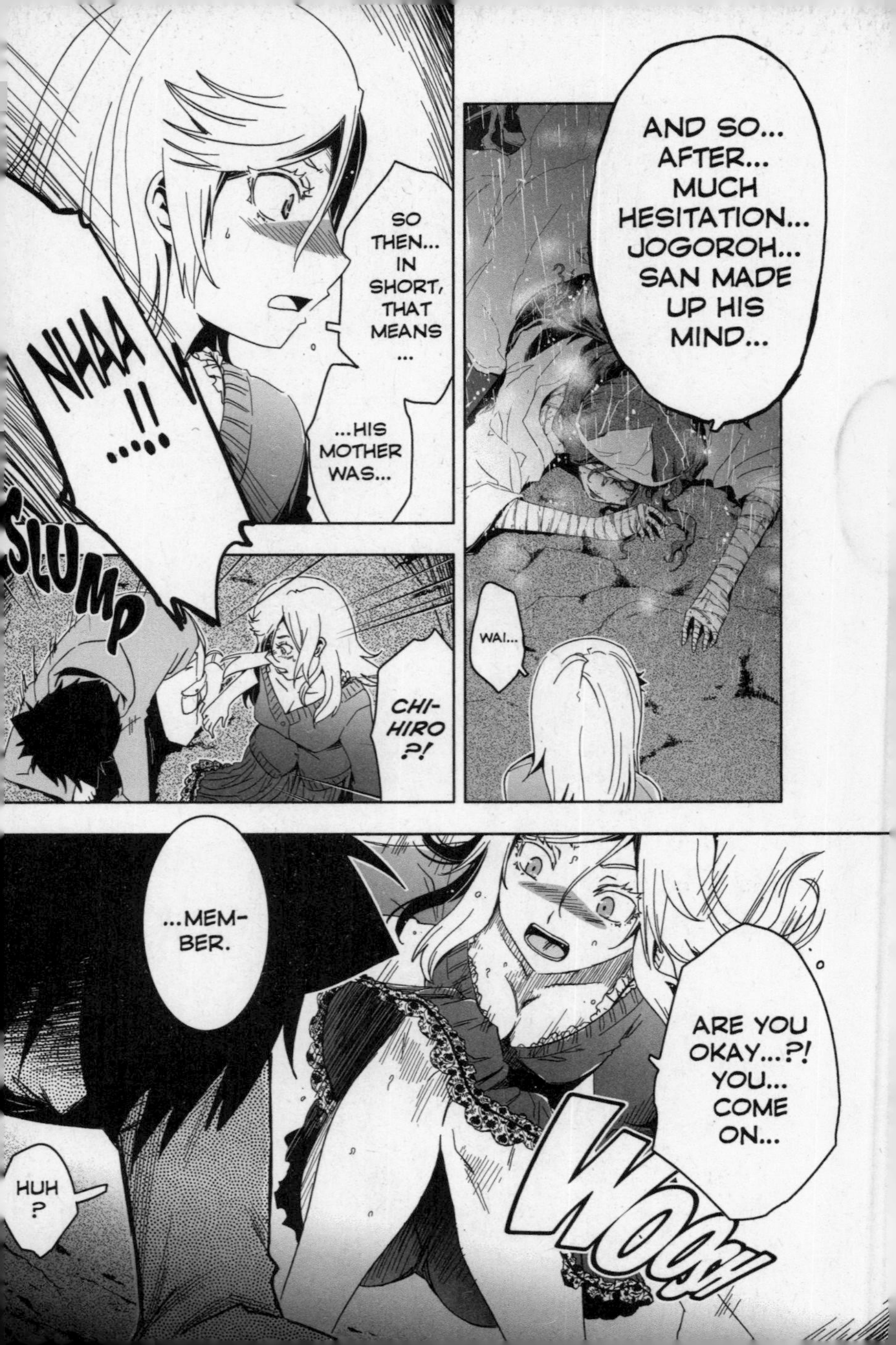
AND SO... AFTER... MUCH HESITATION... JOGOROH... SAN MADE UP HIS MIND...
WAI...
SO THEN... IN SHORT, THAT MEANS ...
...HIS MOTHER WAS...
NHAA !! ...!!
SLUMP
CHI-HIRO ?!
ARE YOU OKAY...?! YOU... COME ON...
...MEM-BER.
HUH ?

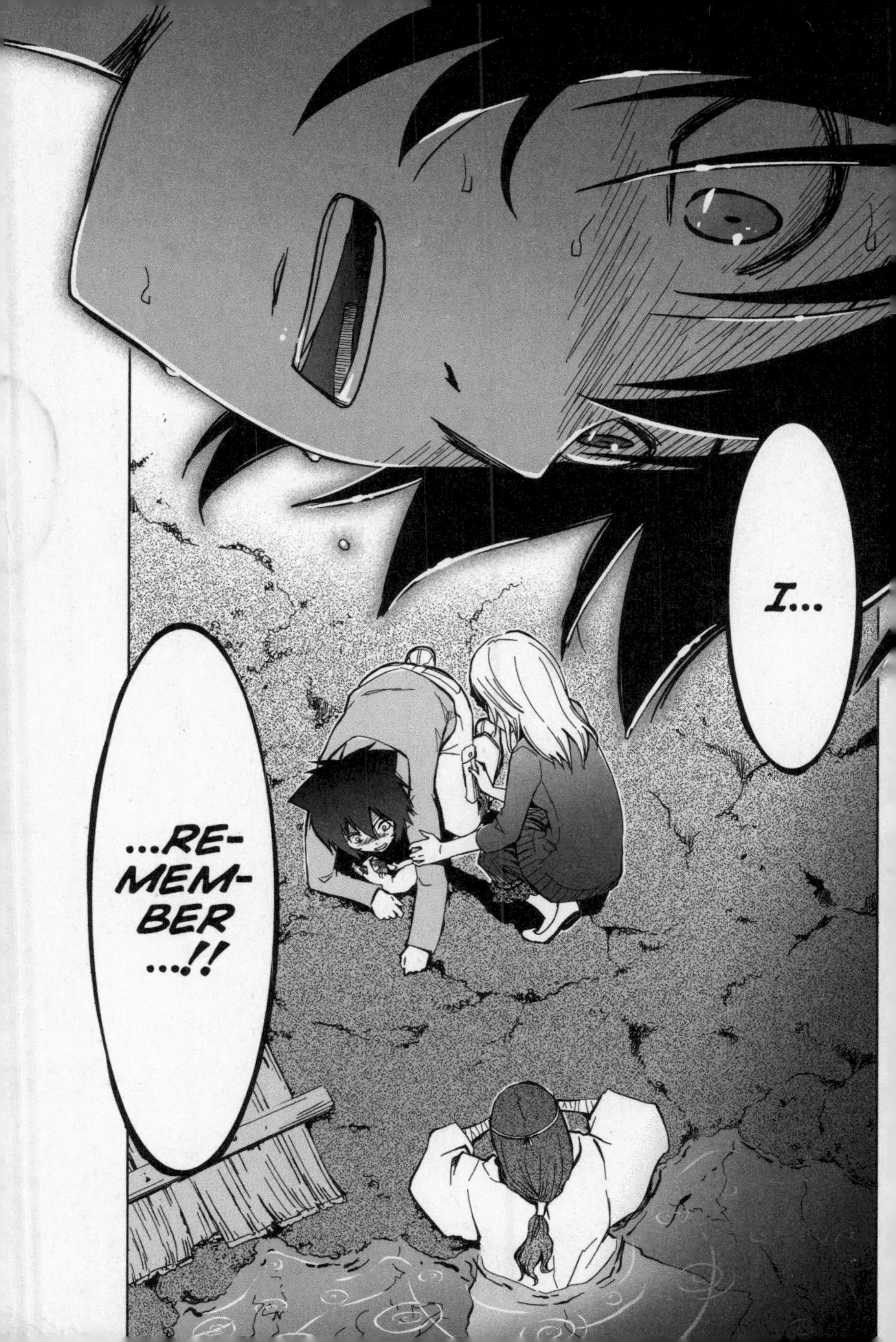
I...
...RE-MEM-BER...!!

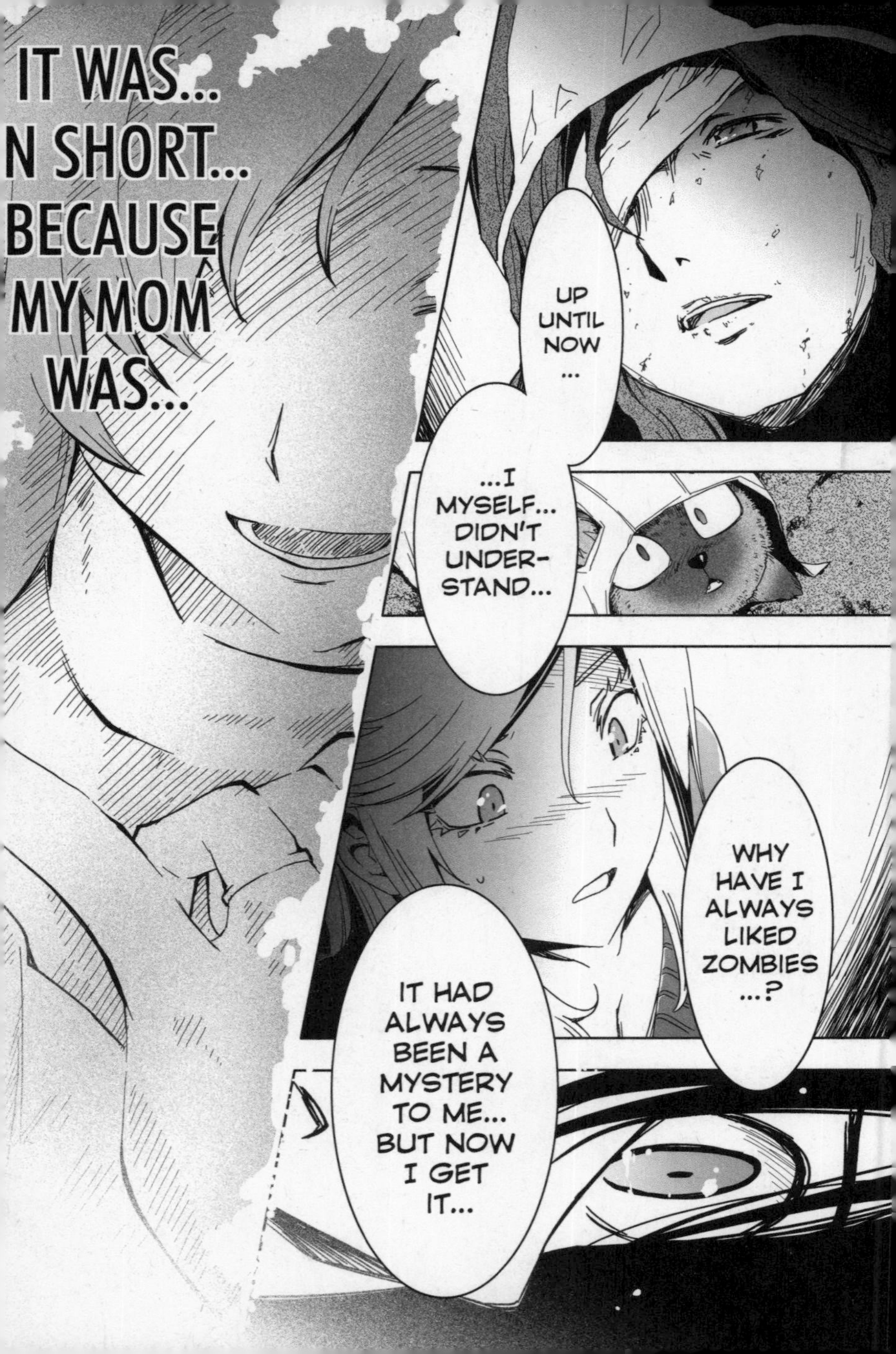
UP UNTIL NOW ...
...I MYSELF... DIDN'T UNDER-STAND...
WHY HAVE I ALWAYS LIKED ZOMBIES ...?
IT HAD ALWAYS BEEN A MYSTERY TO ME... BUT NOW I GET IT...
IT WAS... N SHORT... BECAUSE MY MOM WAS...

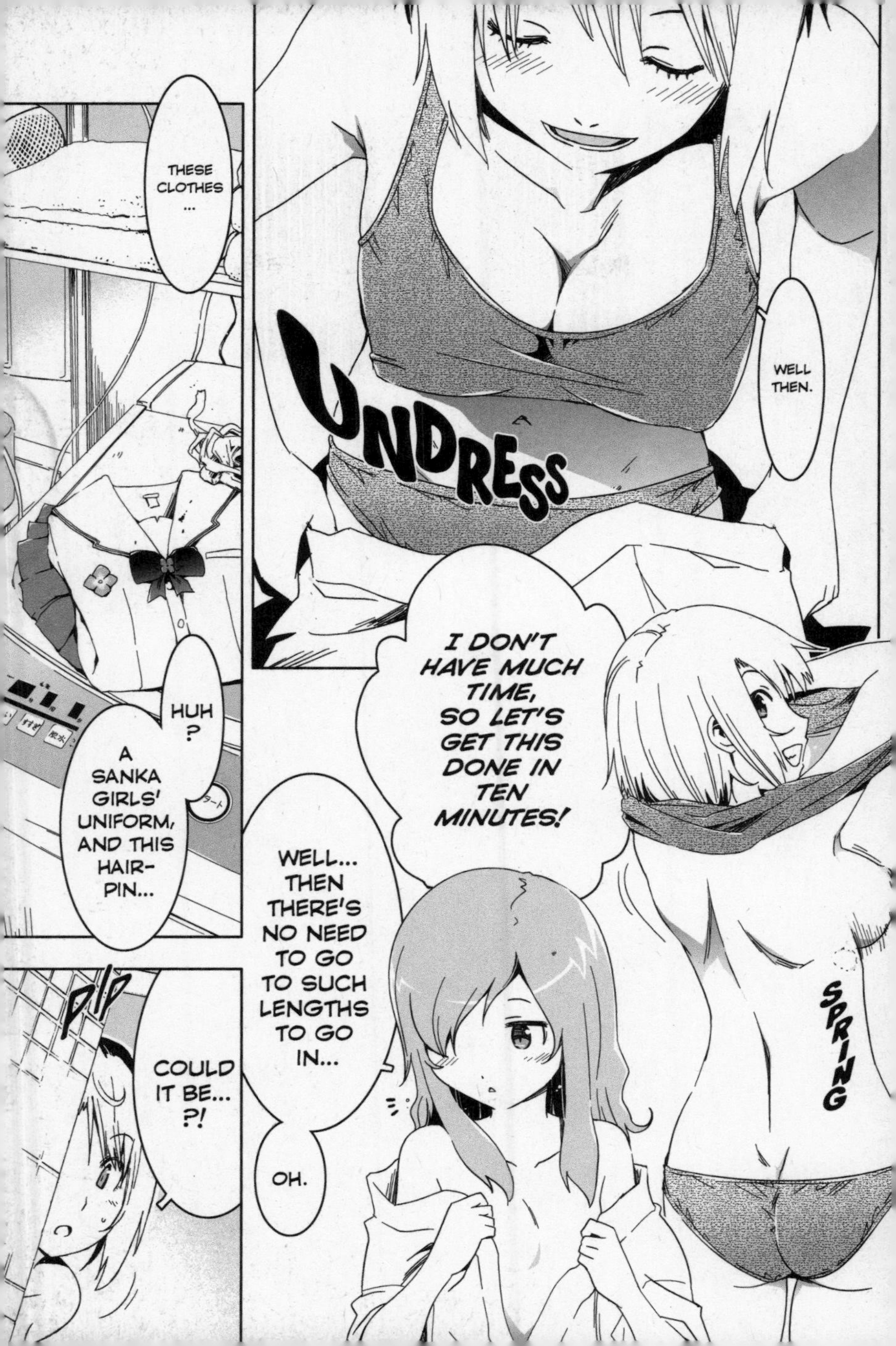
WELL THEN.
UNDRESS
I DON'T HAVE MUCH TIME, SO LET'S GET THIS DONE IN TEN MINUTES!
SPRING
WELL... THEN THERE'S NO NEED TO GO TO SUCH LENGTHS TO GO IN...
OH.
THESE CLOTHES ...
HUH ?
A SANKA GIRLS' UNIFORM, AND THIS HAIR-PIN...
D/D
COULD IT BE... ?!

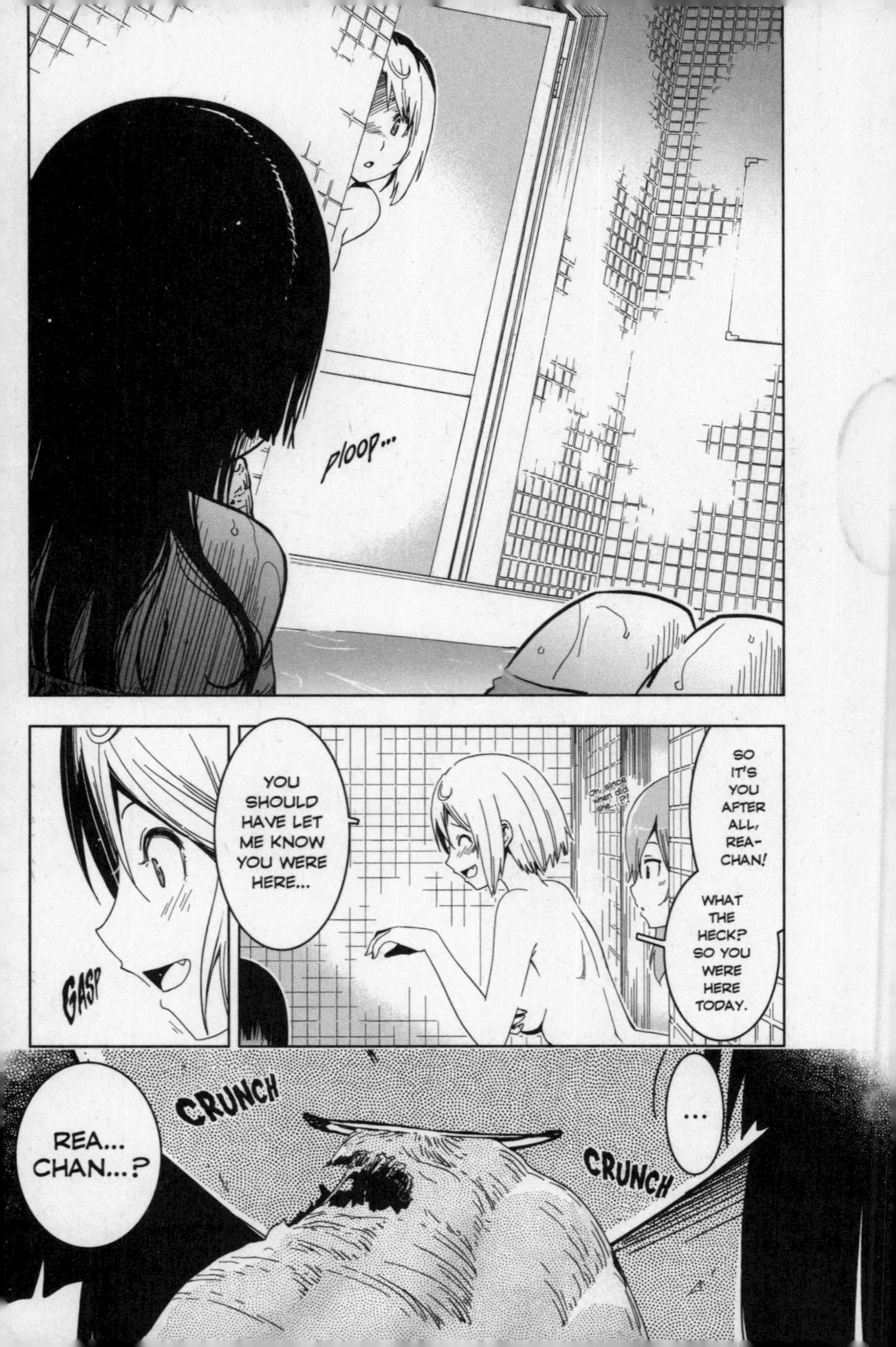
PLOOP...
SO IT'S YOU AFTER ALL, REA-CHAN!
Oh, since when did she...?!
WHAT THE HECK? SO YOU WERE HERE TODAY.
YOU SHOULD HAVE LET ME KNOW YOU WERE HERE...
GASP
...
CRUNCH
CRUNCH
REA... CHAN...?

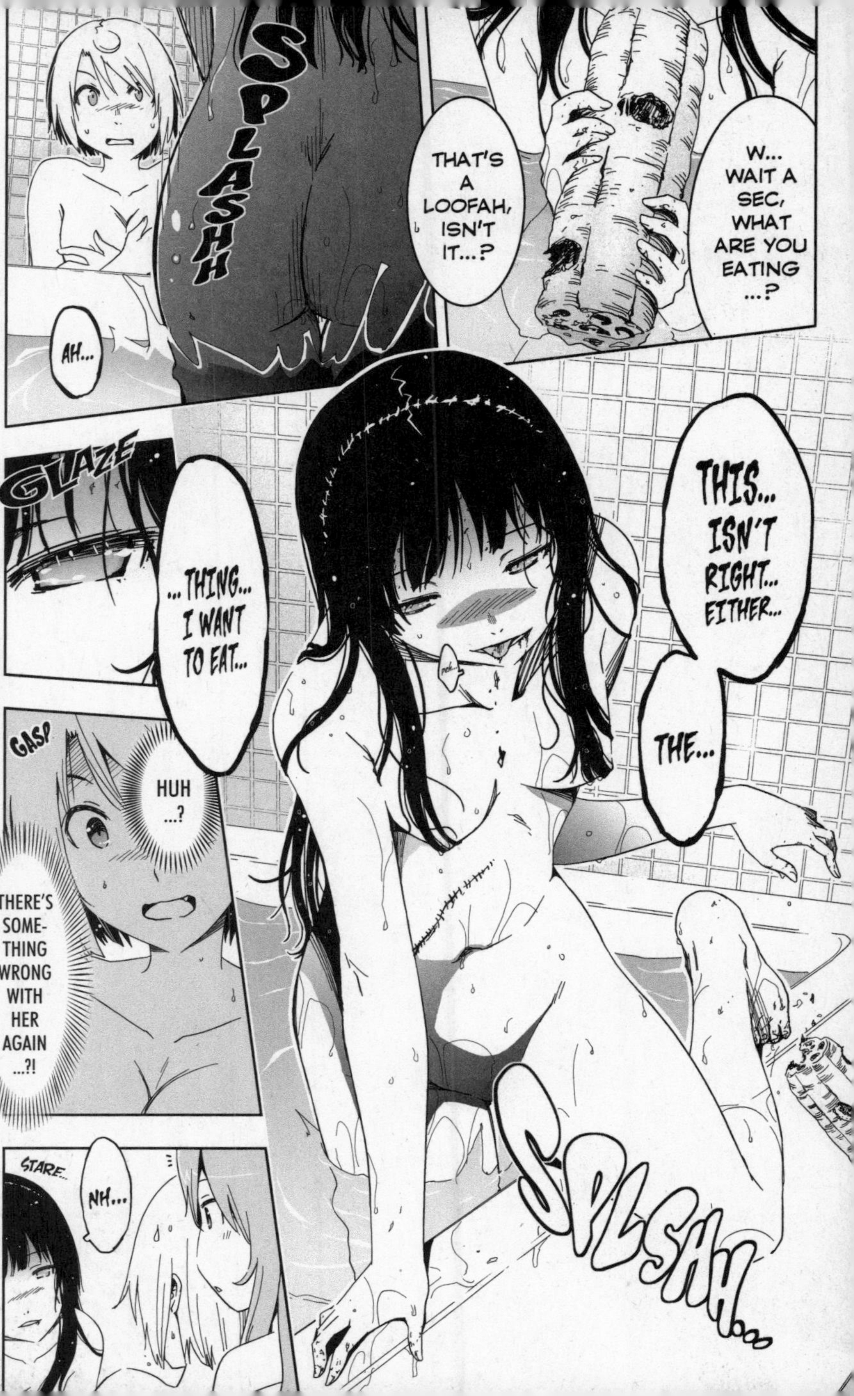
W... WAIT A SEC, WHAT ARE YOU EATING ...?
THAT'S A LOOFAH, ISN'T IT...?
SPLASHH
AH...
THIS... ISN'T RIGHT... EITHER...
THE...
...THING... I WANT TO EAT...
SPLSHH...
GLAZE
GASP
HUH ...?
THERE'S SOME-THING WRONG WITH HER AGAIN ...?!
STARE..
NH...

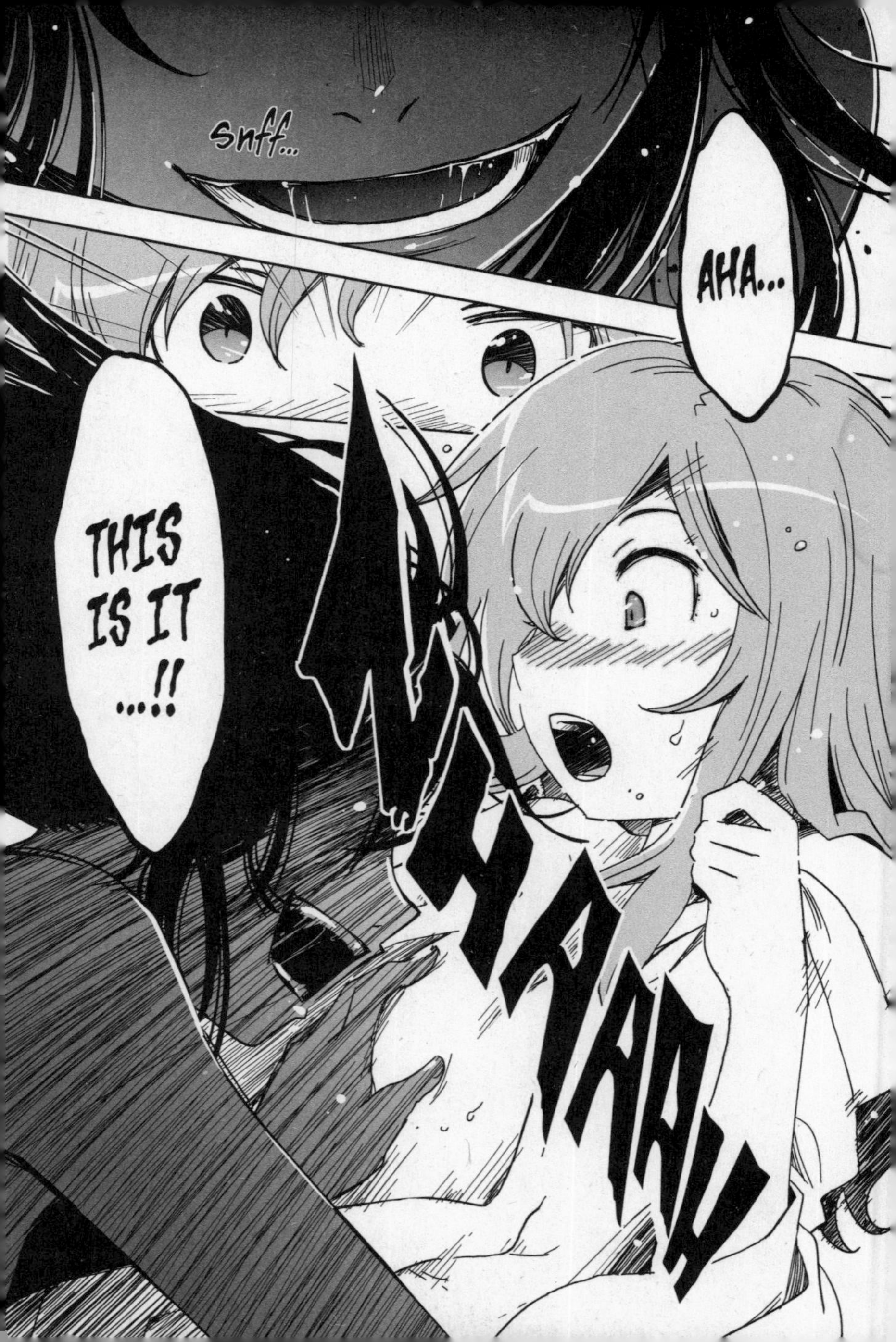
snff...
AHA...
THIS IS IT ...!!
HAAA!

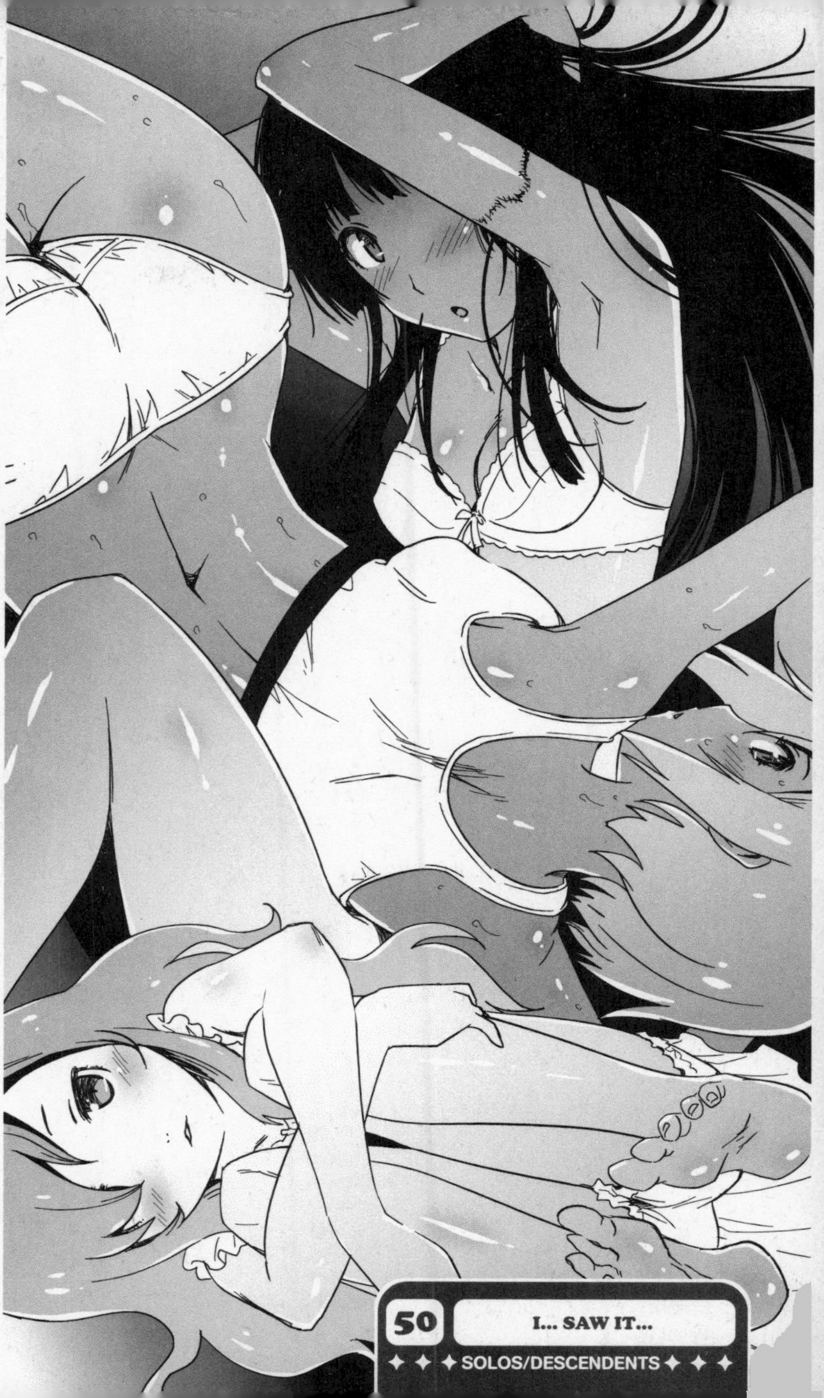
50
I... SAW IT...
SOLOS/DESCENDENTS

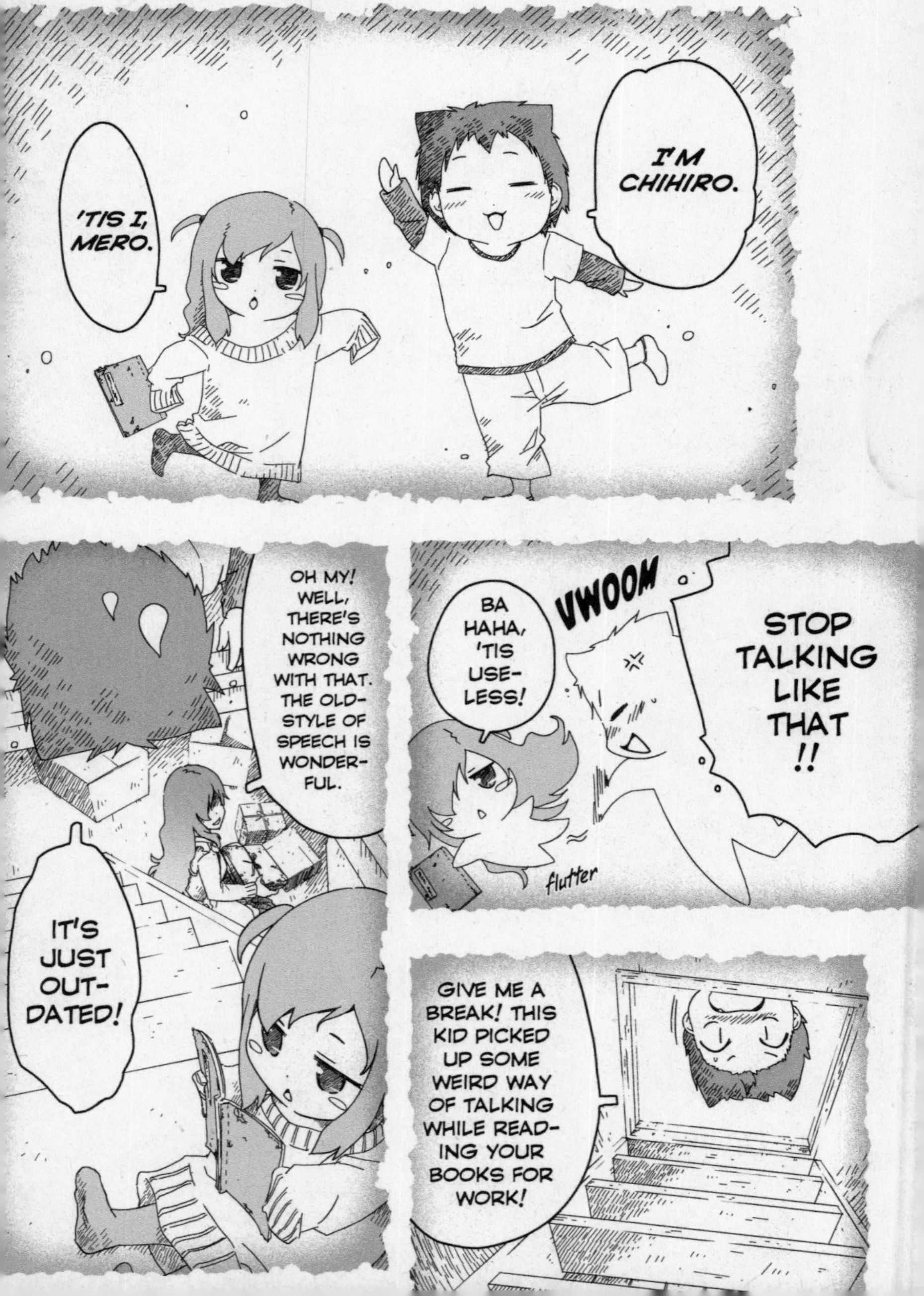
I'M CHIHIRO.
'TIS I, MERO.
STOP TALKING LIKE THAT!!
VWOOM
BA HAHA, 'TIS USELESS!
flutter
GIVE ME A BREAK! THIS KID PICKED UP SOME WEIRD WAY OF TALKING WHILE READING YOUR BOOKS FOR WORK!
OH MY! WELL, THERE'S NOTHING WRONG WITH THAT. THE OLD-STYLE OF SPEECH IS WONDERFUL.
IT'S JUST OUTDATED!

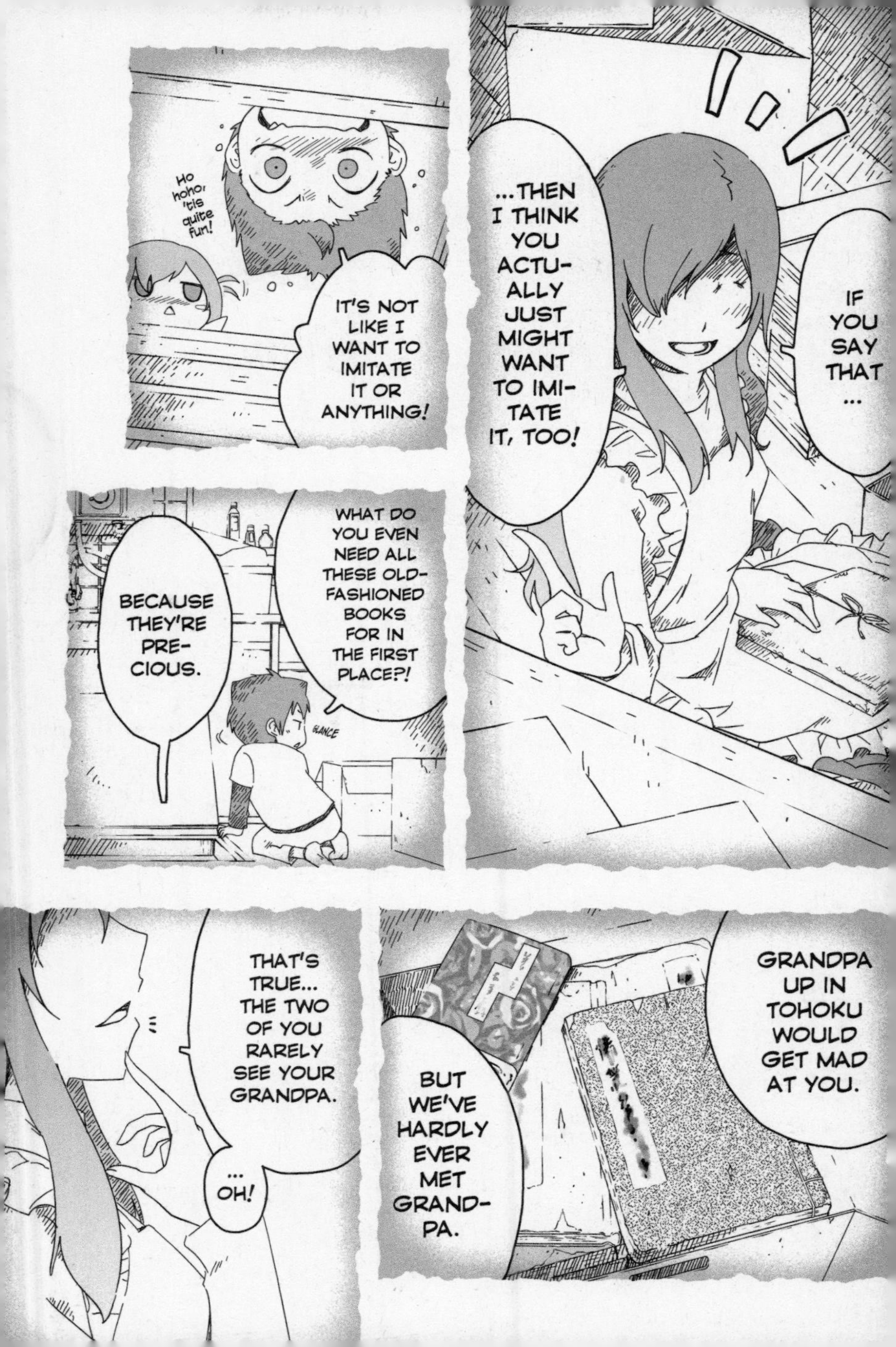

IF YOU SAY THAT...
...THEN I THINK YOU ACTU-ALLY JUST MIGHT WANT TO IMI-TATE IT, TOO!
IT'S NOT LIKE I WANT TO IMITATE IT OR ANYTHING!
Ho hoho, 'tis quite fun!
WHAT DO YOU EVEN NEED ALL THESE OLD-FASHIONED BOOKS FOR IN THE FIRST PLACE?!
GLANCE
BECAUSE THEY'RE PRE-CIOUS.
GRANDPA UP IN TOHOKU WOULD GET MAD AT YOU.
BUT WE'VE HARDLY EVER MET GRAND-PA.
THAT'S TRUE... THE TWO OF YOU RARELY SEE YOUR GRANDPA.
... OH!

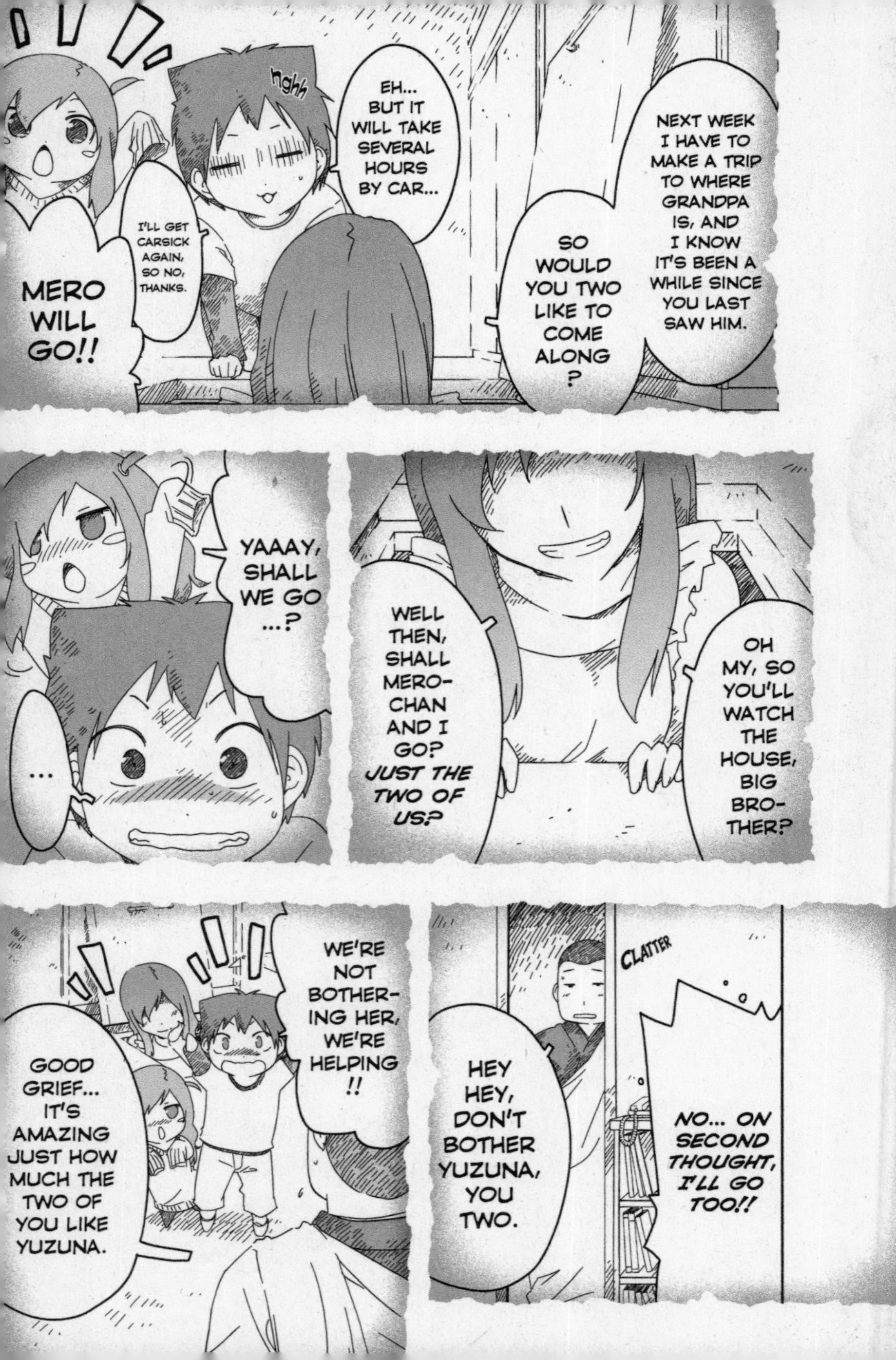
NEXT WEEK I HAVE TO MAKE A TRIP TO WHERE GRANDPA IS, AND I KNOW IT'S BEEN A WHILE SINCE YOU LAST SAW HIM.
SO WOULD YOU TWO LIKE TO COME ALONG?
EH... BUT IT WILL TAKE SEVERAL HOURS BY CAR...
nghh
I'LL GET CARSICK AGAIN, SO NO, THANKS.
MERO WILL GO!!
OH MY, SO YOU'LL WATCH THE HOUSE, BIG BROTHER?
WELL THEN, SHALL MERO-CHAN AND I GO? *JUST THE TWO OF US?*
YAAAY, SHALL WE GO ...?
...
CLATTER
NO... ON SECOND THOUGHT, I'LL GO TOO!!
HEY HEY, DON'T BOTHER YUZUNA, YOU TWO.
WE'RE NOT BOTHERING HER, WE'RE HELPING!!
GOOD GRIEF... IT'S AMAZING JUST HOW MUCH THE TWO OF YOU LIKE YUZUNA.

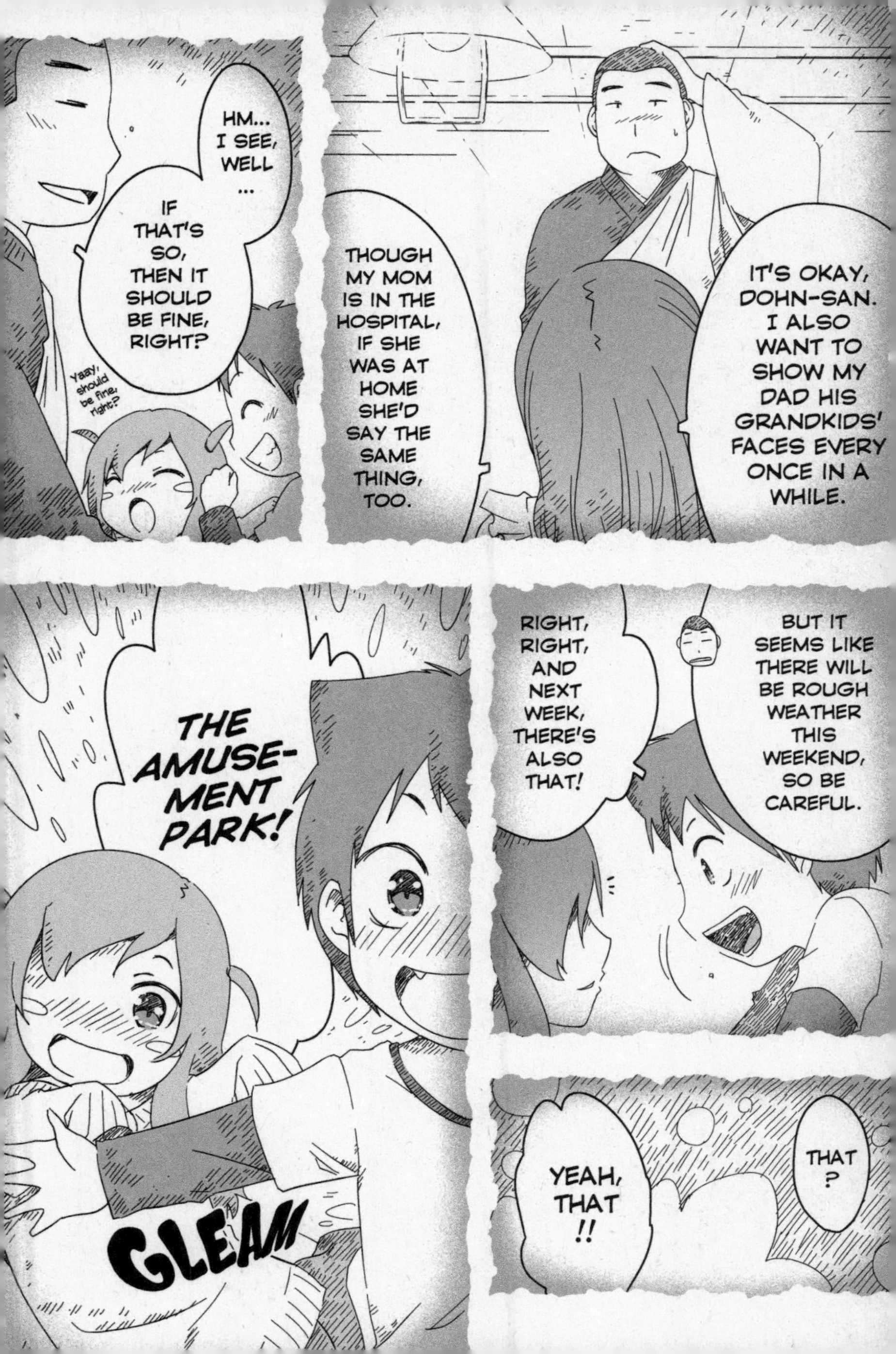
IT'S OKAY, DOHN-SAN. I ALSO WANT TO SHOW MY DAD HIS GRANDKIDS' FACES EVERY ONCE IN A WHILE.
THOUGH MY MOM IS IN THE HOSPITAL, IF SHE WAS AT HOME SHE'D SAY THE SAME THING, TOO.
HM... I SEE, WELL ...
IF THAT'S SO, THEN IT SHOULD BE FINE, RIGHT?
Yaay, should be fine, right?
BUT IT SEEMS LIKE THERE WILL BE ROUGH WEATHER THIS WEEKEND, SO BE CAREFUL.
RIGHT, RIGHT, AND NEXT WEEK, THERE'S ALSO THAT!
THAT?
YEAH, THAT!!
THE AMUSE-MENT PARK!
GLEAM

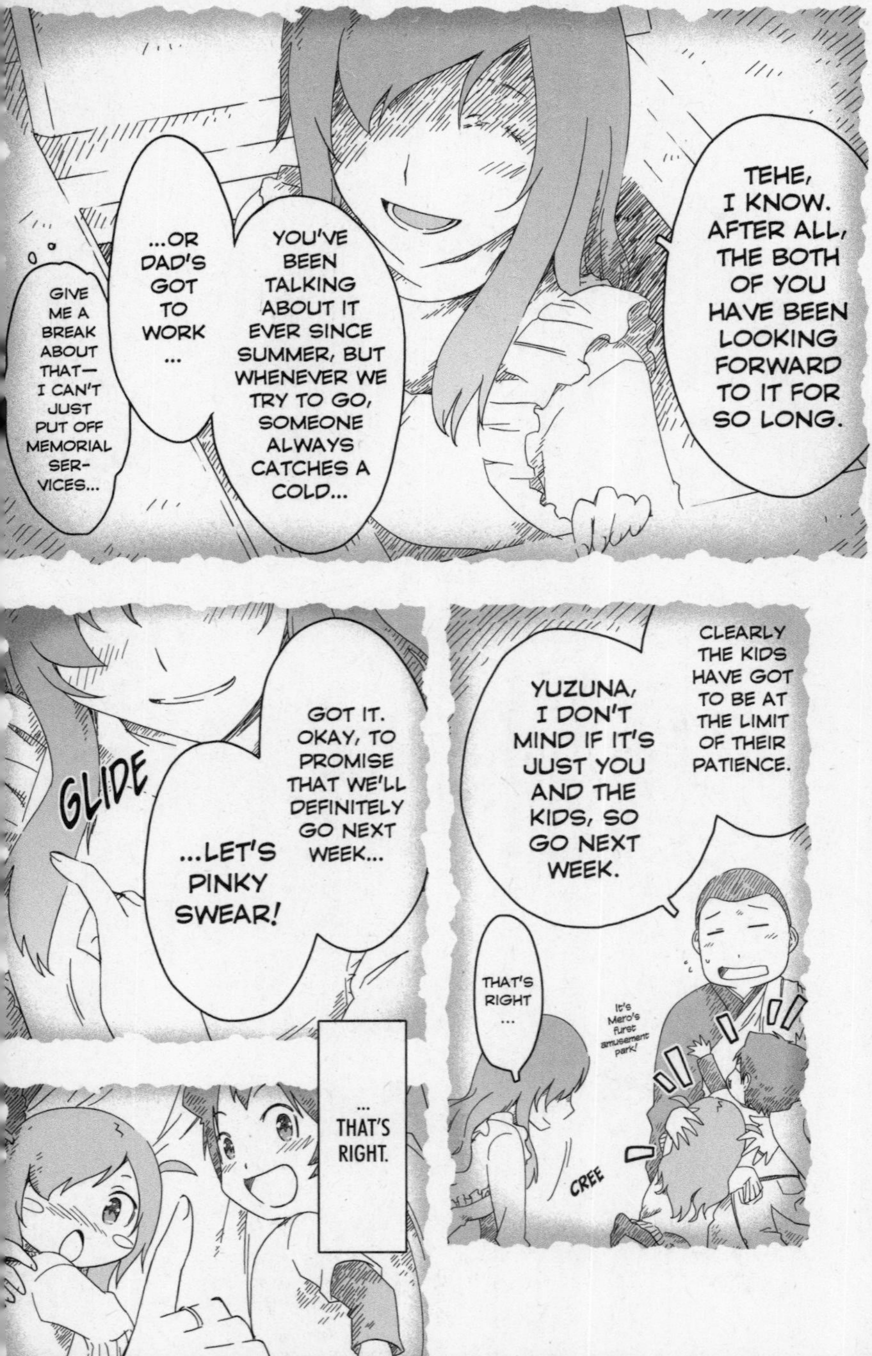
TEHE, I KNOW. AFTER ALL, THE BOTH OF YOU HAVE BEEN LOOKING FORWARD TO IT FOR SO LONG.
YOU'VE BEEN TALKING ABOUT IT EVER SINCE SUMMER, BUT WHENEVER WE TRY TO GO, SOMEONE ALWAYS CATCHES A COLD...
...OR DAD'S GOT TO WORK ...
GIVE ME A BREAK ABOUT THAT— I CAN'T JUST PUT OFF MEMORIAL SER-VICES...
CLEARLY THE KIDS HAVE GOT TO BE AT THE LIMIT OF THEIR PATIENCE.
YUZUNA, I DON'T MIND IF IT'S JUST YOU AND THE KIDS, SO GO NEXT WEEK.
It's Mero's furst amusement park!
THAT'S RIGHT ...
CREE
GOT IT. OKAY, TO PROMISE THAT WE'LL DEFINITELY GO NEXT WEEK...
...LET'S PINKY SWEAR!
GLIDE
... THAT'S RIGHT.

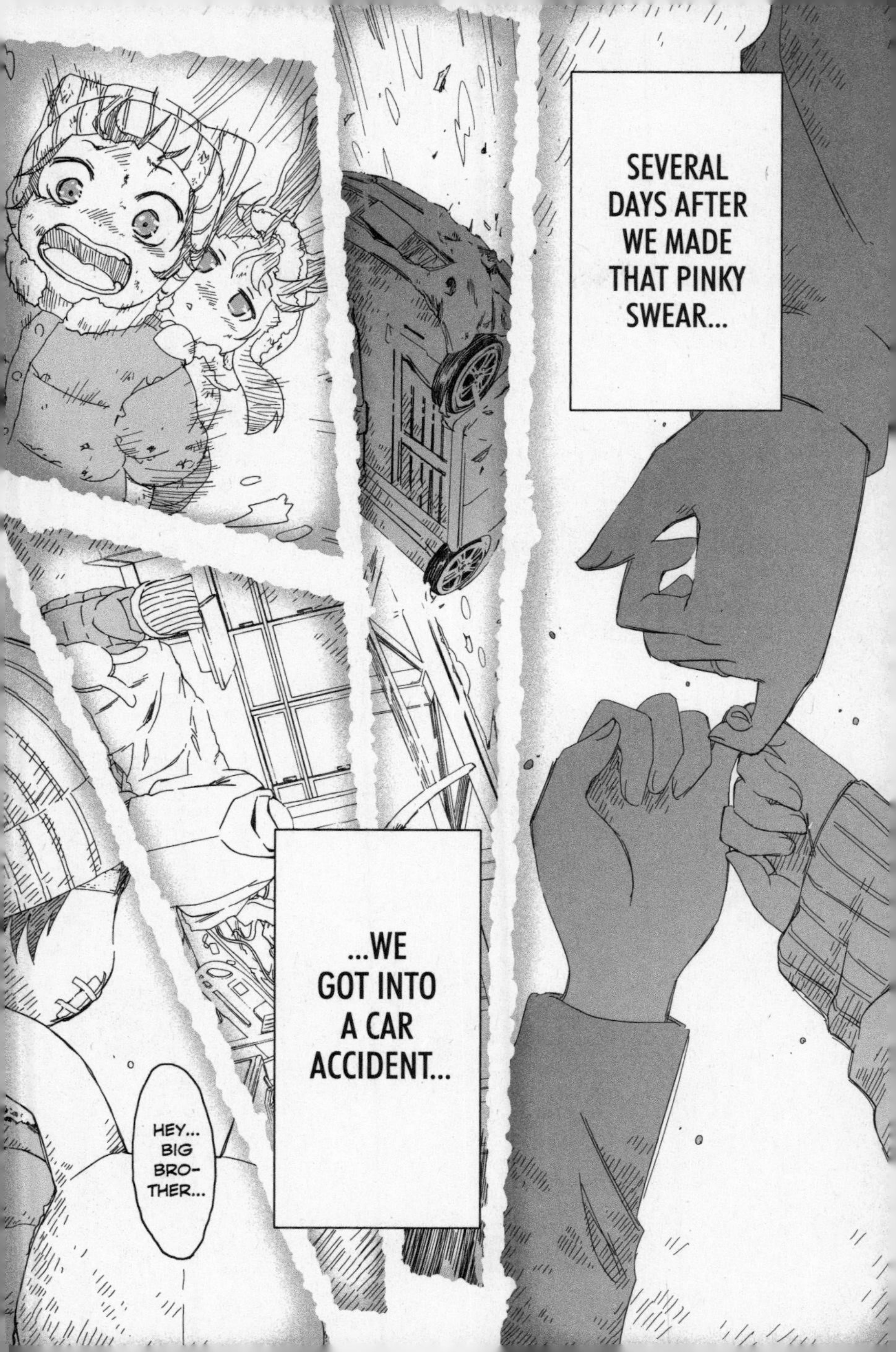
SEVERAL DAYS AFTER WE MADE THAT PINKY SWEAR...
...WE GOT INTO A CAR ACCIDENT...
HEY... BIG BRO-THER...

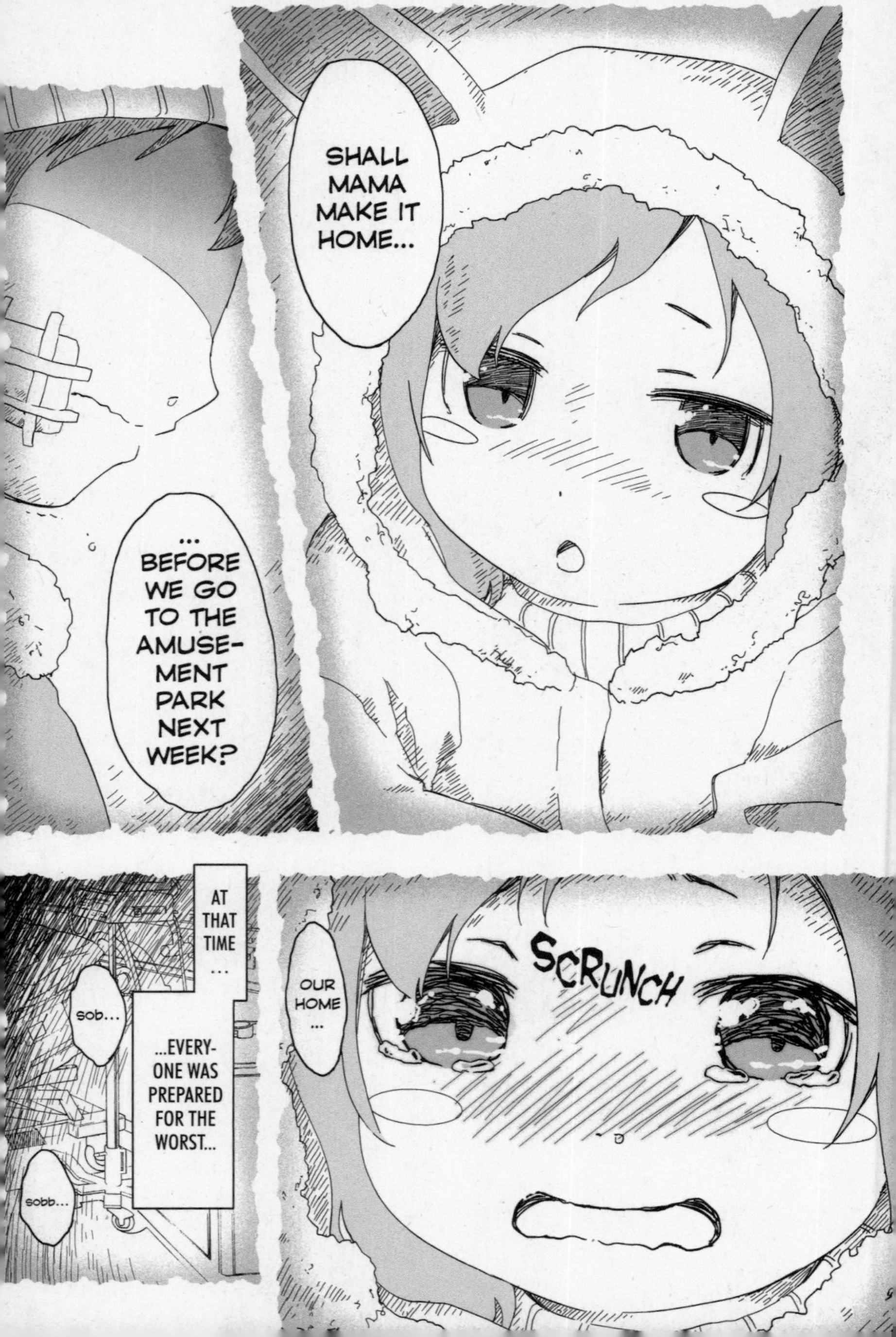
SHALL MAMA MAKE IT HOME...
...BEFORE WE GO TO THE AMUSEMENT PARK NEXT WEEK?
SCRUNCH
OUR HOME...
AT THAT TIME...
...EVERYONE WAS PREPARED FOR THE WORST...
sob...
sobb...

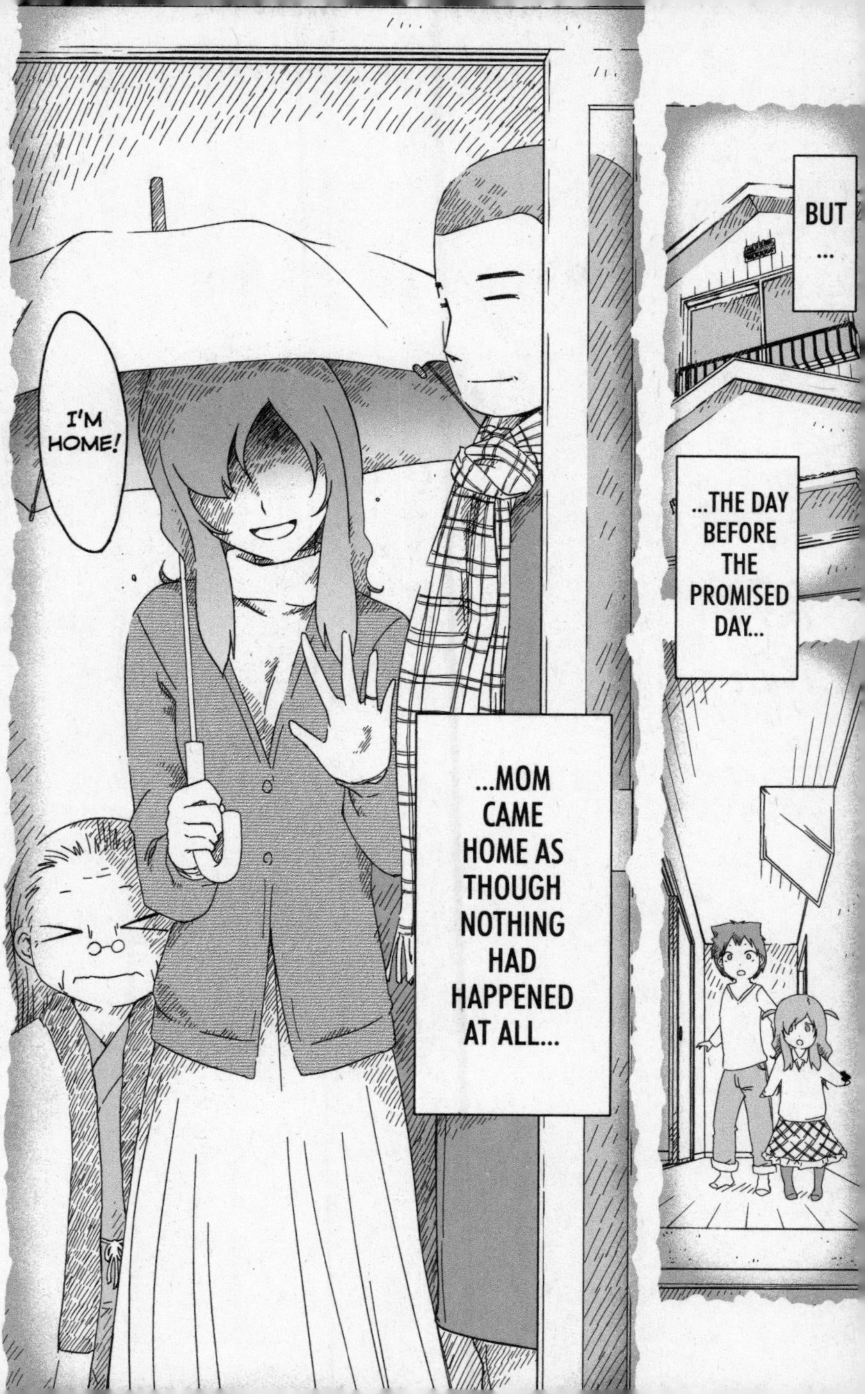
BUT ...
...THE DAY BEFORE THE PROMISED DAY...
...MOM CAME HOME AS THOUGH NOTHING HAD HAPPENED AT ALL...
I'M HOME!

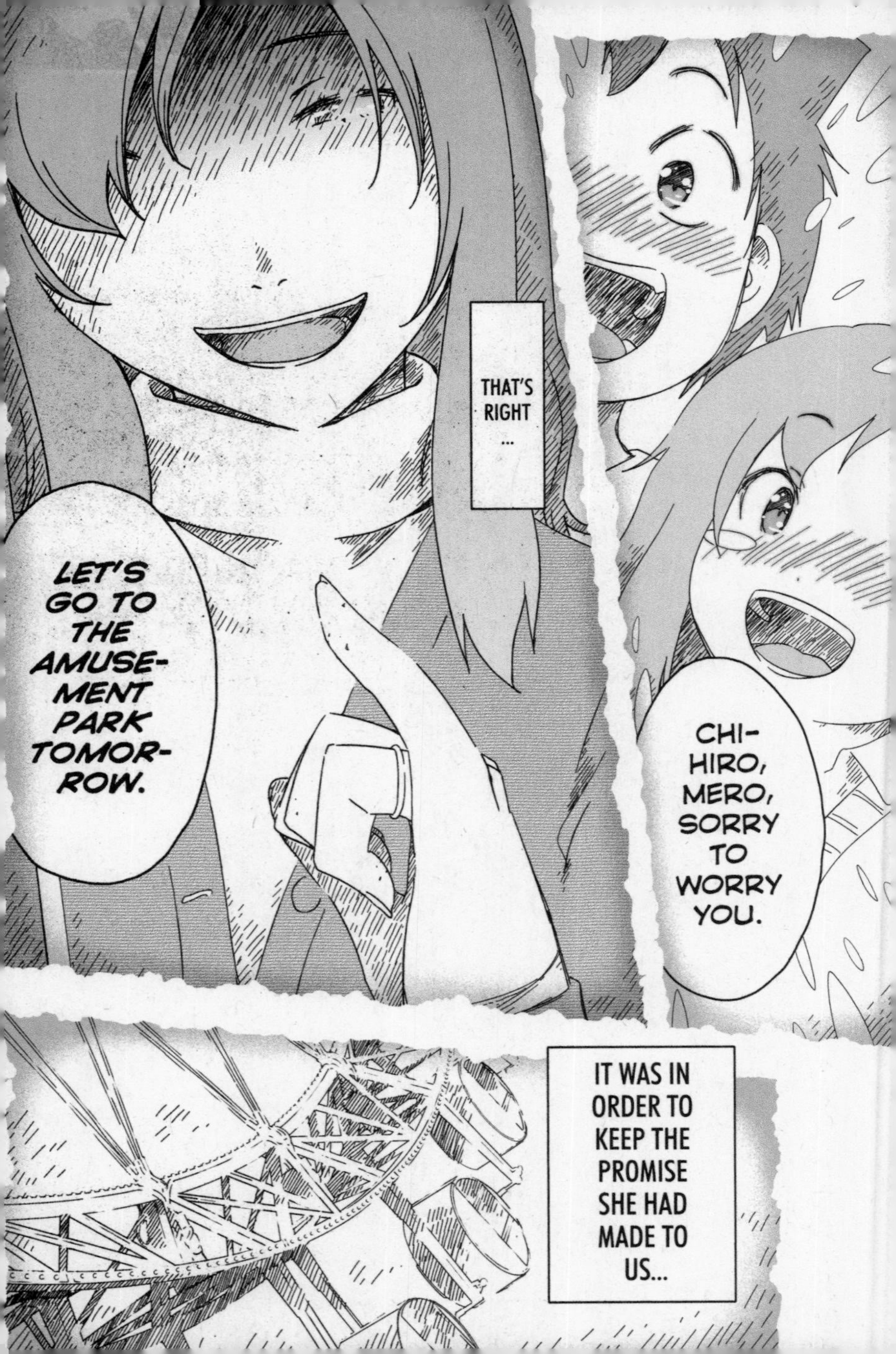
CHI-HIRO, MERO, SORRY TO WORRY YOU.
THAT'S RIGHT...
LET'S GO TO THE AMUSEMENT PARK TOMORROW.
IT WAS IN ORDER TO KEEP THE PROMISE SHE HAD MADE TO US...

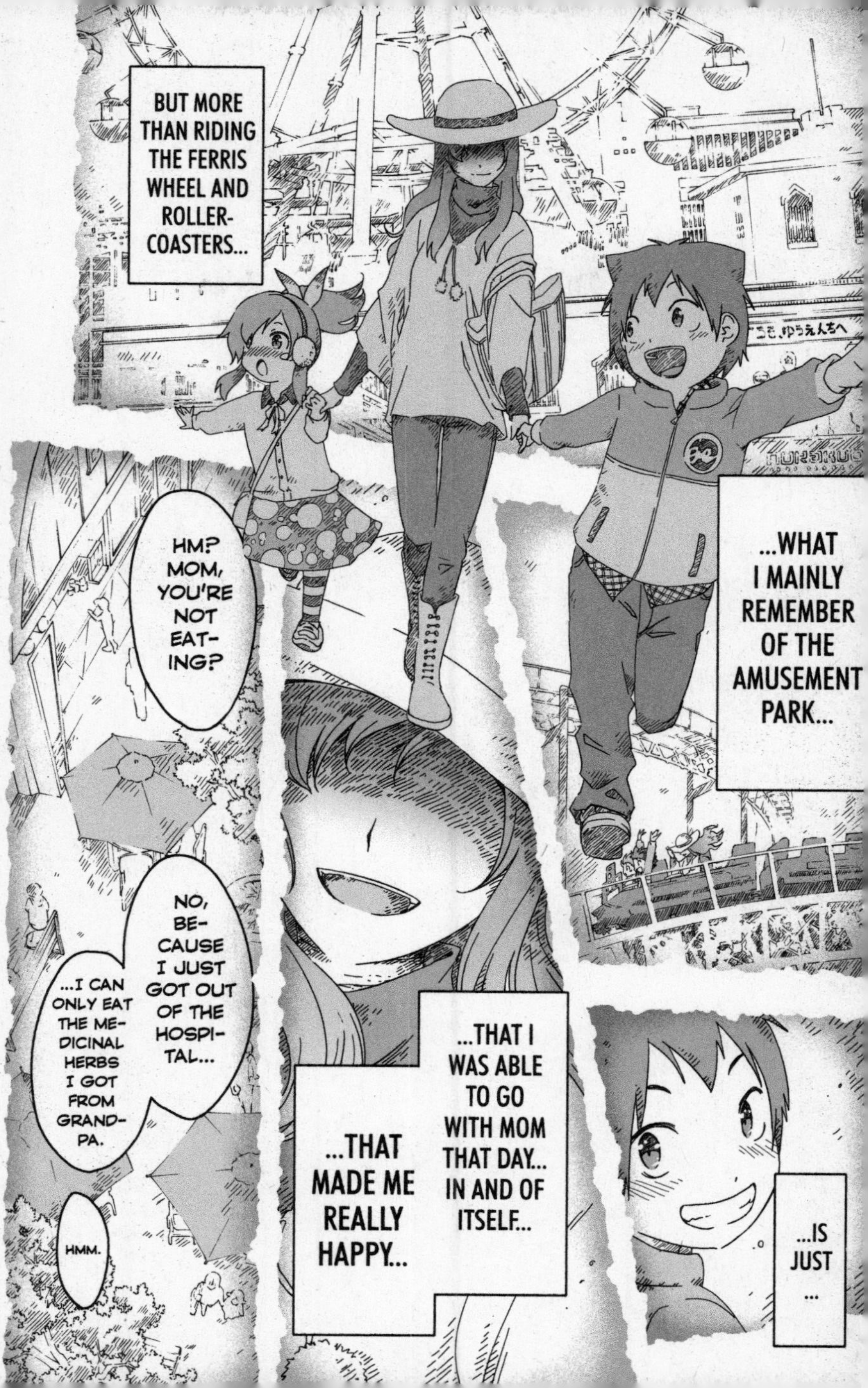
BUT MORE THAN RIDING THE FERRIS WHEEL AND ROLLER-COASTERS...
...WHAT I MAINLY REMEMBER OF THE AMUSEMENT PARK...
HM? MOM, YOU'RE NOT EAT-ING?
NO, BE-CAUSE I JUST GOT OUT OF THE HOSPI-TAL...
...I CAN ONLY EAT THE ME-DICINAL HERBS I GOT FROM GRAND-PA.
HMM.
...IS JUST ...
...THAT I WAS ABLE TO GO WITH MOM THAT DAY... IN AND OF ITSELF...
...THAT MADE ME REALLY HAPPY...

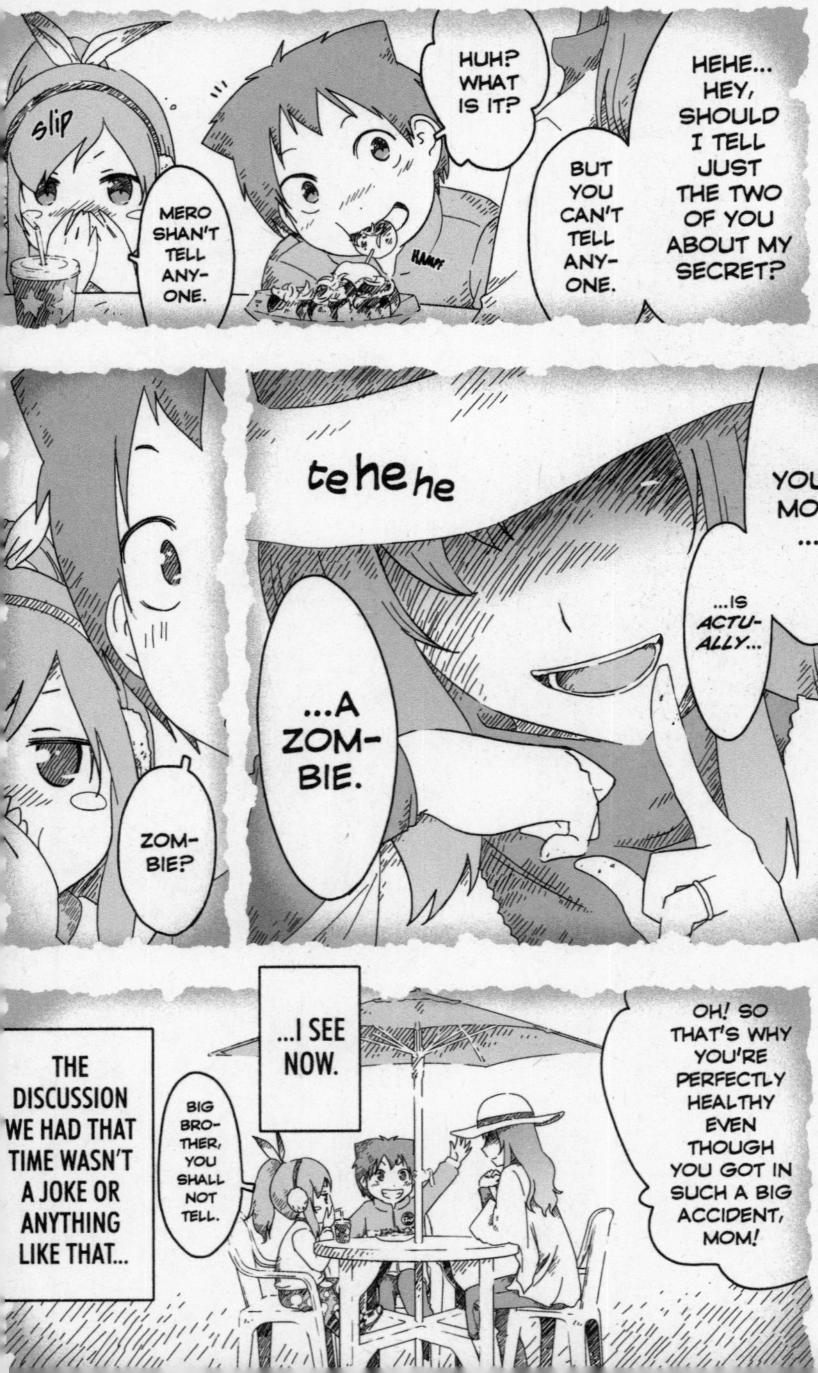
HEHE... HEY, SHOULD I TELL JUST THE TWO OF YOU ABOUT MY SECRET?
BUT YOU CAN'T TELL ANY-ONE.
HUH? WHAT IS IT?
slip
MERO SHAN'T TELL ANY-ONE.
YOUR MOM ...
...IS ACTU-ALLY...
tehehe
...A ZOM-BIE.
ZOM-BIE?
OH! SO THAT'S WHY YOU'RE PERFECTLY HEALTHY EVEN THOUGH YOU GOT IN SUCH A BIG ACCIDENT, MOM!
...I SEE NOW.
BIG BRO-THER, YOU SHALL NOT TELL.
THE DISCUSSION WE HAD THAT TIME WASN'T A JOKE OR ANYTHING LIKE THAT...

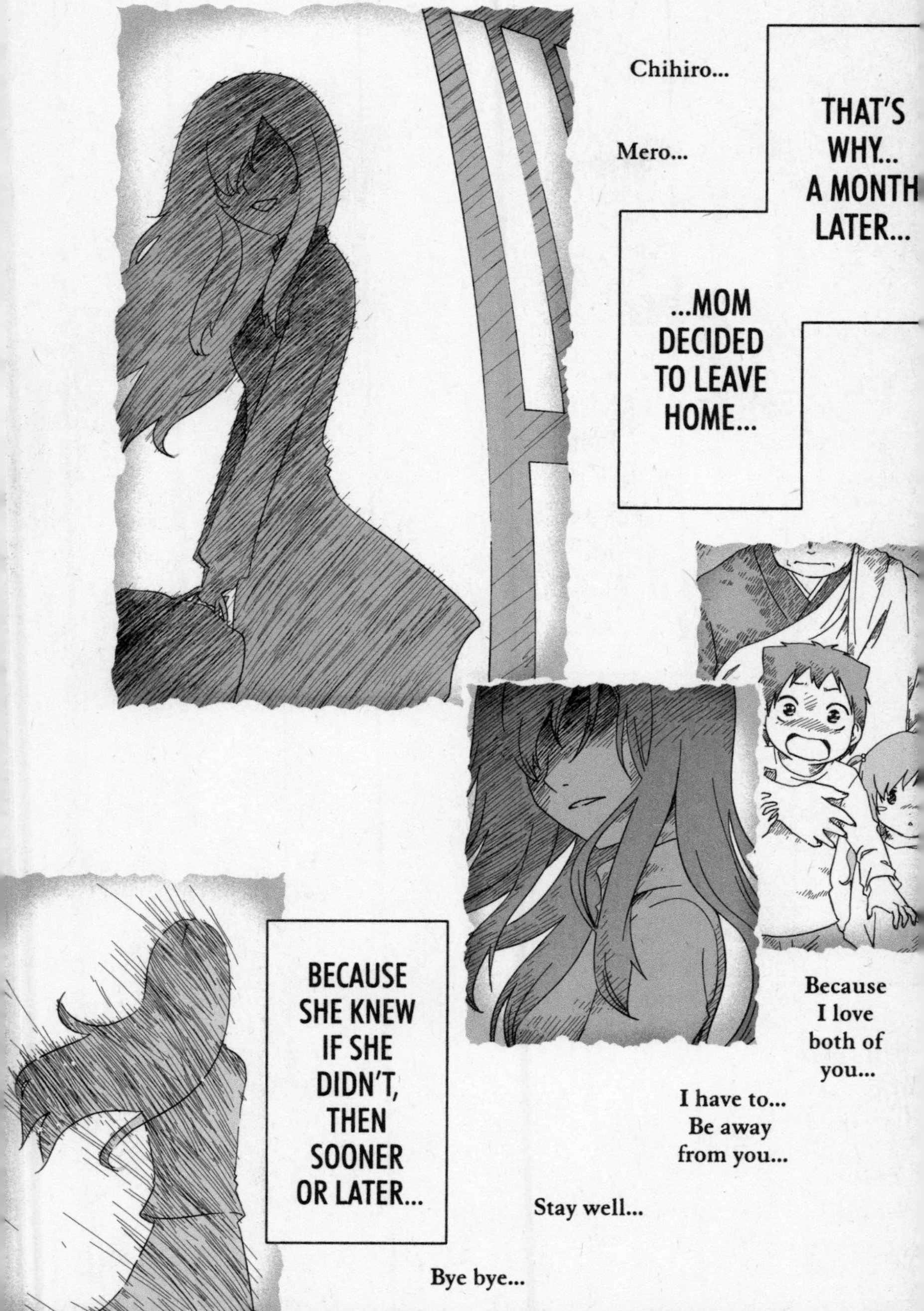
THAT'S WHY... A MONTH LATER...
...MOM DECIDED TO LEAVE HOME...
Chihiro...
Mero...
Because I love both of you...
I have to... Be away from you...
Stay well...
BECAUSE SHE KNEW IF SHE DIDN'T, THEN SOONER OR LATER...
Bye bye...

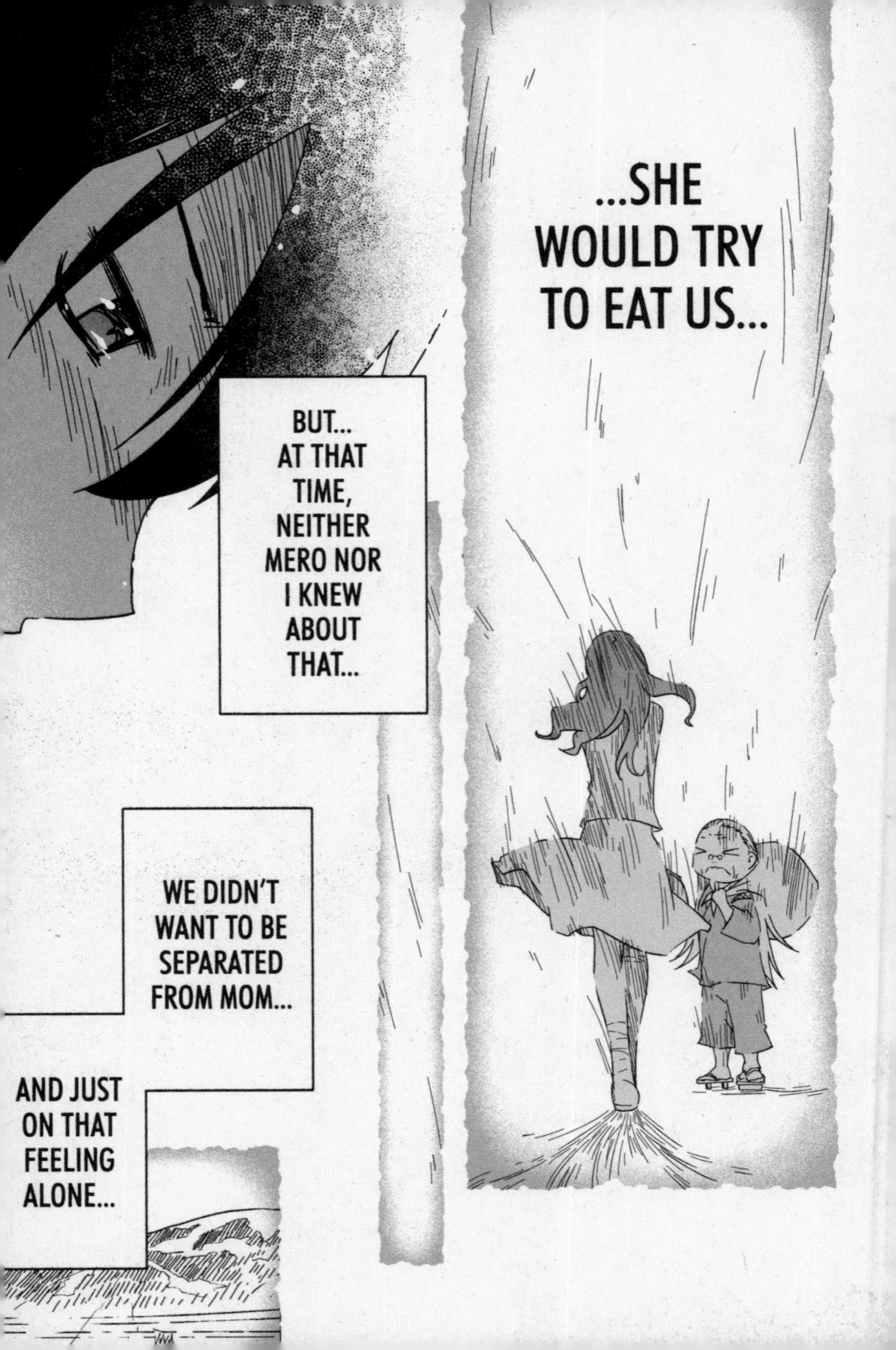
...SHE WOULD TRY TO EAT US...
BUT... AT THAT TIME, NEITHER MERO NOR I KNEW ABOUT THAT...
WE DIDN'T WANT TO BE SEPARATED FROM MOM...
AND JUST ON THAT FEELING ALONE...

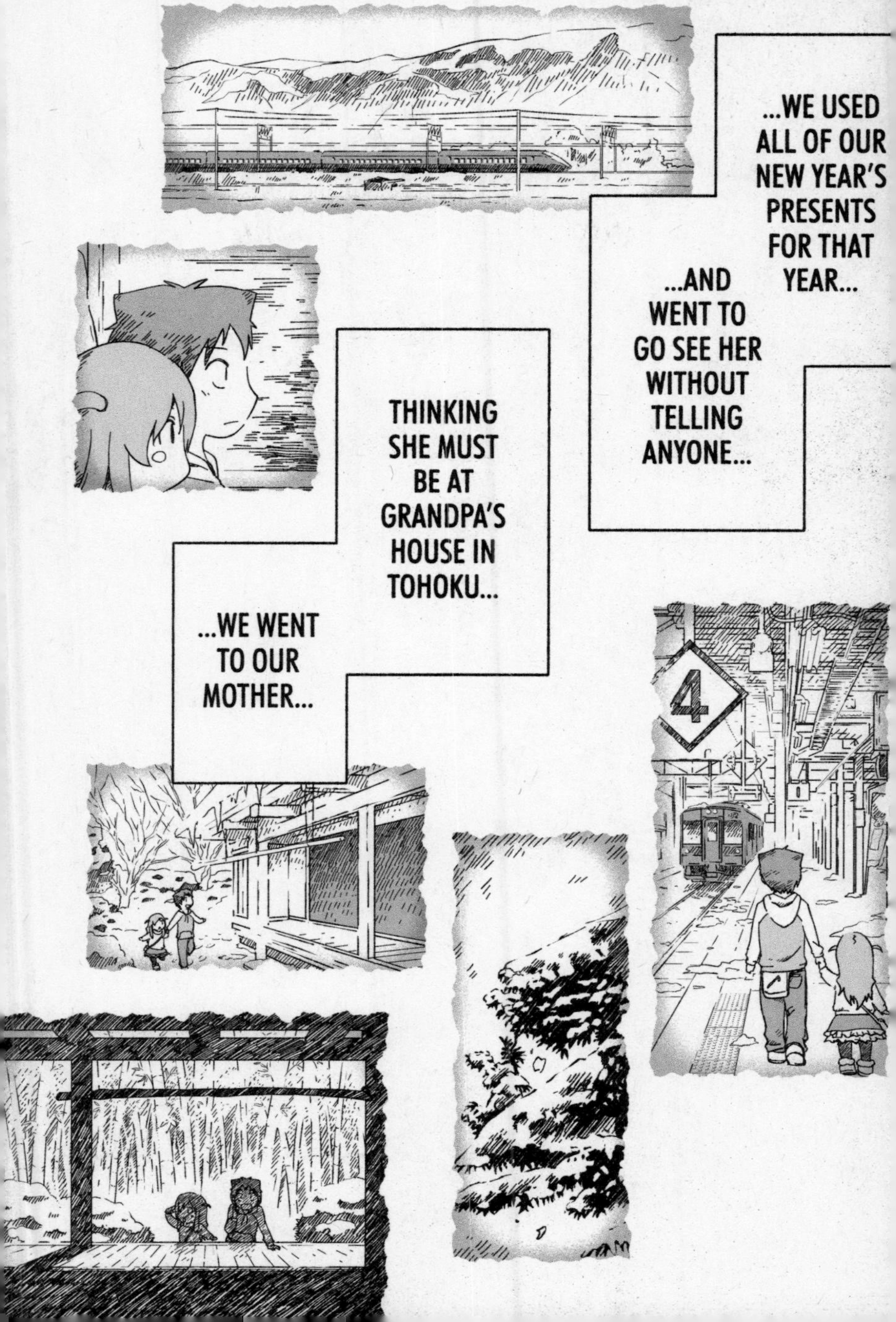
...WE USED ALL OF OUR NEW YEAR'S PRESENTS FOR THAT YEAR...
...AND WENT TO GO SEE HER WITHOUT TELLING ANYONE...
THINKING SHE MUST BE AT GRANDPA'S HOUSE IN TOHOKU...
...WE WENT TO OUR MOTHER...
4

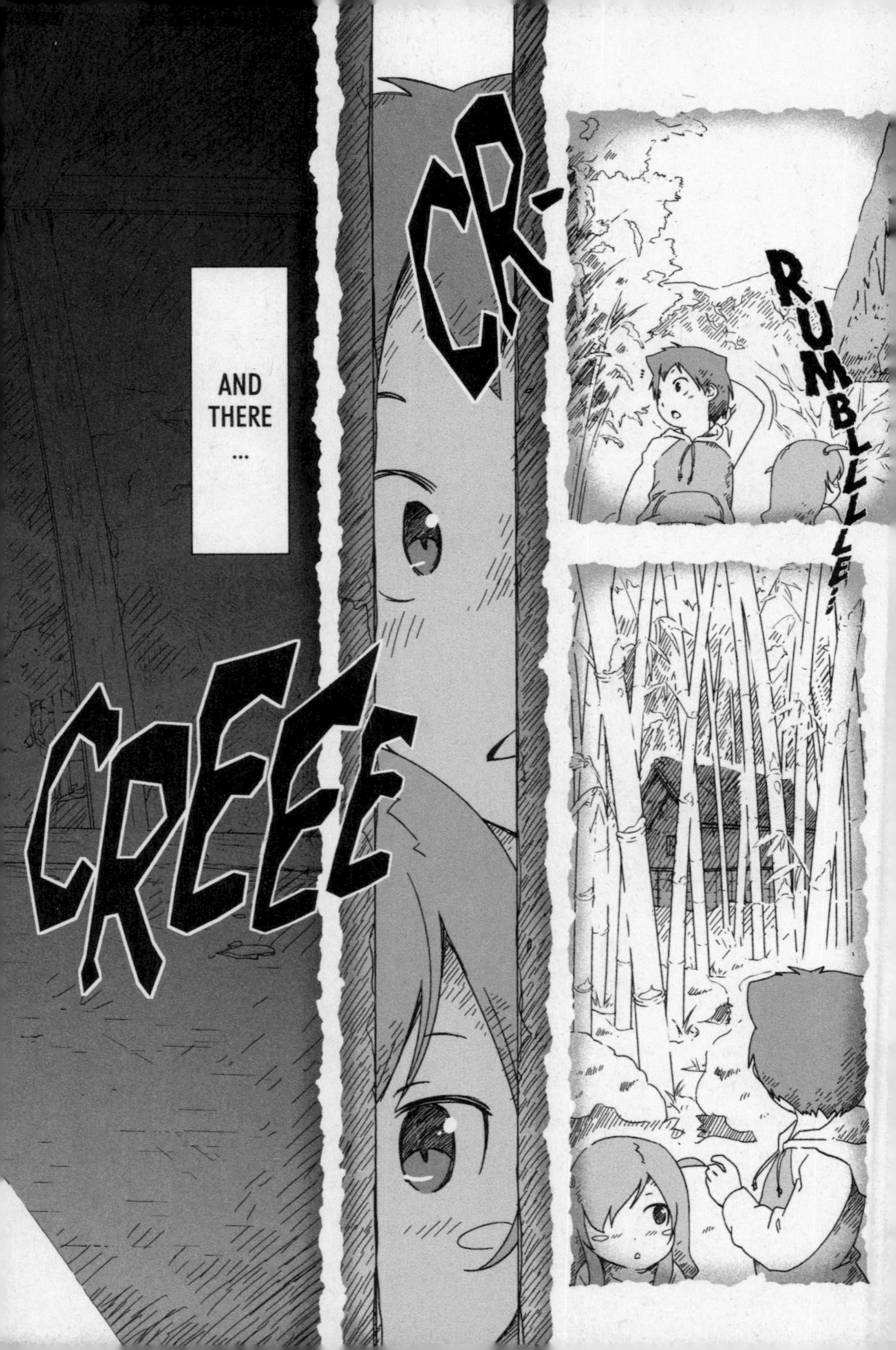
RUMBLLLLE!!
CR-
AND THERE ...
CREEE

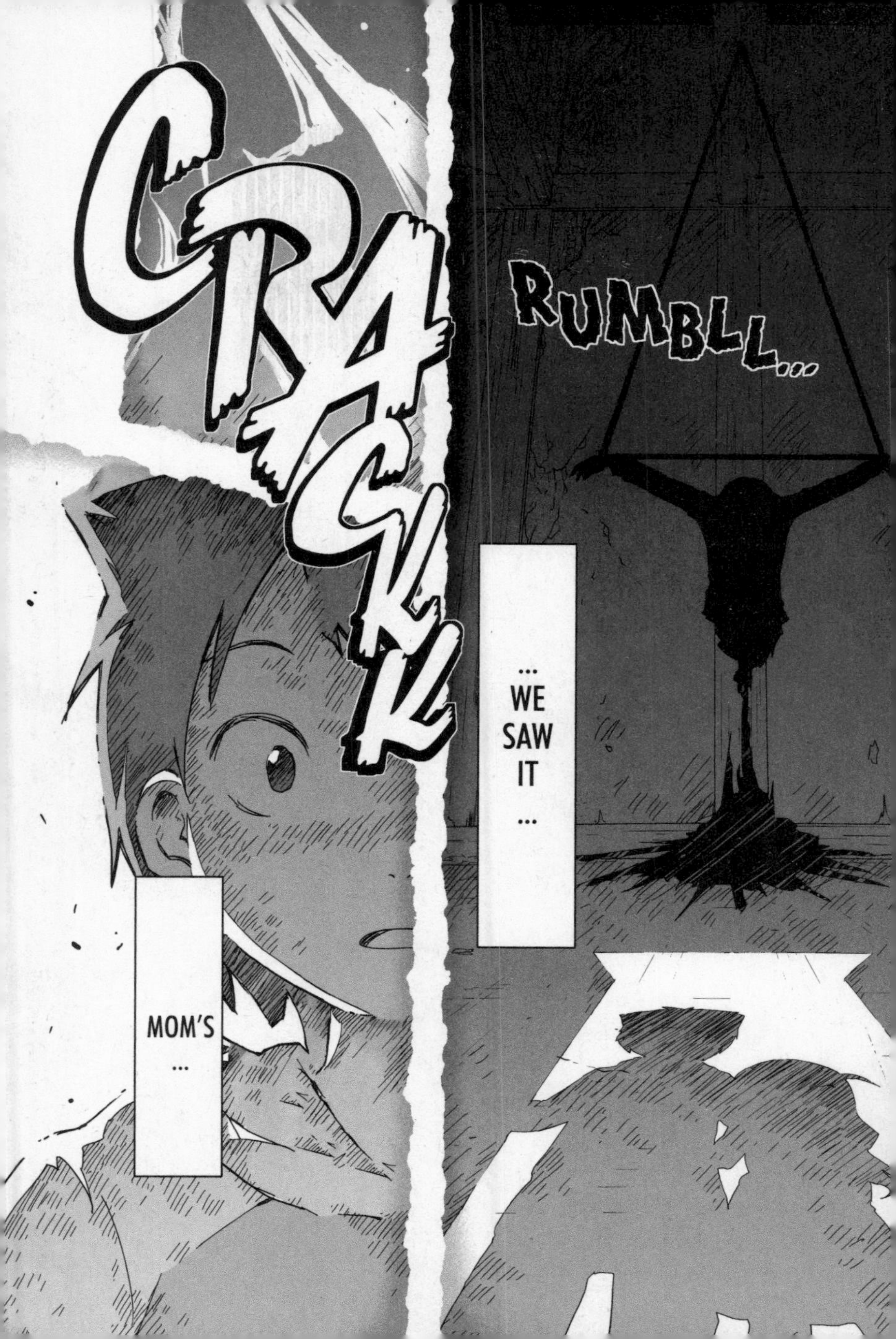
RUMBLL...
... WE SAW IT ...
CRACKL
MOM'S ...

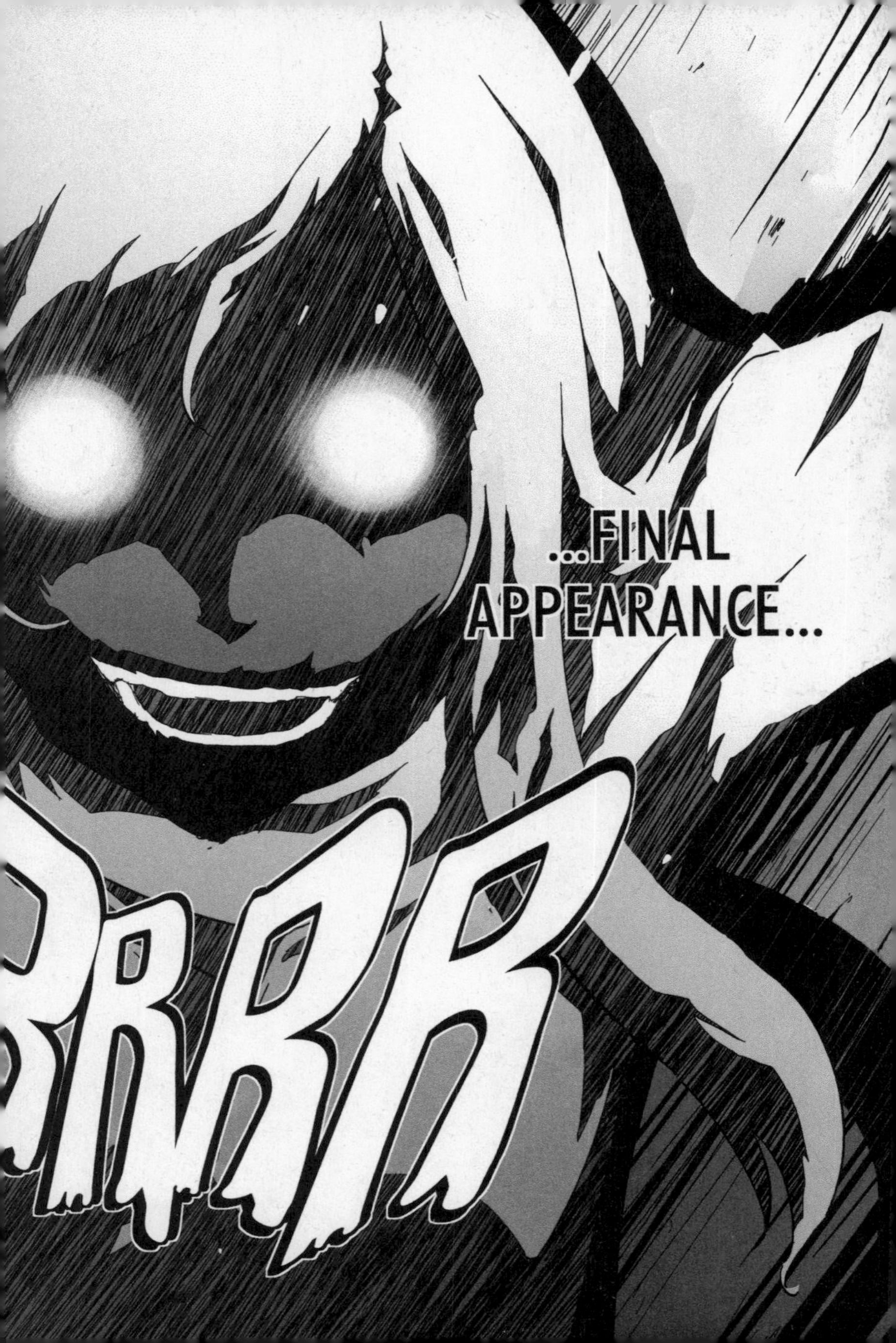
...FINAL APPEARANCE...
RRRR

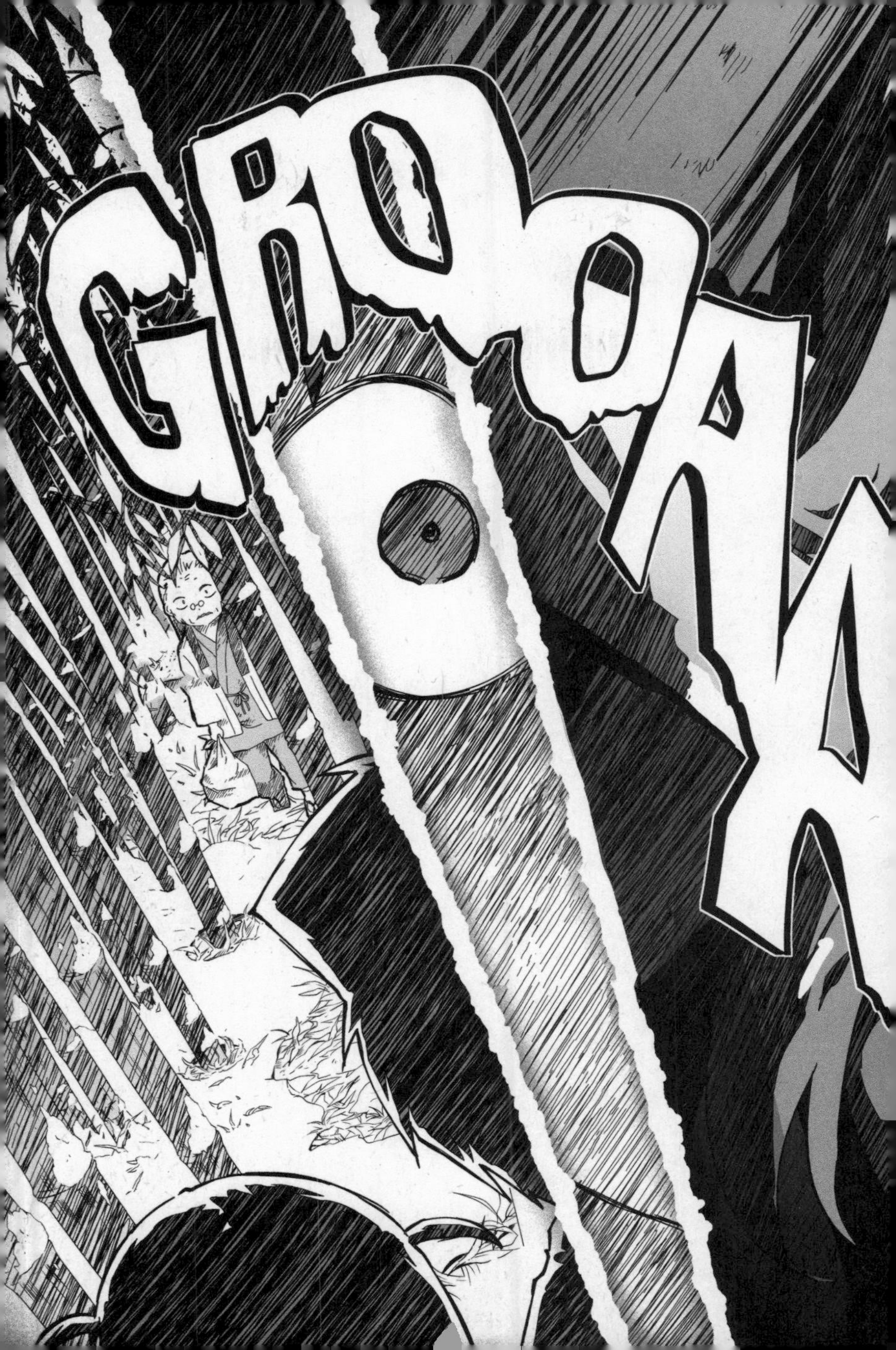
GROOAK

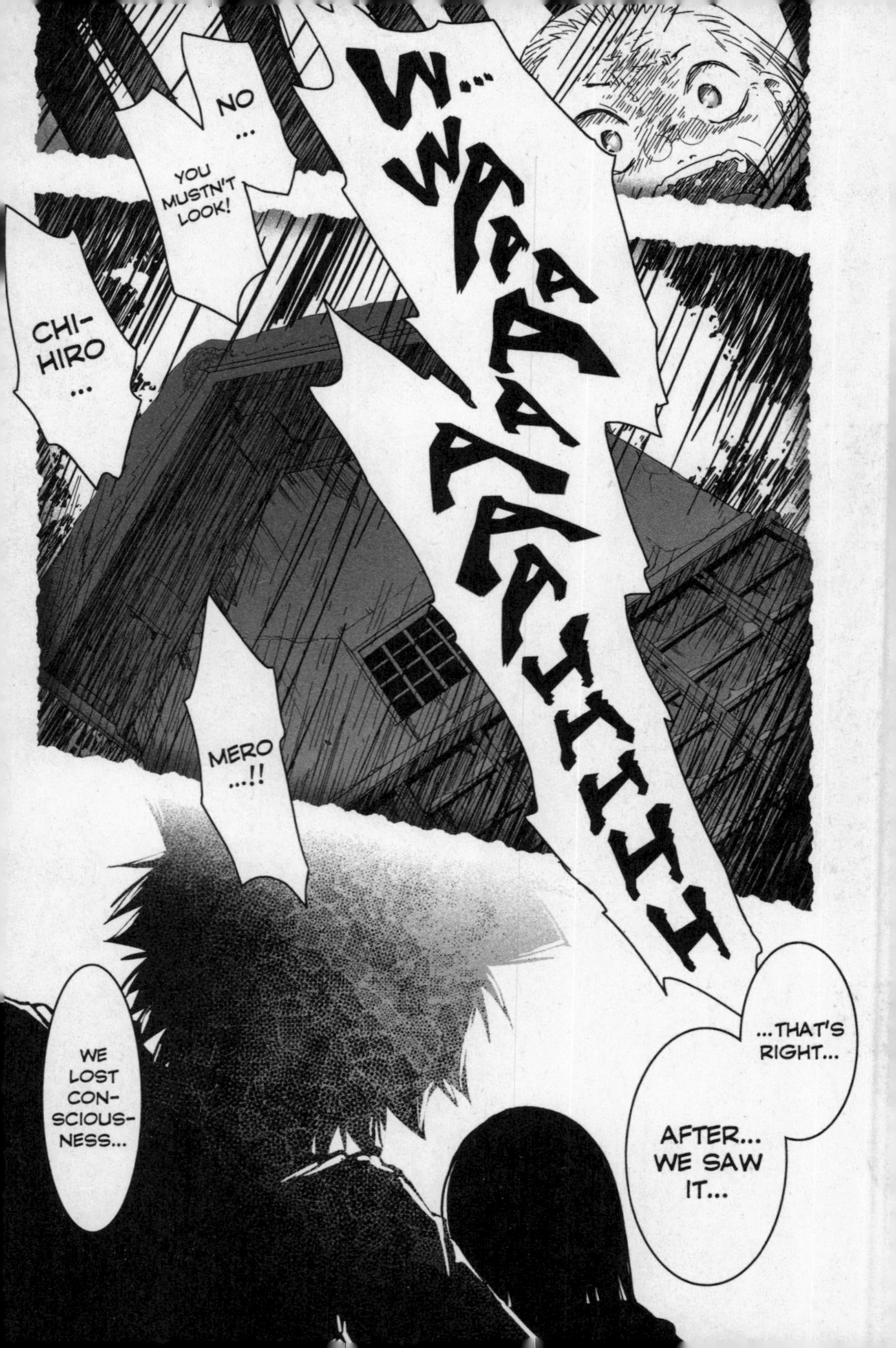
W... WAAAAAAIIIIII
NO ... YOU MUSTN'T LOOK!
CHI-HIRO ...
MERO ...!!
...THAT'S RIGHT... AFTER... WE SAW IT...
WE LOST CON-SCIOUS-NESS...

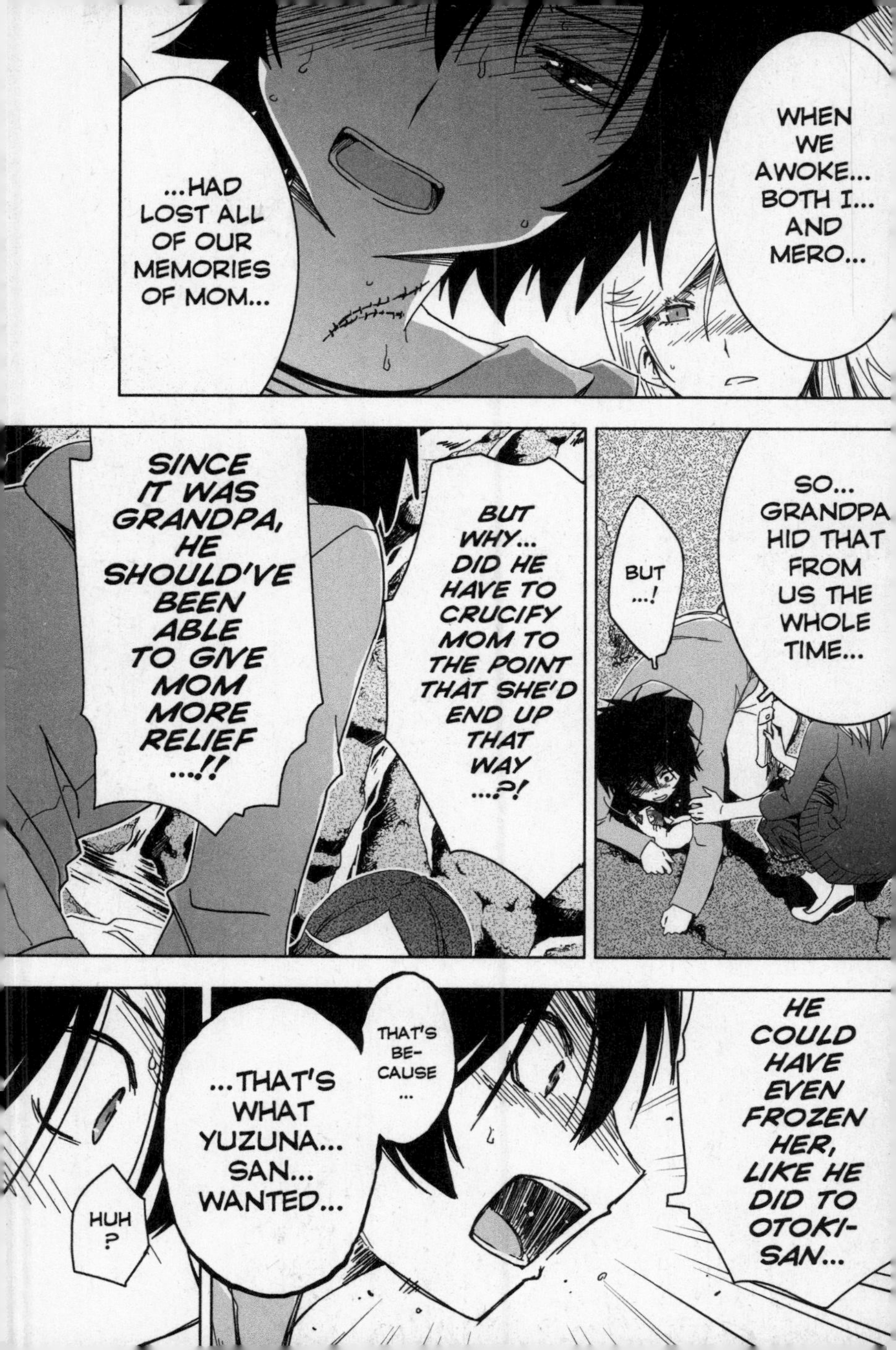

WHEN WE AWOKE... BOTH I... AND MERO...
...HAD LOST ALL OF OUR MEMORIES OF MOM...
SO... GRANDPA HID THAT FROM US THE WHOLE TIME...
BUT ...!
BUT WHY... DID HE HAVE TO CRUCIFY MOM TO THE POINT THAT SHE'D END UP THAT WAY ...?!
SINCE IT WAS GRANDPA, HE SHOULD'VE BEEN ABLE TO GIVE MOM MORE RELIEF ...!!
HE COULD HAVE EVEN FROZEN HER, LIKE HE DID TO OTOKI-SAN...
THAT'S BE-CAUSE ...
...THAT'S WHAT YUZUNA... SAN... WANTED...
HUH ?

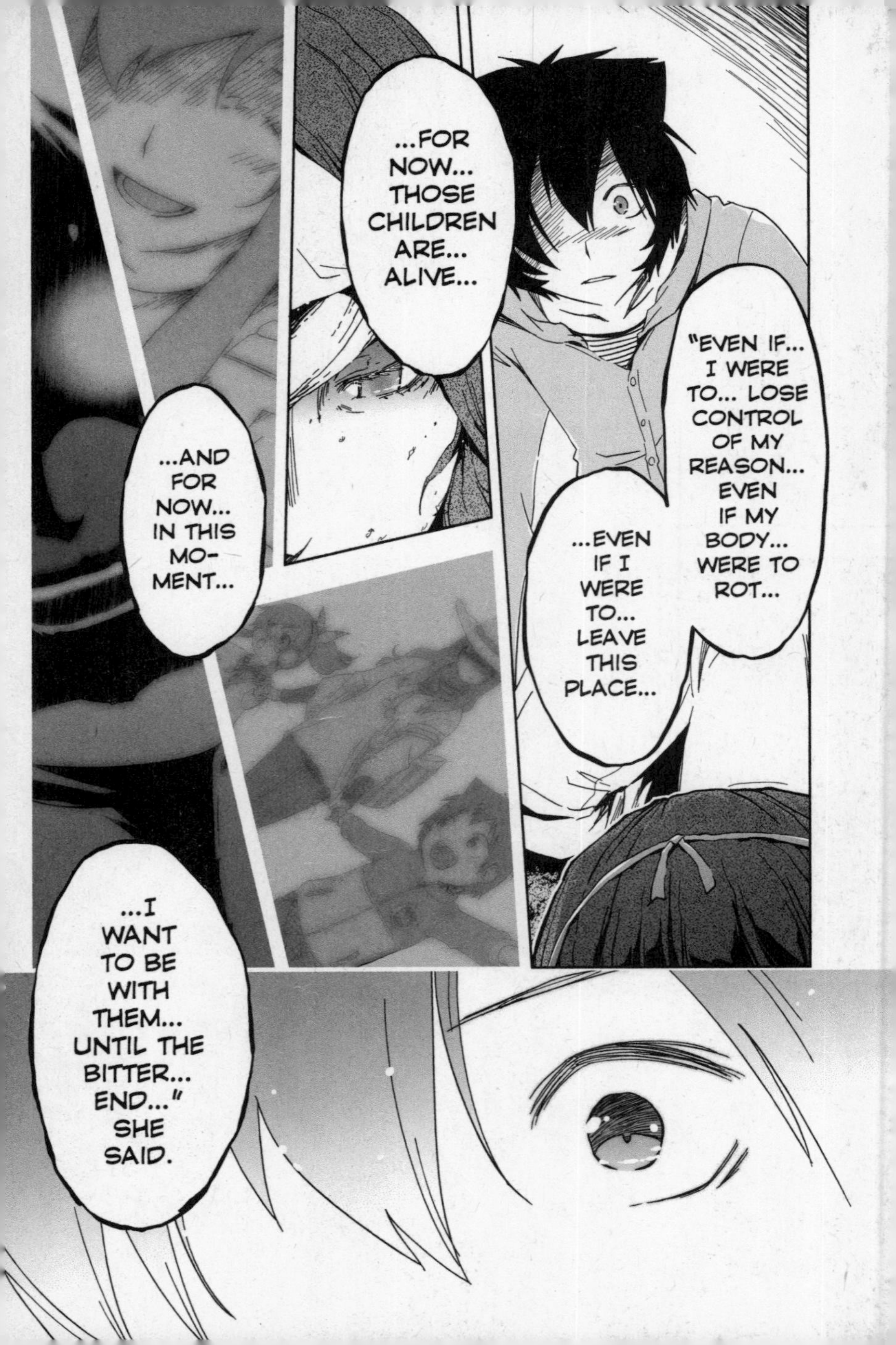
"EVEN IF... I WERE TO... LOSE CONTROL OF MY REASON... EVEN IF MY BODY... WERE TO ROT...
...EVEN IF I WERE TO... LEAVE THIS PLACE...
...FOR NOW... THOSE CHILDREN ARE... ALIVE...
...AND FOR NOW... IN THIS MO-MENT...
...I WANT TO BE WITH THEM... UNTIL THE BITTER... END..." SHE SAID.

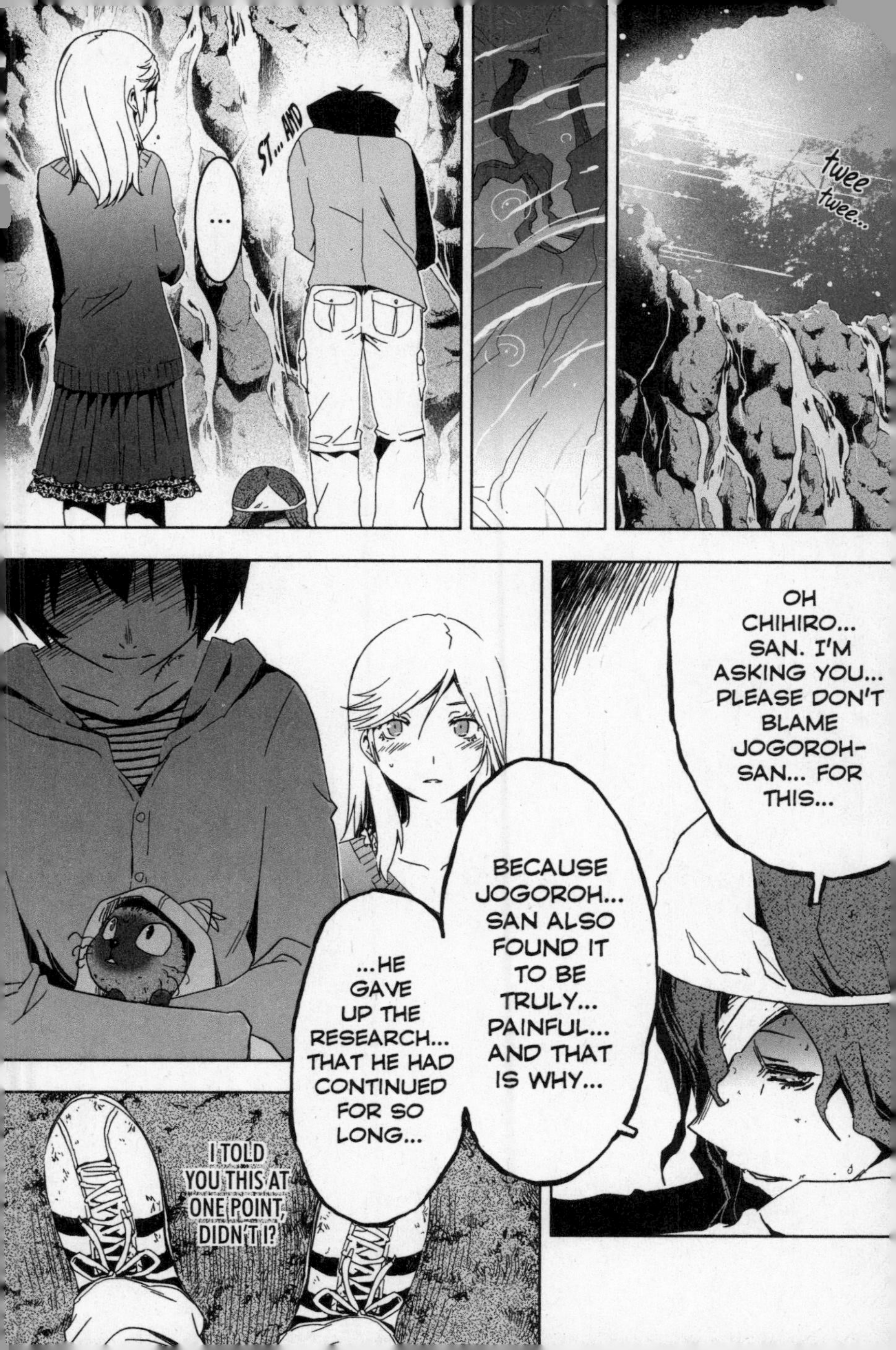
twee twee...
ST... AND
...
OH CHIHIRO... SAN. I'M ASKING YOU... PLEASE DON'T BLAME JOGOROH-SAN... FOR THIS...
BECAUSE JOGOROH... SAN ALSO FOUND IT TO BE TRULY... PAINFUL... AND THAT IS WHY...
...HE GAVE UP THE RESEARCH... THAT HE HAD CONTINUED FOR SO LONG...
I TOLD YOU THIS AT ONE POINT, DIDN'T I?

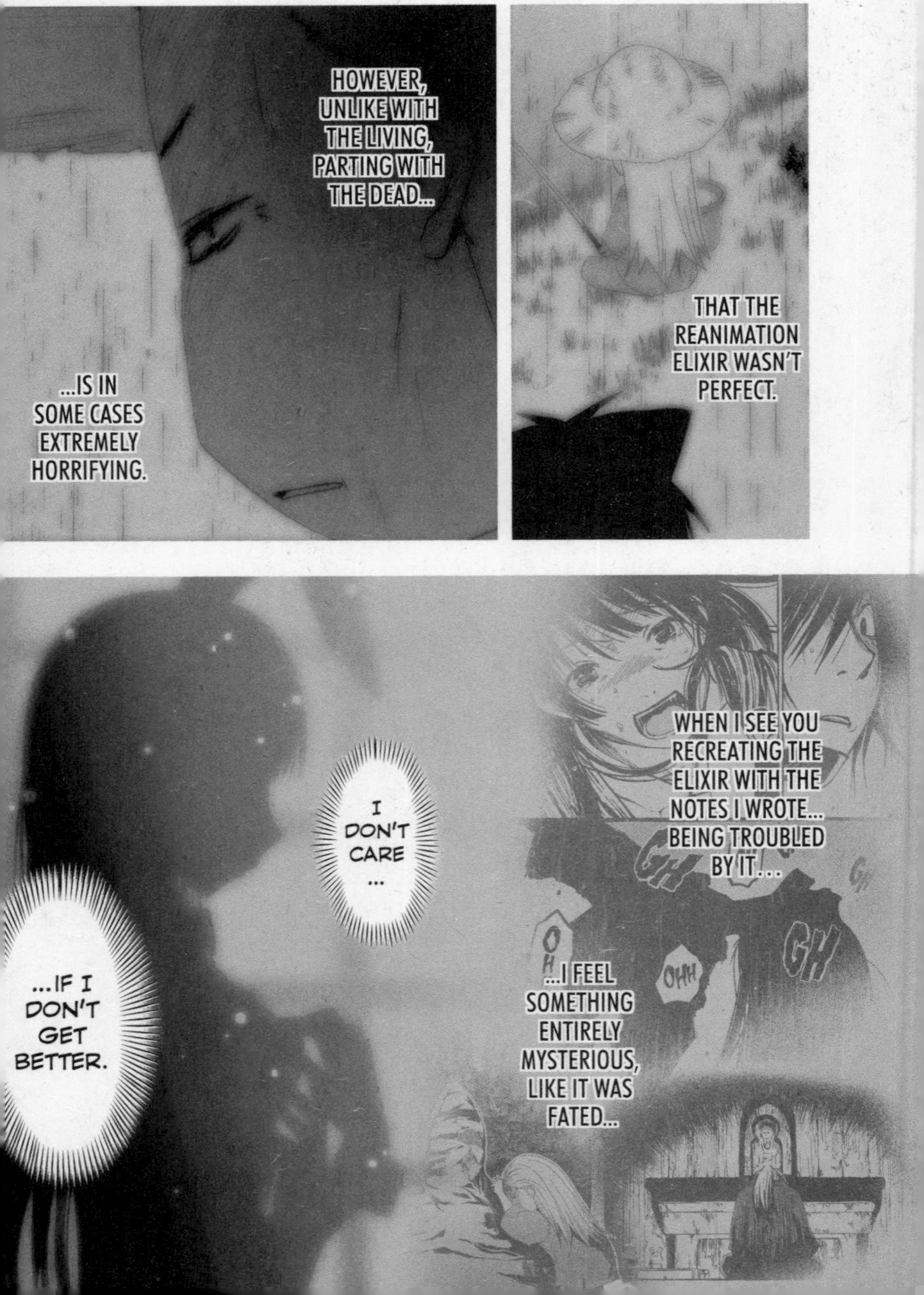
THAT THE REANIMATION ELIXIR WASN'T PERFECT.
HOWEVER, UNLIKE WITH THE LIVING, PARTING WITH THE DEAD...
...IS IN SOME CASES EXTREMELY HORRIFYING.
WHEN I SEE YOU RECREATING THE ELIXIR WITH THE NOTES I WROTE... BEING TROUBLED BY IT...
GH
GH
GH
OHH
OH
...I FEEL SOMETHING ENTIRELY MYSTERIOUS, LIKE IT WAS FATED...
I DON'T CARE...
...IF I DON'T GET BETTER.

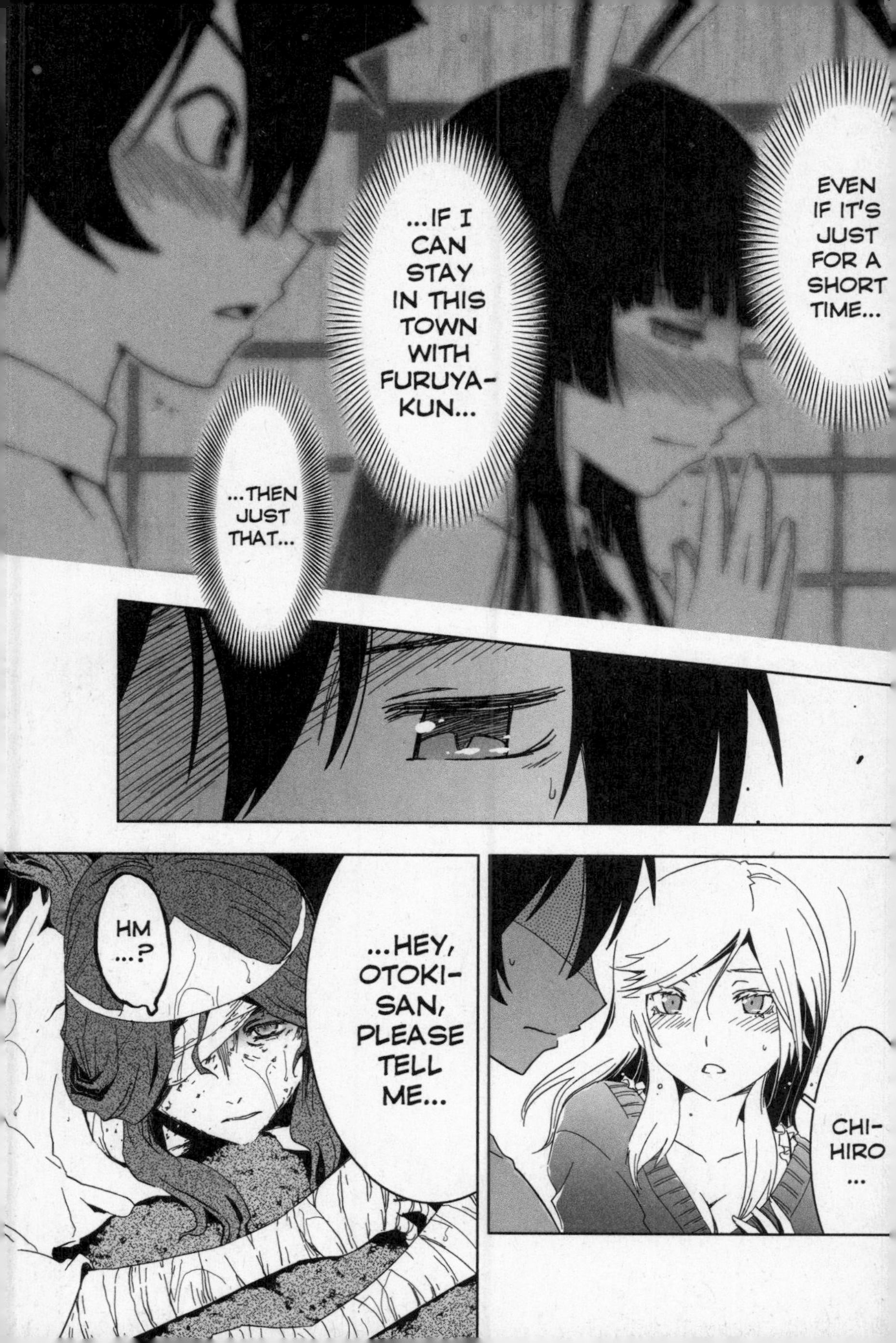
EVEN IF IT'S JUST FOR A SHORT TIME...
...IF I CAN STAY IN THIS TOWN WITH FURUYA-KUN...
...THEN JUST THAT...
CHI-HIRO ...
...HEY, OTOKI-SAN, PLEASE TELL ME...
HM ...?

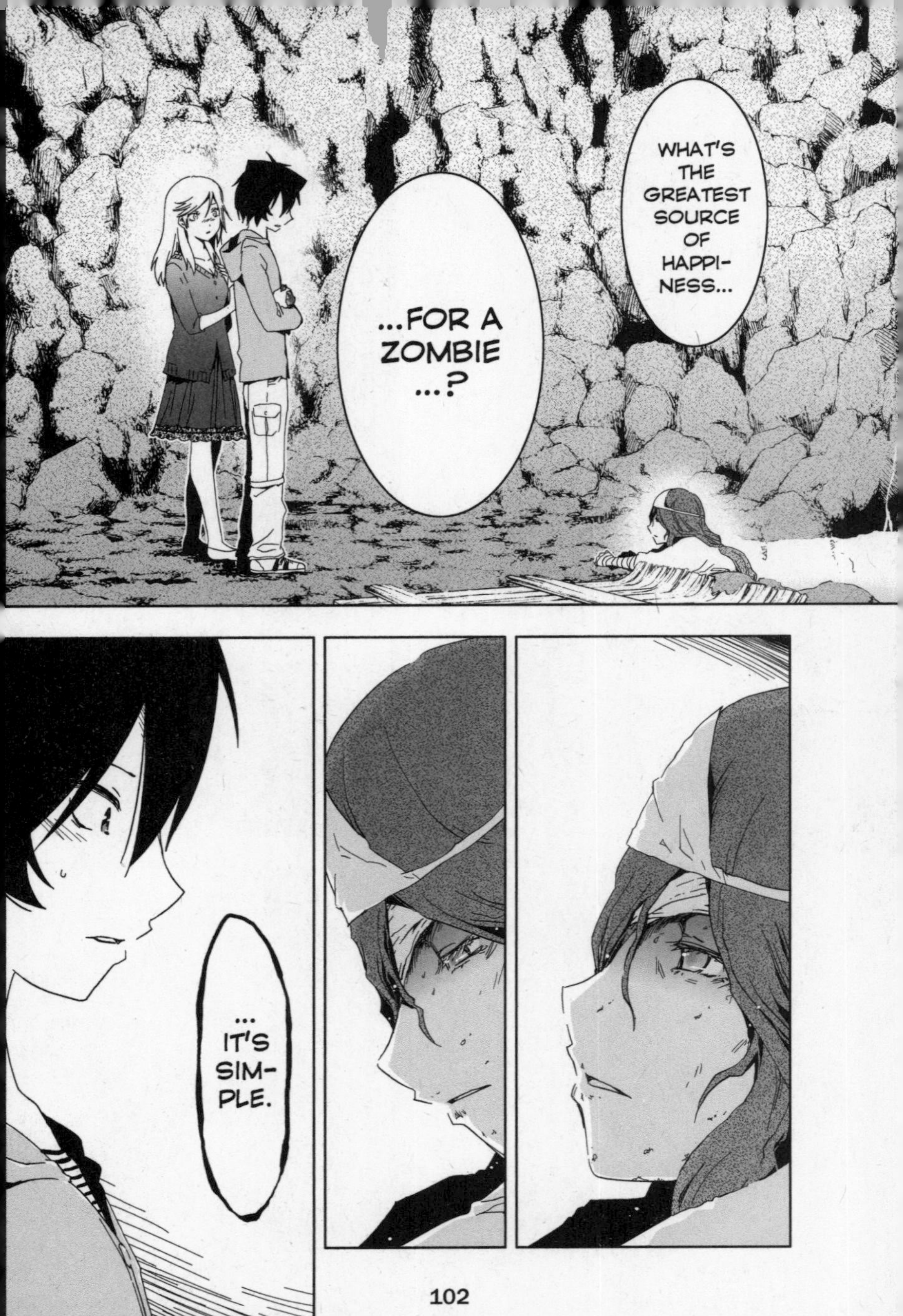
WHAT'S THE GREATEST SOURCE OF HAPPI-NESS...
...FOR A ZOMBIE ...?
... IT'S SIM-PLE.

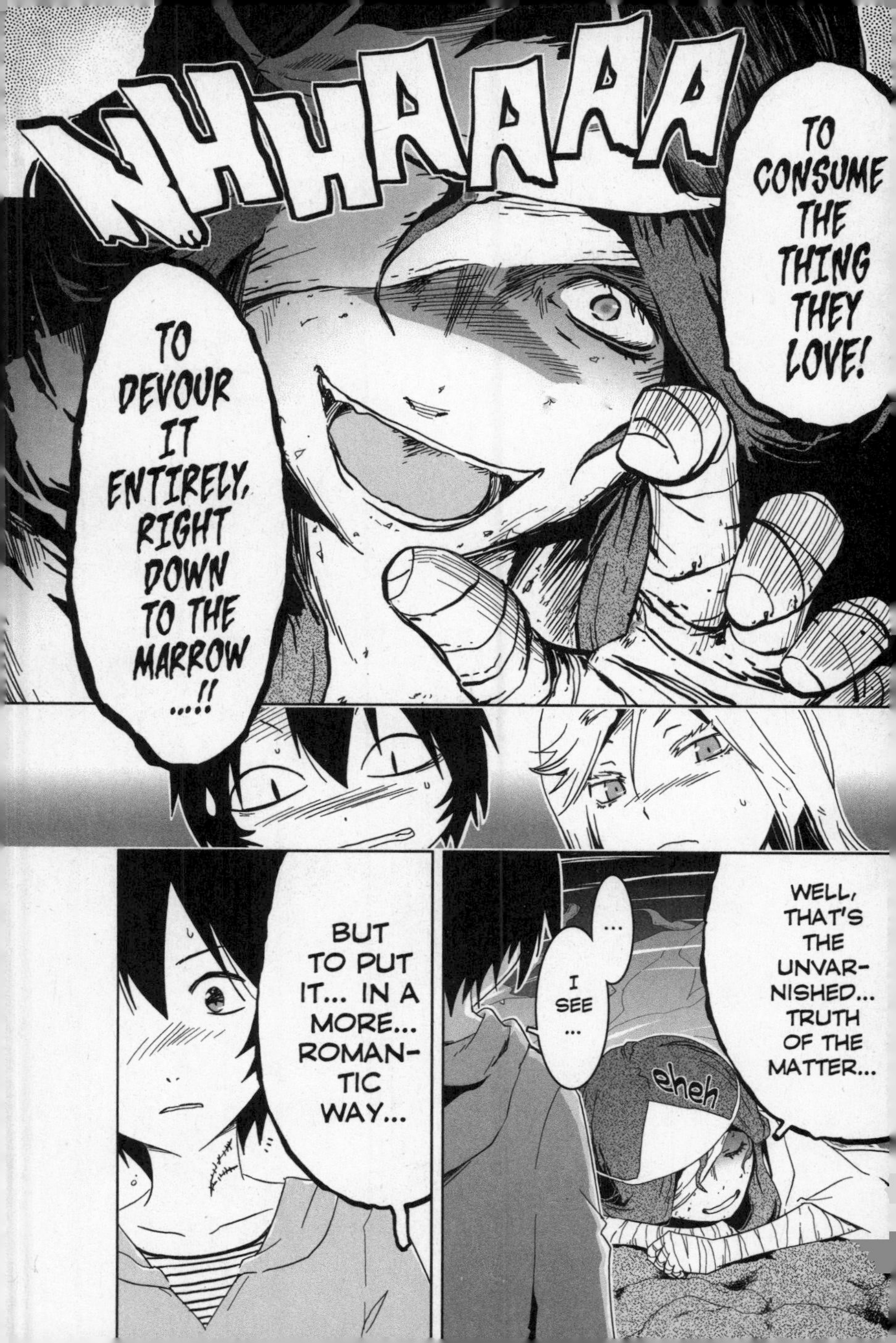
NHHAAAA
TO CONSUME THE THING THEY LOVE!
TO DEVOUR IT ENTIRELY, RIGHT DOWN TO THE MARROW ...!!
WELL, THAT'S THE UNVARNISHED... TRUTH OF THE MATTER...
eheh
...
I SEE ...
BUT TO PUT IT... IN A MORE... ROMANTIC WAY...

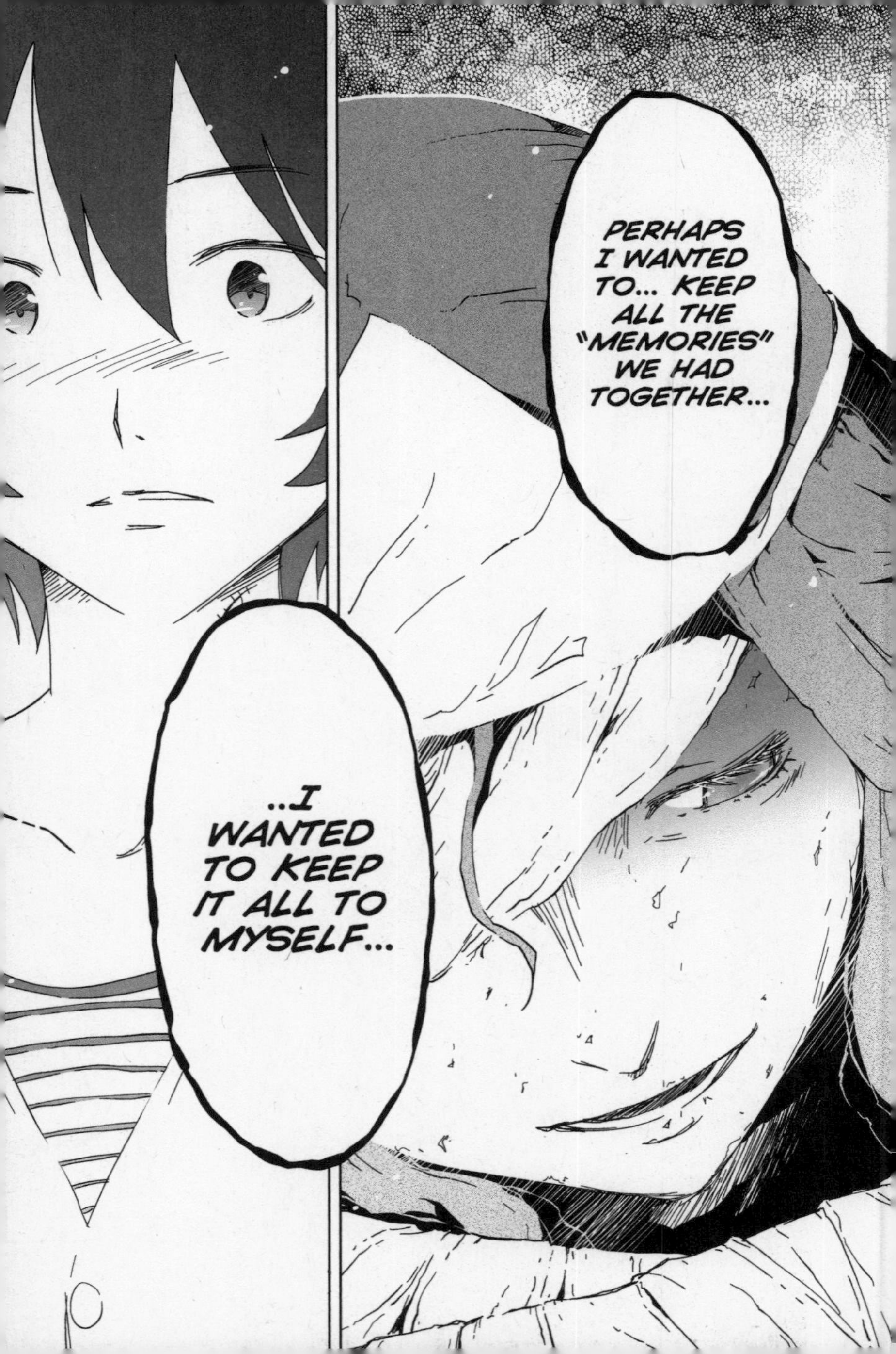
PERHAPS I WANTED TO... KEEP ALL THE "MEMORIES" WE HAD TOGETHER...
...I WANTED TO KEEP IT ALL TO MYSELF...

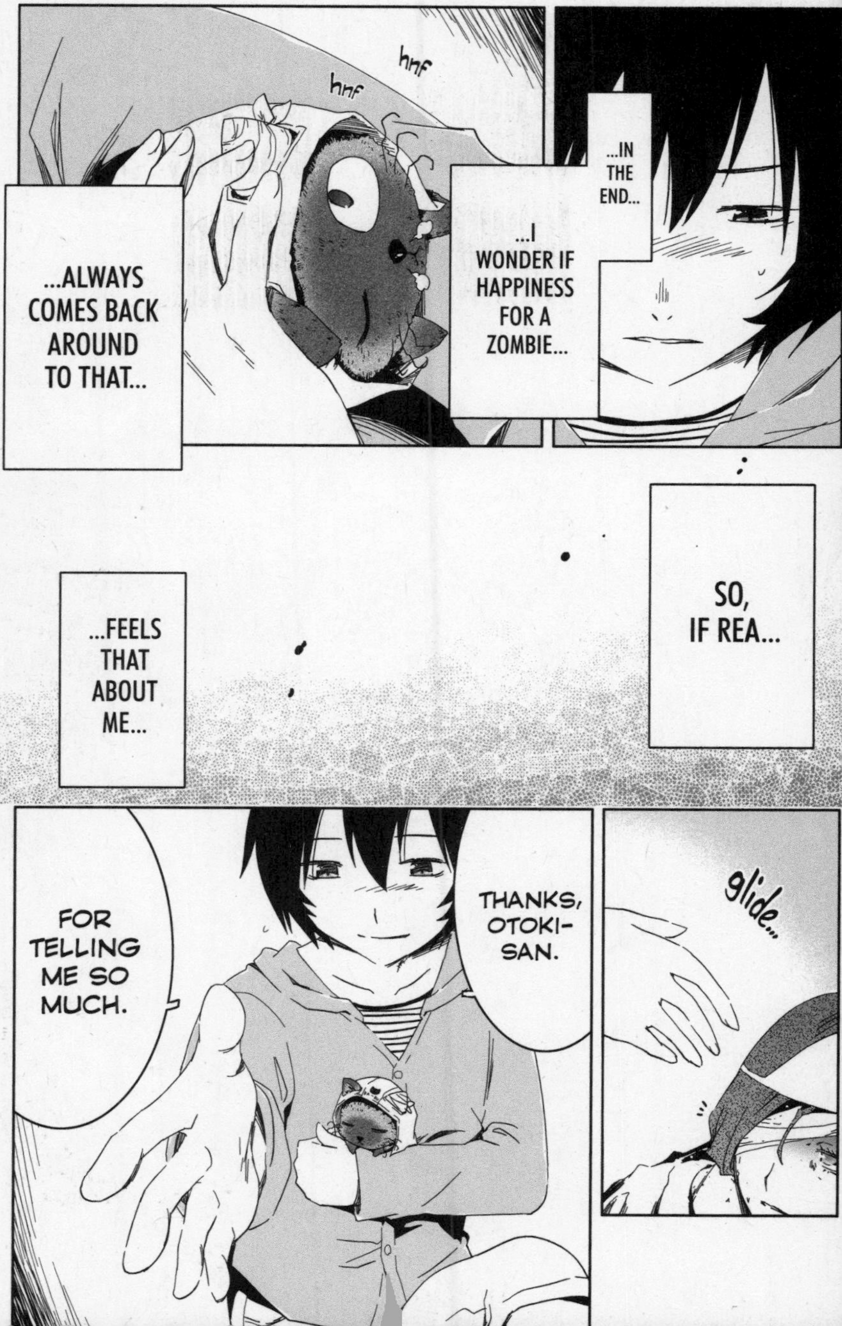
...IN THE END...
...I WONDER IF HAPPINESS FOR A ZOMBIE...
hnf
hnf
...ALWAYS COMES BACK AROUND TO THAT...
SO, IF REA...
...FEELS THAT ABOUT ME...
glide...
THANKS, OTOKI-SAN.
FOR TELLING ME SO MUCH.

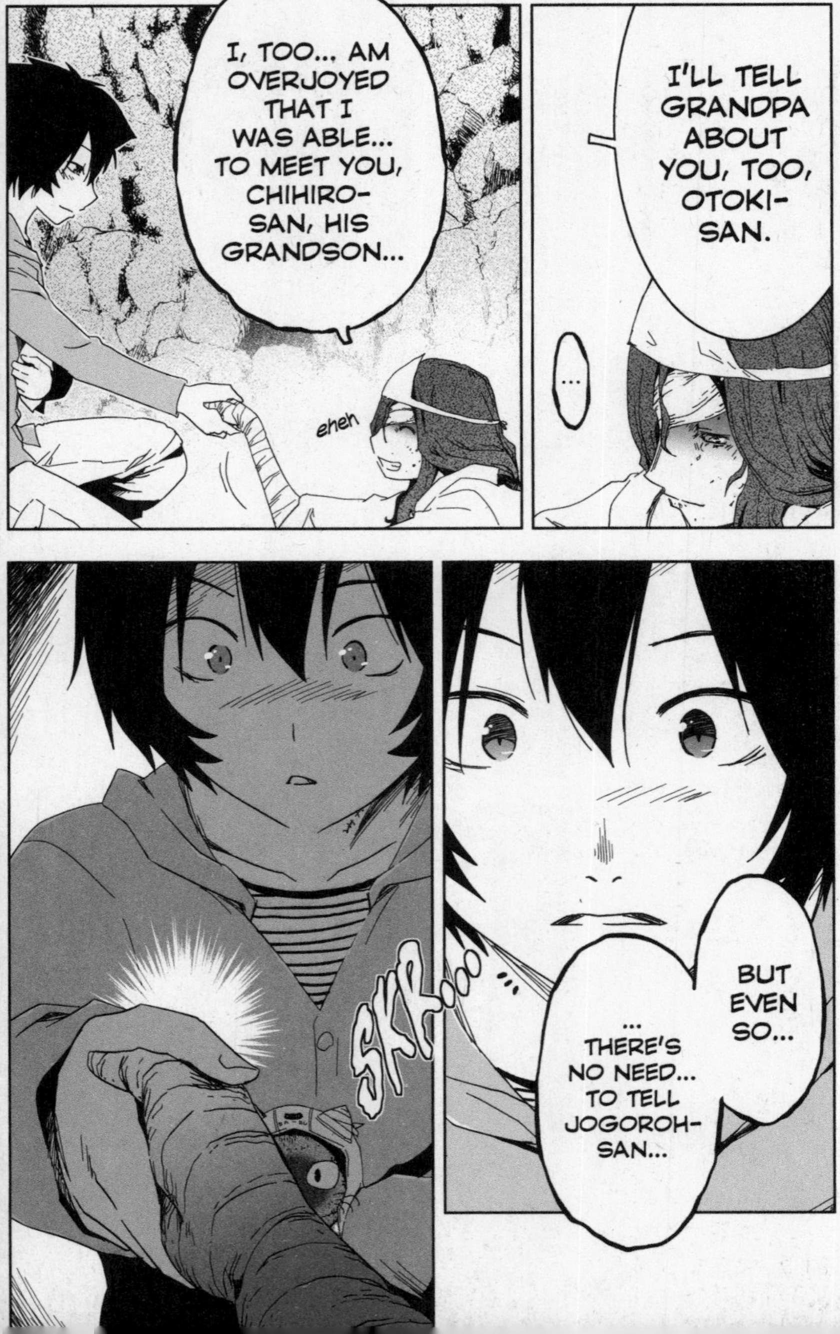
I'LL TELL GRANDPA ABOUT YOU, TOO, OTOKI-SAN.
...
I, TOO..., AM OVERJOYED THAT I WAS ABLE... TO MEET YOU, CHIHIRO-SAN, HIS GRANDSON...
eheh
BUT EVEN SO...
... THERE'S NO NEED... TO TELL JOGOROH-SAN...

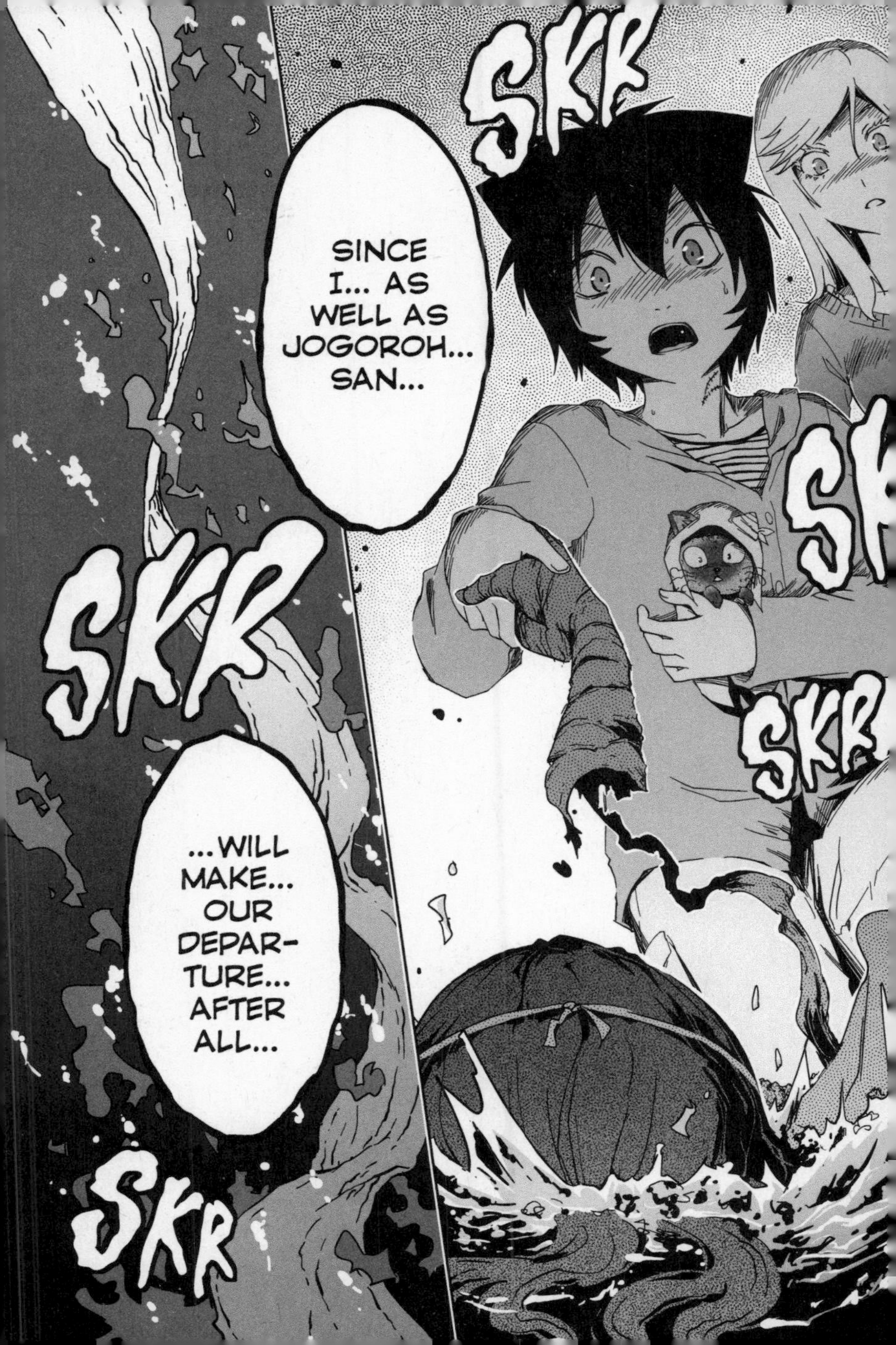
SKR
SKR
SINCE I... AS WELL AS JOGOROH... SAN...
SKR
SKR
...WILL MAKE... OUR DEPARTURE... AFTER ALL...
SKR

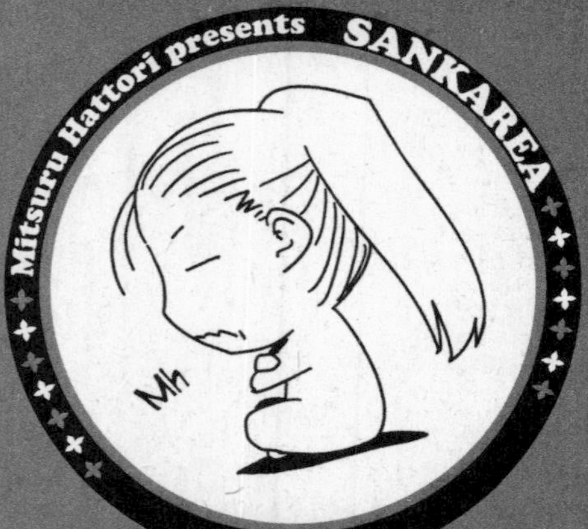
Mitsuru Hattori presents
SANKAREA

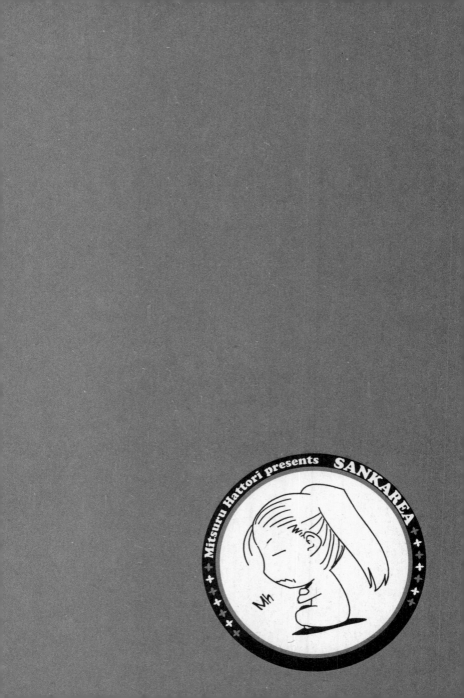

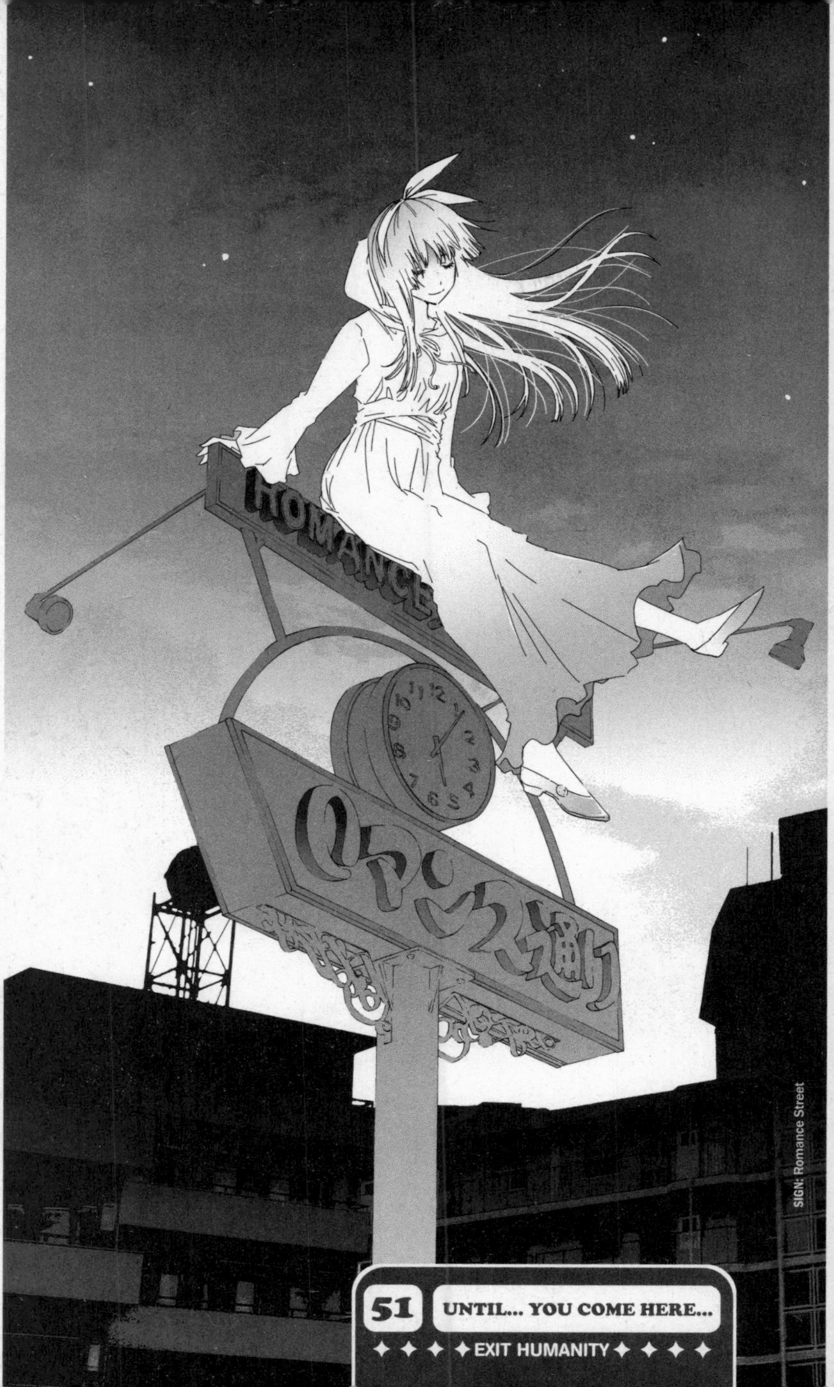
ROMANCE
SIGN: Romance Street
51
UNTIL... YOU COME HERE...
EXIT HUMANITY

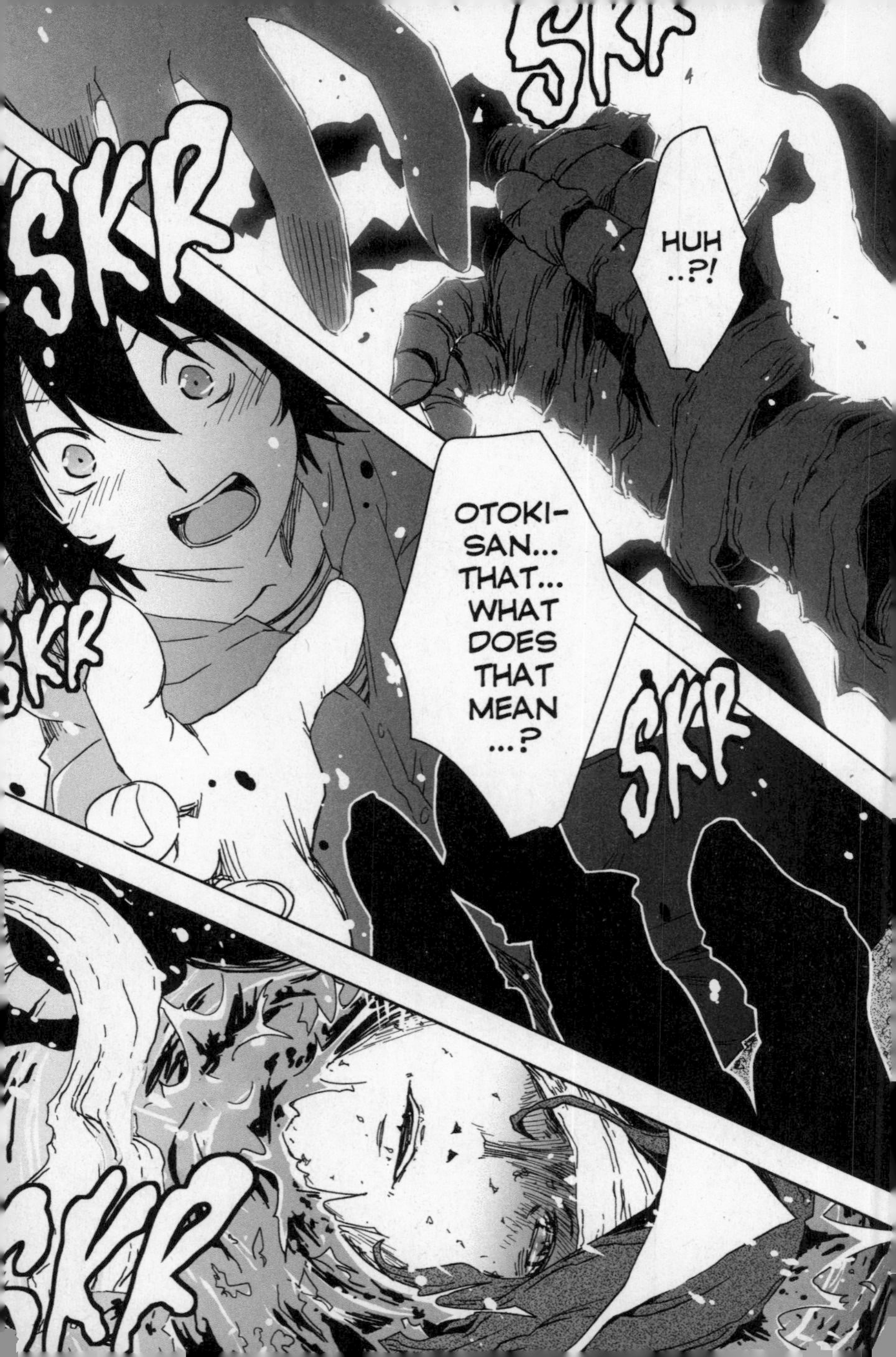
SKR
SKR
HUH ..?!
OTOKI-SAN... THAT... WHAT DOES THAT MEAN ...?
SKR
SKR
SKR

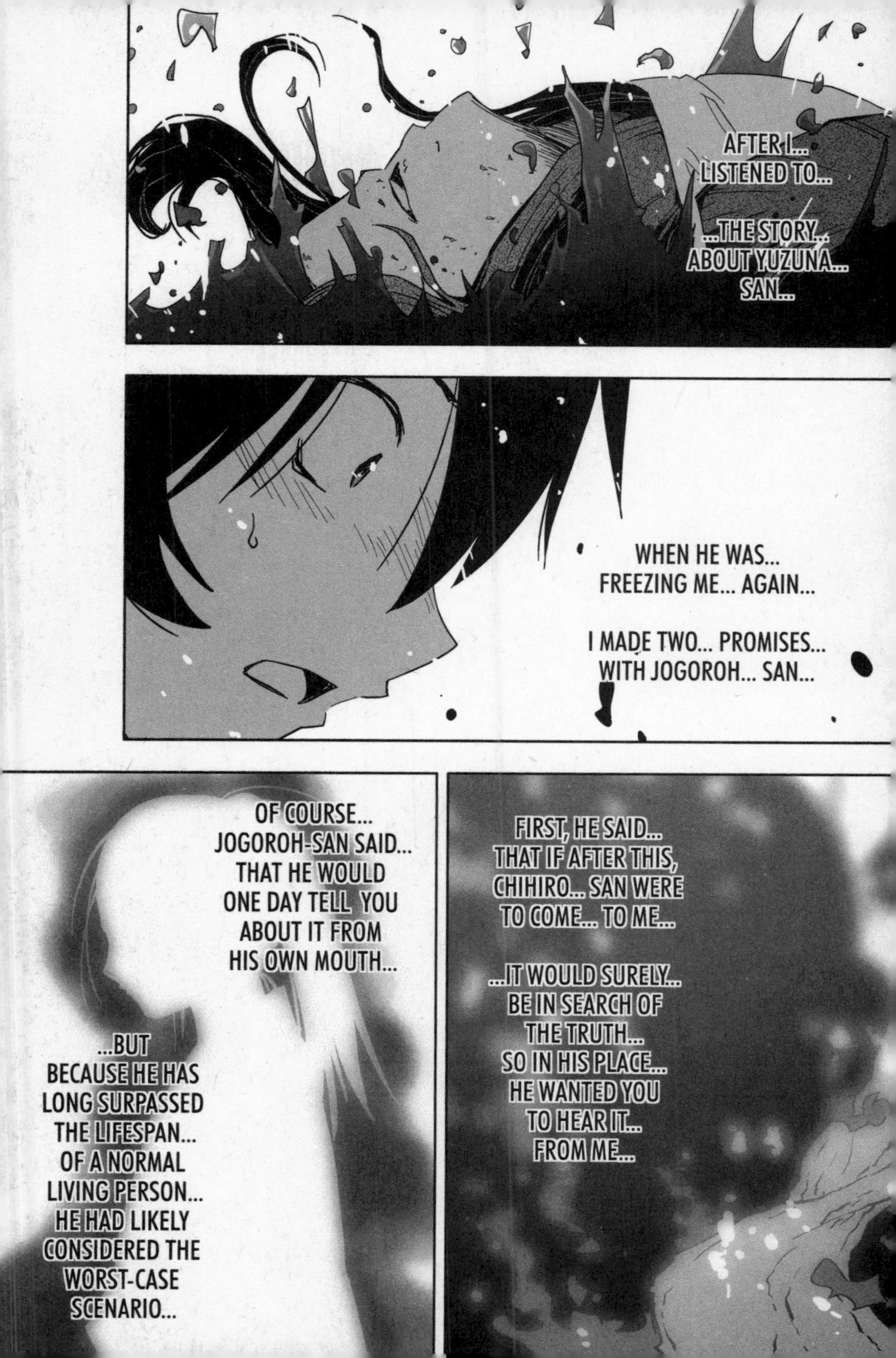
AFTER I... LISTENED TO...
...THE STORY... ABOUT YUZUNA... SAN...
WHEN HE WAS... FREEZING ME... AGAIN...
I MADE TWO... PROMISES... WITH JOGOROH... SAN...
FIRST, HE SAID... THAT IF AFTER THIS, CHIHIRO... SAN WERE TO COME... TO ME...
...IT WOULD SURELY... BE IN SEARCH OF THE TRUTH... SO IN HIS PLACE... HE WANTED YOU TO HEAR IT... FROM ME...
OF COURSE... JOGOROH-SAN SAID... THAT HE WOULD ONE DAY TELL YOU ABOUT IT FROM HIS OWN MOUTH...
...BUT BECAUSE HE HAS LONG SURPASSED THE LIFESPAN... OF A NORMAL LIVING PERSON... HE HAD LIKELY CONSIDERED THE WORST-CASE SCENARIO...

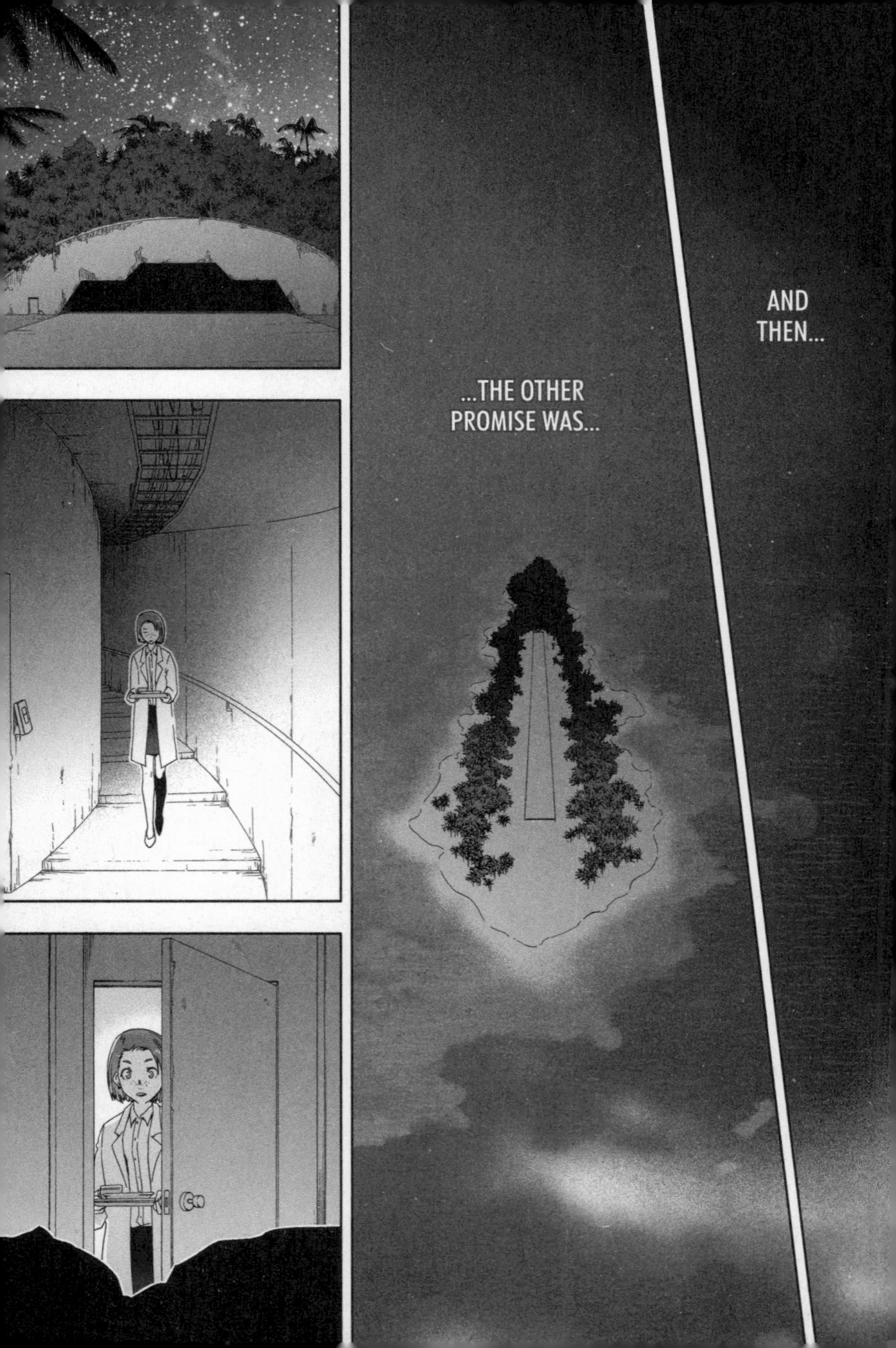
AND THEN...
...THE OTHER PROMISE WAS...

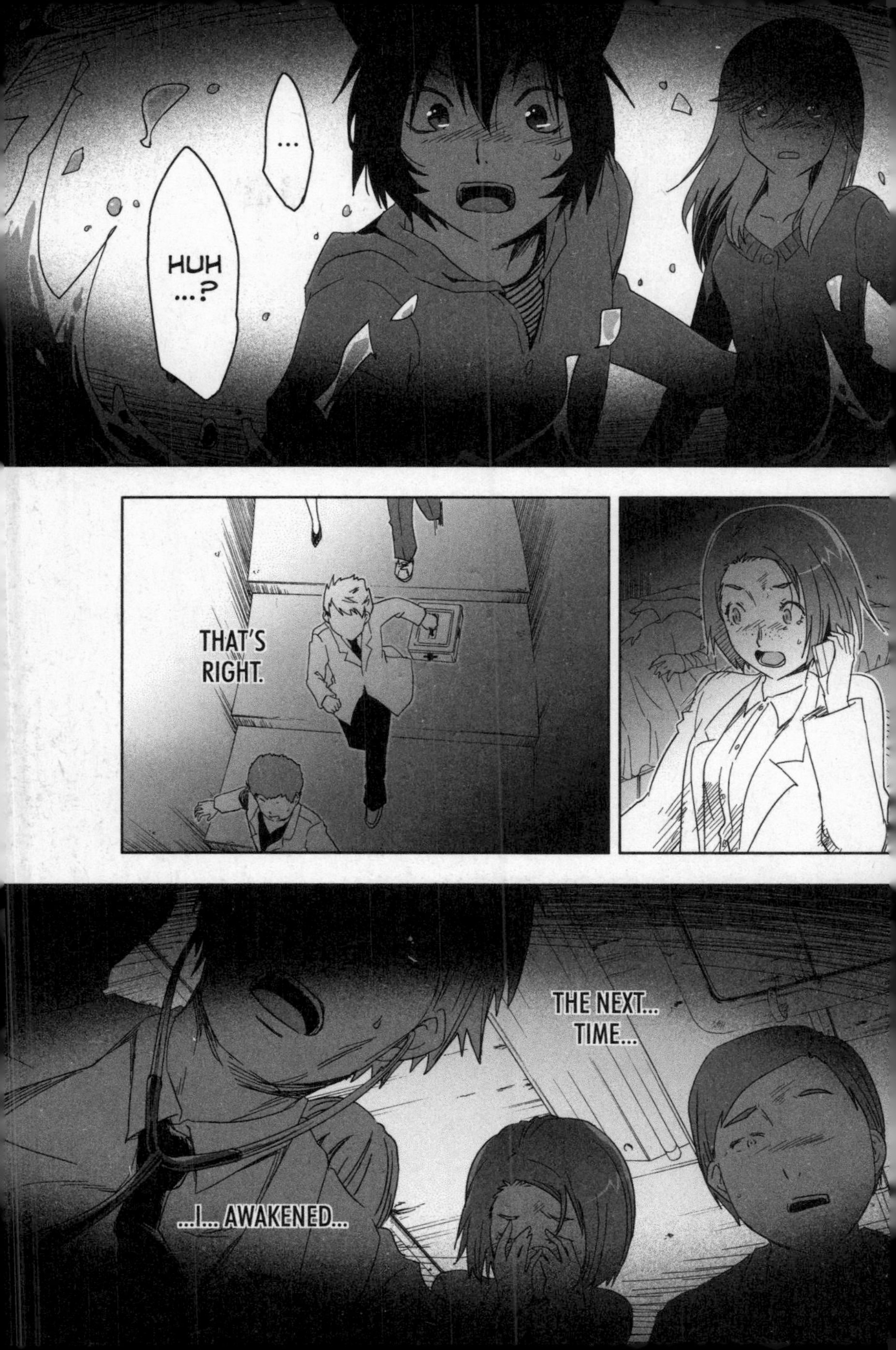
...
HUH ...?
THAT'S RIGHT.
THE NEXT... TIME...
...I... AWAKENED...

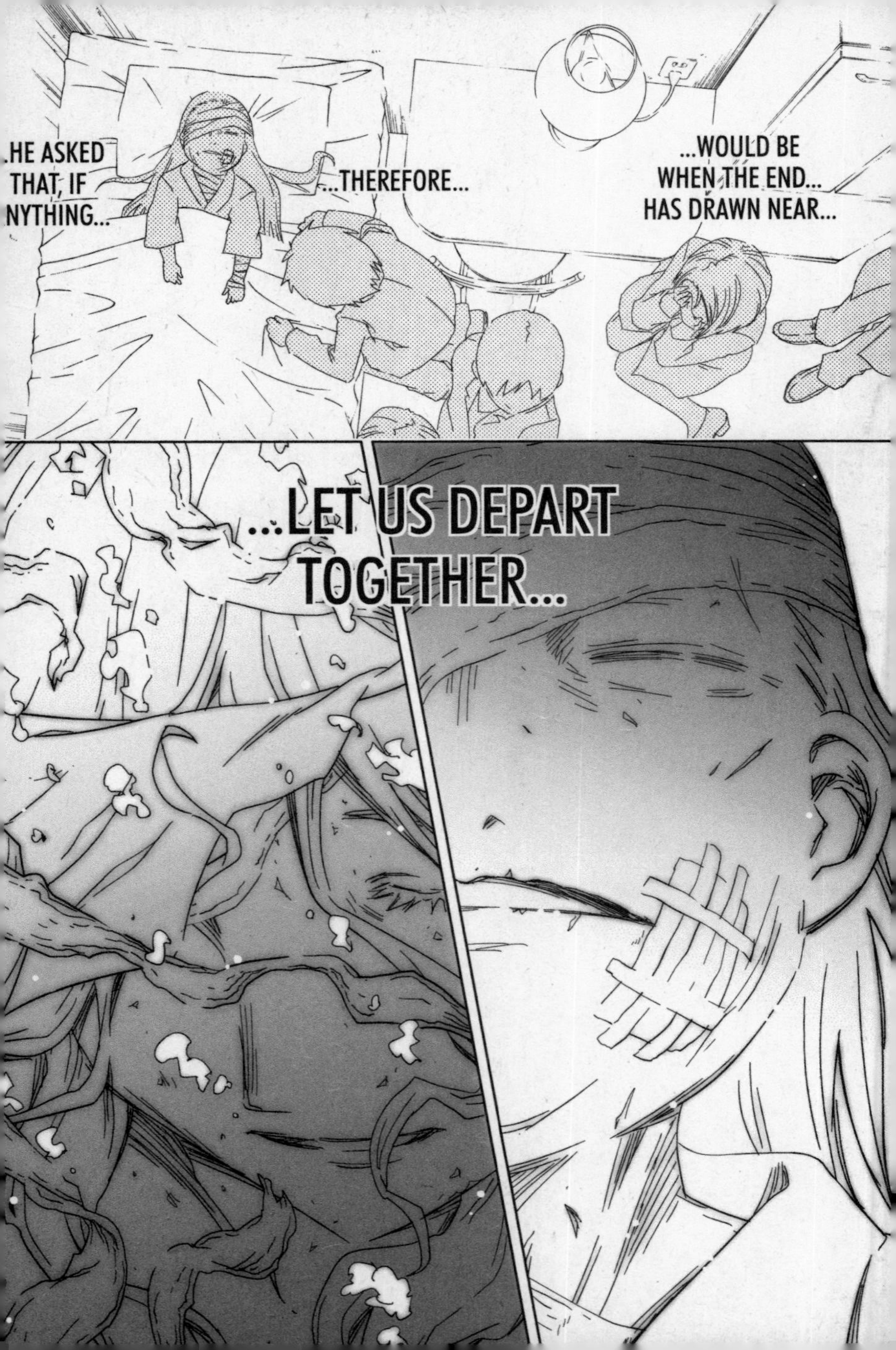
...WOULD BE WHEN THE END... HAS DRAWN NEAR...
...THEREFORE...
.HE ASKED THAT, IF NYTHING...
...LET US DEPART TOGETHER...

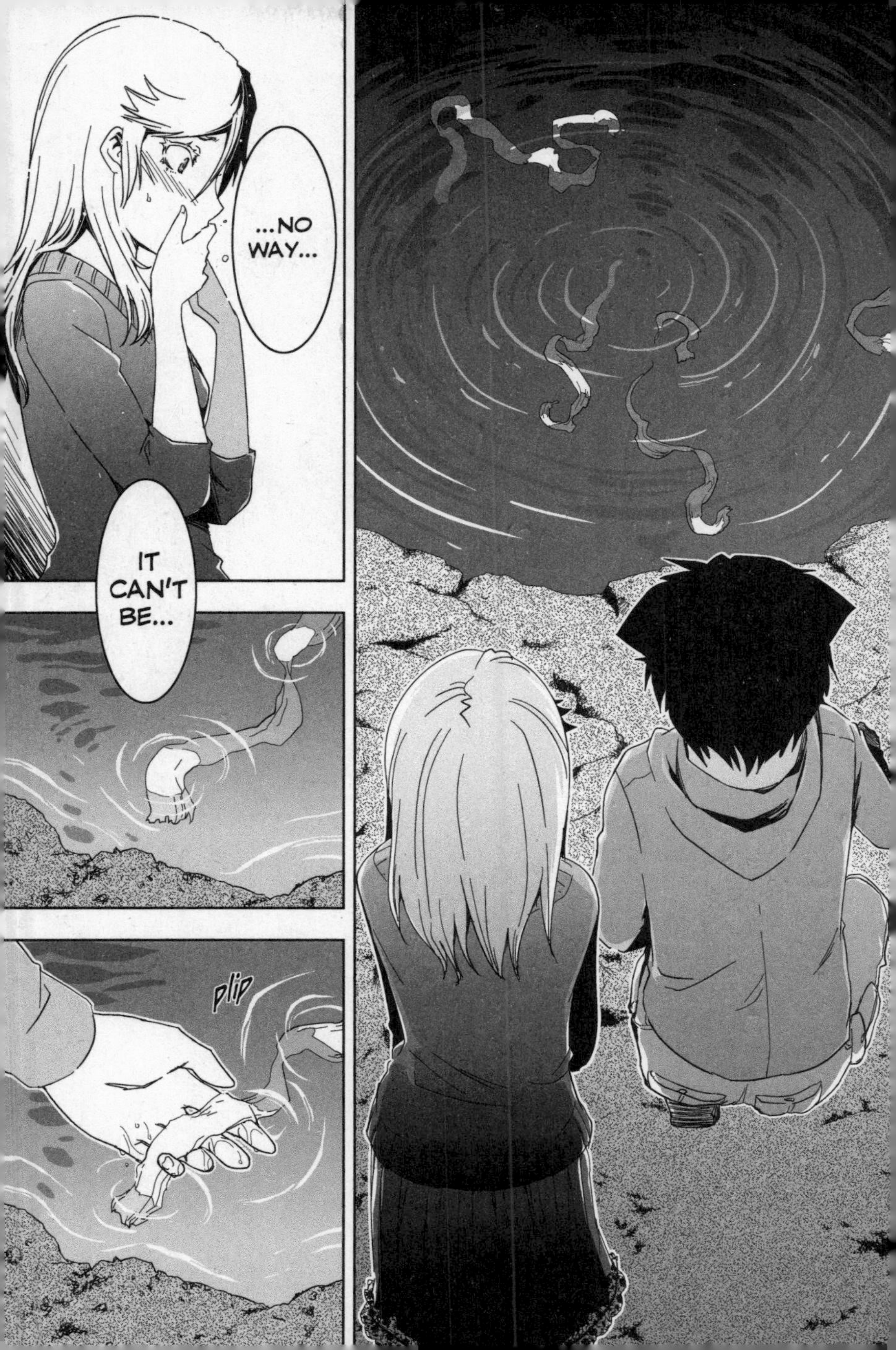
...NO WAY...
IT CAN'T BE...
plip

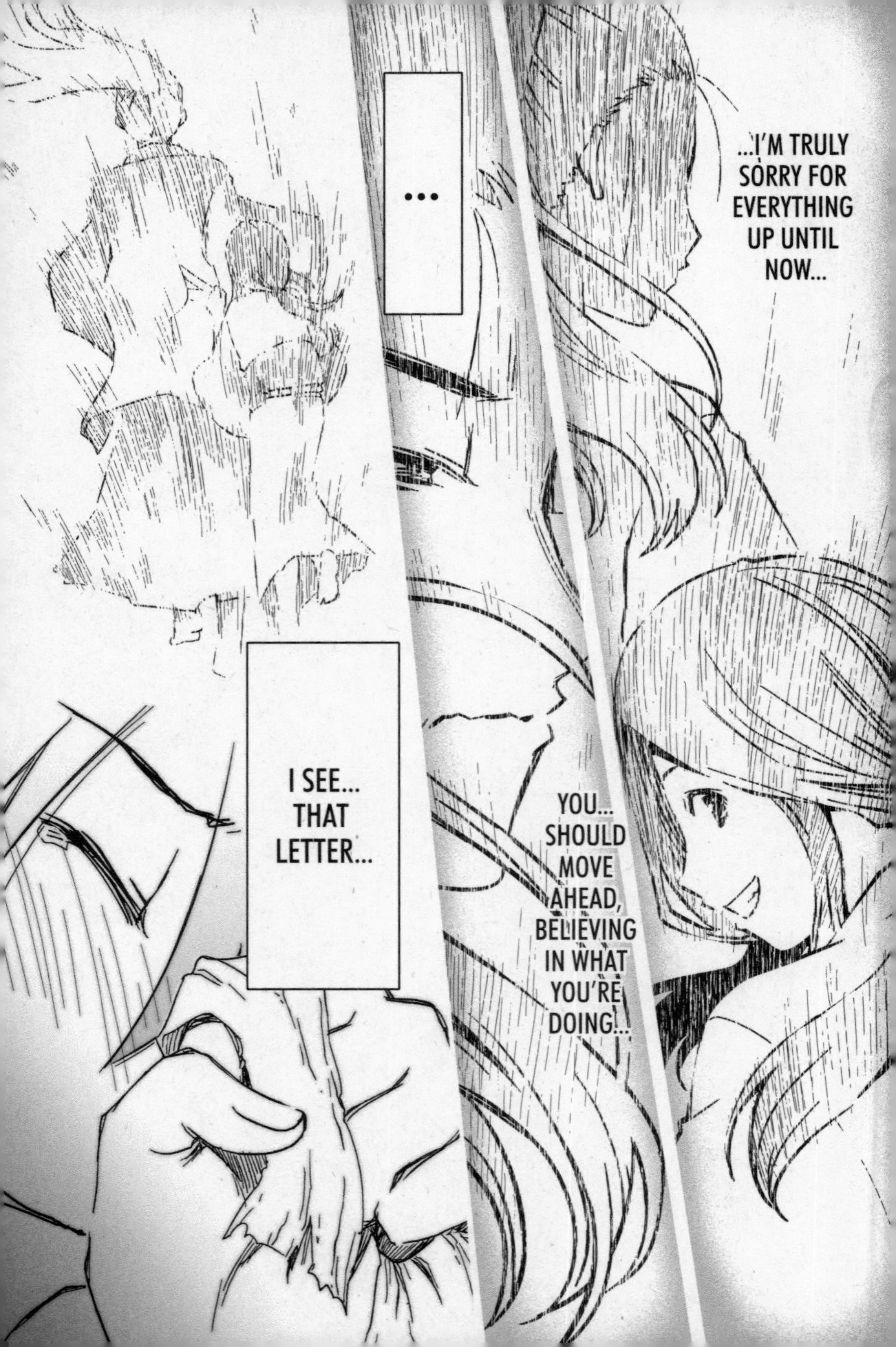
...I'M TRULY SORRY FOR EVERYTHING UP UNTIL NOW...
YOU... SHOULD MOVE AHEAD, BELIEVING IN WHAT YOU'RE DOING...
...
I SEE... THAT LETTER...

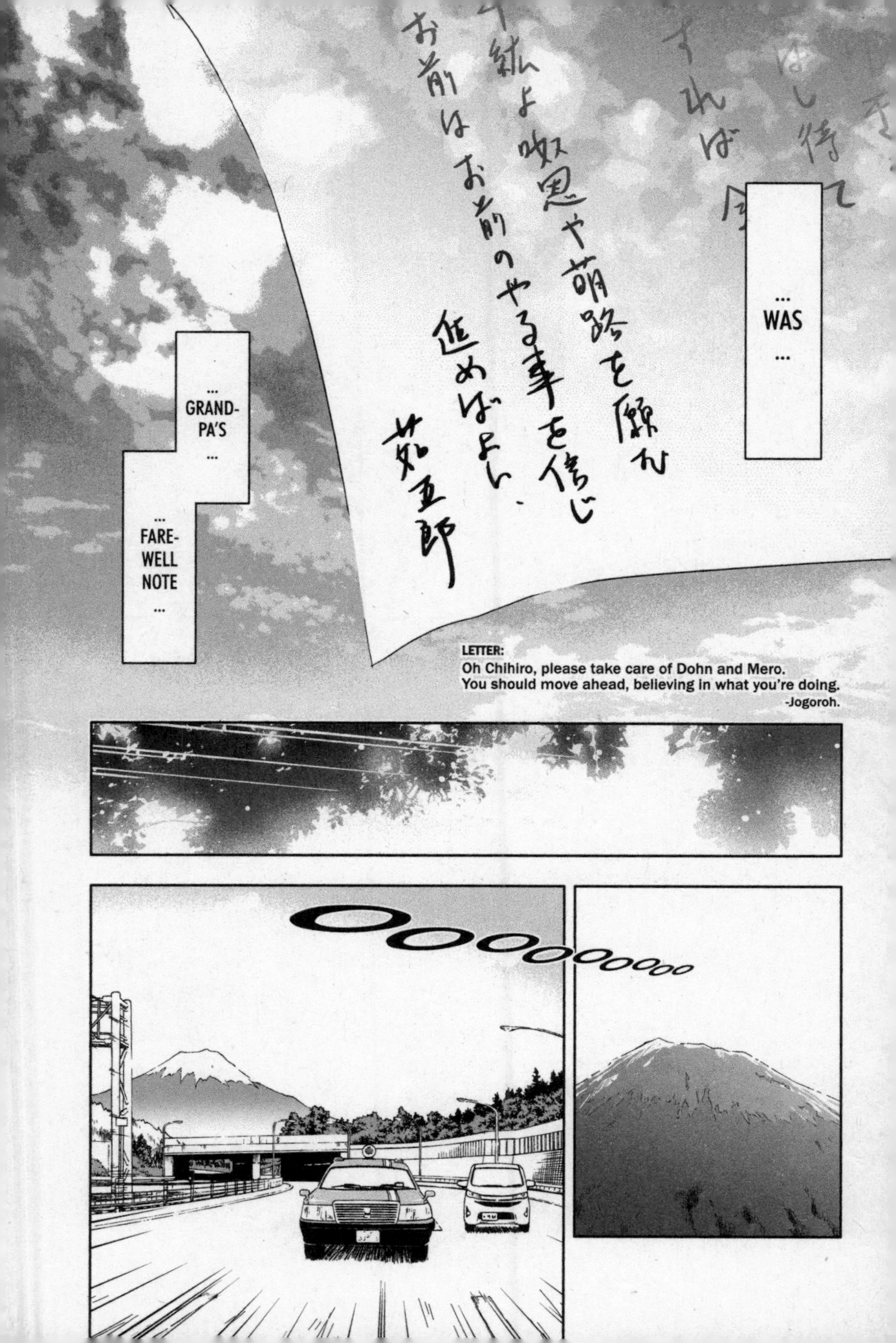
... WAS ...
... GRAND-PA'S ...
... FARE-WELL NOTE ...
お前はお前のやる事を信じ
進めばよい
LETTER:
Oh Chihiro, please take care of Dohn and Mero.
You should move ahead, believing in what you're doing.
-Jogoroh.
OOOOOoooo

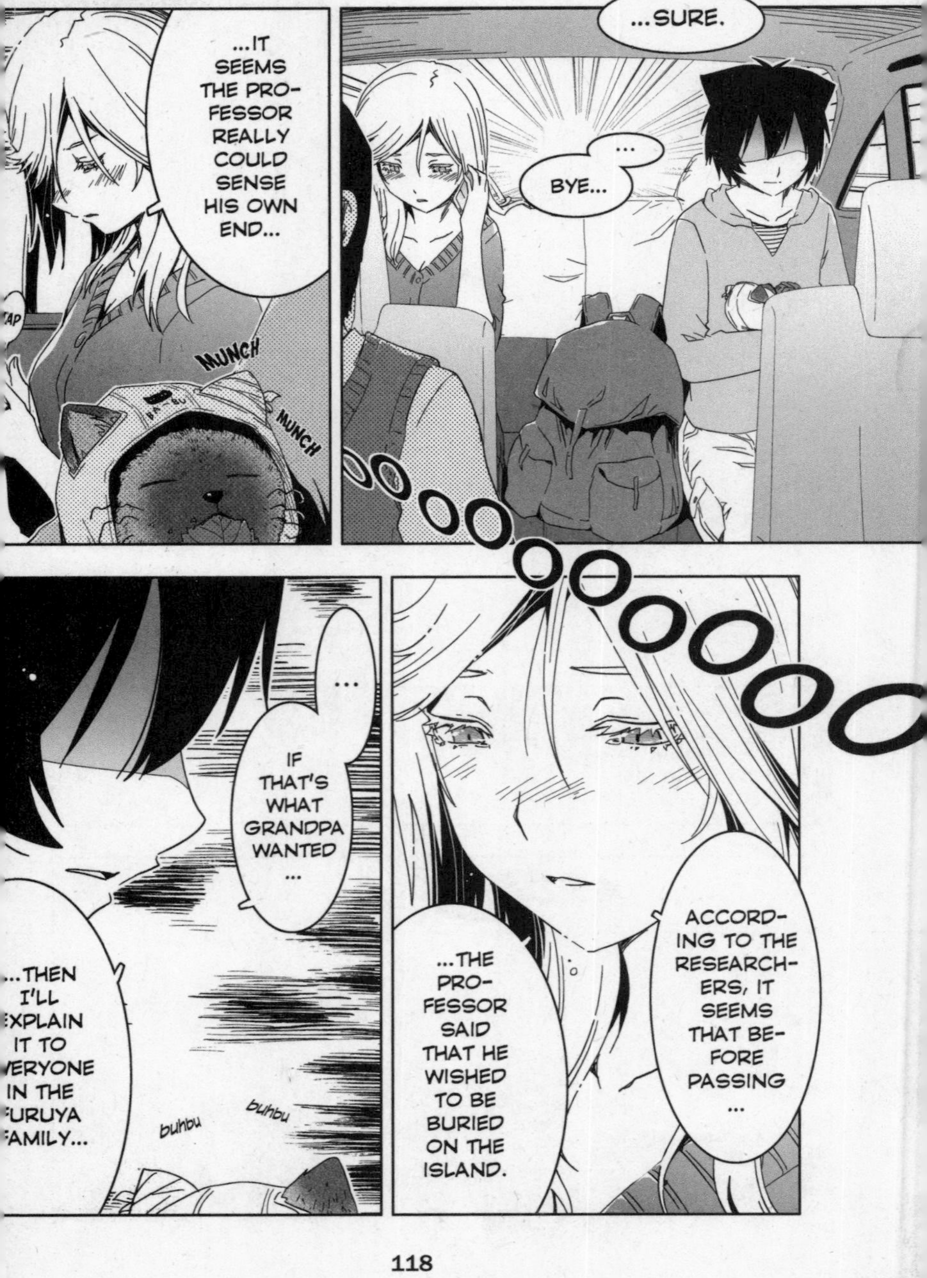
...SURE.
... BYE...
...IT SEEMS THE PRO-FESSOR REALLY COULD SENSE HIS OWN END...
AP
MUNCH
MUNCH
OOOOOOOOOOOOOO
ACCORD-ING TO THE RESEARCH-ERS, IT SEEMS THAT BE-FORE PASSING ...
...THE PRO-FESSOR SAID THAT HE WISHED TO BE BURIED ON THE ISLAND.
...
IF THAT'S WHAT GRANDPA WANTED ...
...THEN I'LL EXPLAIN IT TO VERYONE IN THE FURUYA AMILY...
buhbu
buhbu

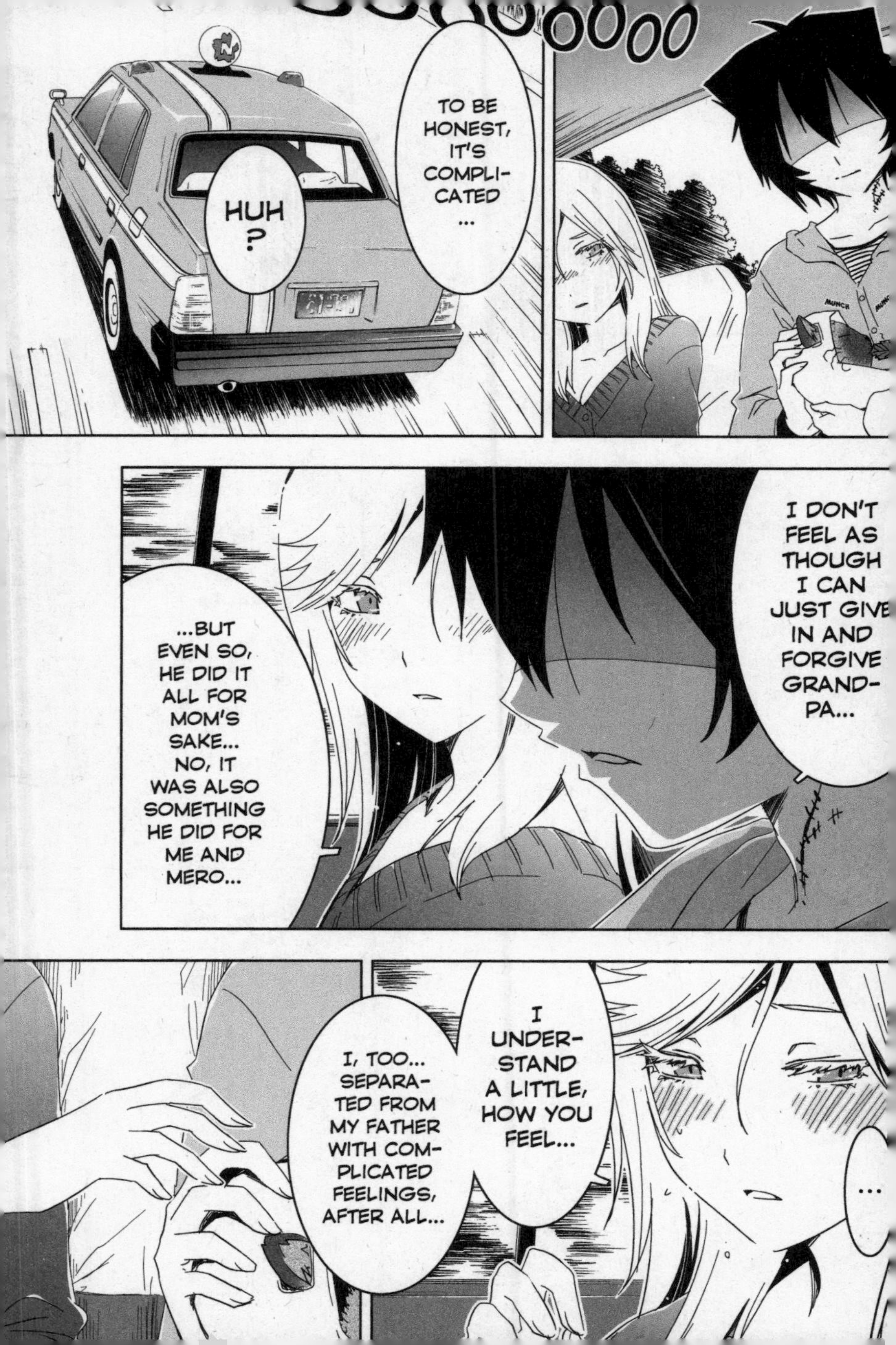
OOOOO
TO BE HONEST, IT'S COMPLICATED ...
HUH ?
I DON'T FEEL AS THOUGH I CAN JUST GIVE IN AND FORGIVE GRANDPA...
...BUT EVEN SO, HE DID IT ALL FOR MOM'S SAKE... NO, IT WAS ALSO SOMETHING HE DID FOR ME AND MERO...
...
I UNDERSTAND A LITTLE, HOW YOU FEEL...
I, TOO... SEPARATED FROM MY FATHER WITH COMPLICATED FEELINGS, AFTER ALL...

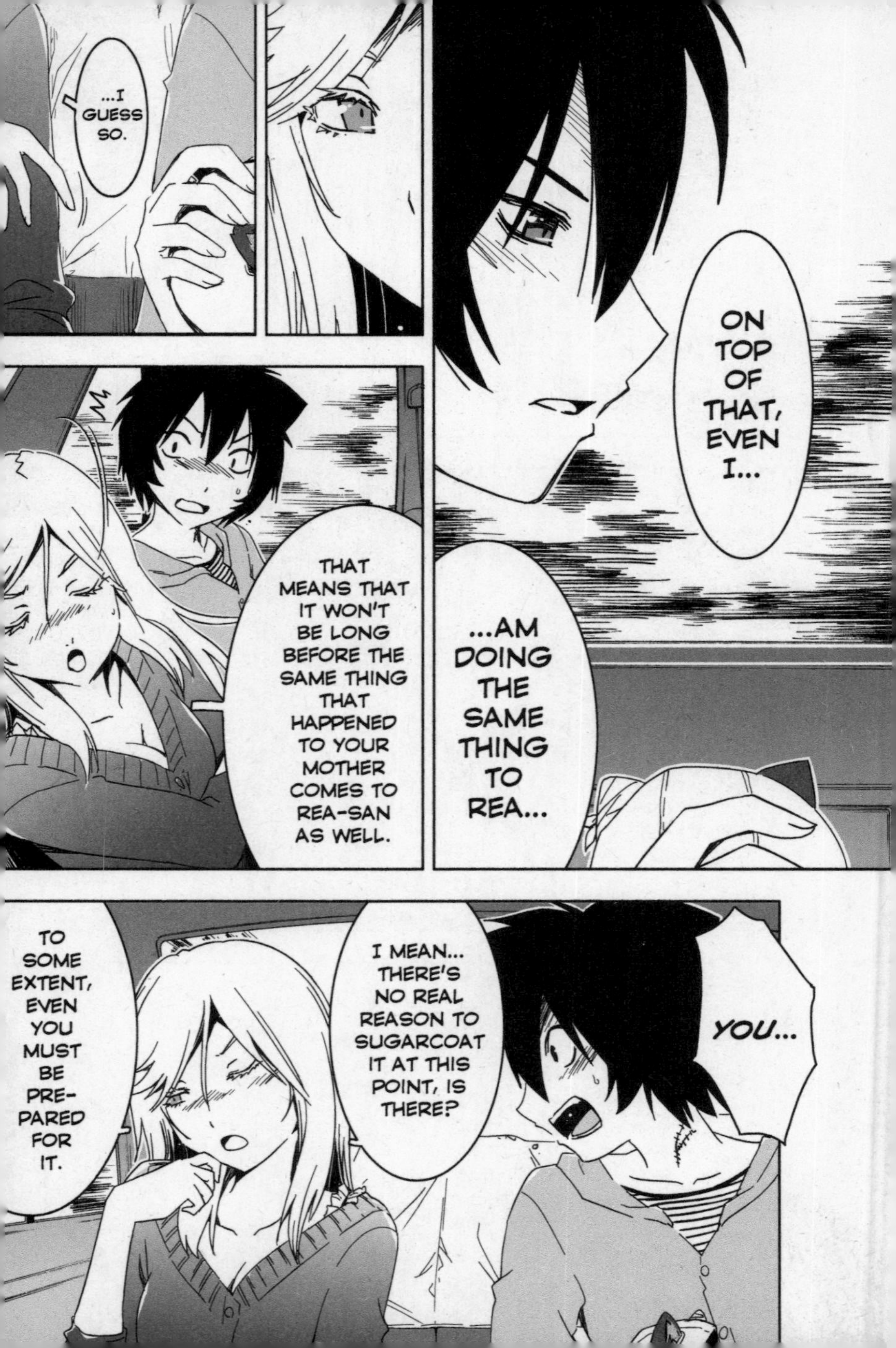
ON TOP OF THAT, EVEN I...
...AM DOING THE SAME THING TO REA...
...I GUESS SO.
THAT MEANS THAT IT WON'T BE LONG BEFORE THE SAME THING THAT HAPPENED TO YOUR MOTHER COMES TO REA-SAN AS WELL.
YOU...
I MEAN... THERE'S NO REAL REASON TO SUGARCOAT IT AT THIS POINT, IS THERE?
TO SOME EXTENT, EVEN YOU MUST BE PRE-PARED FOR IT.

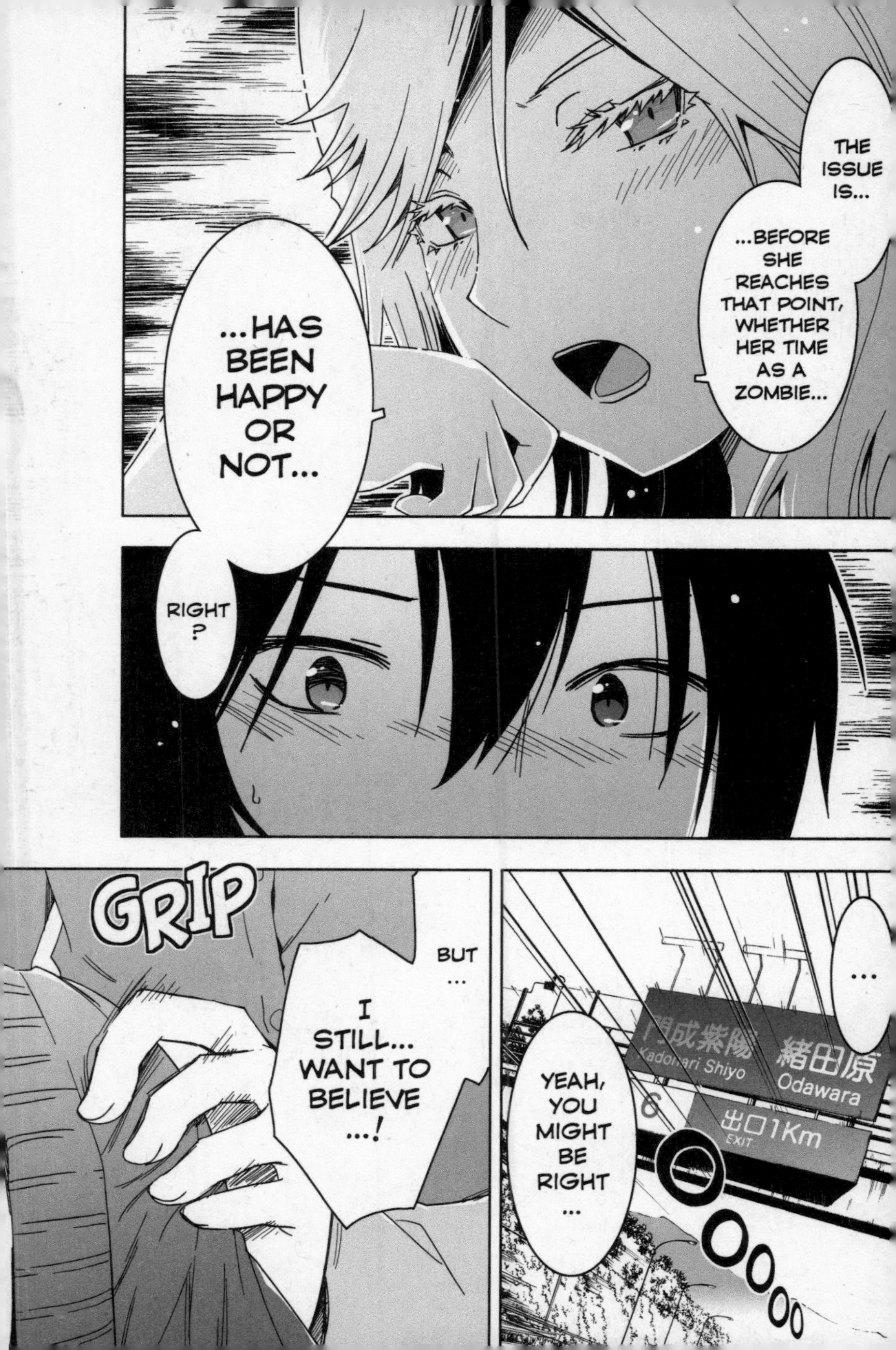
THE ISSUE IS...
...BEFORE SHE REACHES THAT POINT, WHETHER HER TIME AS A ZOMBIE...
...HAS BEEN HAPPY OR NOT...
RIGHT?
...
YEAH, YOU MIGHT BE RIGHT...
Kadonari Shiyo
Odawara
EXIT
GRIP
BUT...
I STILL... WANT TO BELIEVE...!

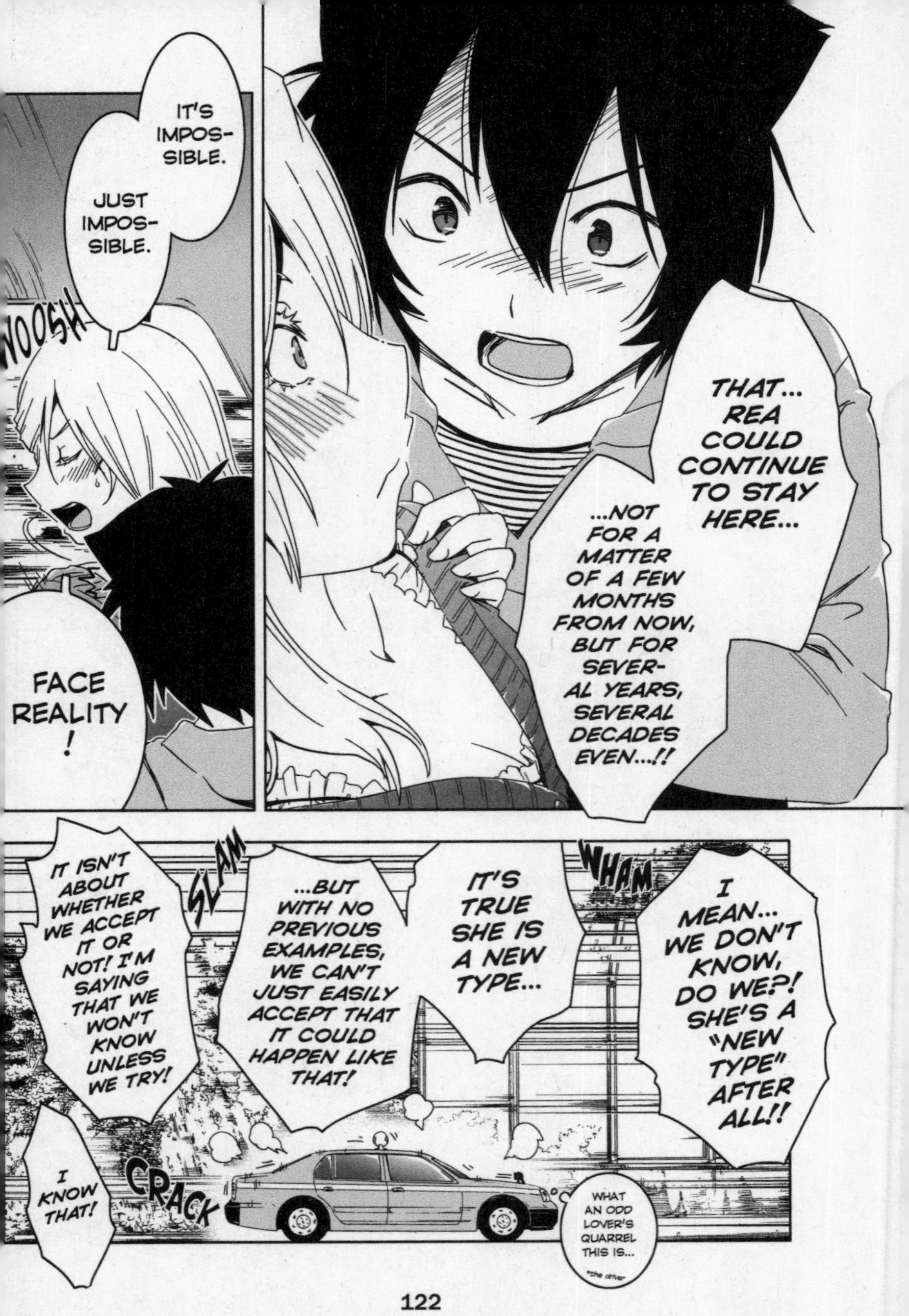
THAT... REA COULD CONTINUE TO STAY HERE...
...NOT FOR A MATTER OF A FEW MONTHS FROM NOW, BUT FOR SEVERAL YEARS, SEVERAL DECADES EVEN...!!
IT'S IMPOSSIBLE.
JUST IMPOSSIBLE.
WOOSH
FACE REALITY!
I MEAN... WE DON'T KNOW, DO WE?! SHE'S A "NEW TYPE" AFTER ALL!!
WHAM
IT'S TRUE SHE IS A NEW TYPE...
...BUT WITH NO PREVIOUS EXAMPLES, WE CAN'T JUST EASILY ACCEPT THAT IT COULD HAPPEN LIKE THAT!
SLAM
IT ISN'T ABOUT WHETHER WE ACCEPT IT OR NOT! I'M SAYING THAT WE WON'T KNOW UNLESS WE TRY!
WHAT AN ODD LOVER'S QUARREL THIS IS...
*the driver
CRACK
I KNOW THAT!

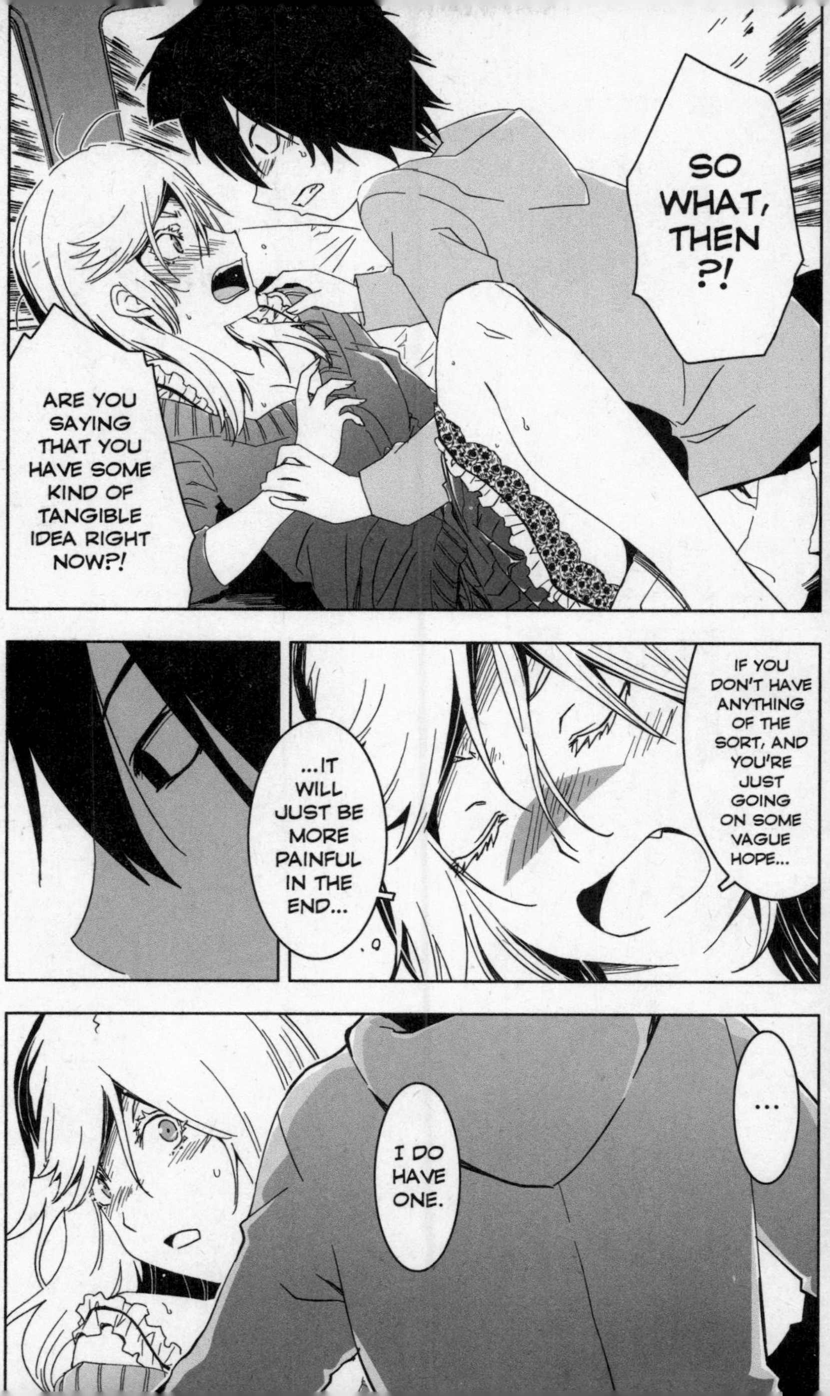
SO WHAT, THEN ?!
ARE YOU SAYING THAT YOU HAVE SOME KIND OF TANGIBLE IDEA RIGHT NOW?!
IF YOU DON'T HAVE ANYTHING OF THE SORT, AND YOU'RE JUST GOING ON SOME VAGUE HOPE...
...IT WILL JUST BE MORE PAINFUL IN THE END...
...
I DO HAVE ONE.

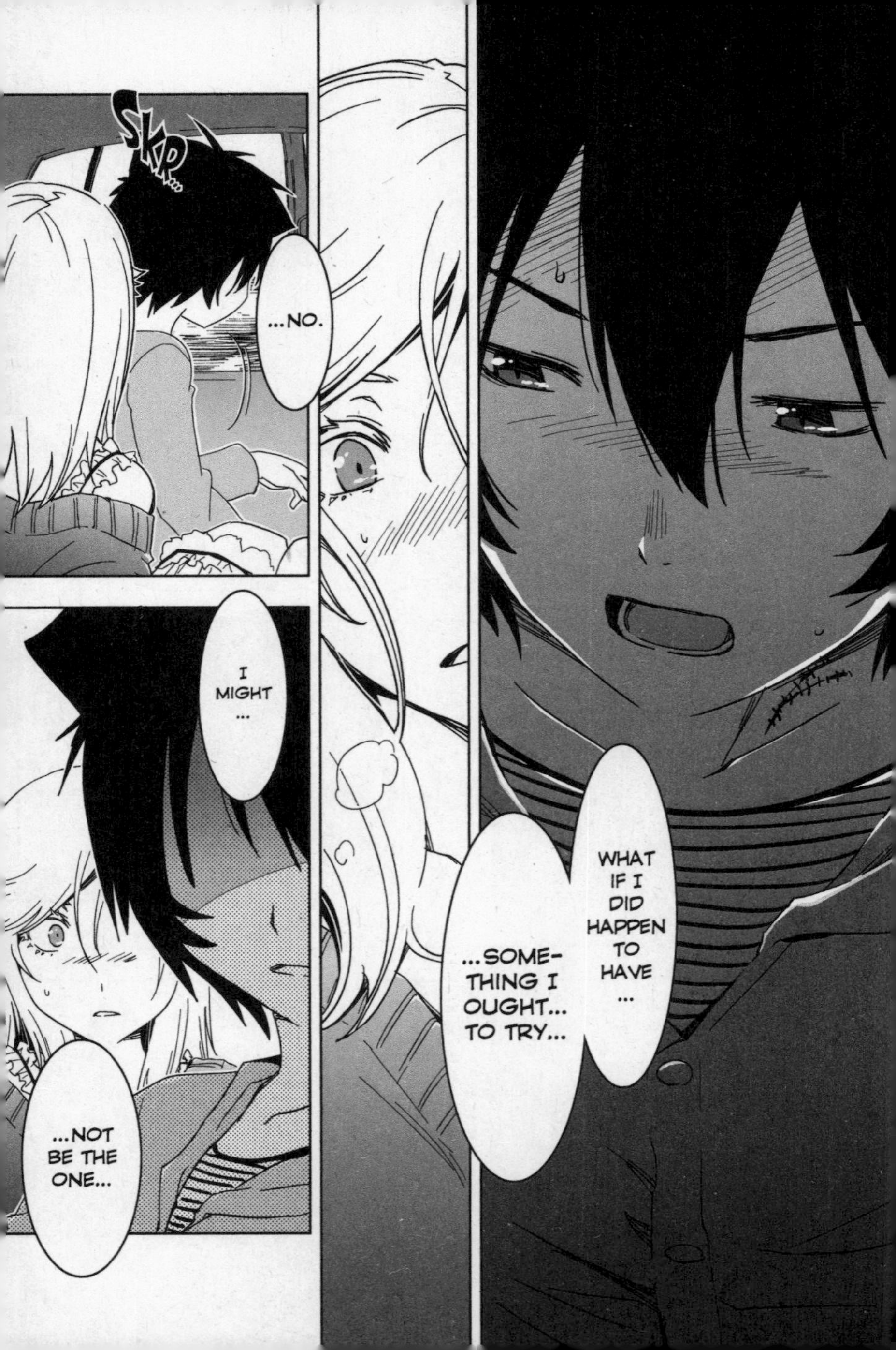
WHAT IF I DID HAPPEN TO HAVE ...
...SOME-THING I OUGHT... TO TRY...
SKR...
...NO.
I MIGHT ...
...NOT BE THE ONE...

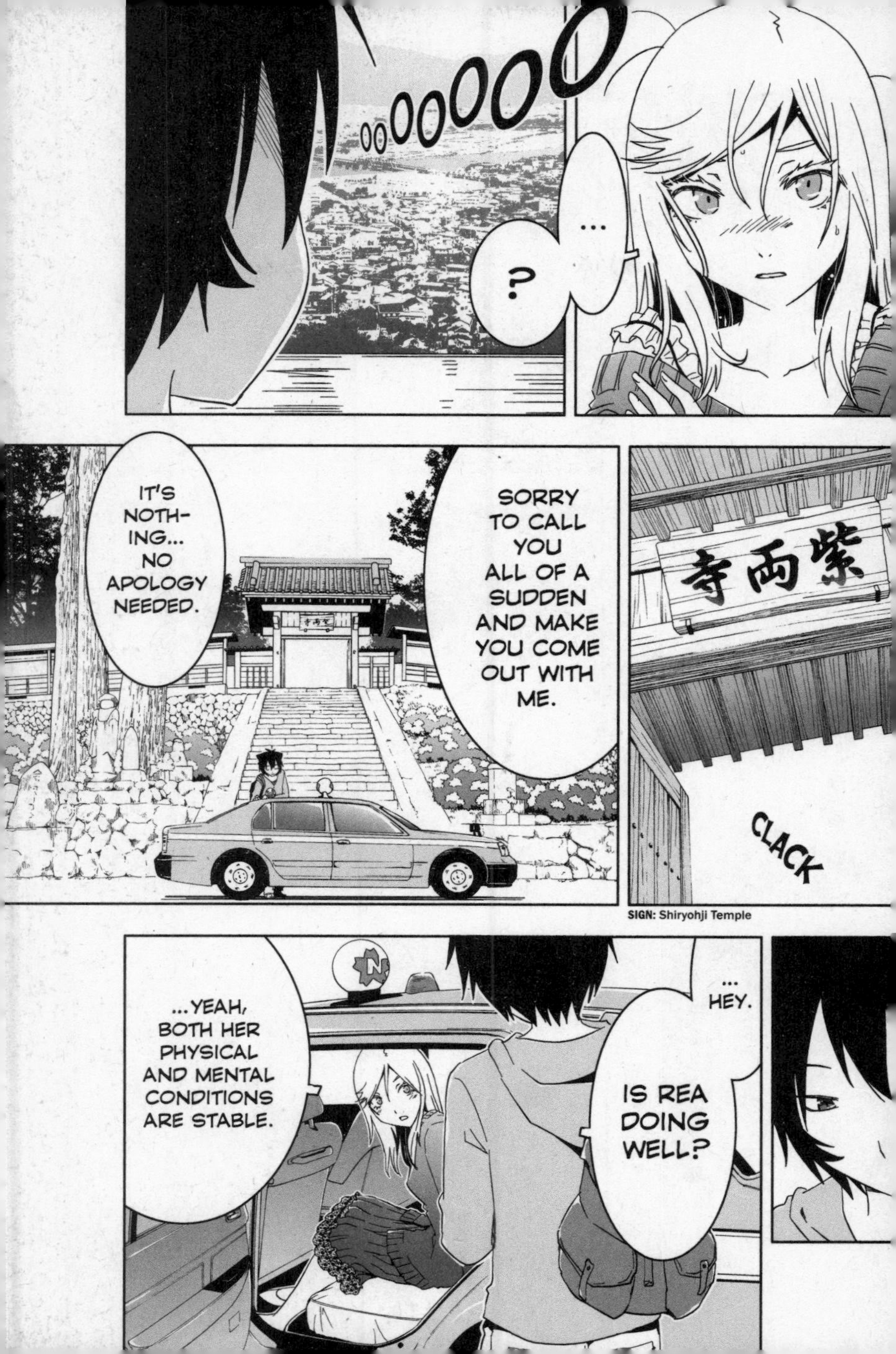
...
?
OOOOOOO
紫両寺
CLACK
SORRY TO CALL YOU ALL OF A SUDDEN AND MAKE YOU COME OUT WITH ME.
IT'S NOTH-ING... NO APOLOGY NEEDED.
...HEY.
IS REA DOING WELL?
...YEAH, BOTH HER PHYSICAL AND MENTAL CONDITIONS ARE STABLE.
SIGN: Shiryohji Temple

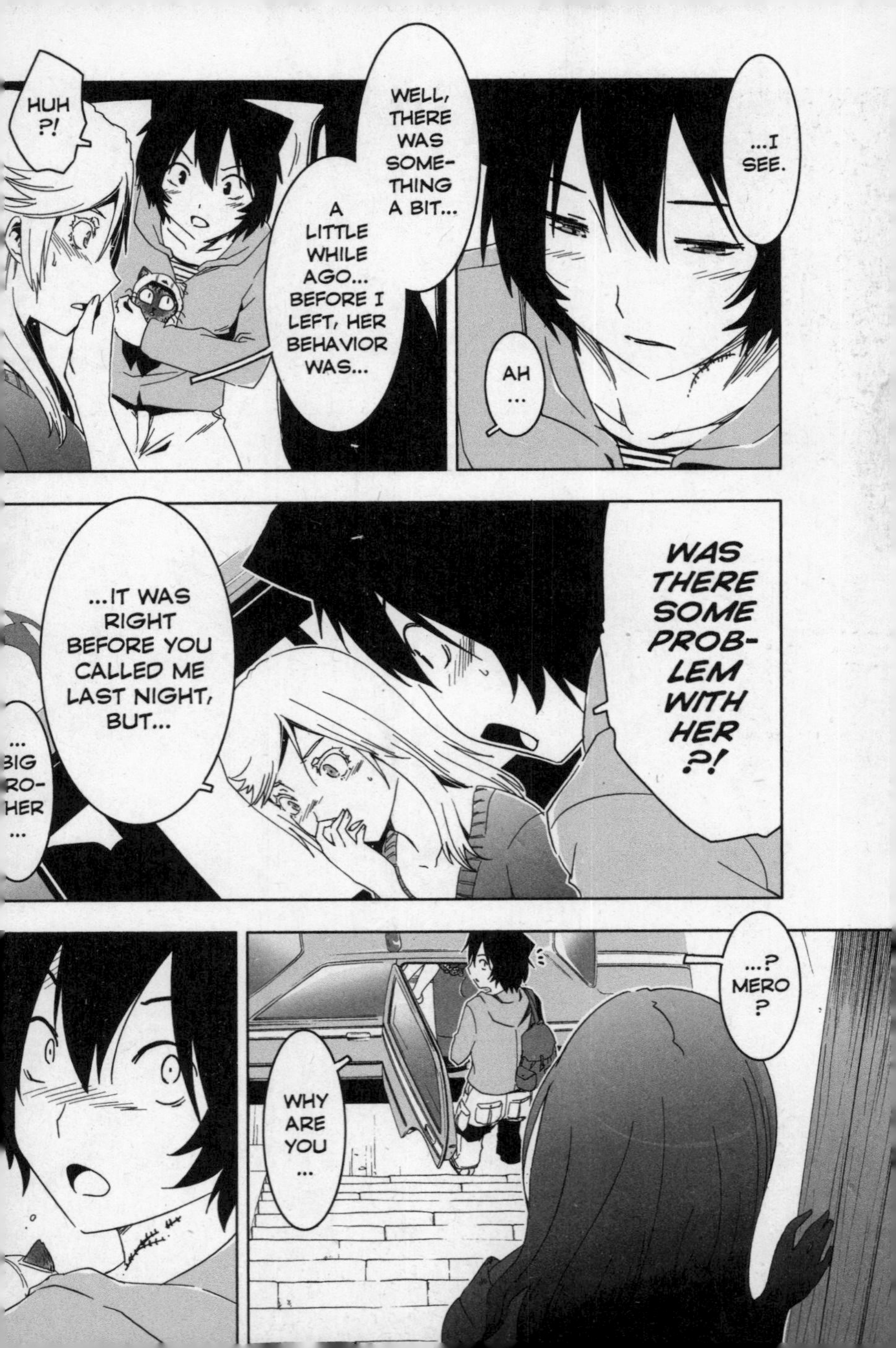
...I SEE.
AH ...
WELL, THERE WAS SOME- THING A BIT...
A LITTLE WHILE AGO... BEFORE I LEFT, HER BEHAVIOR WAS...
HUH ?!
WAS THERE SOME PROB- LEM WITH HER ?!
...IT WAS RIGHT BEFORE YOU CALLED ME LAST NIGHT, BUT...
... BIG RO- HER ...
...? MERO ?
WHY ARE YOU ...

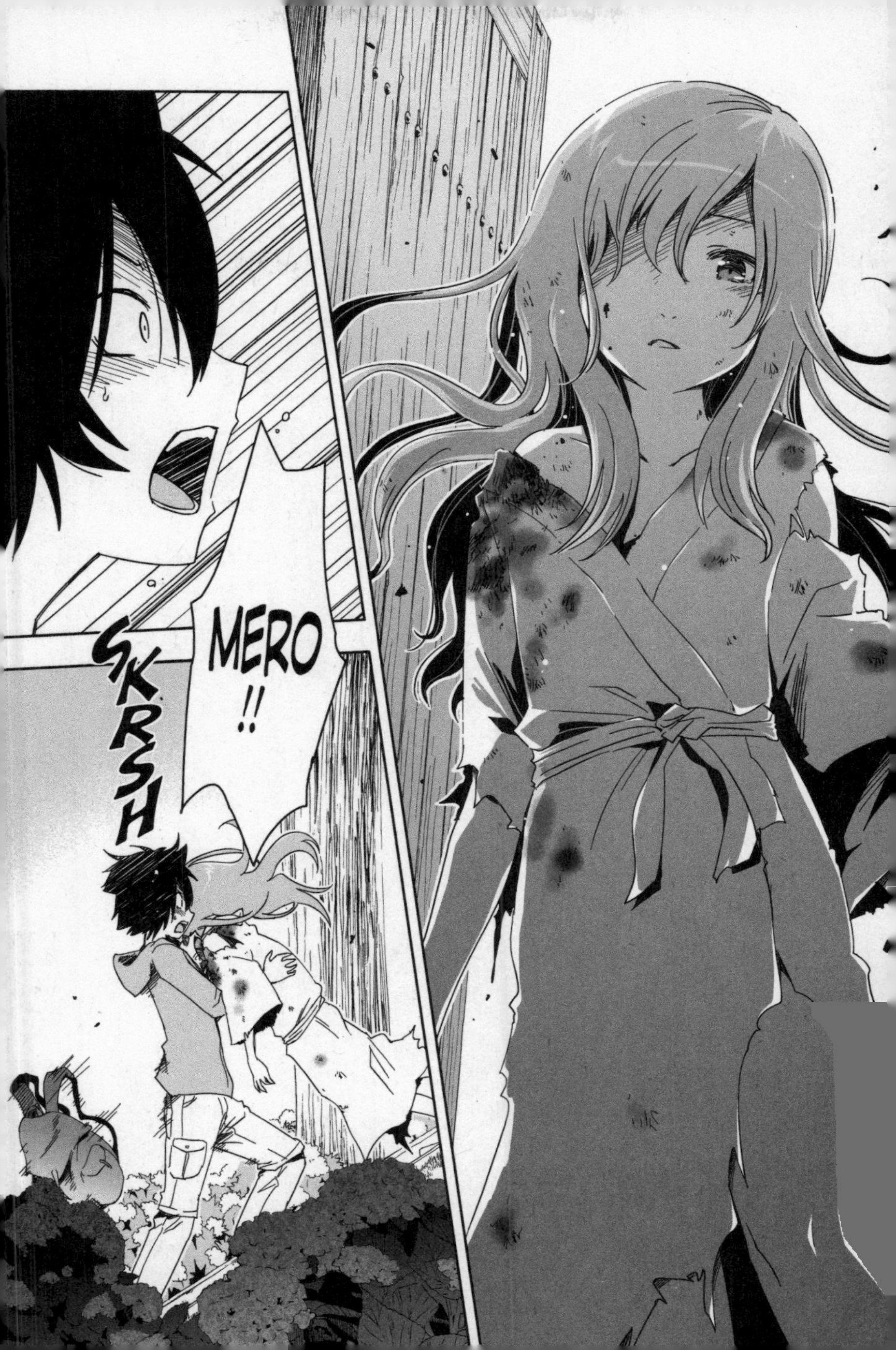
MERO !!
SKRSH

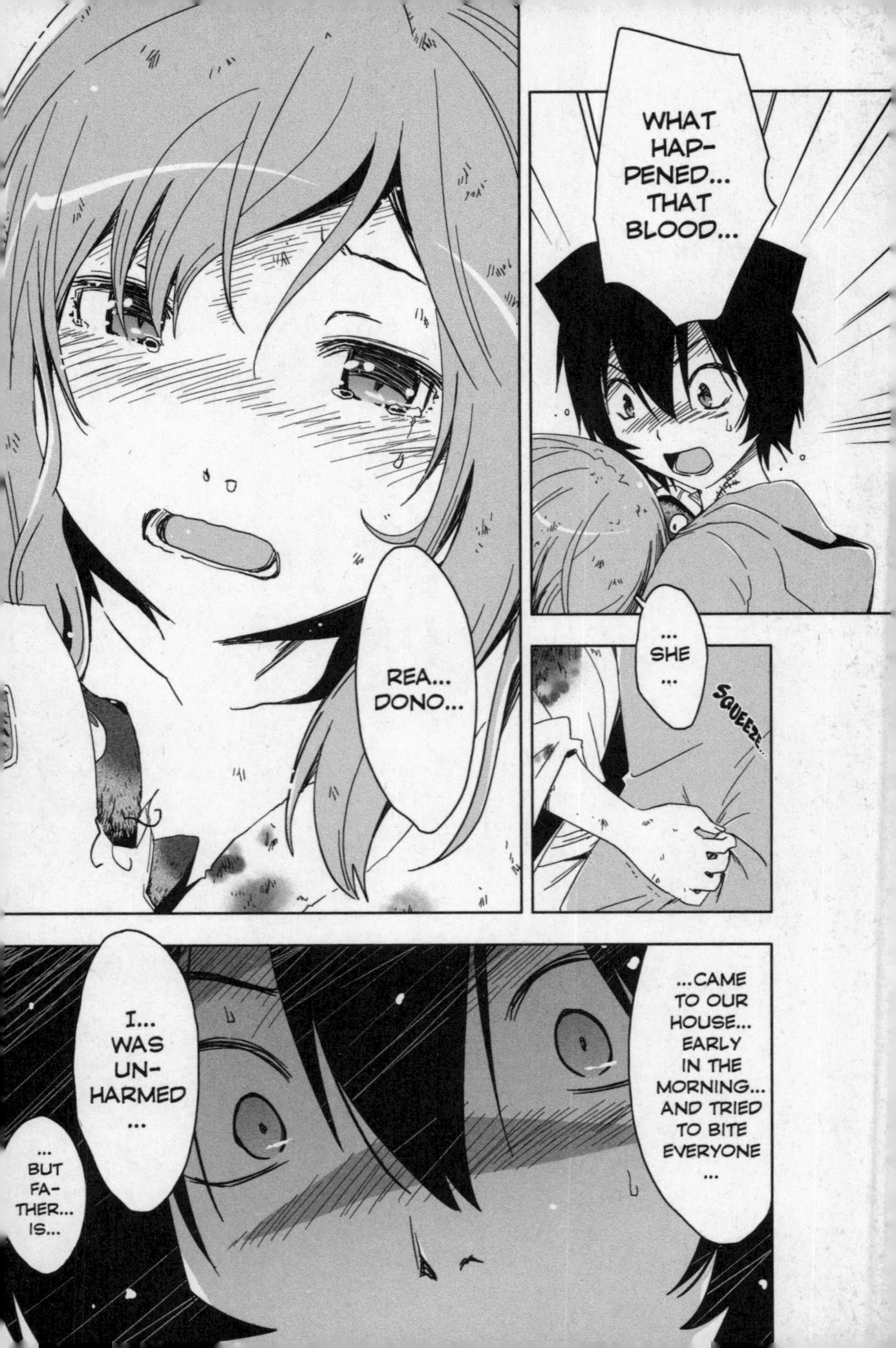
WHAT HAP-PENED... THAT BLOOD...
...SHE...
SQUEEZE...
REA... DONO...
...CAME TO OUR HOUSE... EARLY IN THE MORNING... AND TRIED TO BITE EVERYONE...
I... WAS UN-HARMED...
...BUT FA-THER... IS...

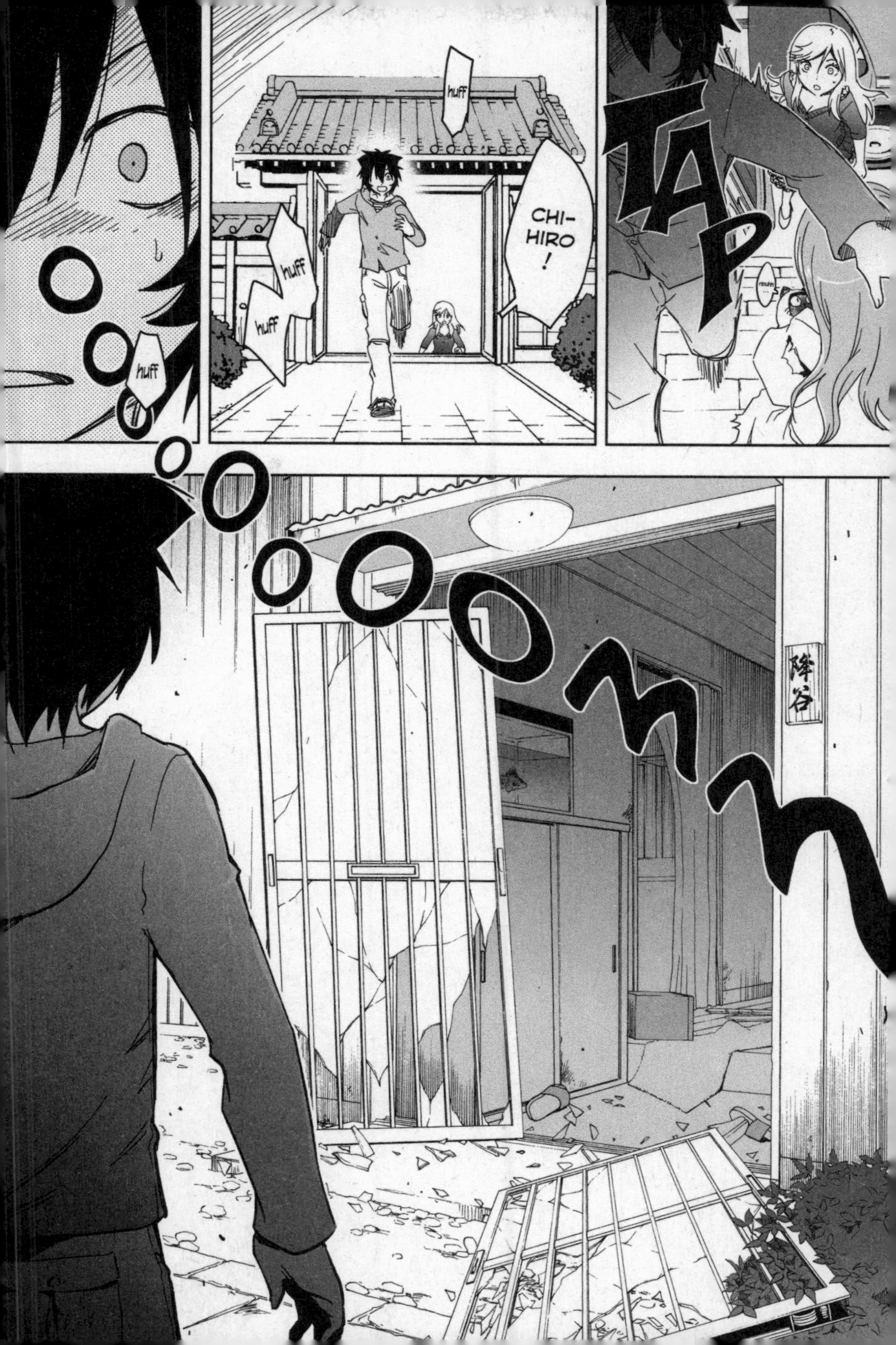
TAP
huff
CHI-HIRO!
huff
huff
huff
降谷

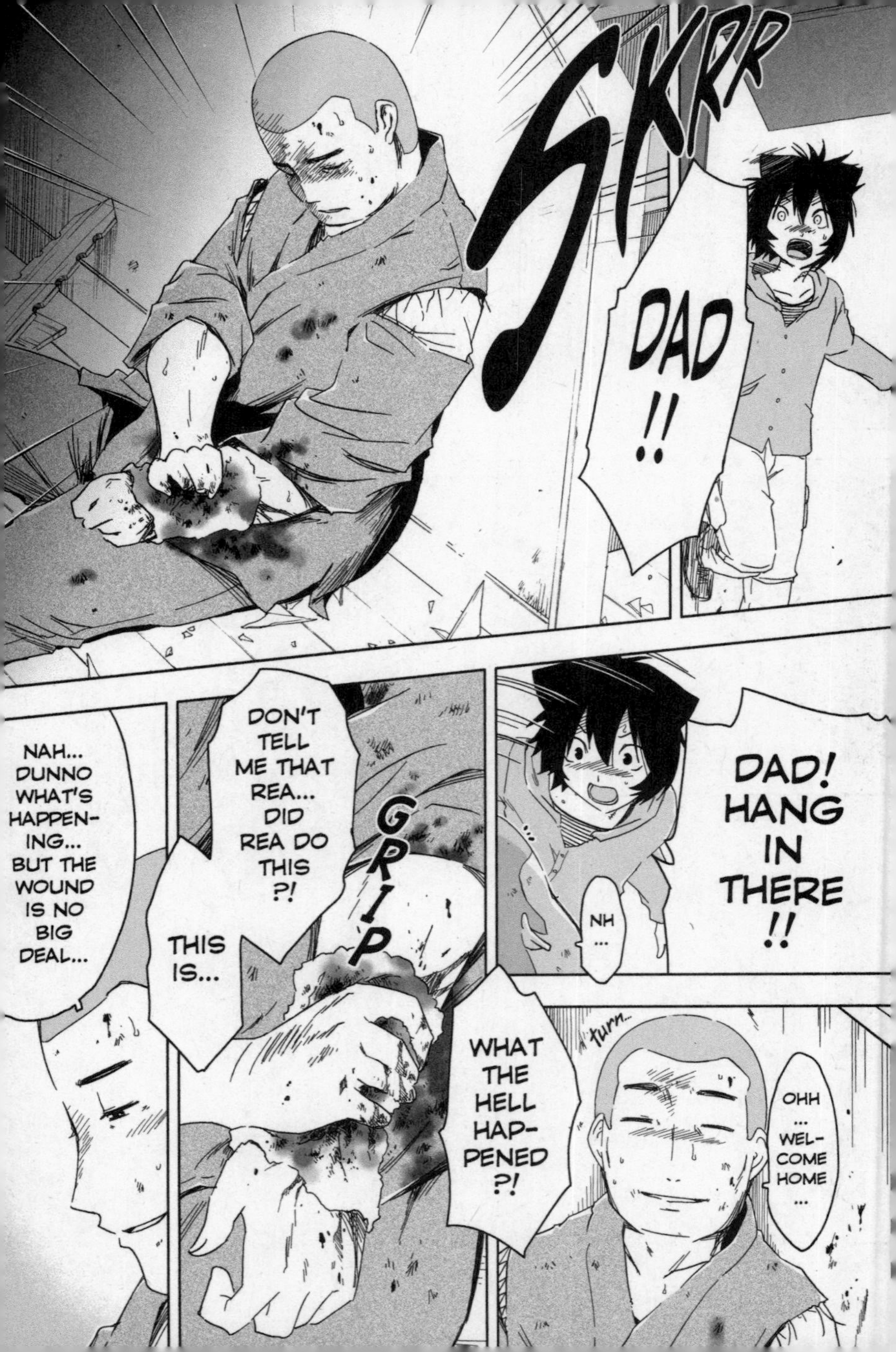
SKRR
DAD!!
DAD! HANG IN THERE!!
NH...
turn..
OHH... WELCOME HOME...
WHAT THE HELL HAPPENED?!
DON'T TELL ME THAT REA... DID REA DO THIS?!
GRIP
THIS IS...
NAH... DUNNO WHAT'S HAPPENING... BUT THE WOUND IS NO BIG DEAL...

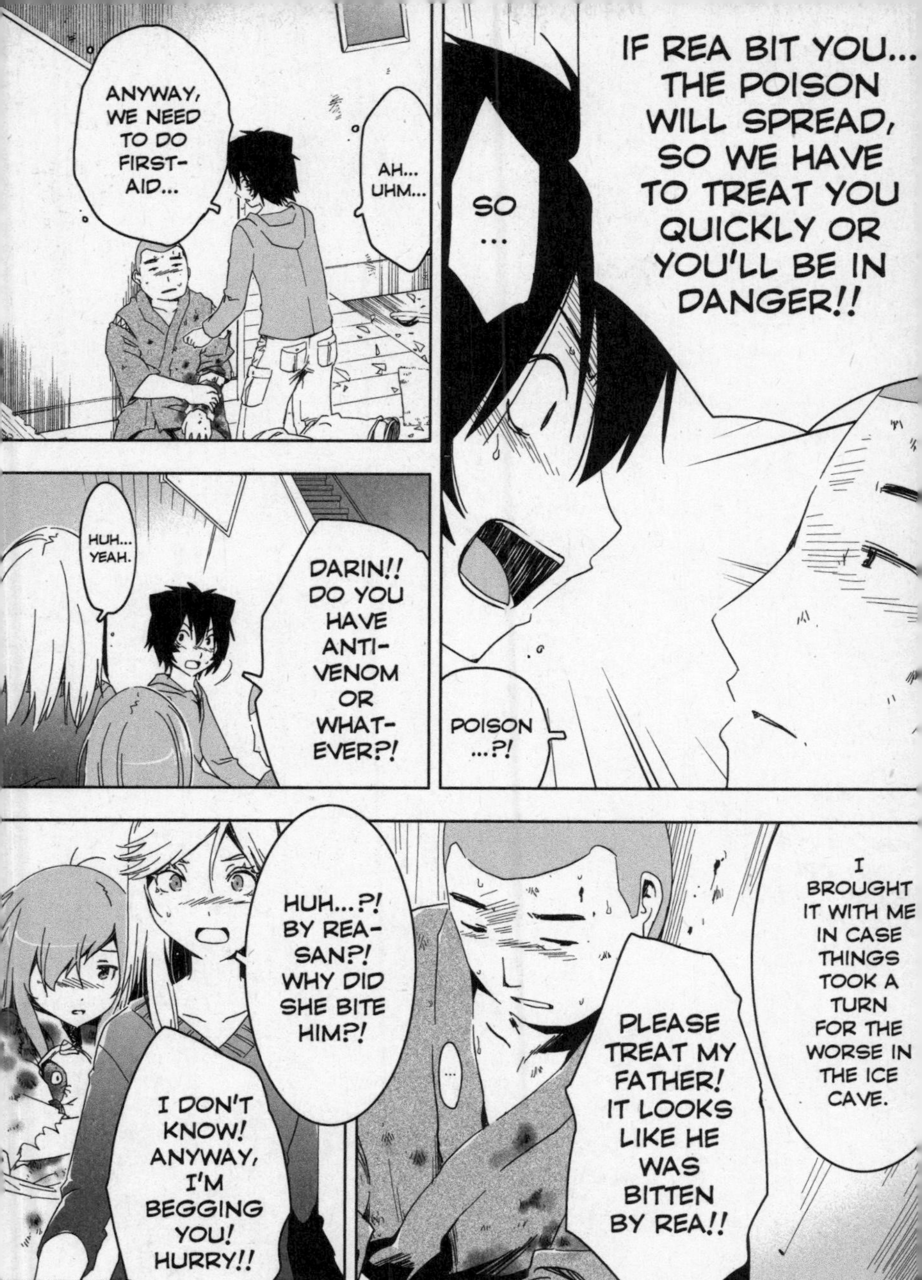
IF REA BIT YOU... THE POISON WILL SPREAD, SO WE HAVE TO TREAT YOU QUICKLY OR YOU'LL BE IN DANGER!!
SO ...
POISON ...?!
AH... UHM...
ANYWAY, WE NEED TO DO FIRST-AID...
DARIN!! DO YOU HAVE ANTI-VENOM OR WHAT-EVER?!
HUH... YEAH.
I BROUGHT IT WITH ME IN CASE THINGS TOOK A TURN FOR THE WORSE IN THE ICE CAVE.
PLEASE TREAT MY FATHER! IT LOOKS LIKE HE WAS BITTEN BY REA!!
...
HUH...?! BY REA-SAN?! WHY DID SHE BITE HIM?!
I DON'T KNOW! ANYWAY, I'M BEGGING YOU! HURRY!!

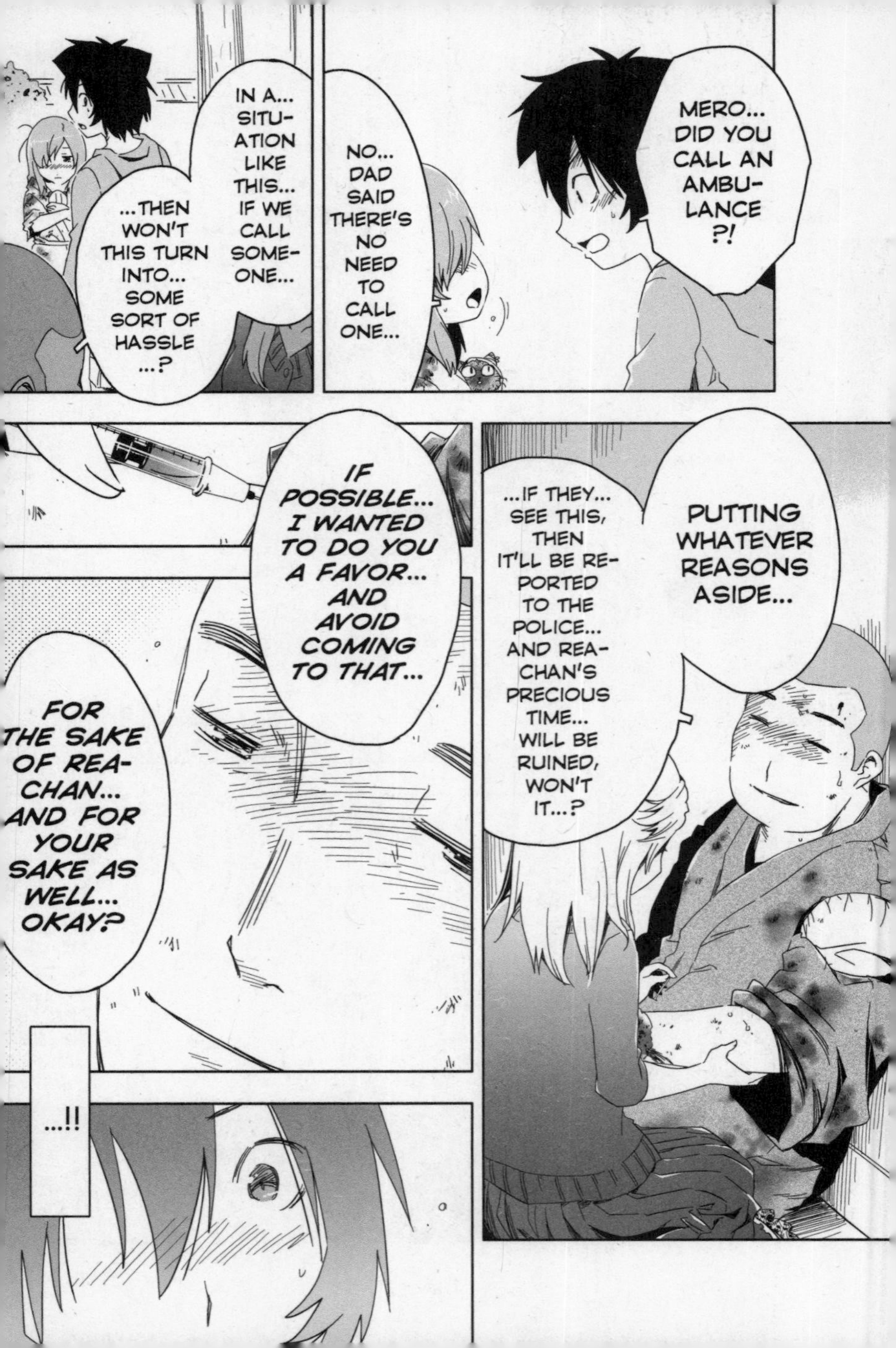
MERO... DID YOU CALL AN AMBULANCE?!
NO... DAD SAID THERE'S NO NEED TO CALL ONE...
IN A... SITUATION LIKE THIS... IF WE CALL SOMEONE...
...THEN WON'T THIS TURN INTO... SOME SORT OF HASSLE...?
PUTTING WHATEVER REASONS ASIDE...
...IF THEY... SEE THIS, THEN IT'LL BE REPORTED TO THE POLICE... AND REA-CHAN'S PRECIOUS TIME... WILL BE RUINED, WON'T IT...?
IF POSSIBLE... I WANTED TO DO YOU A FAVOR... AND AVOID COMING TO THAT...
FOR THE SAKE OF REA-CHAN... AND FOR YOUR SAKE AS WELL... OKAY?
...!!

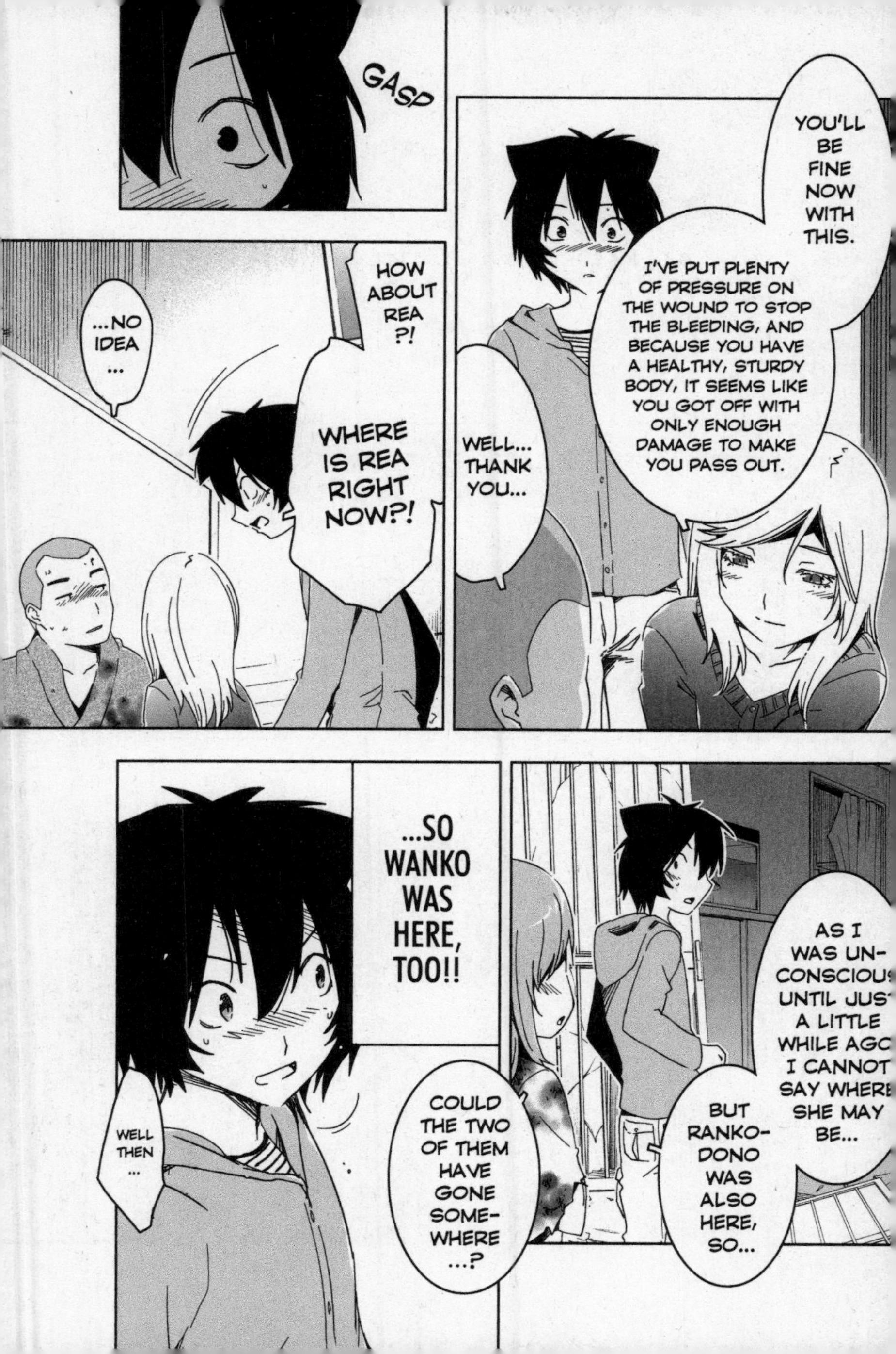
YOU'LL BE FINE NOW WITH THIS.
I'VE PUT PLENTY OF PRESSURE ON THE WOUND TO STOP THE BLEEDING, AND BECAUSE YOU HAVE A HEALTHY, STURDY BODY, IT SEEMS LIKE YOU GOT OFF WITH ONLY ENOUGH DAMAGE TO MAKE YOU PASS OUT.
WELL... THANK YOU...
GASP
HOW ABOUT REA?!
WHERE IS REA RIGHT NOW?!
...NO IDEA...
AS I WAS UN-CONSCIOUS UNTIL JUST A LITTLE WHILE AGO I CANNOT SAY WHERE SHE MAY BE...
BUT RANKO-DONO WAS ALSO HERE, SO...
COULD THE TWO OF THEM HAVE GONE SOME-WHERE...?
...SO WANKO WAS HERE, TOO!!
WELL THEN...

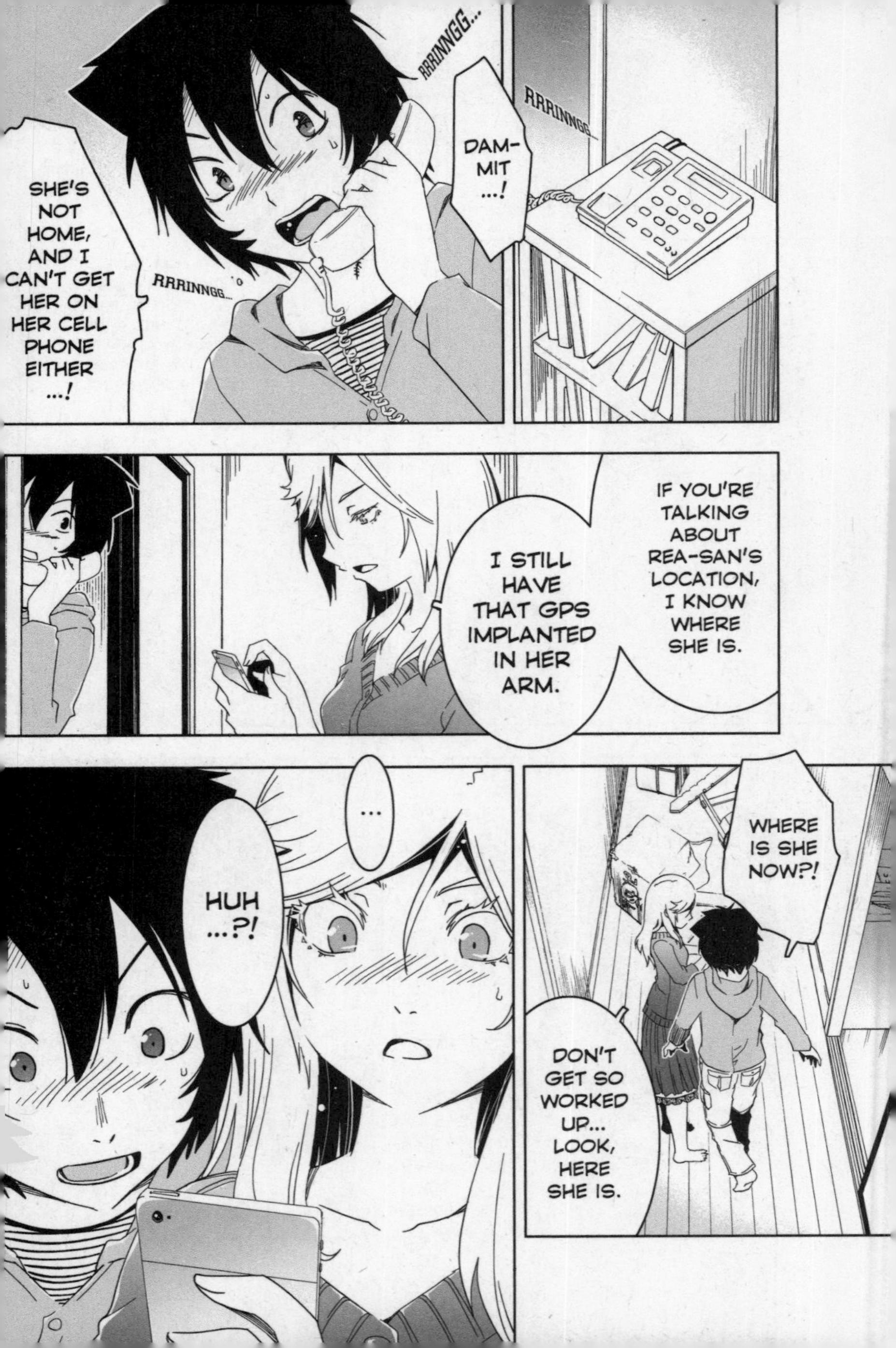
RRRINNGG...
RRRINNGG...
DAM-MIT ...!
RRRINNGG...
SHE'S NOT HOME, AND I CAN'T GET HER ON HER CELL PHONE EITHER ...!
IF YOU'RE TALKING ABOUT REA-SAN'S LOCATION, I KNOW WHERE SHE IS.
I STILL HAVE THAT GPS IMPLANTED IN HER ARM.
WHERE IS SHE NOW?!
DON'T GET SO WORKED UP... LOOK, HERE SHE IS.
...
HUH ...?!

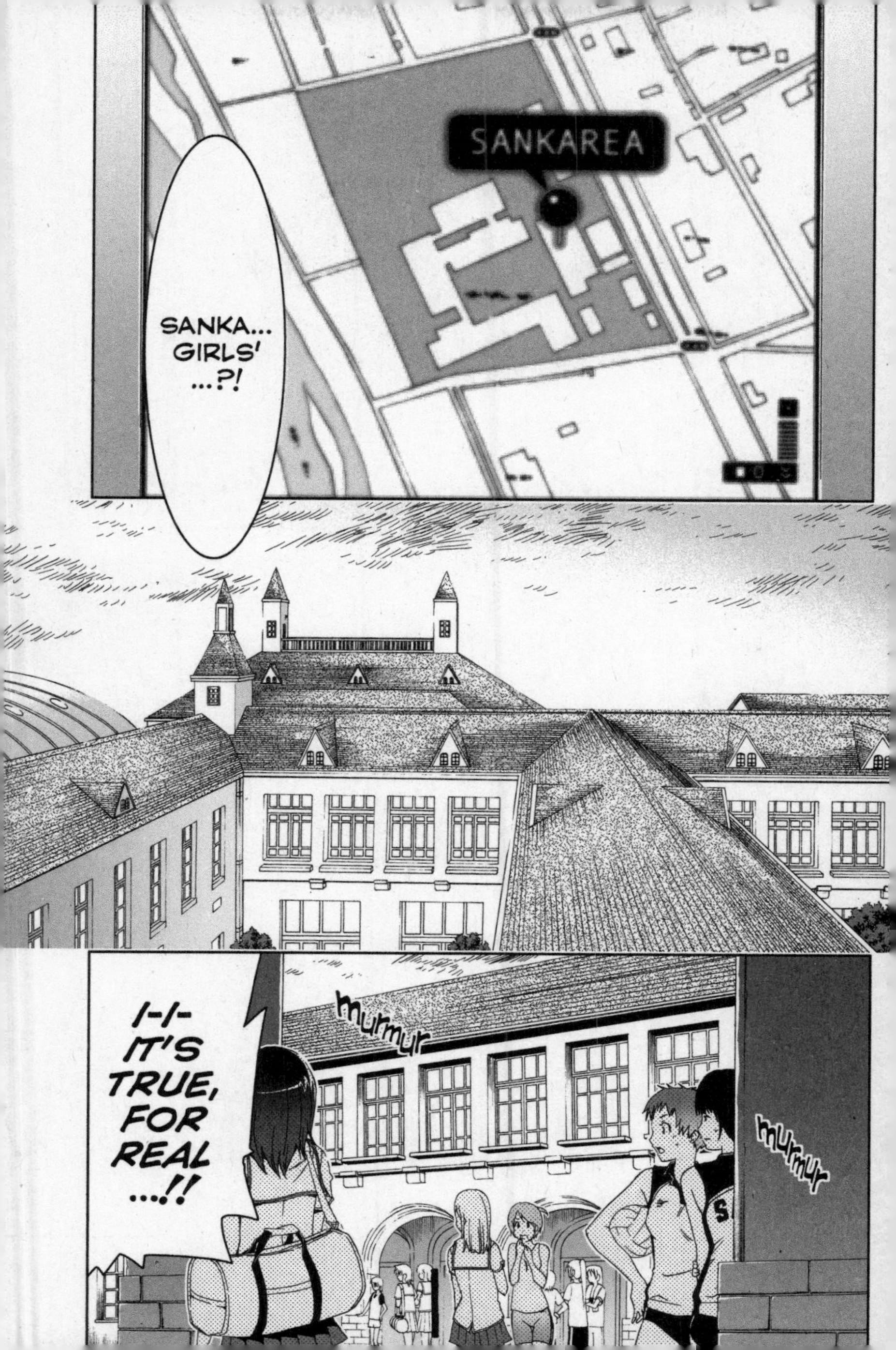
SANKAREA
SANKA... GIRLS' ...?!
murmur
murmur
I-I-IT'S TRUE, FOR REAL...!!

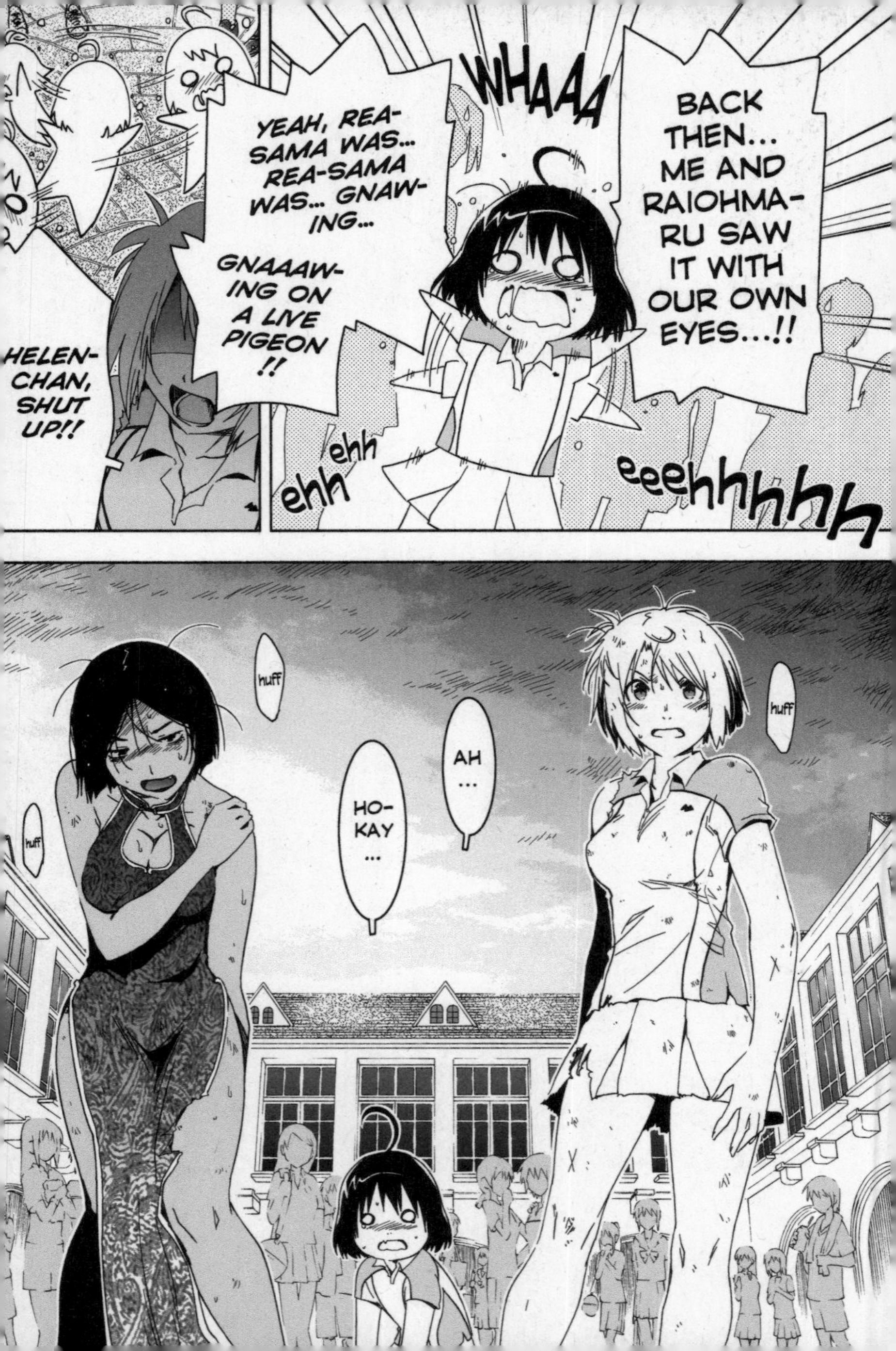
BACK THEN... ME AND RAIOHMA-RU SAW IT WITH OUR OWN EYES...!!
WHAAAA
eeehhhhhh
YEAH, REA-SAMA WAS... REA-SAMA WAS... GNAW-ING...
GNAAAW-ING ON A LIVE PIGEON !!
ehh
ehh
HELEN-CHAN, SHUT UP!!
huff
AH ...
HO-KAY ...
huff
huff

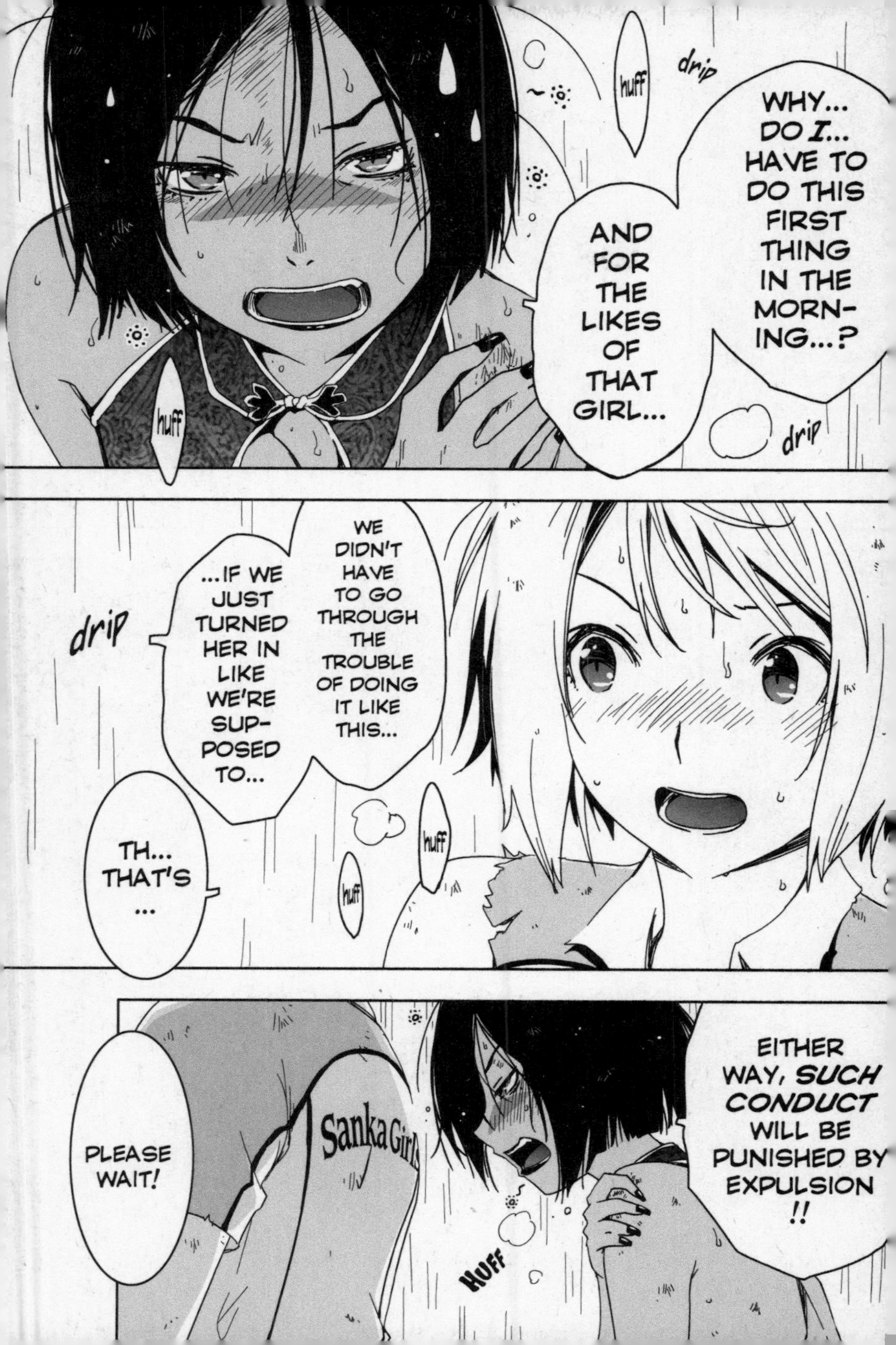
drip
WHY... DO *I*... HAVE TO DO THIS FIRST THING IN THE MORNING...?
huff
AND FOR THE LIKES OF THAT GIRL...
drip
huff
WE DIDN'T HAVE TO GO THROUGH THE TROUBLE OF DOING IT LIKE THIS...
...IF WE JUST TURNED HER IN LIKE WE'RE SUPPOSED TO...
huff
huff
drip
TH... THAT'S ...
EITHER WAY, *SUCH CONDUCT* WILL BE PUNISHED BY EXPULSION!!
HUFF
Sanka Girls
PLEASE WAIT!

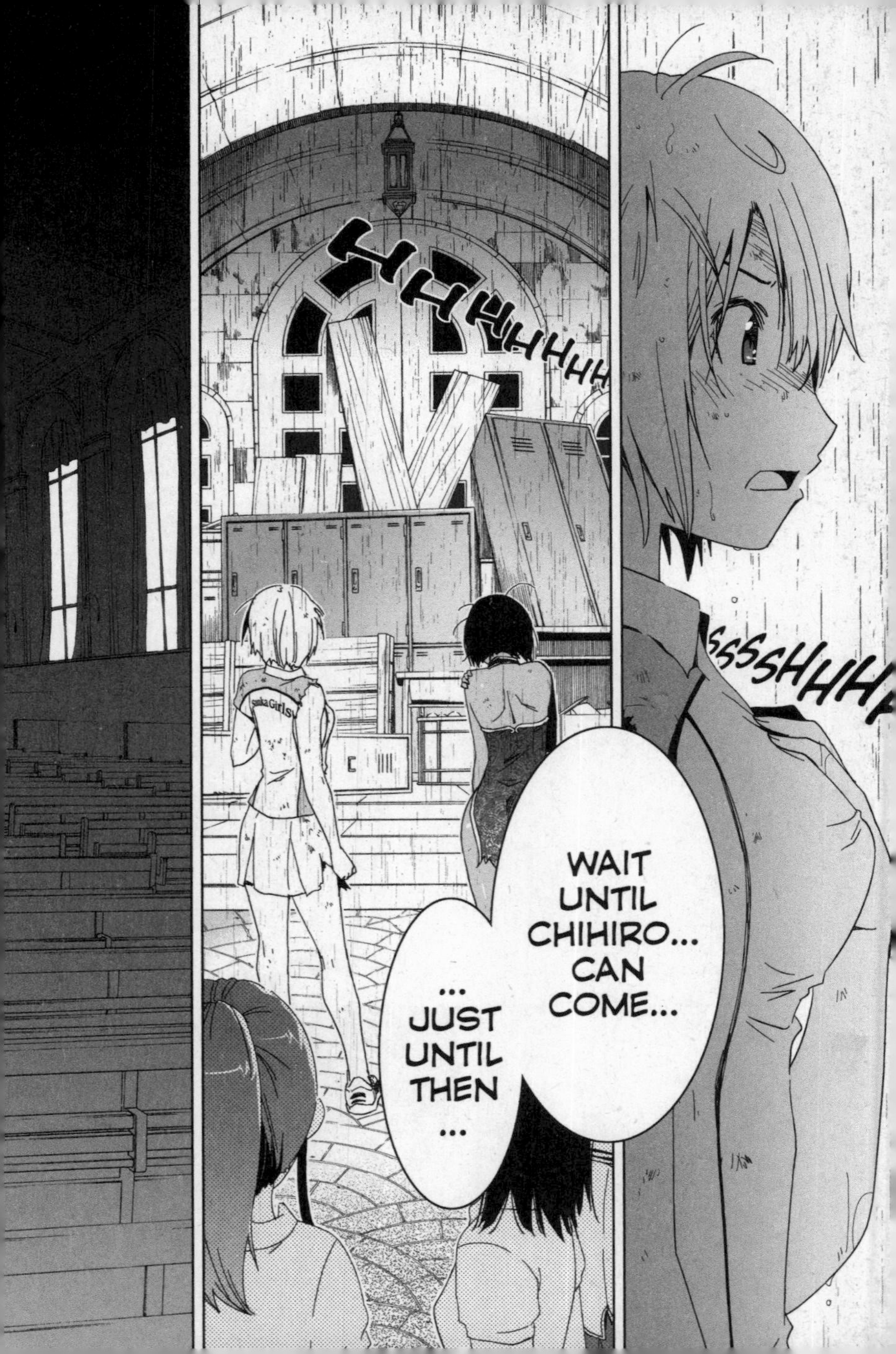
SSSSHHH
WAIT UNTIL CHIHIRO... CAN COME...
...JUST UNTIL THEN...
HHHHHHHH

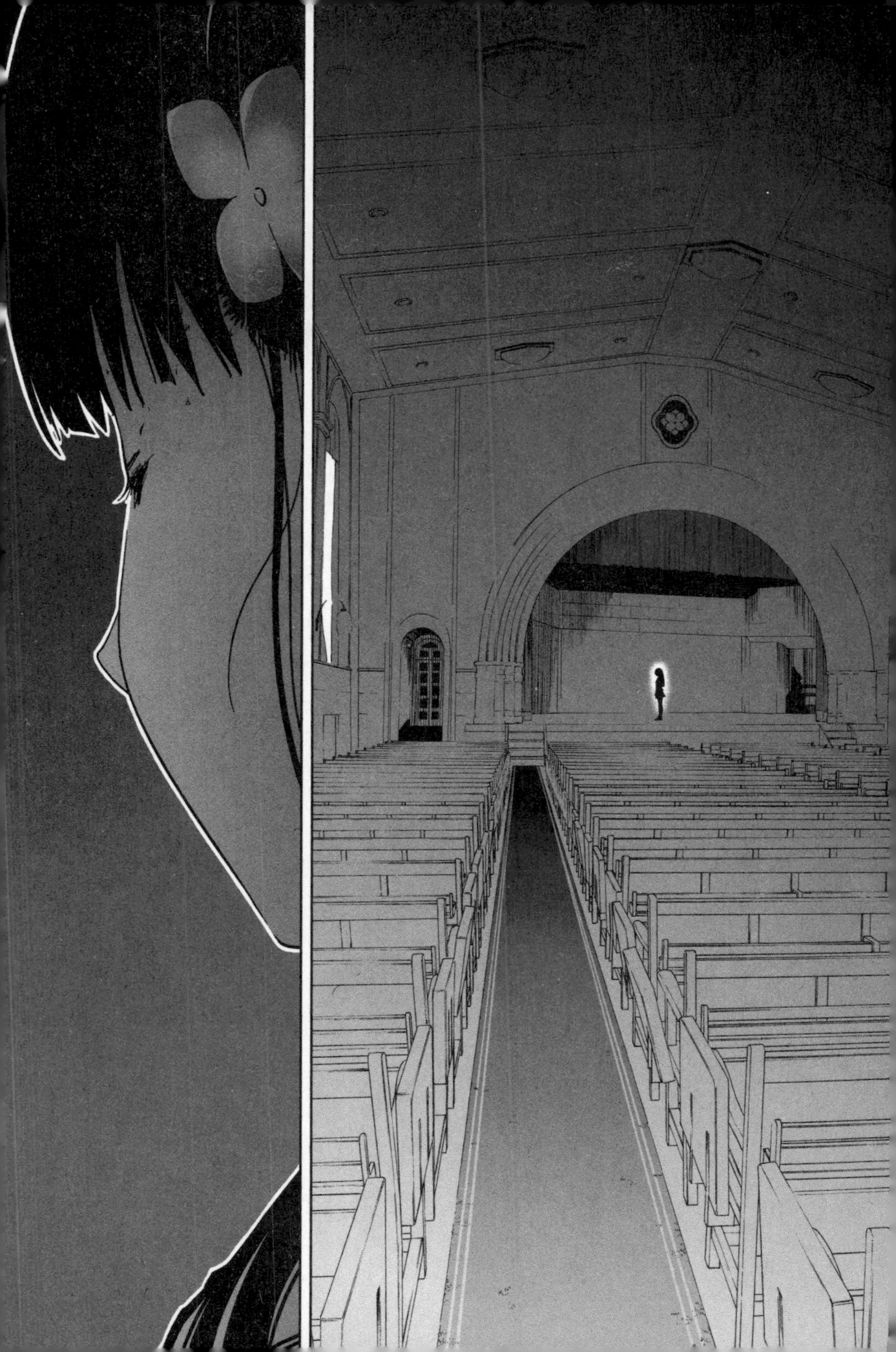

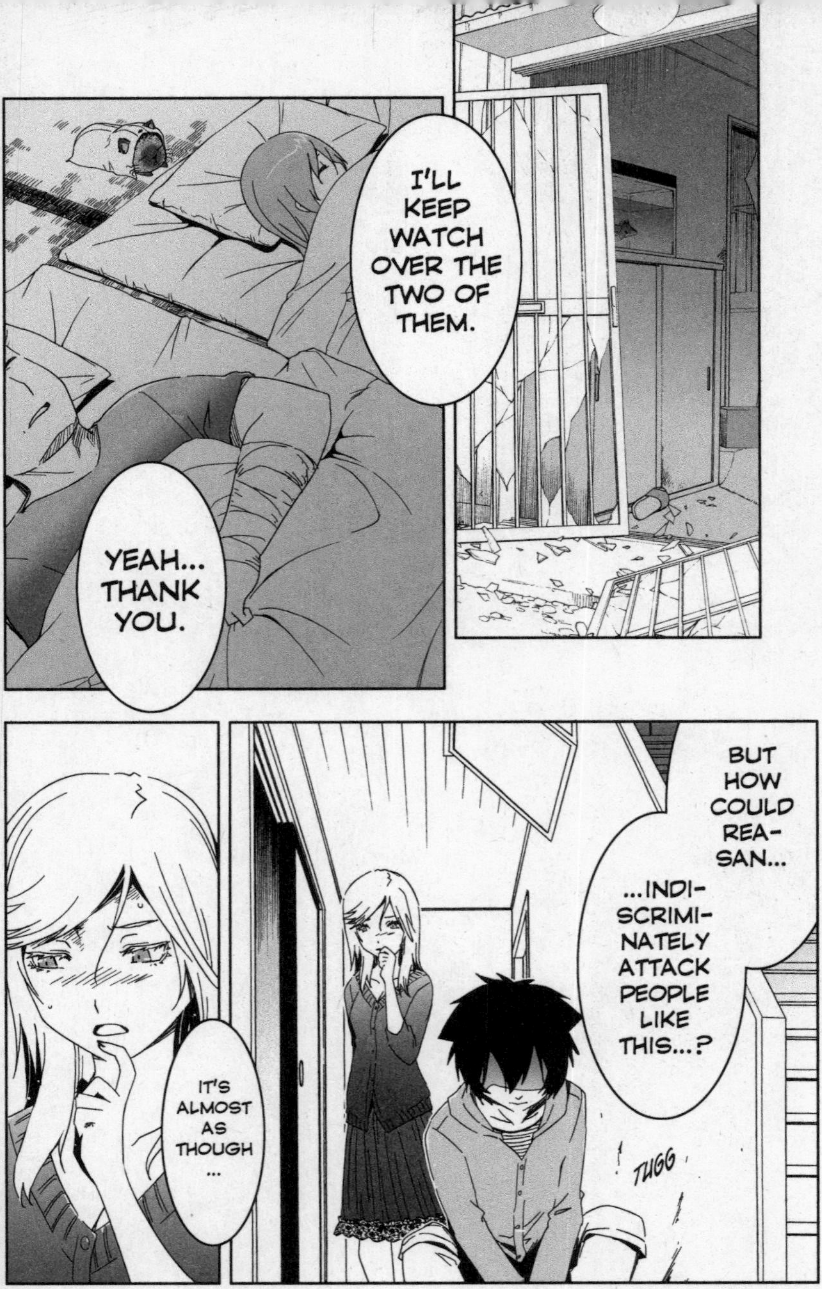
I'LL KEEP WATCH OVER THE TWO OF THEM.
YEAH... THANK YOU.
BUT HOW COULD REA-SAN...
...INDI-SCRIMI-NATELY ATTACK PEOPLE LIKE THIS...?
TUGG
IT'S ALMOST AS THOUGH ...

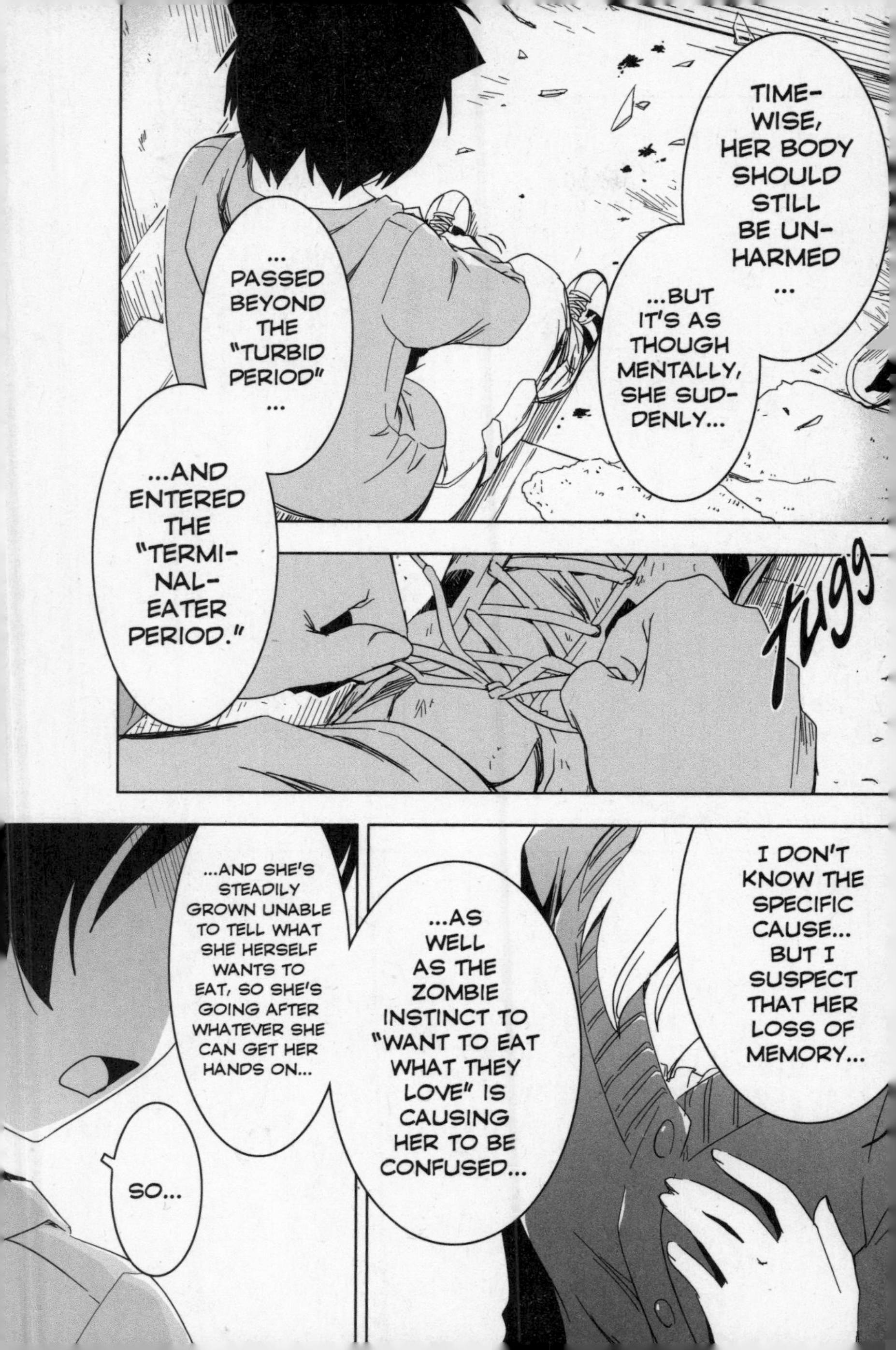
TIME-WISE, HER BODY SHOULD STILL BE UNHARMED ...
...BUT IT'S AS THOUGH MENTALLY, SHE SUDDENLY...
... PASSED BEYOND THE "TURBID PERIOD" ...
...AND ENTERED THE "TERMINAL-EATER PERIOD."
Tugg
I DON'T KNOW THE SPECIFIC CAUSE... BUT I SUSPECT THAT HER LOSS OF MEMORY...
...AS WELL AS THE ZOMBIE INSTINCT TO "WANT TO EAT WHAT THEY LOVE" IS CAUSING HER TO BE CONFUSED...
...AND SHE'S STEADILY GROWN UNABLE TO TELL WHAT SHE HERSELF WANTS TO EAT, SO SHE'S GOING AFTER WHATEVER SHE CAN GET HER HANDS ON...
SO...

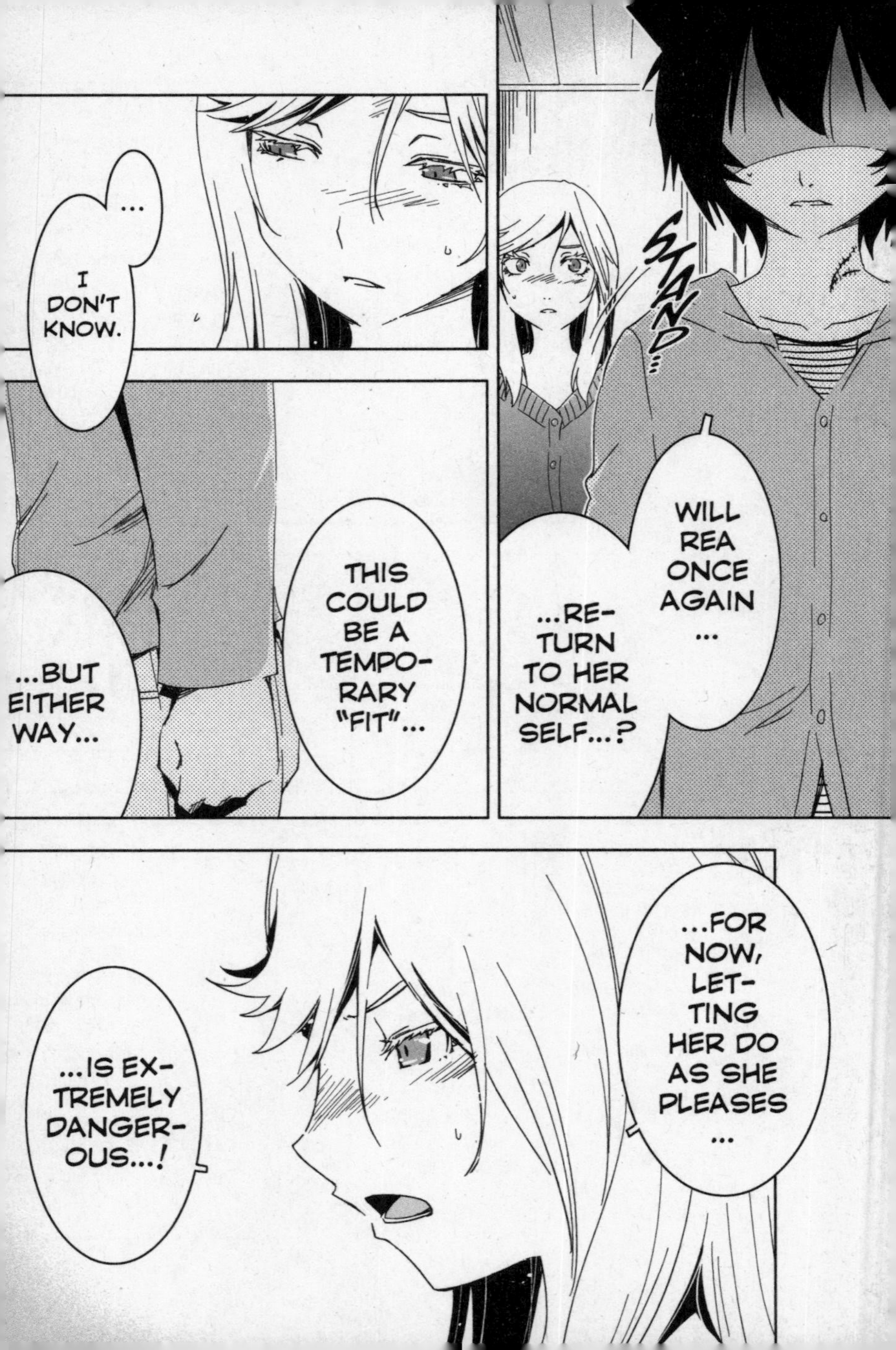
STAND...
WILL REA ONCE AGAIN ...
...RE-TURN TO HER NORMAL SELF...?
...
I DON'T KNOW.
THIS COULD BE A TEMPO-RARY "FIT"...
...BUT EITHER WAY...
...FOR NOW, LET-TING HER DO AS SHE PLEASES ...
...IS EX-TREMELY DANGER-OUS...!

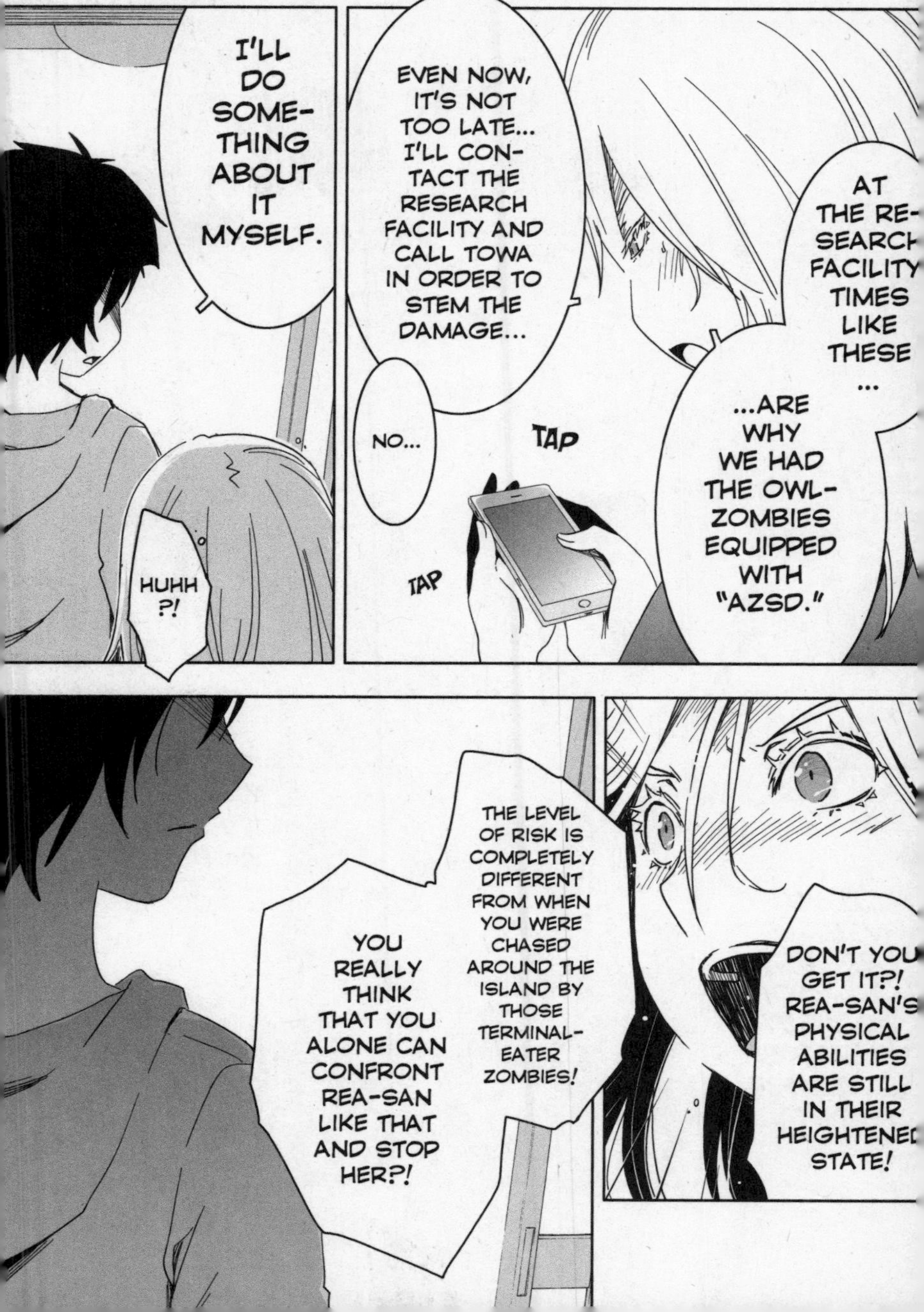
AT THE RE-SEARCH FACILITY TIMES LIKE THESE...
...ARE WHY WE HAD THE OWL-ZOMBIES EQUIPPED WITH "AZSD."
EVEN NOW, IT'S NOT TOO LATE... I'LL CON-TACT THE RESEARCH FACILITY AND CALL TOWA IN ORDER TO STEM THE DAMAGE...
TAP
NO...
TAP
I'LL DO SOME-THING ABOUT IT MYSELF.
HUHH?!
DON'T YOU GET IT?! REA-SAN'S PHYSICAL ABILITIES ARE STILL IN THEIR HEIGHTENED STATE!
THE LEVEL OF RISK IS COMPLETELY DIFFERENT FROM WHEN YOU WERE CHASED AROUND THE ISLAND BY THOSE TERMINAL-EATER ZOMBIES!
YOU REALLY THINK THAT YOU ALONE CAN CONFRONT REA-SAN LIKE THAT AND STOP HER?!

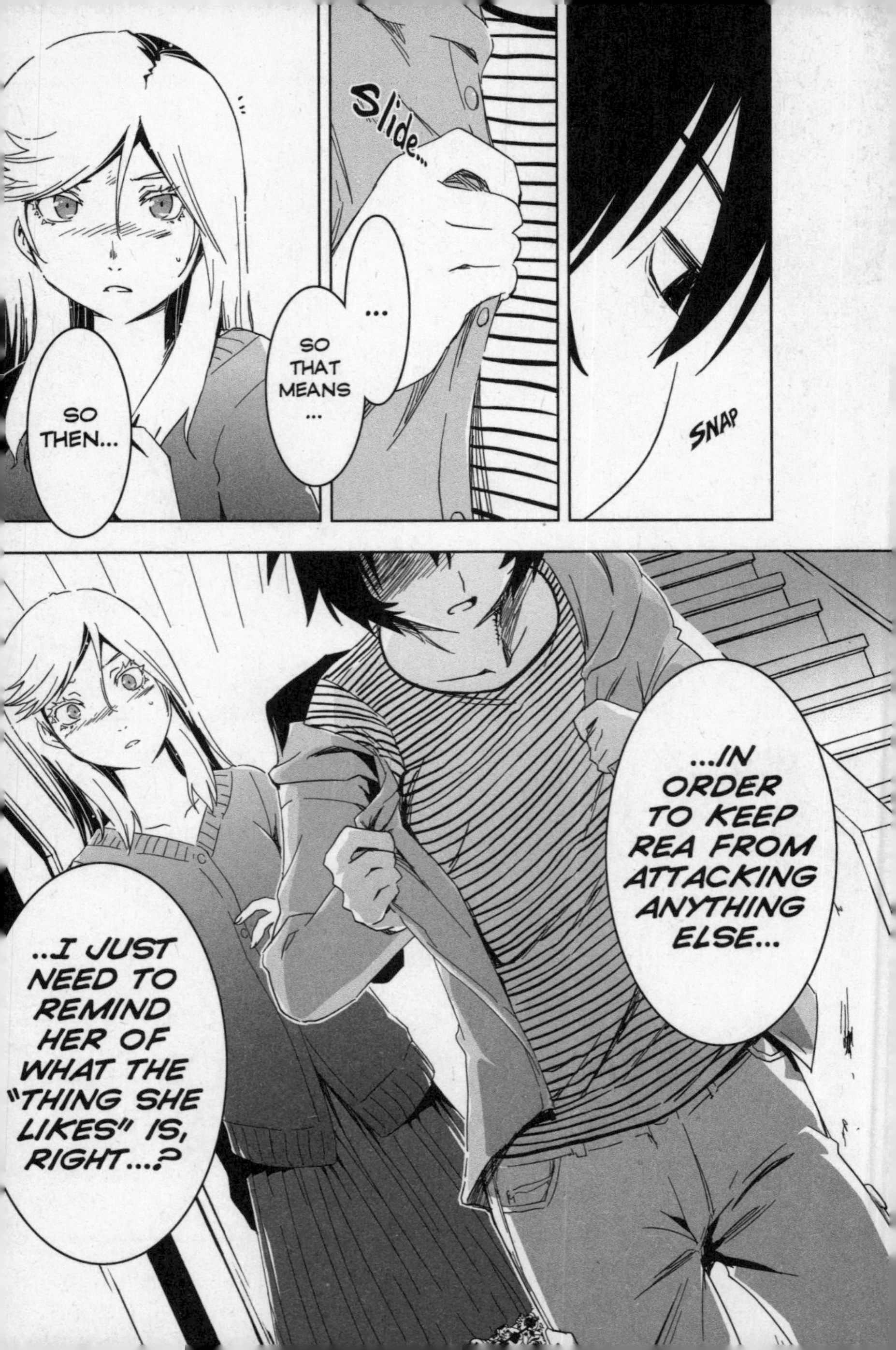
SNAP
Slide...
...
SO THAT MEANS...
SO THEN...
...IN ORDER TO KEEP REA FROM ATTACKING ANYTHING ELSE...
...I JUST NEED TO REMIND HER OF WHAT THE "THING SHE LIKES" IS, RIGHT...?

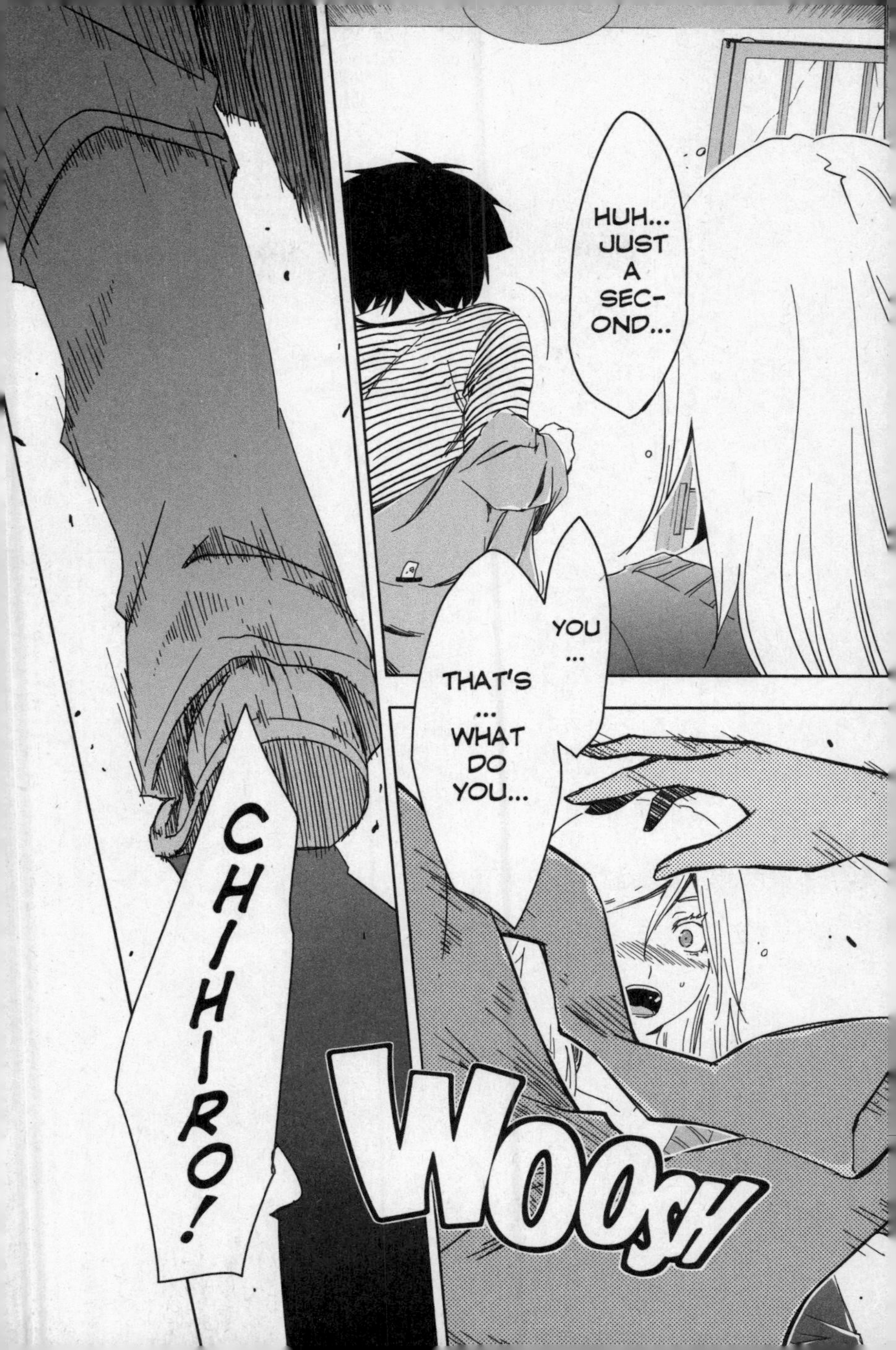
HUH... JUST A SEC-OND...
YOU ... THAT'S ... WHAT DO YOU...
WOOSH
CHIHIRO!

SANKAREA

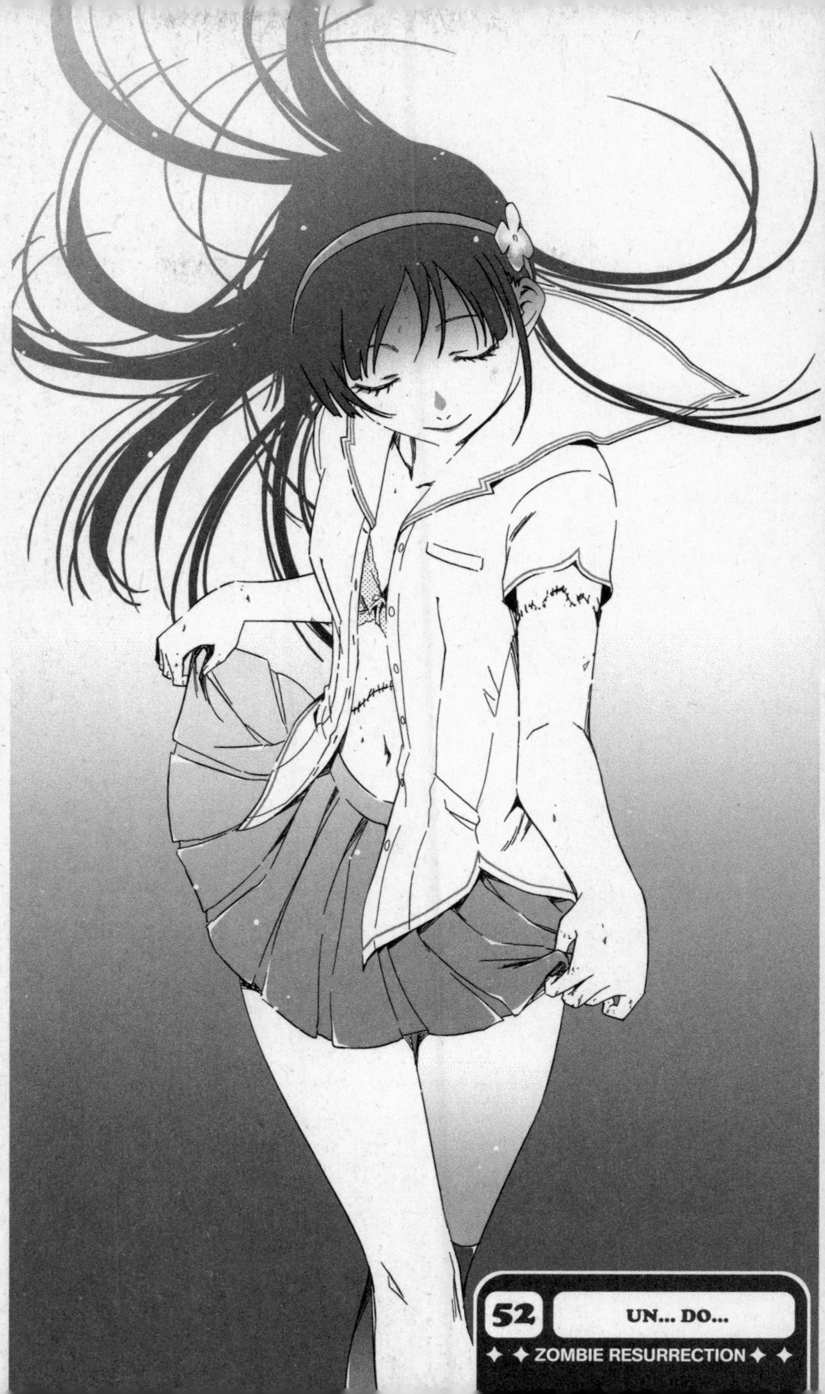
52
UN... DO...
ZOMBIE RESURRECTION

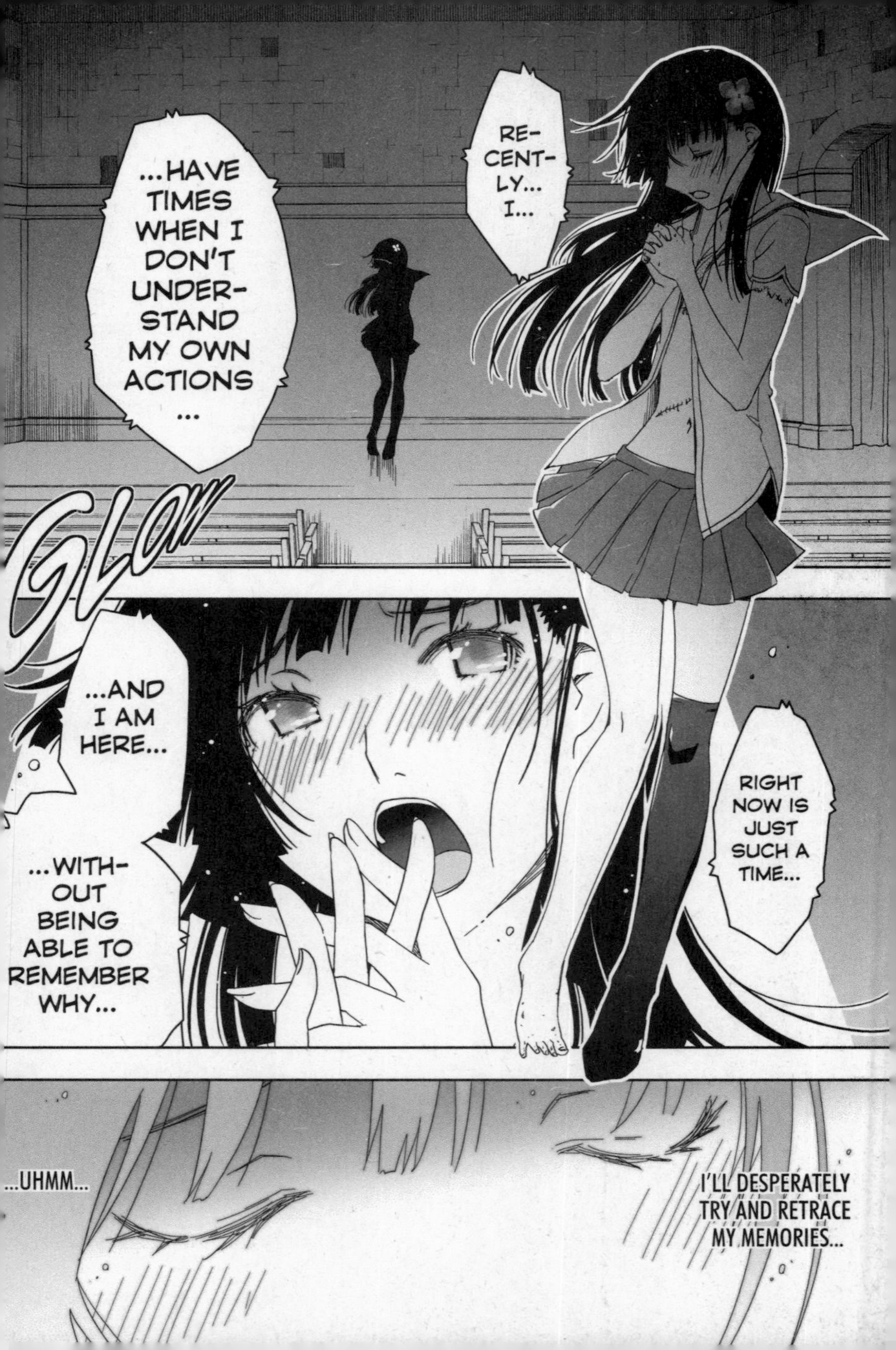

RE-CENT-LY... I...
...HAVE TIMES WHEN I DON'T UNDER-STAND MY OWN ACTIONS ...
RIGHT NOW IS JUST SUCH A TIME...
...AND I AM HERE...
...WITH-OUT BEING ABLE TO REMEMBER WHY...
I'LL DESPERATELY TRY AND RETRACE MY MEMORIES...
...UHMM...

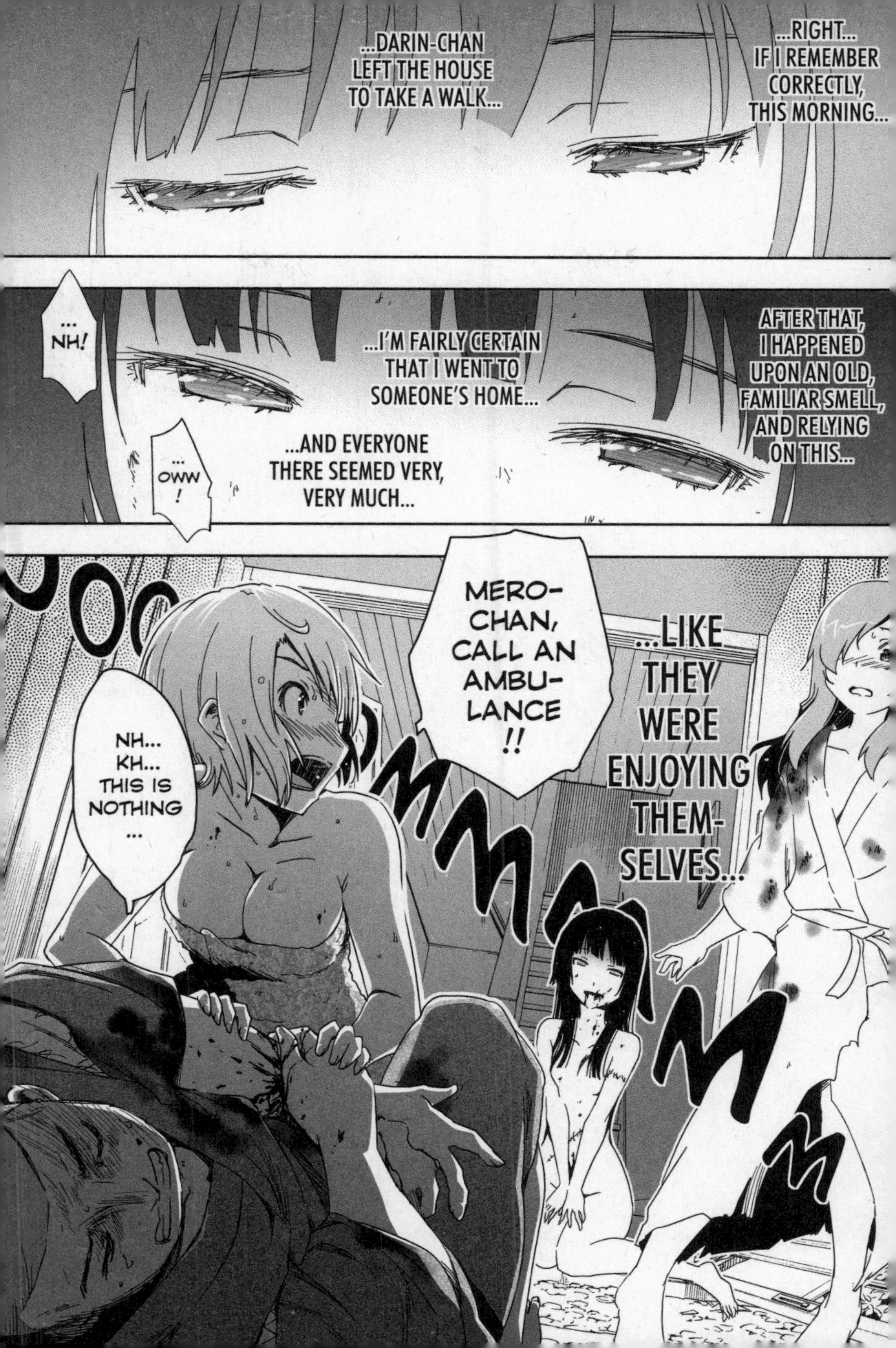
...RIGHT... IF I REMEMBER CORRECTLY, THIS MORNING...
...DARIN-CHAN LEFT THE HOUSE TO TAKE A WALK...
AFTER THAT, I HAPPENED UPON AN OLD, FAMILIAR SMELL, AND RELYING ON THIS...
...I'M FAIRLY CERTAIN THAT I WENT TO SOMEONE'S HOME...
...AND EVERYONE THERE SEEMED VERY, VERY MUCH...
... NH!
... OWW!
...LIKE THEY WERE ENJOYING THEMSELVES...
MERO-CHAN, CALL AN AMBULANCE!!
NH... KH... THIS IS NOTHING...

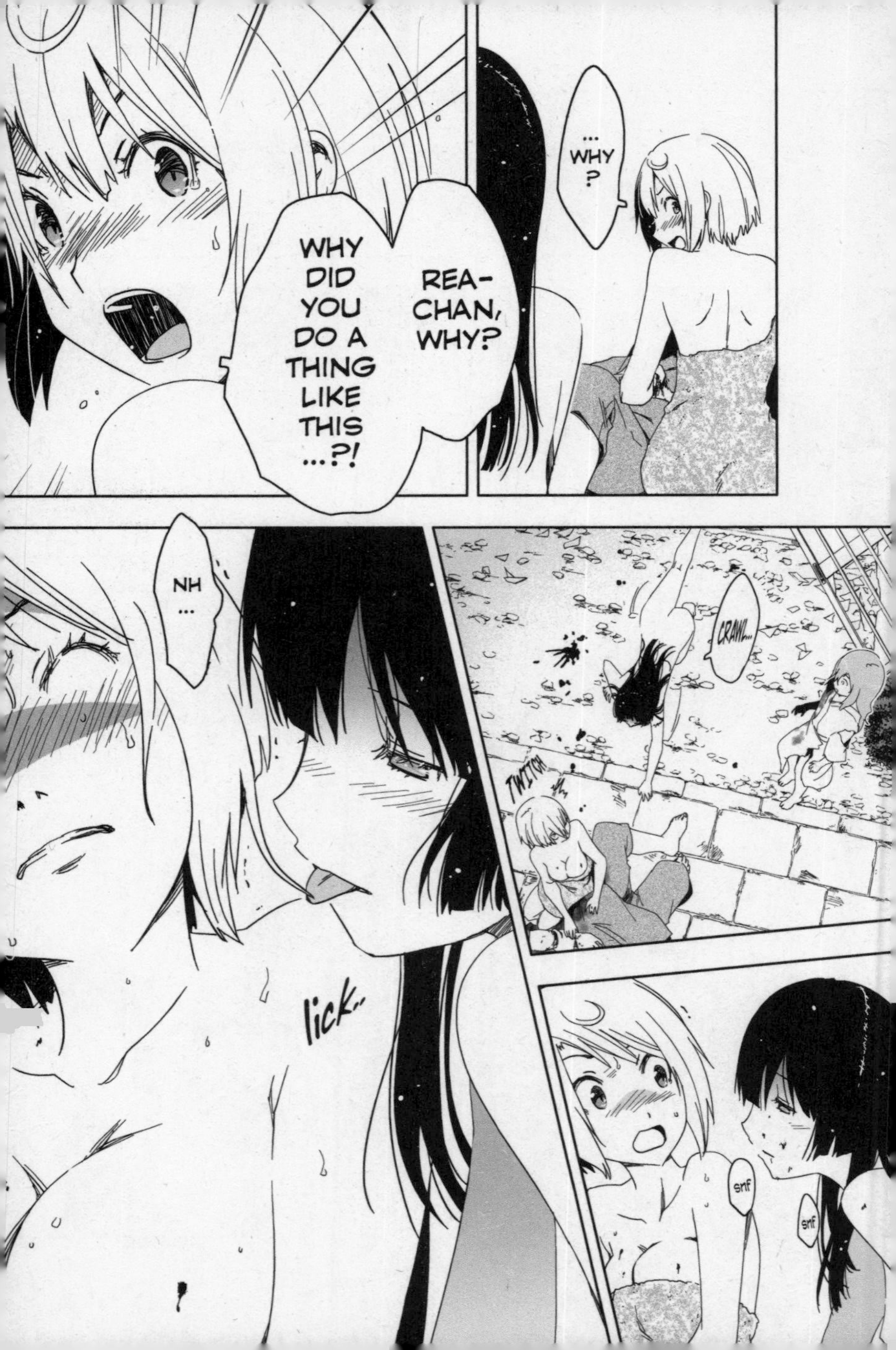

...WHY?
REA-CHAN, WHY?
WHY DID YOU DO A THING LIKE THIS ...?!
CRAWL...
TWITCH
snf
snf
NH...
lick..

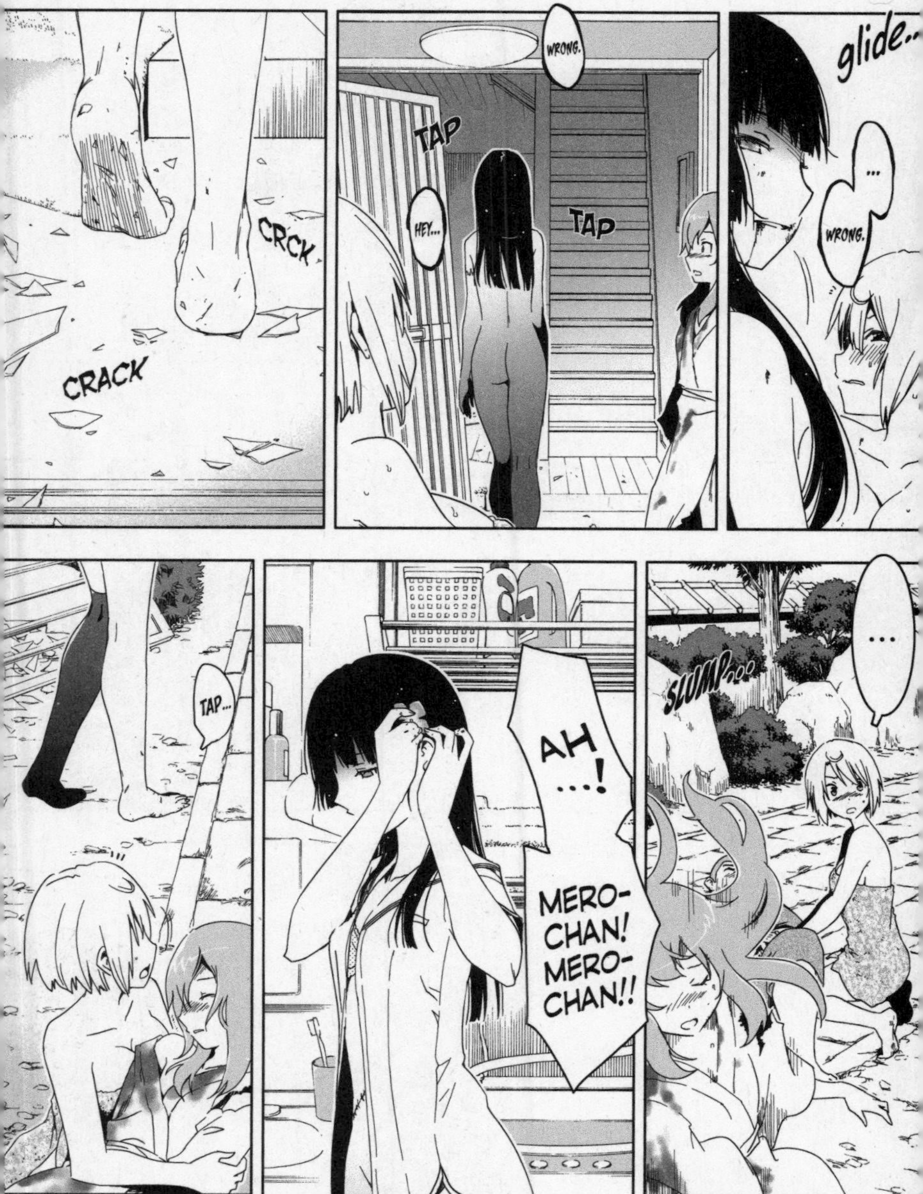
glide...
...
WRONG.
WRONG.
TAP
HEY...
TAP
CRCK
CRACK
...
...
SLUMP...
AH...!
MERO-CHAN! MERO-CHAN!!
TAP...

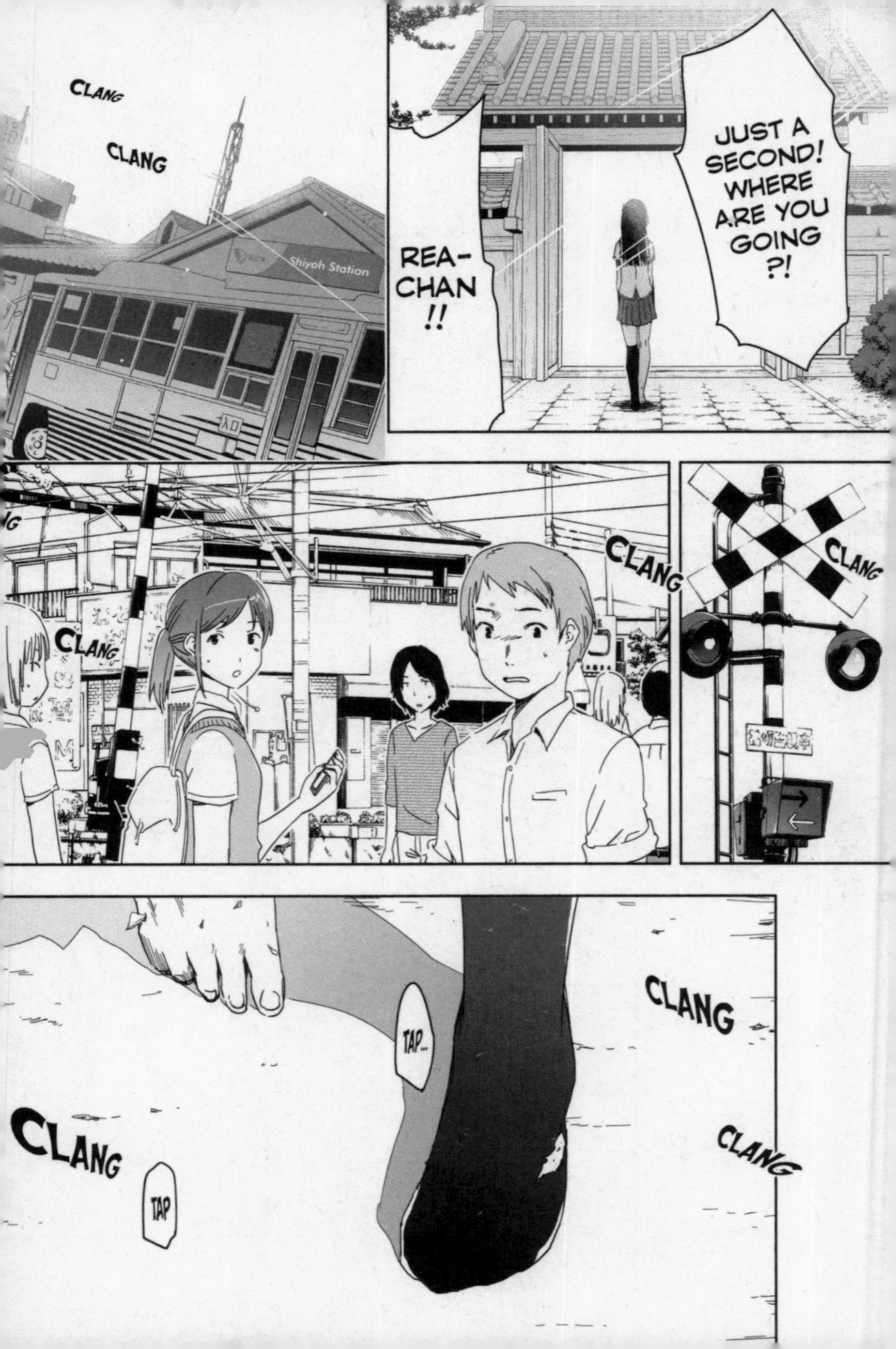
JUST A SECOND! WHERE ARE YOU GOING ?!
REA-CHAN !!
CLANG
CLANG
Shiyoh Station
CLANG
CLANG
CLANG
CLANG
CLANG
TAP...
CLANG
TAP

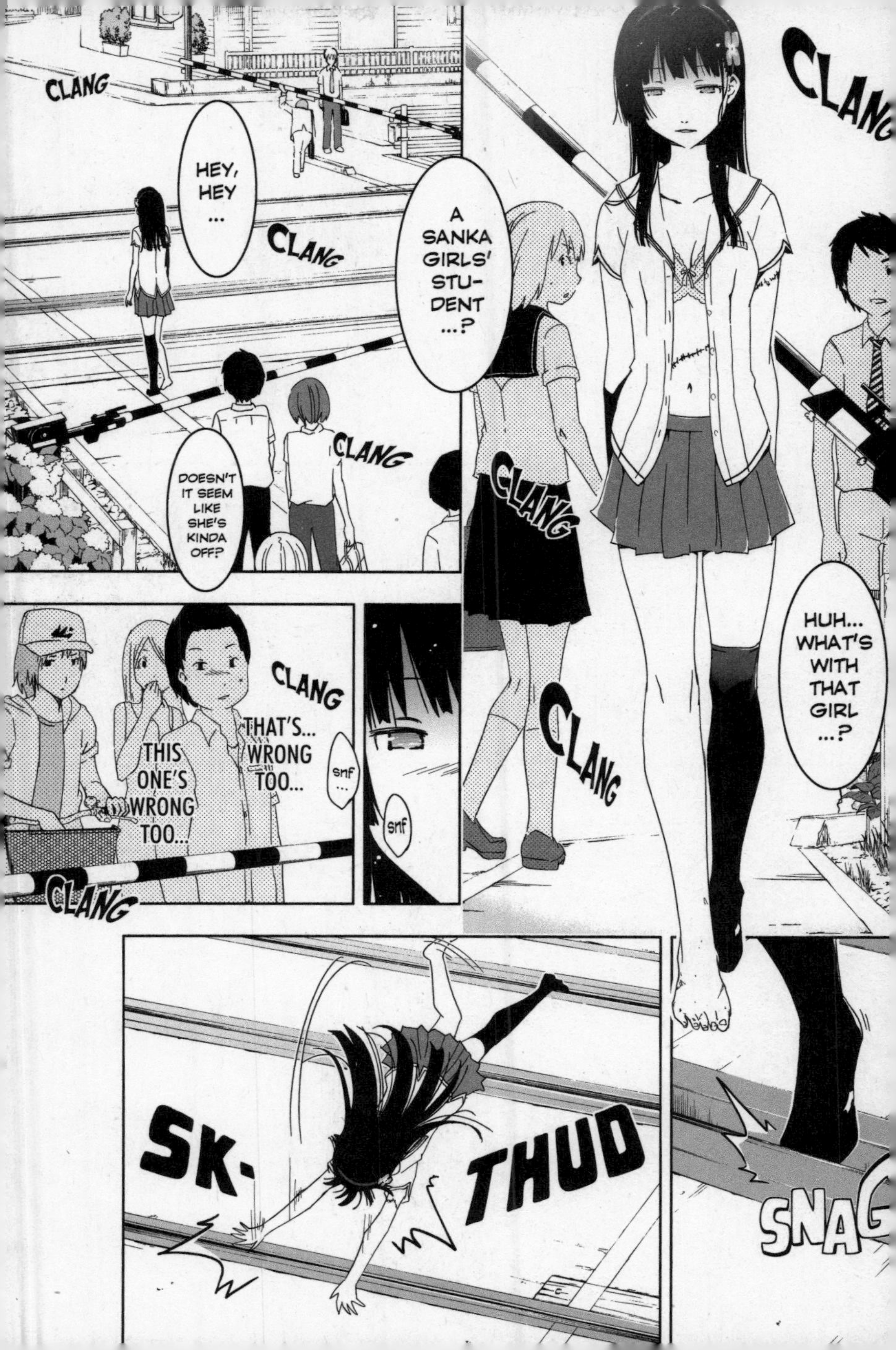

CLANG
CLANG
CLANG
HUH... WHAT'S WITH THAT GIRL ...?
A SANKA GIRLS' STU-DENT ...?
HEY, HEY ...
CLANG
CLANG
CLANG
DOESN'T IT SEEM LIKE SHE'S KINDA OFF?
snf ...
snf
CLANG
THAT'S... WRONG TOO...
THIS ONE'S WRONG TOO...
CLANG
SNAG
SK-
THUD

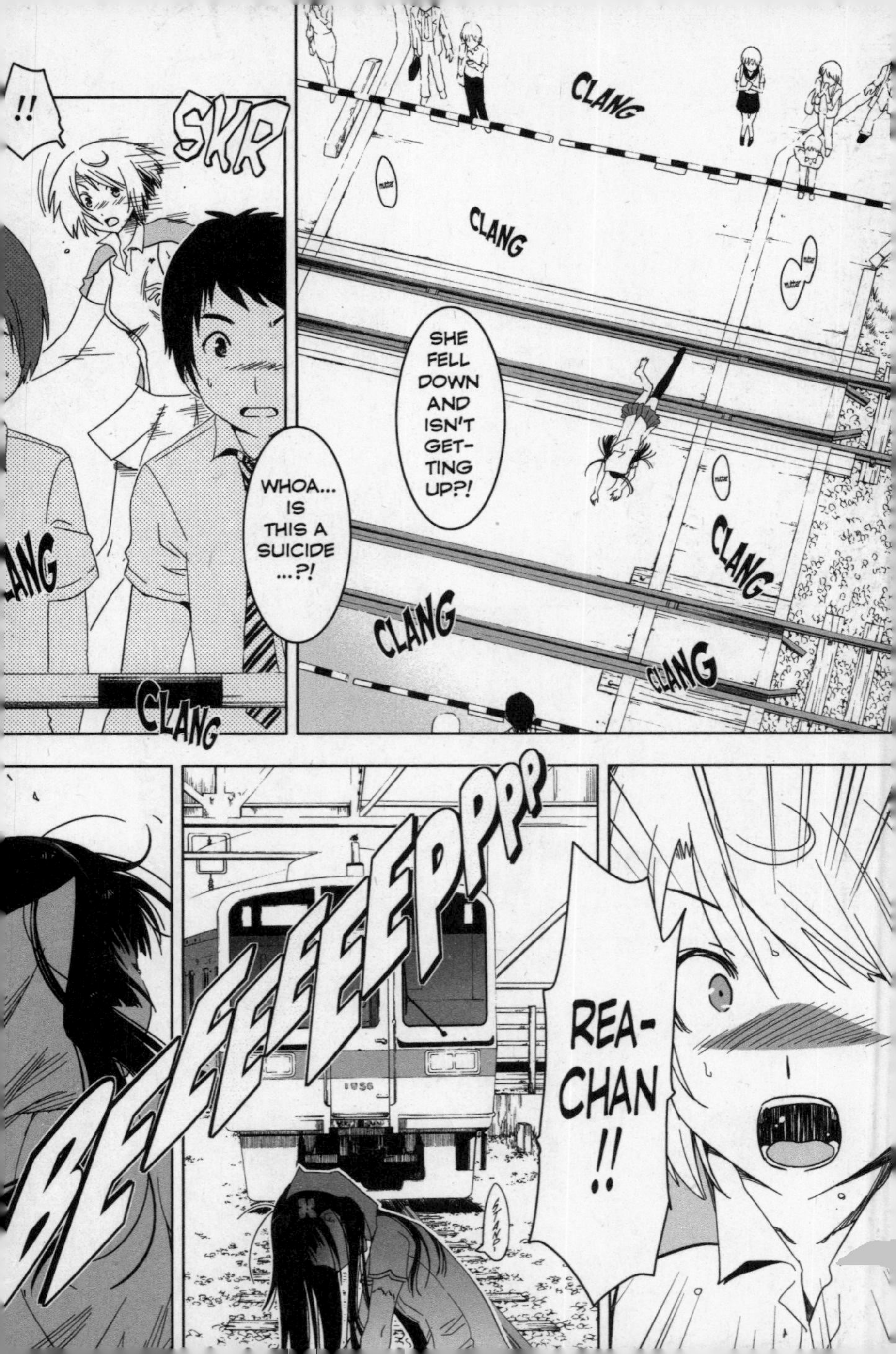
CLANG
mutter
CLANG
mutter
mutter
SHE FELL DOWN AND ISN'T GET-TING UP?!
mutter
CLANG
CLANG
CLANG
!!
SKR
WHOA... IS THIS A SUICIDE ...?!
ANG
CLANG
REA-CHAN!!
BZEEEEEPPP!
STAMP!

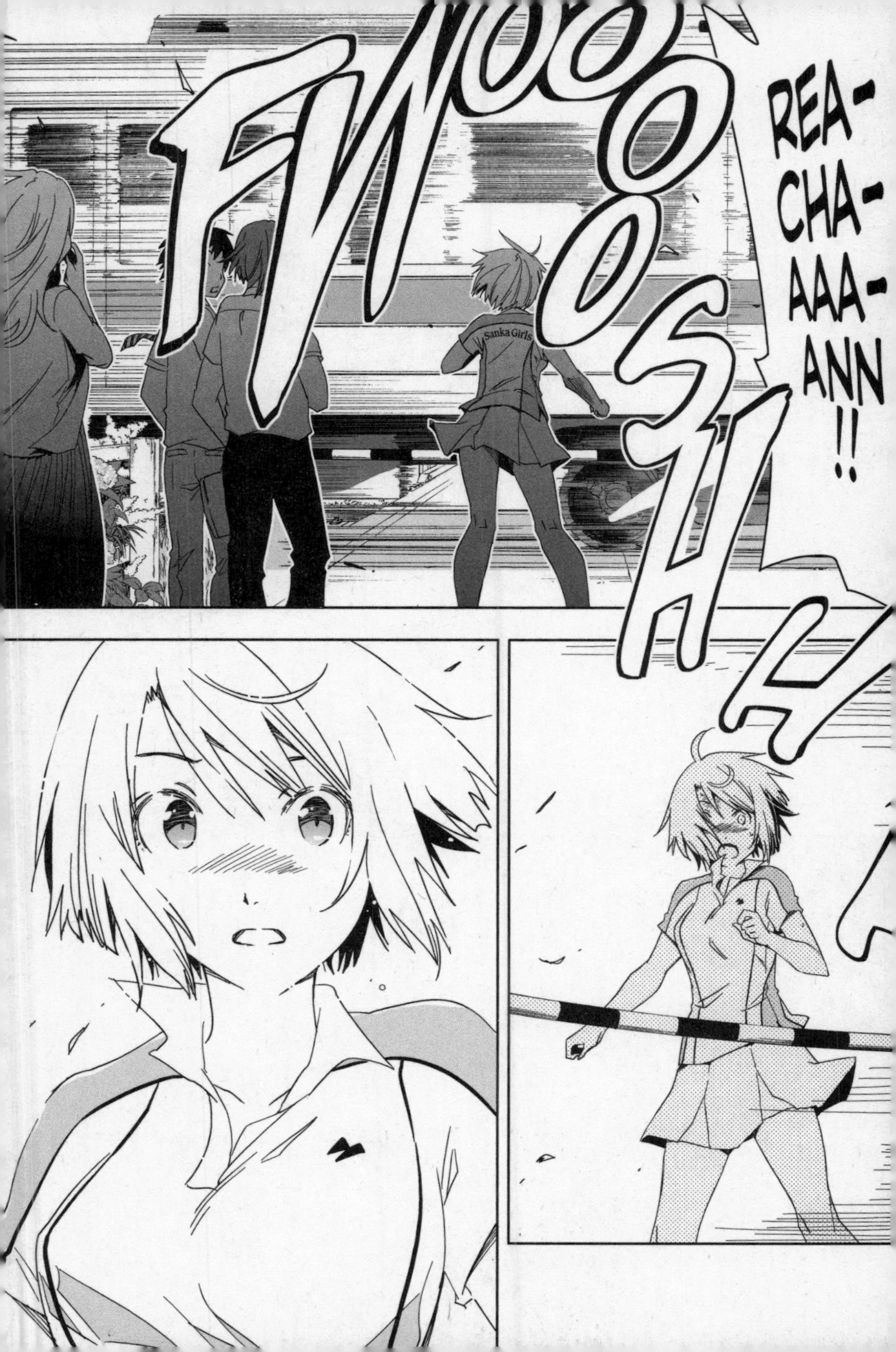
REA-
CHA-
AAA-
ANN
!!
FWOOOOOSHHH
Sanka Girls

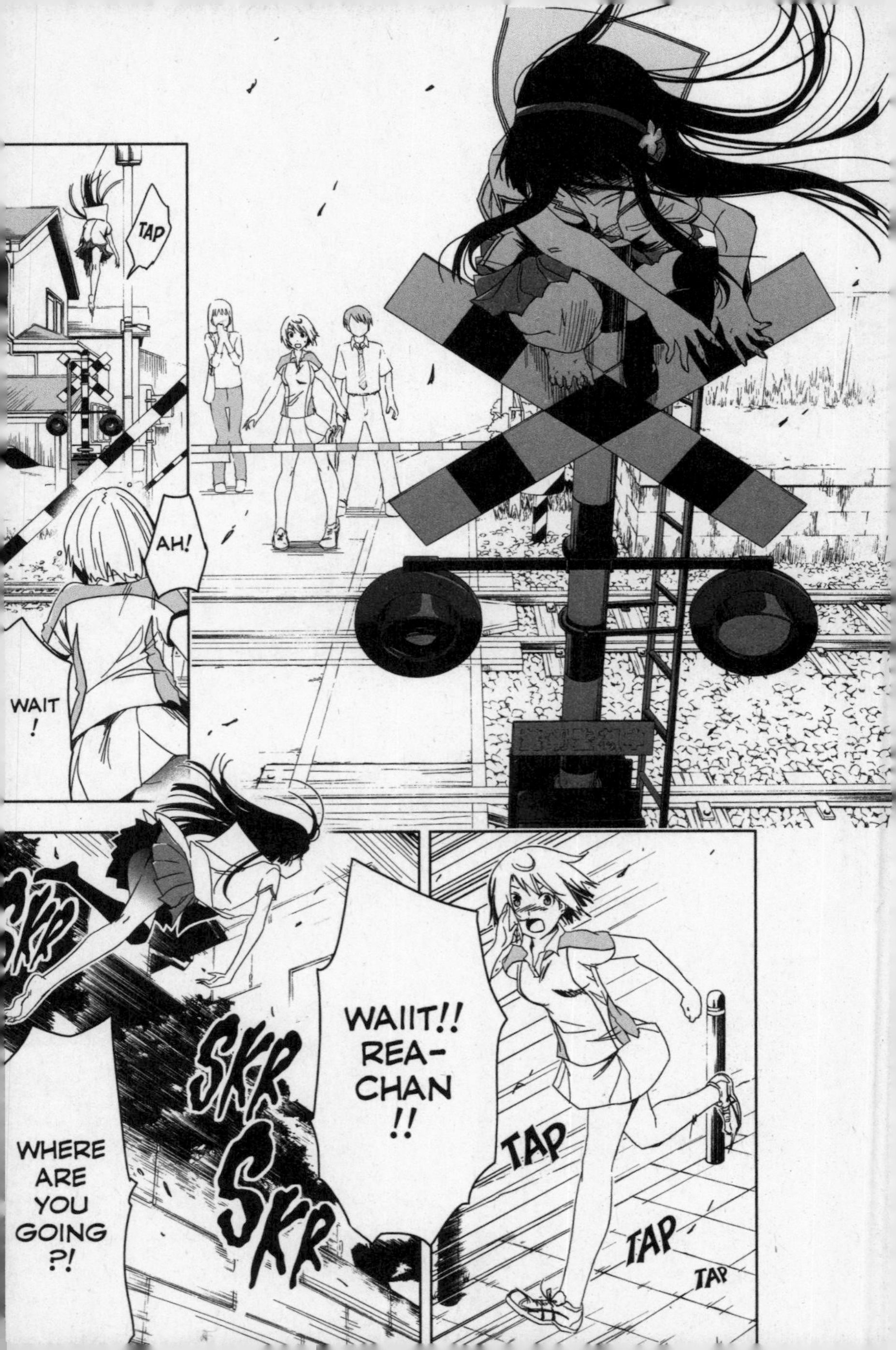
TAP
AH!
WAIT!
WAIIT!! REA-CHAN!!
TAP
TAP
TAP
SKR
SKR
SKR
WHERE ARE YOU GOING?!

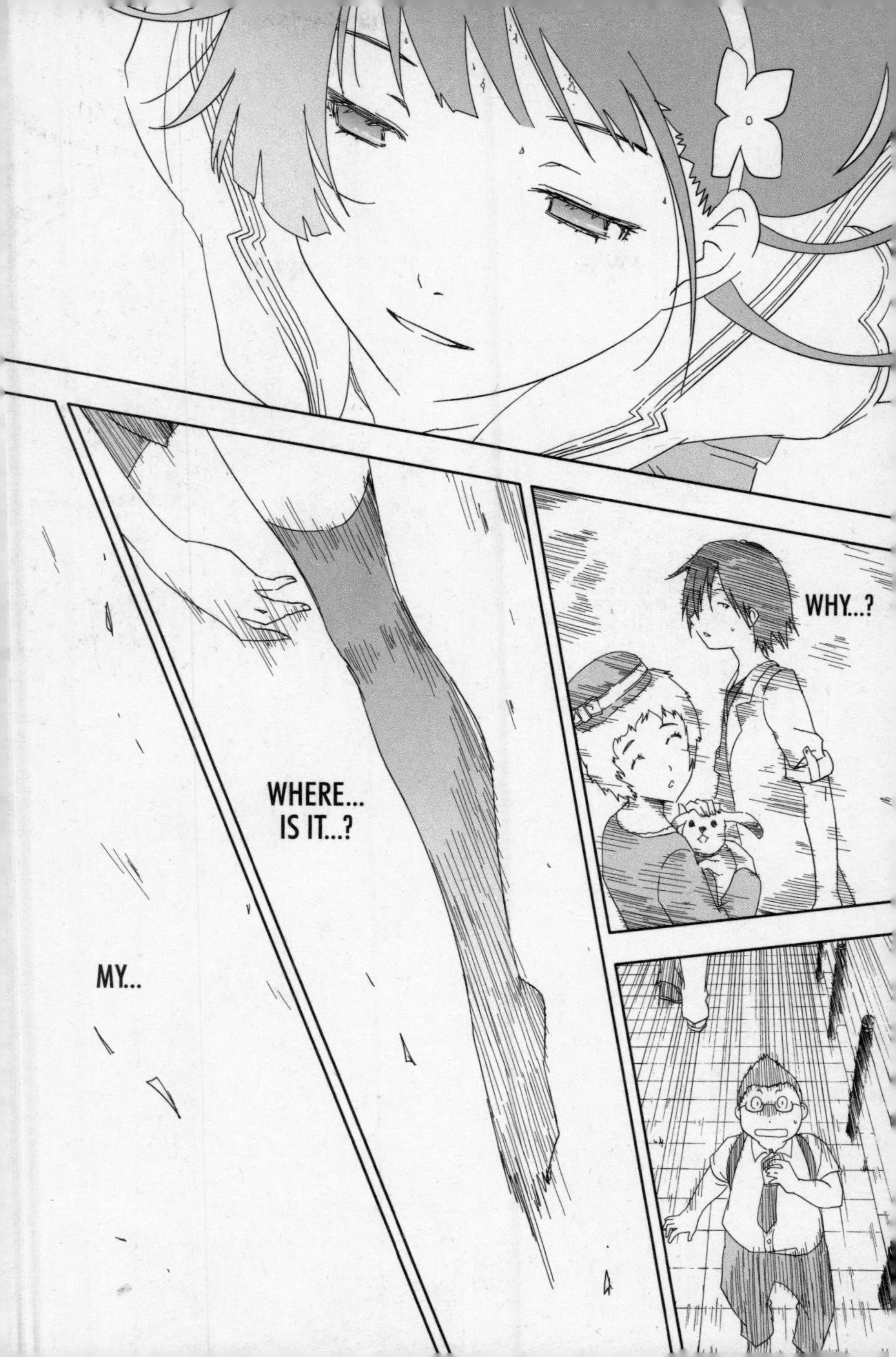
WHY...?
WHERE... IS IT...?
MY...

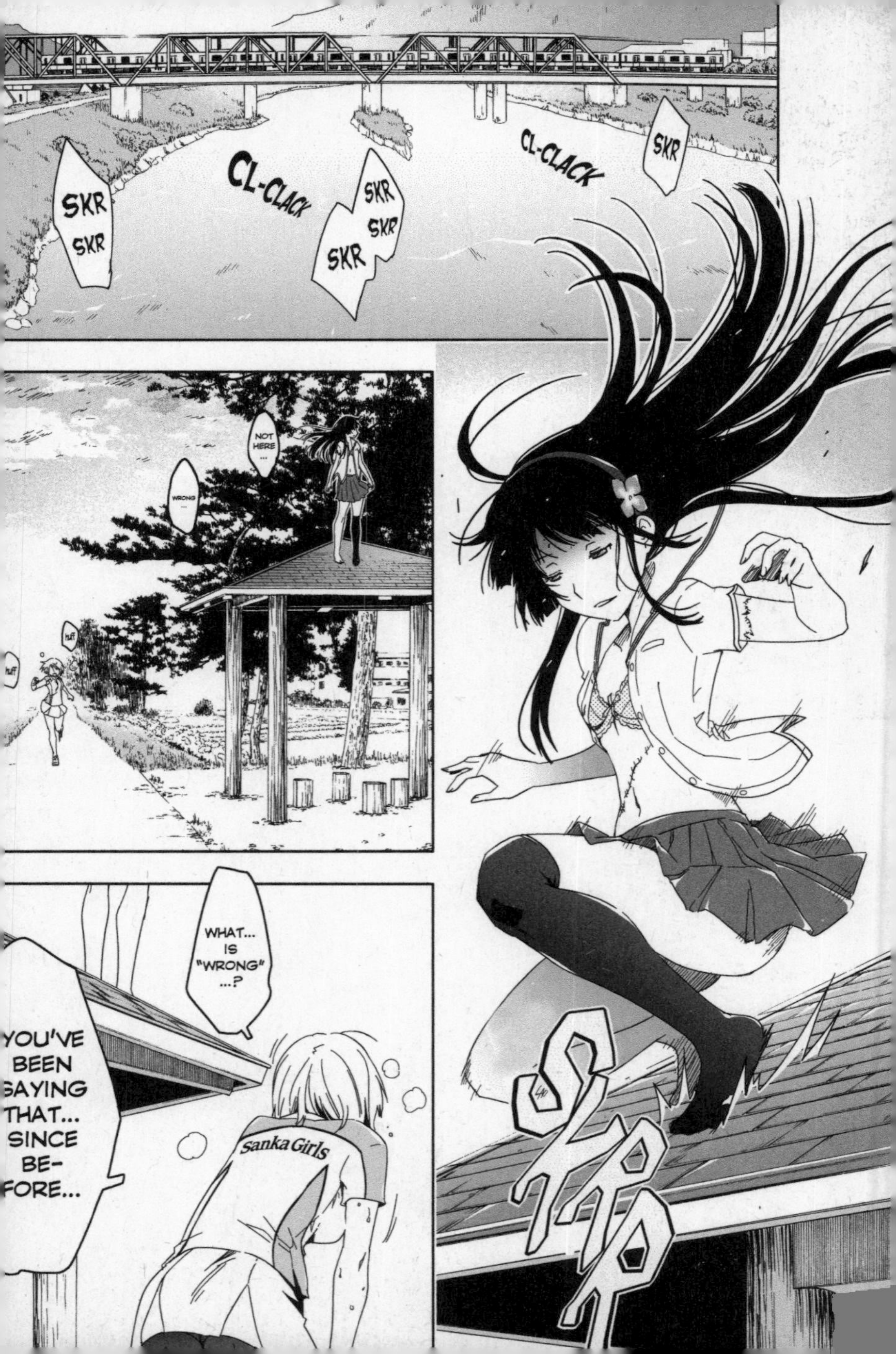
SKR
CL-CLACK
SKR SKR SKR
CL-CLACK
SKR SKR
SKR
NOT HERE ...
WRONG ...
huff
huff
WHAT... IS "WRONG" ...?
YOU'VE BEEN SAYING THAT... SINCE BE-FORE...
Sanka Girls

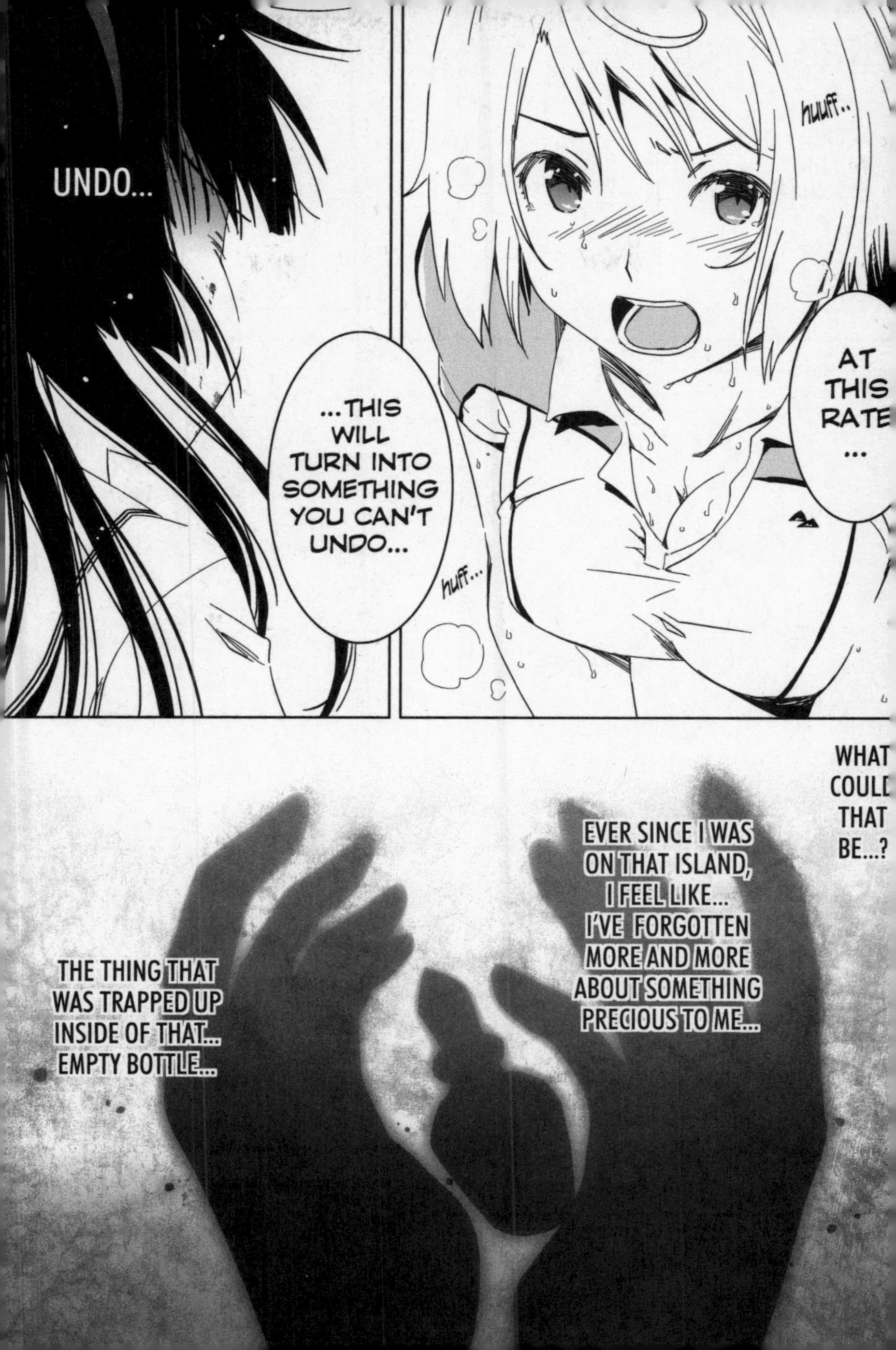
huuff..
AT THIS RATE...
huff...
...THIS WILL TURN INTO SOMETHING YOU CAN'T UNDO...
UNDO...
WHAT COULD THAT BE...?
EVER SINCE I WAS ON THAT ISLAND, I FEEL LIKE... I'VE FORGOTTEN MORE AND MORE ABOUT SOMETHING PRECIOUS TO ME...
THE THING THAT WAS TRAPPED UP INSIDE OF THAT... EMPTY BOTTLE...

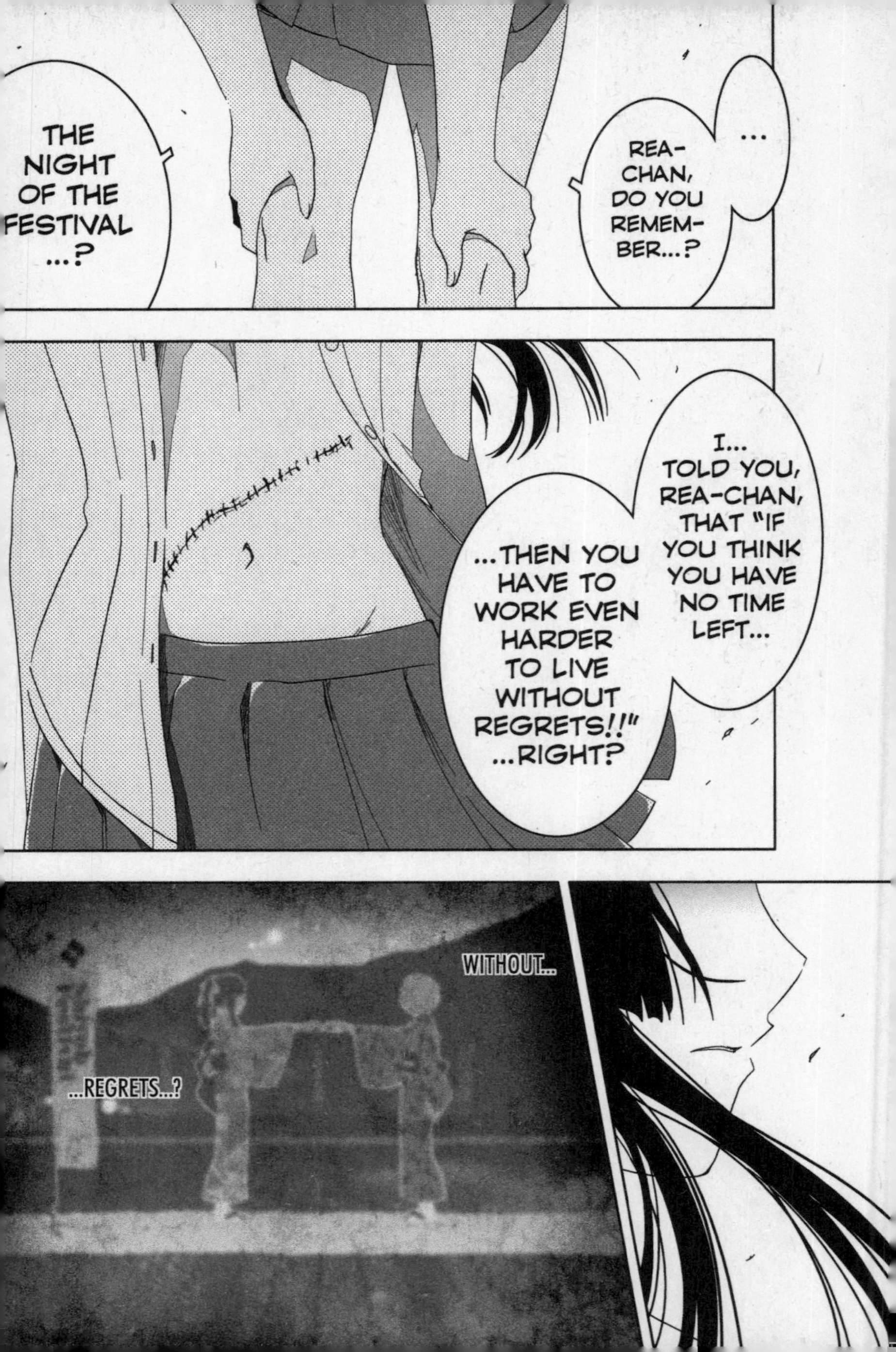
...
REA-CHAN, DO YOU REMEMBER...?
THE NIGHT OF THE FESTIVAL ...?
I... TOLD YOU, REA-CHAN, THAT "IF YOU THINK YOU HAVE NO TIME LEFT...
...THEN YOU HAVE TO WORK EVEN HARDER TO LIVE WITHOUT REGRETS!!" ...RIGHT?
WITHOUT...
...REGRETS...?

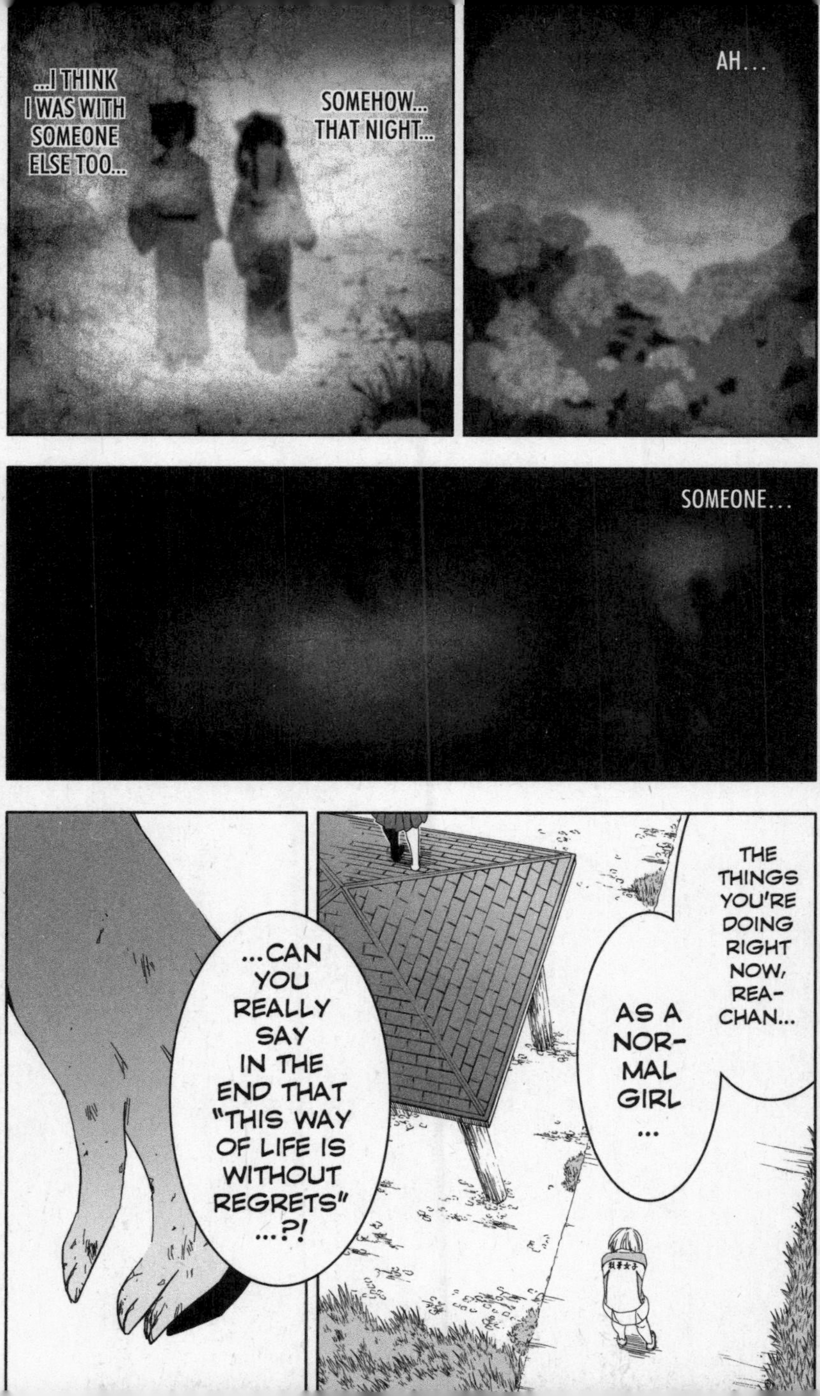
AH...
SOMEHOW... THAT NIGHT...
...I THINK I WAS WITH SOMEONE ELSE TOO...
SOMEONE...
THE THINGS YOU'RE DOING RIGHT NOW, REA-CHAN...
AS A NOR-MAL GIRL ...
...CAN YOU REALLY SAY IN THE END THAT "THIS WAY OF LIFE IS WITHOUT REGRETS" ...?!

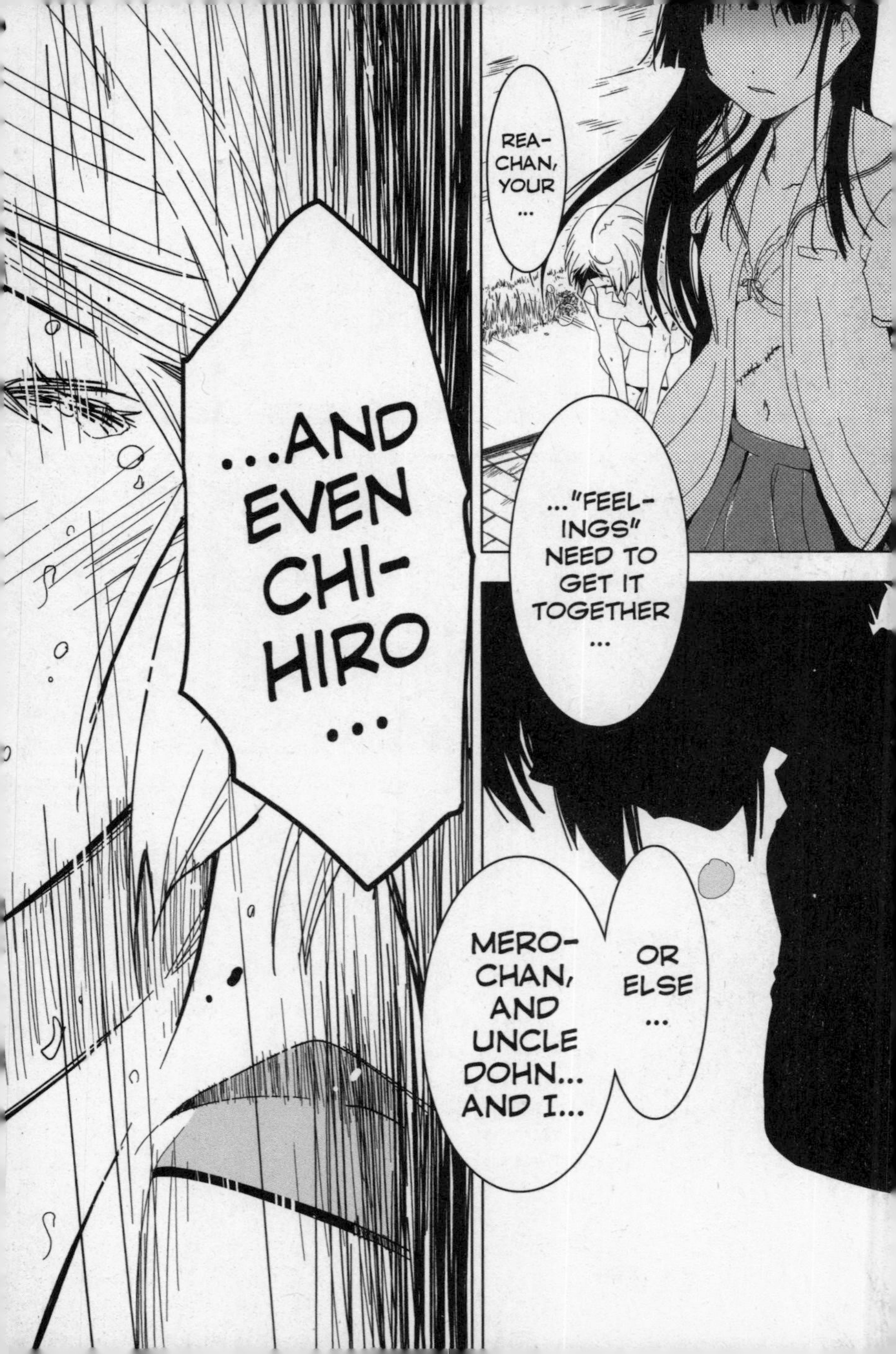
REA-CHAN, YOUR ...
..."FEEL-INGS" NEED TO GET IT TOGETHER ...
OR ELSE ...
MERO-CHAN, AND UNCLE DOHN... AND I...
...AND EVEN CHI-HIRO ...

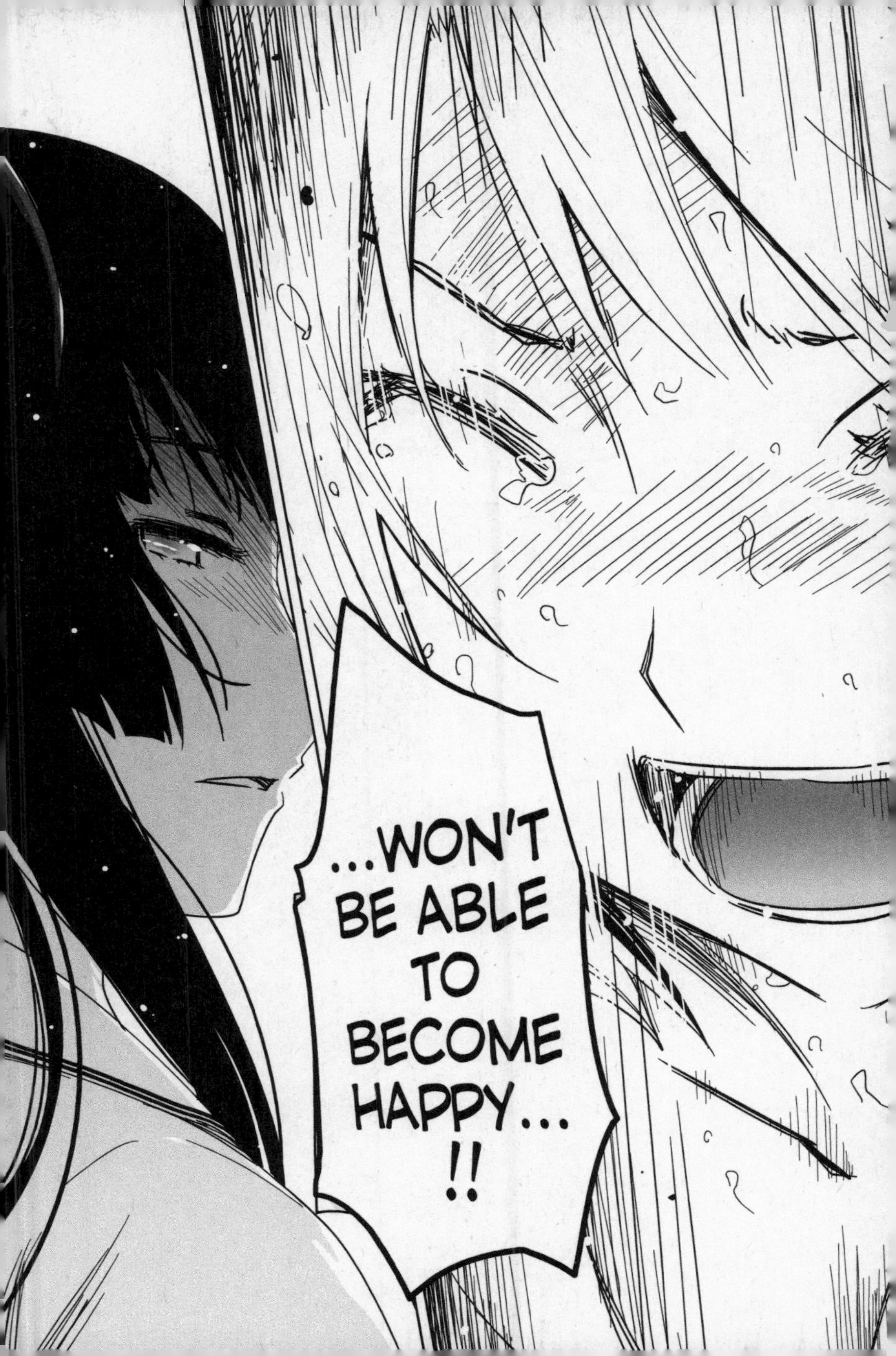
...WON'T BE ABLE TO BECOME HAPPY... !!

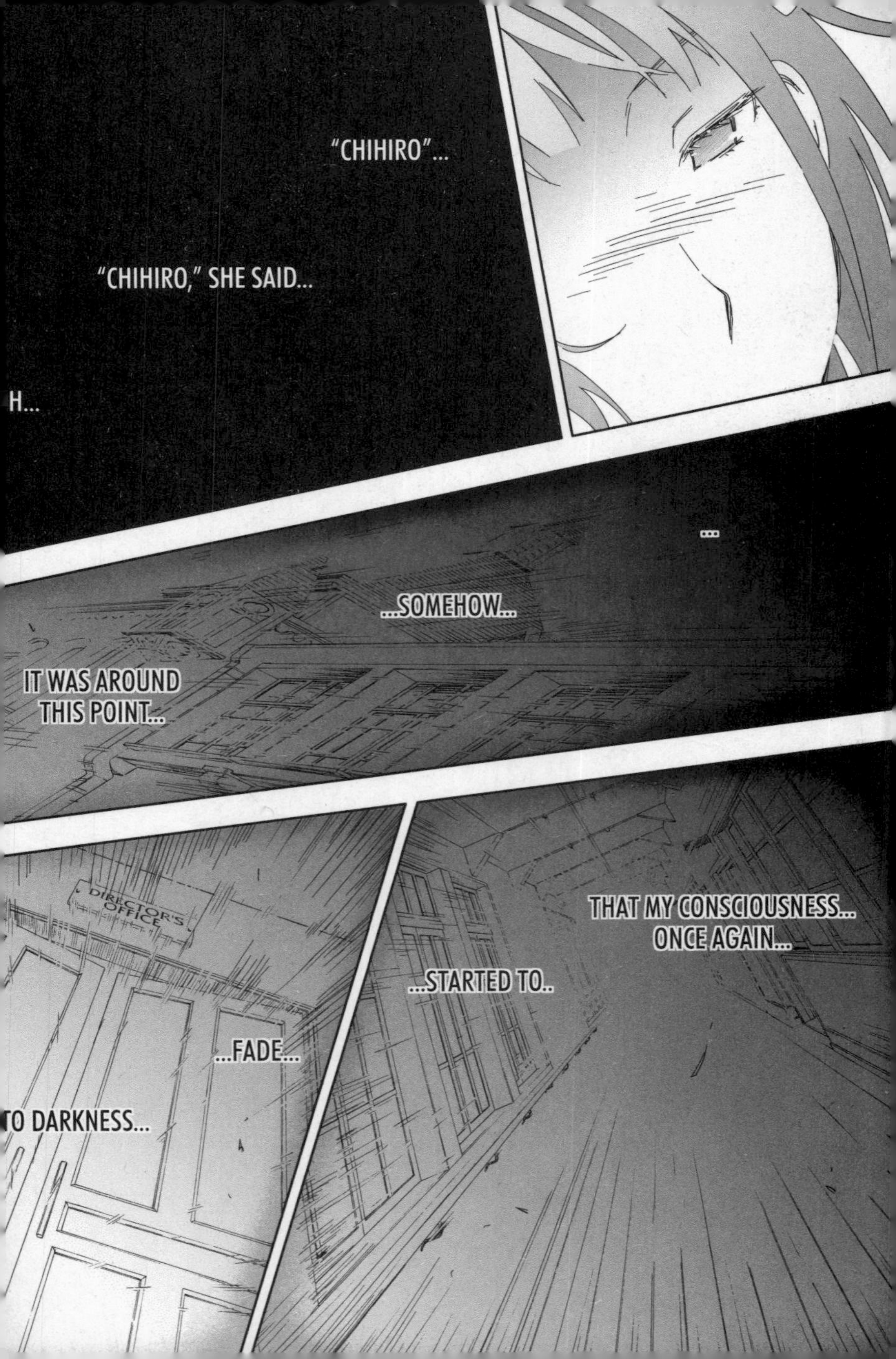
"CHIHIRO"...
"CHIHIRO," SHE SAID...
H...
...
...SOMEHOW...
IT WAS AROUND THIS POINT...
THAT MY CONSCIOUSNESS... ONCE AGAIN...
...STARTED TO..
DIRECTOR'S OFFICE
...FADE...
TO DARKNESS...

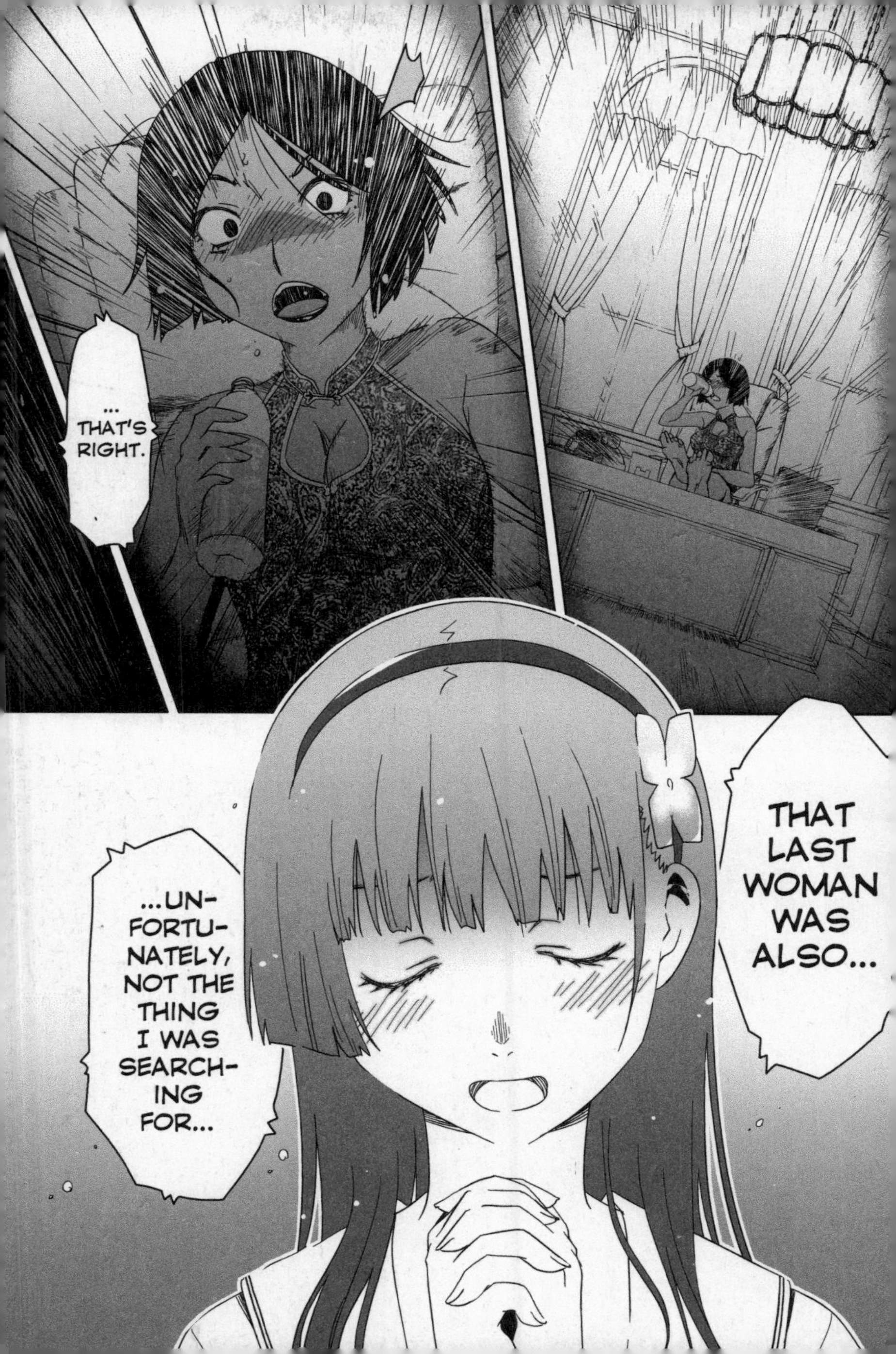

... THAT'S RIGHT.
THAT LAST WOMAN WAS ALSO...
...UN-FORTUNATELY, NOT THE THING I WAS SEARCH-ING FOR...

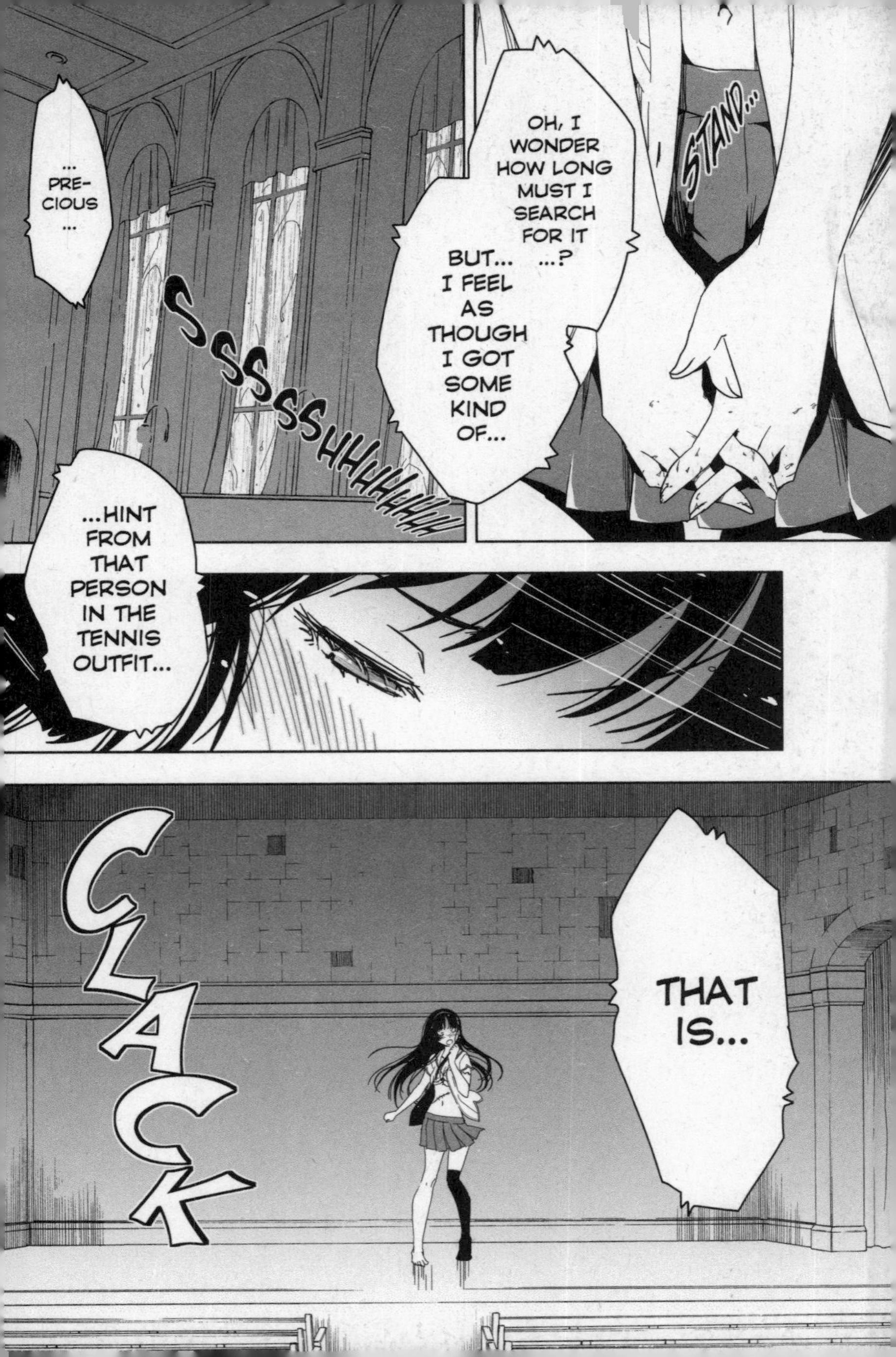
STAND...
OH, I WONDER HOW LONG MUST I SEARCH FOR IT ...?
BUT... I FEEL AS THOUGH I GOT SOME KIND OF...
... PRE-CIOUS ...
SSSSSHHHHHHHHH
...HINT FROM THAT PERSON IN THE TENNIS OUTFIT...
THAT IS...
CLACK

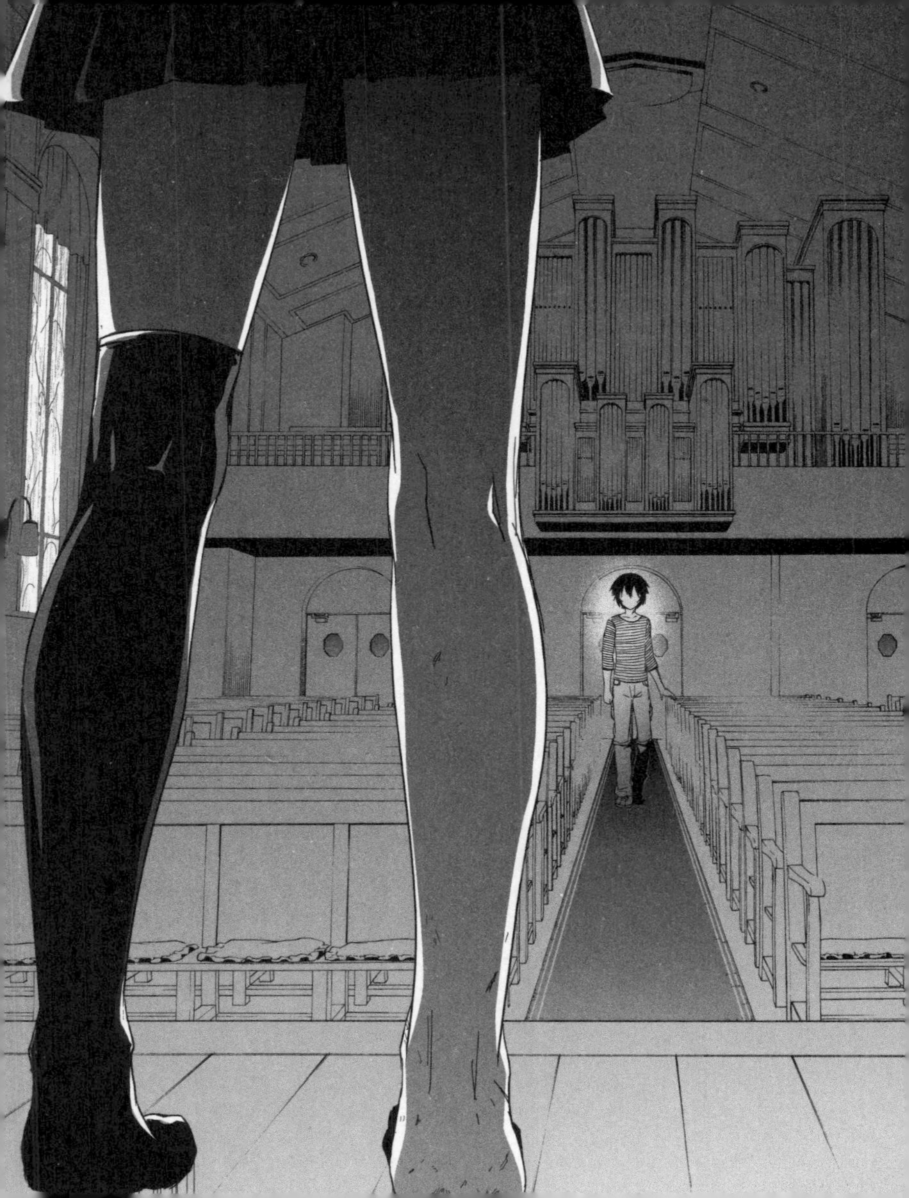

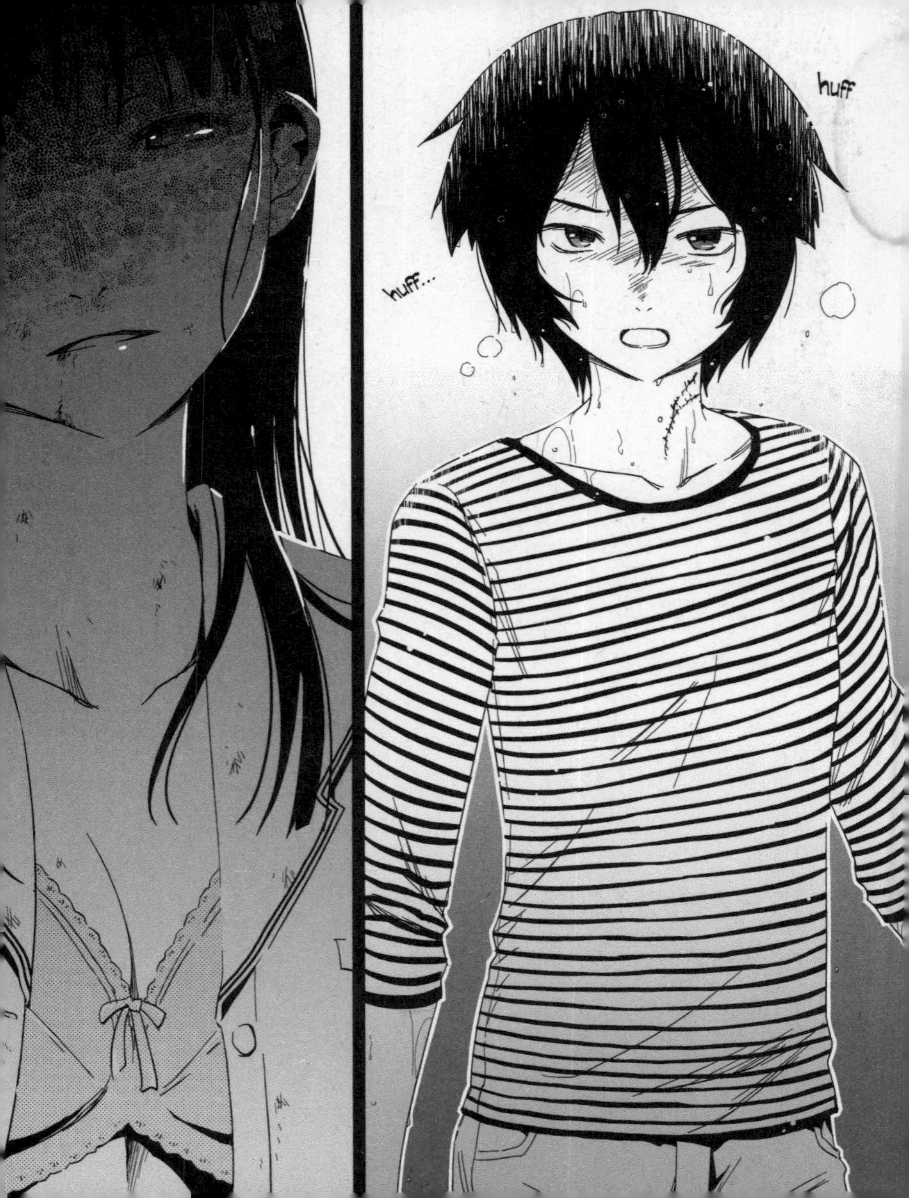
huff
huff...

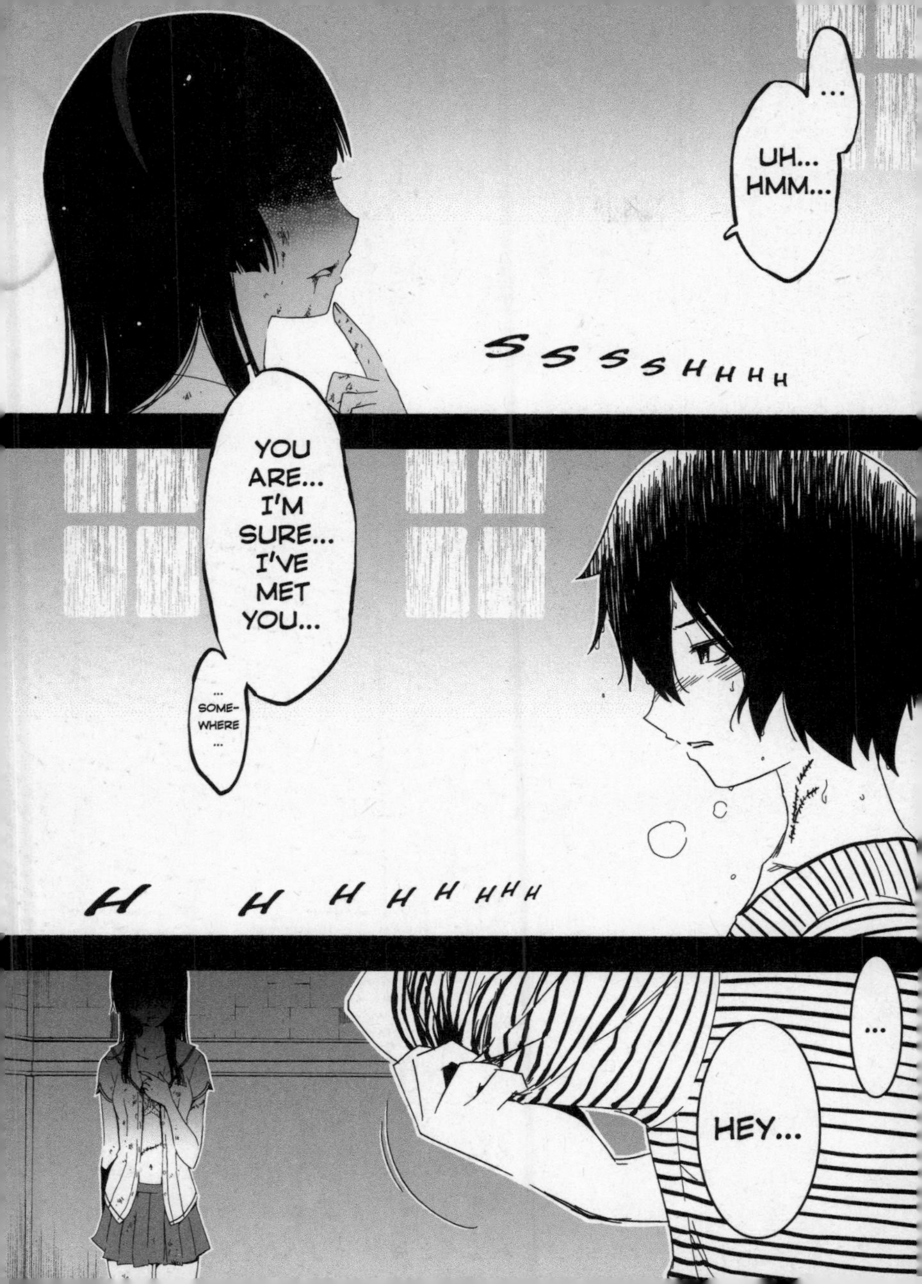

... UH... HMM...
SSSSHHHH
YOU ARE... I'M SURE... I'VE MET YOU...
... SOME-WHERE ...
HHHHHHHH
...
HEY...

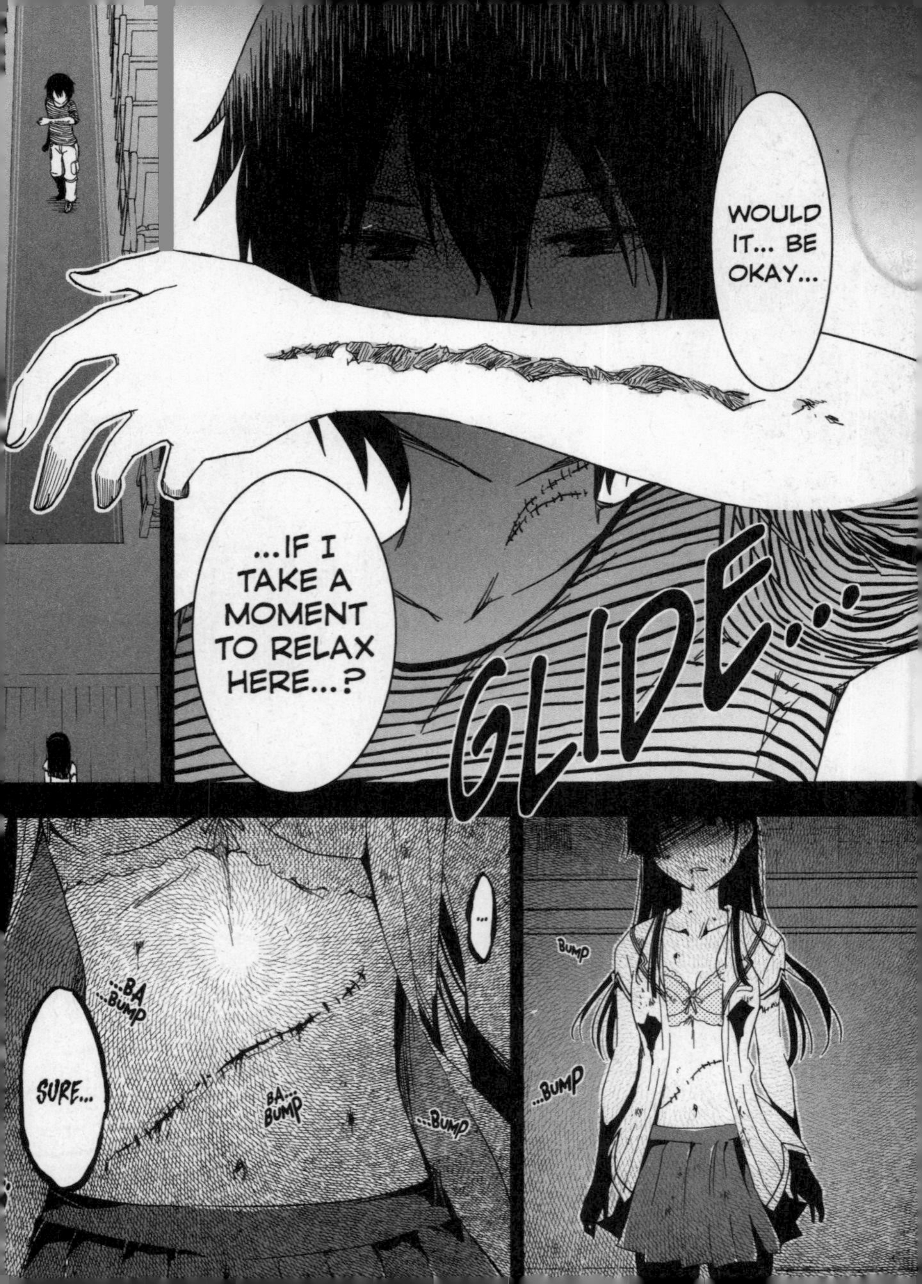
WOULD IT... BE OKAY...
...IF I TAKE A MOMENT TO RELAX HERE...?
GLIDE...
BUMP
...BUMP
...
...BA ...BUMP
BA... BUMP
...BUMP
SURE...

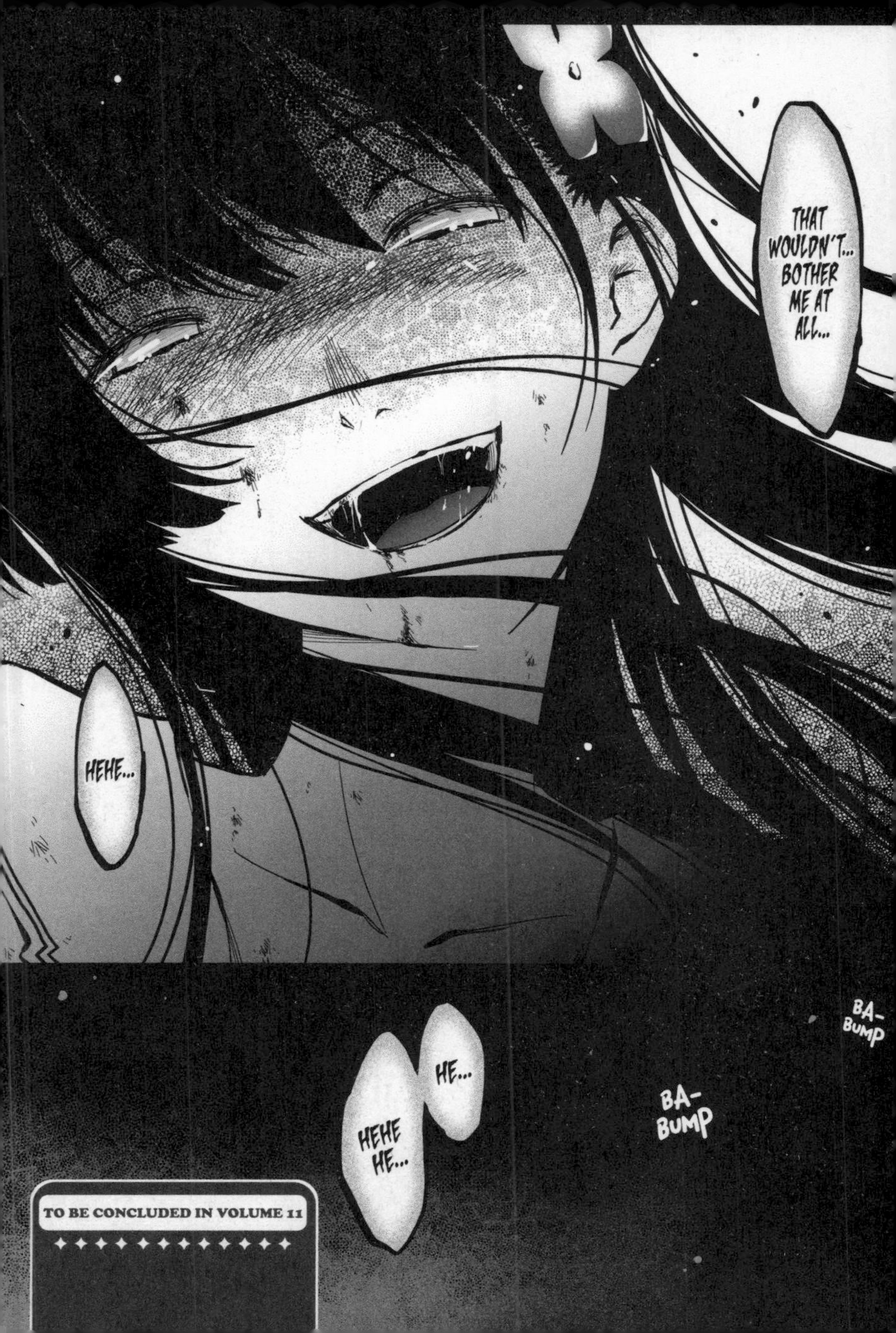
THAT WOULDN'T... BOTHER ME AT ALL...
HEHE...
BA-BUMP
BA-BUMP
HE...
HEHE HE...
TO BE CONCLUDED IN VOLUME 11

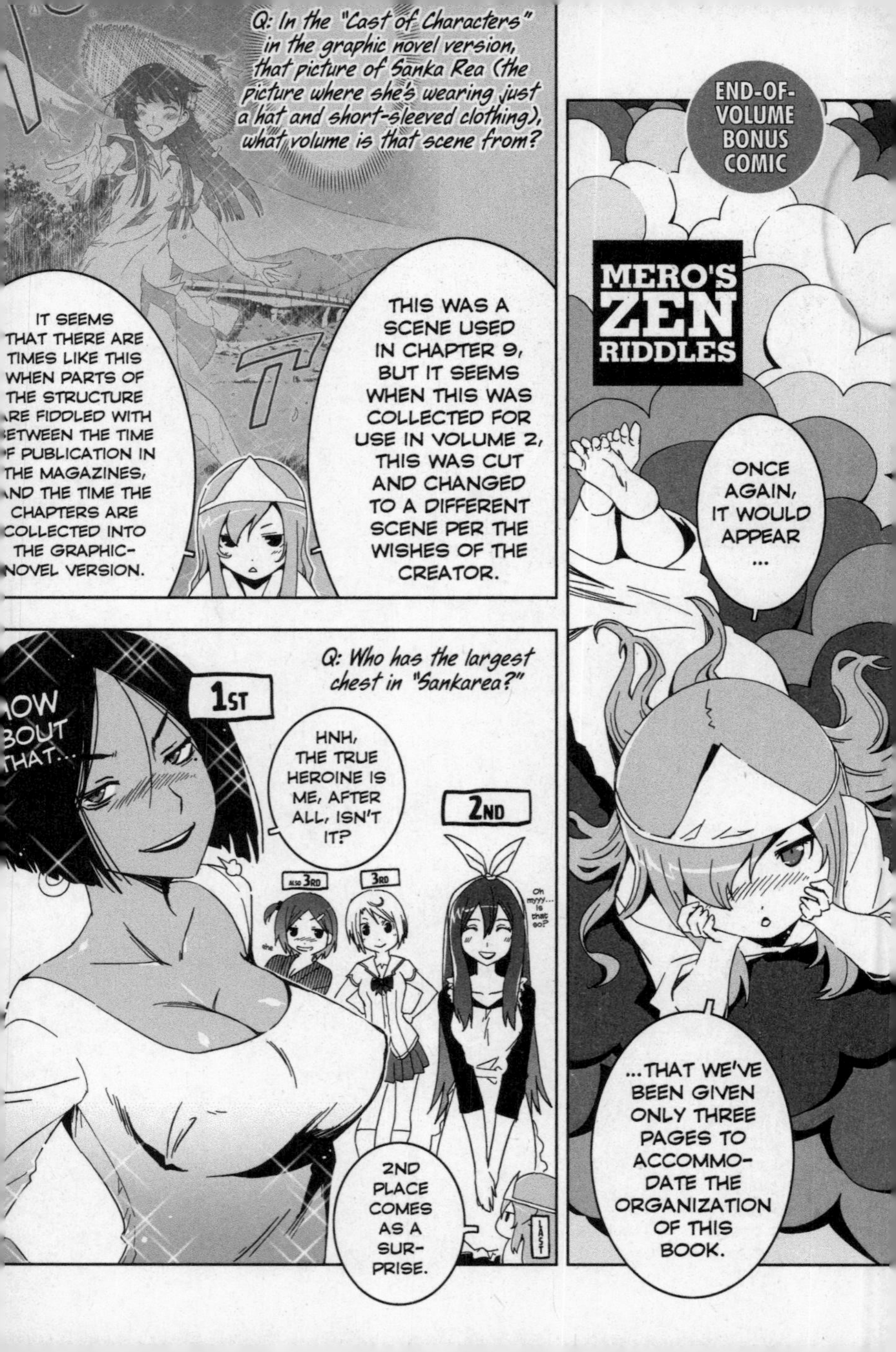
END-OF-VOLUME BONUS COMIC
MERO'S ZEN RIDDLES
ONCE AGAIN, IT WOULD APPEAR ...
...THAT WE'VE BEEN GIVEN ONLY THREE PAGES TO ACCOMMO-DATE THE ORGANIZATION OF THIS BOOK.
Q: In the "Cast of Characters" in the graphic novel version, that picture of Sanka Rea (the picture where she's wearing just a hat and short-sleeved clothing), what volume is that scene from?
THIS WAS A SCENE USED IN CHAPTER 9, BUT IT SEEMS WHEN THIS WAS COLLECTED FOR USE IN VOLUME 2, THIS WAS CUT AND CHANGED TO A DIFFERENT SCENE PER THE WISHES OF THE CREATOR.
IT SEEMS THAT THERE ARE TIMES LIKE THIS WHEN PARTS OF THE STRUCTURE RE FIDDLED WITH ETWEEN THE TIME F PUBLICATION IN THE MAGAZINES, ND THE TIME THE CHAPTERS ARE COLLECTED INTO THE GRAPHIC-NOVEL VERSION.
Q: Who has the largest chest in "Sankarea?"
1ST
2ND
HNH, THE TRUE HEROINE IS ME, AFTER ALL, ISN'T IT?
Oh myyy... is that so?
3RD
ALSO 3RD
ehe
2ND PLACE COMES AS A SUR-PRISE.
LAST

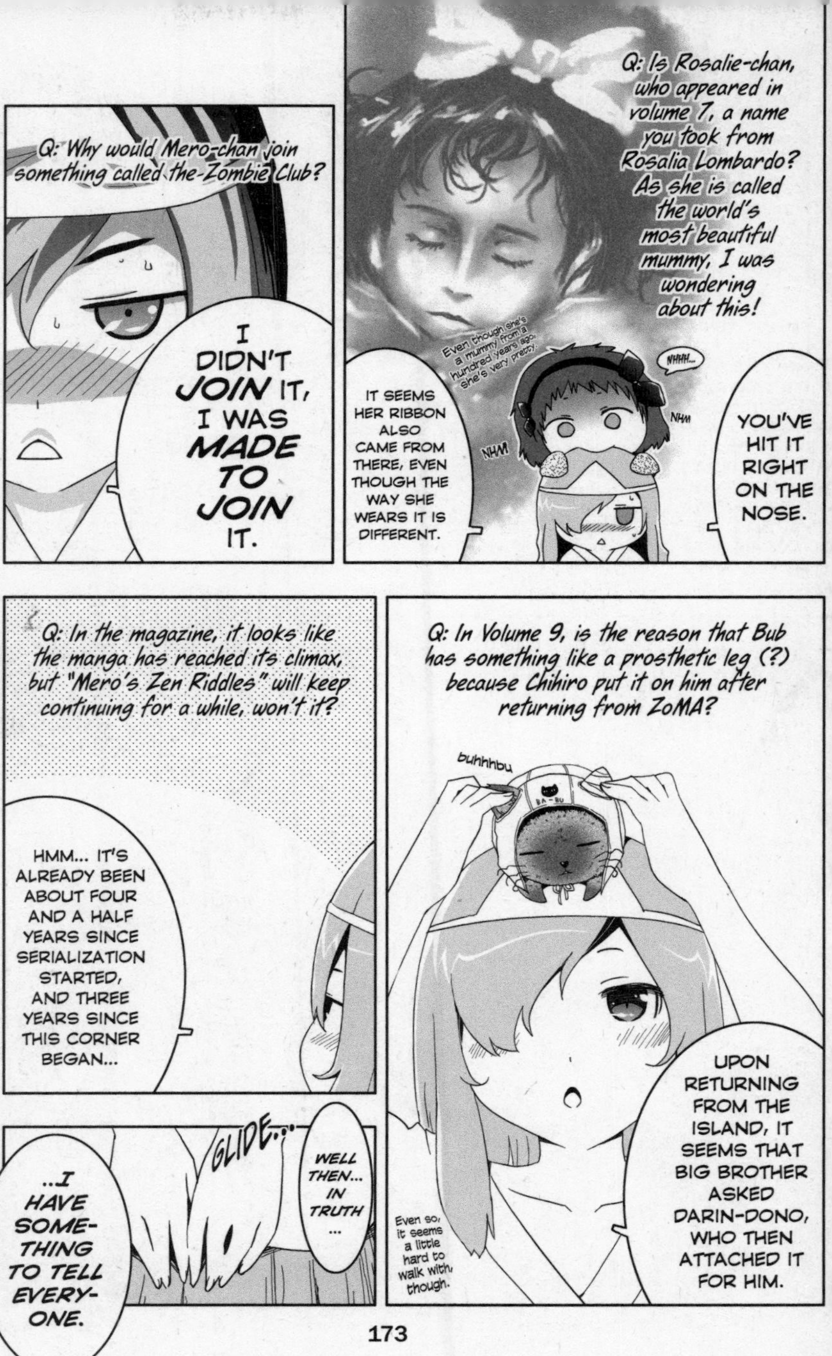

Q: Is Rosalie-chan, who appeared in volume 7, a name you took from Rosalia Lombardo? As she is called the world's most beautiful mummy, I was wondering about this!
NHHH...
YOU'VE HIT IT RIGHT ON THE NOSE.
NHM
NHM
Even though she's a mummy from a hundred years ago, she's very pretty.
IT SEEMS HER RIBBON ALSO CAME FROM THERE, EVEN THOUGH THE WAY SHE WEARS IT IS DIFFERENT.
Q: Why would Mero-chan join something called the Zombie Club?
I DIDN'T JOIN IT, I WAS MADE TO JOIN IT.
Q: In Volume 9, is the reason that Bub has something like a prosthetic leg (?) because Chihiro put it on him after returning from ZoMA?
buhhhbu
BA-BU
UPON RETURNING FROM THE ISLAND, IT SEEMS THAT BIG BROTHER ASKED DARIN-DONO, WHO THEN ATTACHED IT FOR HIM.
Even so, it seems a little hard to walk with, though.
Q: In the magazine, it looks like the manga has reached its climax, but "Mero's Zen Riddles" will keep continuing for a while, won't it?
HMM... IT'S ALREADY BEEN ABOUT FOUR AND A HALF YEARS SINCE SERIALIZATION STARTED, AND THREE YEARS SINCE THIS CORNER BEGAN...
GLIDE...
WELL THEN... IN TRUTH...
...I HAVE SOMETHING TO TELL EVERYONE.

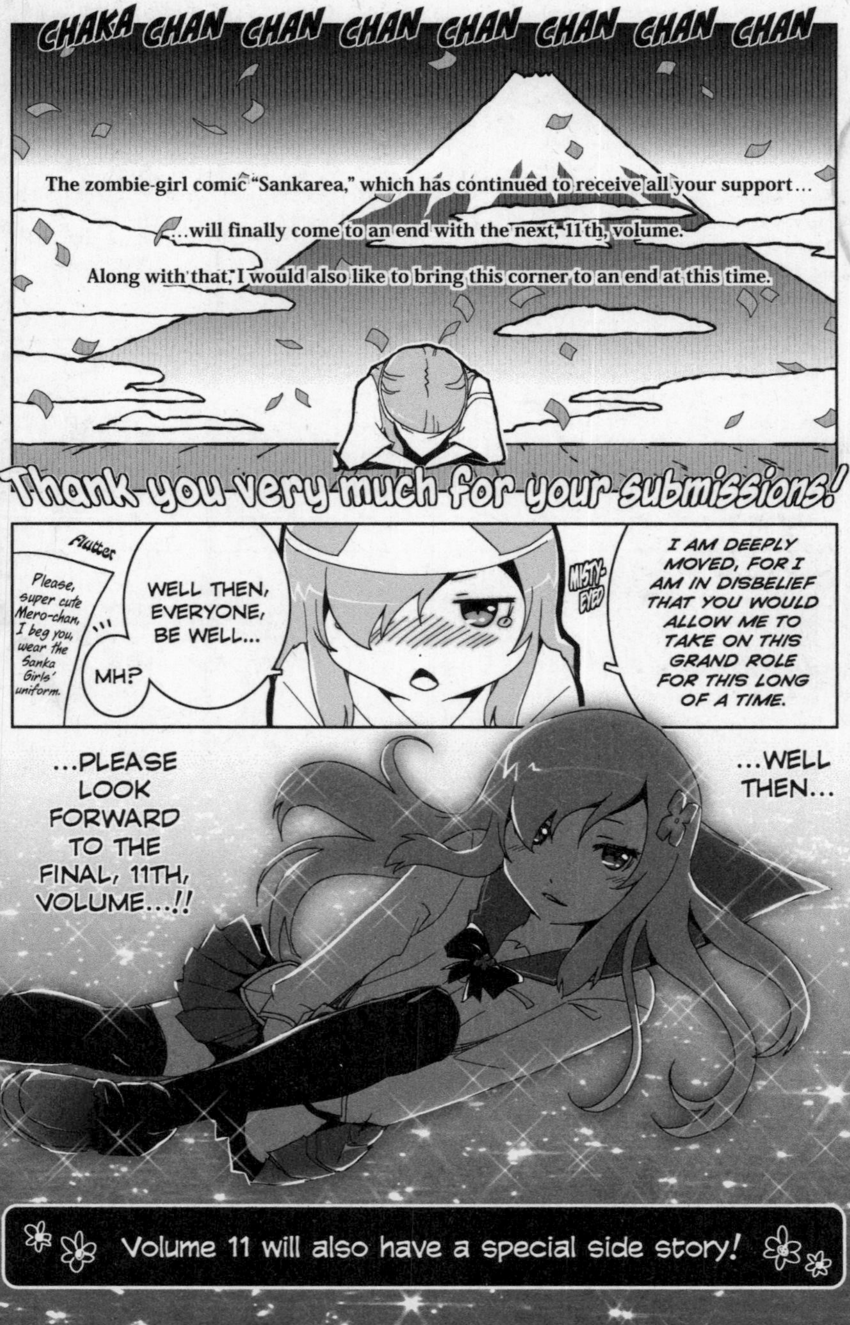
CHAKA CHAN CHAN CHAN CHAN CHAN CHAN CHAN
The zombie-girl comic "Sankarea," which has continued to receive all your support...
...will finally come to an end with the next, 11th, volume.
Along with that, I would also like to bring this corner to an end at this time.
Thank you very much for your submissions!
I AM DEEPLY MOVED, FOR I AM IN DISBELIEF THAT YOU WOULD ALLOW ME TO TAKE ON THIS GRAND ROLE FOR THIS LONG OF A TIME.
MISTY-EYED
WELL THEN, EVERYONE, BE WELL...
...
MH?
Flutter
Please, super cute Mero-chan, I beg you, wear the Sanka Girls' uniform.
...WELL THEN...
...PLEASE LOOK FORWARD TO THE FINAL, 11TH, VOLUME...!!
Volume 11 will also have a special side story!

TRANSLATION NOTES

Page 8: Ou
The Ou Mountains are a range of mountains in Tohoku, Honshu, Japan. They are the longest in Japan and reach from Aomori to the northern part of Kanto.

Page 8: Tenpo
Tenpo was the name of an era that lasted from 1830 to 1844. It's well known as a time of unrest and the period during which one of the worst famines in Japanese history occurred.

Page 8: Meiji
The Meiji period was an era that lasted from 1868 to 1912. This is the period during which Japanese society changed fundamentally and structurally from a closed feudal society to a more modern and international nation-state.

Page 9: Meiji Restoration
The Meiji Restoration was the event that led to the Meiji Period, during which the ruling warrior Shogunate was disbanded and the Emperor was reinstated as the figural head of Japan.

Page 11: The Great Famine
The Great Tenpo Famine began in 1833 and lasted until 1837. It was the worst ever in northern Honshu, and caused by cold and flooding that occurred early in the year.

Page 60: Get's
A popular catchphrase of the Japanese comedian Dandy Sakano. "Get's" was popular in the early 2000s, but would now sound outdated and cheesy.

Page 62: Tohoku
Tohoku is the northeastern region of Honshu, the main island of Japan.

Page 91: New Year's presents
Japanese children are usually given money by their parents and older relatives as presents for the New Year celebration. In Japanese this is called *otoshidama*.

Page 108: Mh
In the original Japanese, the Chinese character for "nothing" is written here. Because it can be pronounced as "mu," this makes it into somewhat of a pun.

The unknown

MUNCH
MUNCH
MUNCH
MUNCH
whew
HOT WATER
...Hm? Are you wondering, "What happened to outer space" ..?
HOT WATER
Well, I suppose ...
...This is the very middle of space, though.
VAWOOOMMM

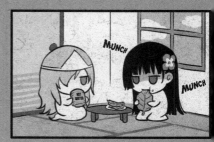

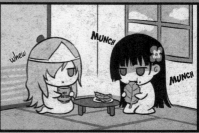

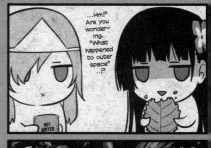

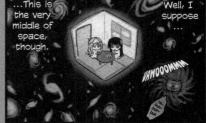

Sankarea: Undying Love volume 10 is a work of fiction. Names, characters, places, and incidents are the products of the author's imagination or are used fictitiously. Any resemblance to actual events, locales, or persons, living or dead, is entirely coincidental.

A Kodansha Comics Trade Paperback Original.

Published in the United States by Kodansha Comics, an imprint of Kodansha USA Publishing, LLC, New York.

Publication rights for this English edition arranged through Kodansha Ltd., Tokyo.

First published in Japan in 2014 by Kodansha Ltd., Tokyo, as Sankarea, volume 10.

ISBN 978-1-61262-581-2

Printed in the United States of America.

www.kodanshacomics.com

9 8 7 6 5 4 3 2 1

Translation: Lindsey Akashi
Lettering: Evan Hayden
Editing: Ajani Oloye
Kodansha Comics edition cover design: Phil Balsman